The Viet Nam War / *The American War*

The Viet Nam War
The American War

Images and Representations
in Euro-American and
Vietnamese Exile Narratives

Renny Christopher

University of Massachusetts Press   *Amherst*

Printed in the United States of America
LC 95-19687
ISBN 1-55849-008-6 (cloth); 009-4 (pbk.)
Designed by Milenda Nanok Lee
Set in Monotype Bembo by Keystone Typesetting, Inc.
Printed and bound by Braun-Brumfield, Inc.
Library of Congress Cataloging-in-Publication Data
Christopher Renny.
    The Viet Nam War/the American war : images and representations in
Euro-American and Vietnamese exile narratives / Renny Christopher.
        p.   cm.
    Includes bibliographical references and index.
    ISBN 1–55849–008–6 (alk. paper). — ISBN 1–55849–009–4 (pbk. : alk. paper)
    1. Vietnamese Conflict, 1961–1975—Literature and the conflict.
2. American literature—20th century—History and criticism.
3. Vietnamese Americans—Biography—History and criticism.
4. Vietnamese literature—20th century—History and criticsm.
5. Vietnam—Exiles—Biography—History and criticism.
6. Literature, Comparative—American and Vietnamese.
7. Literature, Comparative—Vietnamese and American.
8. Soldiers' writings, American—History and criticism.
9. War stories, American—History and criticism.
10. Vietnam—In literature.   11. Narration (Rhetoric)   I. Title.
PS228.V5C47   1995
813'.5409358—dc20   95-19687
                                                          CIP

British Library Cataloguing in Publication data are available.

This book is published with the support and cooperation of the University
of Massachusetts Boston.

Acknowledgments for permission to reprint selections from previously published
material appear on the last printed page of this book.

The United States . . . desires only that these peoples should be left
in peace to work out their own destinies in their own way . . .
—Gulf of Tonkin Resolution, U.S. Congress

Không có gì qúy hỏn độc-lập và tụ-do.
(Nothing is more important than independence and freedom.)
—Hồ Chí Minh

Contents

Preface

I came to write this book because I experienced a complete turnaround in my perceptions of what I, like most Americans, used to call "Vietnam," and what I now call "the American war in Viet Nam." That transformation came about largely through my reading of noncanonical works concerning that war. My aim in this book is to work toward bringing my readers around to the same transformation, but the only way to experience that transformation completely is to read the primary sources I discuss in chapter 2 and in the third section of chapter 4.

My first knowledge of the war came during my earliest childhood in rural California, from watching the news on television. The war lasted for my entire youth; it was always there, small, on the television screen. The chronology of the war lies like an overlay in my mind on the chronology of my childhood. I was born in 1957—the year after the elections failed to take place that were supposed to unify North and South Viet Nam according to the Geneva accords. There were already American "advisors" in the country, and it had started to become a regular feature in the news. I was six when Diem and Kennedy were assassinated. I do not remember Diem; I remember not Kennedy's death, but his funeral: the black horse with the empty boots backwards in the stirrups. I was in second grade when the infamous Tonkin Gulf incident took place. I have a vague memory of Johnson's voice droning, and Johnson looking very earnest, and my mother disapproving of everything he did.

I was eight when the man who would become my husband fifteen years later went with the earliest marines to Chu Lai to build the landing strip there, from which so many planes would take off for the next eight years. From the years 1967 to 1969 I remember vividly four news events: the deaths of Robert Kennedy and Martin Luther King, Jr., "Tet" (which I have now learned to call the Tet Offensive of 1968, or Tết Mậu Thân), and the lunar landing. There was news of the war every night, like background noise, and that background noise focused on the American boys fighting the war.

My family followed that typical 1960s practice of eating dinner in front of the six o'clock news. We watched Huntley and Brinkley. My brother and I regularly said "Good night, Chet," "Good night, David," at bedtime. From the time I was old enough to pay attention, I heard about mythical places called "eye corps" and the Mekong Delta (that name particularly sticks in my mind, because I knew, at least, what a delta was, so I could make some sense of it). No one ever pointed it out to me on a world map to make it real, and for years I thought vaguely that Viet Nam must be somewhere near Japan. Some of the footage I saw on the news looked just like California—dusty, rolling hills. Other pictures looked like nothing at all, to me. Vietnamese villages were as alien, and unreal, as pictures of the moon, and they were often shown back to back, Viet Nam and the moon, separated by commercials for cars and dish detergent.

When I was fifteen I truly believed that the country of Viet Nam had no electricity, because all I saw on television were shots of thatched huts. No news perspective showed me that this was the countryside, the analog to where I lived. I have no memory of seeing Saigon on the news.

In high school, I had a friend who wore a POW bracelet. Viet Nam was part of the furniture for us, but it was distant, unreal. In 1973, for the first time in my memory, I experienced a December devoid of appeals to "bring our boys home for Christmas." The season seemed somehow empty to me— I missed those appeals for years afterward.

In that same year, at the age of sixteen, I became involved with a U.S. veteran of the war. He had been a lieutenant; his father, a retired colonel, had meant for him to be a career officer, but he had been so disillusioned by the war that he left the army after his tour in Viet Nam. He told me war stories. He told me about patrolling with his mechanized cavalry platoon around the Michelin rubber plantation: the United States Army received word each week from the plantation managers about where they would be harvesting, and the army avoided those areas in their patrols. That was what disillusioned him and made him leave the army. His story changed me, as an American, from a true believer into a cynic. I no longer believed in the righteousness of the war, as I had from the time I began thinking about it. I came to believe, as he did, that it was a fuck up, because it was mismanaged. Nevertheless, at that point, I still believed in U.S. good intentions.

In 1975, I sat in a college dormitory and watched the fall of Saigon—the final act in the television drama. The Vietnam Veterans Memorial covers the years 1958 to 1975: the years of my life from age one to age eighteen. Along with most Americans, for me the "fall of Saigon" was not only the end of the war, but also the end of any consciousness of the nation of Viet Nam. But it did not end my consciousness of the war. My relationship with the former lieutenant had changed me. I started trying to find out everything I could about the war. That meant, for me, reading novels and personal narratives that I found in the library and at used book sales. The first two books about the war I can remember reading were Philip Caputo's *A Rumor of War* and James Webb's *Fields of Fire*.

In 1981 I married a U.S. veteran of the war. He had been in the marines for seven years, had run away from home on his seventeenth birthday to join, to escape from his family. He found what he was looking for in the marines and intended to make it a career, until, in his second enlistment, he was sent to Viet Nam. He, too, became disillusioned and left the marines. He would talk about the war only when he was drunk. We were divorced after two years, but I carried with me the effects of having been married to someone with a bad case of post-traumatic stress disorder.

My desire to understand the experience of these men, and my own experiences with them and with the war on television, increased. I continued reading and started writing fiction about U.S. veterans and their families. My focus was unwaveringly on the effect of the war on Americans, and nothing in my reading steered me in any other direction. I read the oral histories by Al Santoli and Mark Baker, and more novels and personal narratives, mostly those in the center or at the periphery of the canon, although as I continued reading I was led far afield into such obscure books as Jim Morris's *War Story*, William E. Holland's *Let a Soldier Die*, Stephen Thorpe's *Walking Wounded*, and Newton Thornburg's *Cutter and Bone*. I read pretty much indiscriminately. I did not have much education when I began, having dropped out of college shortly after I started. These books were, overwhelmingly, by white American men, because that was what I found in the bookstores and the city library. Those are the books that came to hand to an American reader with a bad high school education and a year and a half of college.

Eventually my life changed. I went back to college, then I went to graduate school and got a master's degree from San Jose State University, a culturally diverse and wonderful place. After receiving my degree, I taught there for a year before entering the doctoral program at the University of California, Santa Cruz (UCSC). My perspective had started to shift, because while teaching at San Jose State I encountered many Vietnamese students.

I taught the upper-division writing requirement, a course that incorporated a standard final exam taken by all students enrolled in sections of the course. The exams were graded in common by all instructors teaching sections of the course, in a mass reading held on a Saturday. In my first semester there, the assigned topic was "Describe a journey."

During that Saturday I read about fifty stories of Vietnamese students' escapes from Viet Nam—"boat people" stories. In one stroke, my perception of the war altered drastically. Despite the dozens and dozens of books I had read, these were stories I knew nothing of. I read an essay by a student who had walked, with his family, across Cambodia to Thailand. I read an essay by a young woman who had been on a boat boarded by Thai pirates; her grandfather had dressed her as a boy, so she was the only woman on the boat who was not raped and murdered.

I realized that there was more involved in the war than I, as an American, had ever been led to believe. But I still did not know much. I read James Freeman's oral history of Vietnamese refugees, *Hearts of Sorrow*. But I still did not know much. When I entered the doctoral program, I thought I wanted to write about the underrepresentation of working-class and minority writers in the canon of "Vietnam War" (I still called it that) literature. In my first year at UCSC, I won the library's book collection contest for my collection of Viet Nam literature; my collection did not contain a single work by a Vietnamese author, and my essay focused on novels and narratives detailing the experiences of, for the most part, white American men.

Then I happened on an article called "Teaching Vietnam through Vietnamese Sources," by David Berman, which led me to the novel *Blue Dragon, White Tiger*. I also came upon Le Ly Hayslip's autobiography in a used bookstore—it was still only in hardback then, and had not sold that well before it was heavily promoted in paperback.

At the same time as I started teaching at San Jose State, I became involved with the third American veteran in my life. Dan Scripture had been in military intelligence and had spent a year in language school, learning Vietnamese. He had entered the army as a college graduate, already opposed to the war, with a sophisticated understanding of the history and politics that lay behind the war.

Dan was different from my previous veteran lovers in other ways, too. He had already spent time in veterans' rap groups when he and I met, and after we had lived together for a year, I joined a rap group for partners of veterans. We started teaching about the war together—first in a team-taught American Studies course in summer school, and then in a course cosponsored by the University Extension and VFW Post 5888. In the beginning, both of these courses focused on myths and realities of the war—American myths and realities.

In 1987, with Dan and his daughter, I made my first trip to the Vietnam Veterans Memorial in Washington. Standing before it, the three of us looked at our faces reflected back in the black granite and looked into all the pain the war had caused in our lives.

Now, as my perspective started to shift, I pursued Vietnamese works with the same dedication with which I had previously sought American works about the war. At UCSC I developed a mentoring relationship with a Vietnamese American student, a creative writing major trying to work her own immigration story into a novel. I now saw the war—the American War in Viet Nam—in a new perspective. I saw how my perceptions had been shaped by my culture; I saw how U.S. discourse about the war systematically excludes the Vietnamese context of the war. This discourse had made the war a solely American phenomenon for me; reading the Vietnamese exile writers showed me what I had missed.

As I pursued these issues, Dan's interest in Vietnamese language and culture reawakened. He pointed me toward sources to help me understand the Vietnamese context, and he blew the dust off his thick Vietnamese-English dictionary to show me the meanings of terms that I was encountering for the first time. We both shifted from writing "Vietnam" to "Viet Nam," meaning the country, not the war. The focus of our summer school course began to change, as well. We developed a course called "The Viet Nam War through Asian Sources," although we never got a chance to teach it.

Now I am learning Vietnamese with the ultimate goal of translating Vietnamese American authors who are publishing in the U.S. Vietnamese-language press. When I go to the Vietnam Veterans Memorial in Washington, or to the California Vietnam Veterans Memorial in Sacramento, in my mind's eye I also see the memorials in Viet Nam. I have pictures of them, taken by David Berman, on my desk. In every town a vertical stone rising above the thatch and tile roofs of the houses is inscribed "Tổ Quốc Ghi Cúng Các Liệt Sĩ" (The fatherland remembers the sacrifice of each fallen soldier). The stone memorials of Viet Nam and the stone memorials of America have come together for me now, memorializing the shared past and the shared destiny of our two countries.

A few acknowledgments are in order. I want to thank first Dan Scripture, without whom I would not have entered the doctoral program at UCSC, and without whose inspiration I would have had a much harder time gaining what familiarity I have with my Vietnamese and Vietnamese American sources. His criticisms of drafts of this work made it a much better work than it would have otherwise been.

Another special thanks to my Vietnamese American students, both at San Jose State University and at the University of California, Santa Cruz, especially Lucille Hahn Clark, for opening my eyes with their stories and providing me with the shift in perspective that enabled me to conceptualize this book.

Thanks also to my writing group: Leslie Bow, Elena Creef, Ellen Hart, Ekua Omosupe, and Miriam Wallace. For two years, this group made the writing process much less painful. Finally, thanks to Professor Susan Gillman, who not only encouraged me, but also helped me shape the writing.

The Viet Nam War / *The American War*

ONE

Introduction

Let's bomb them back into the stone age.
—Air Force General Curtis LeMay

The wise man shuts his mouth,
the strong man folds his arms.
—Vietnamese proverb

The Vietnamese are absent from the history of American policy
formation, just as much as they are absent from most of these
novels. They were in the scenery, but they were not anything that
we were really looking at. And this is a big part of why the effort
turned out to be so costly and so unsuccessful.
—Arnold Isaacs

If we are not the parents of little Vietnam, then surely we are the
godparents.
—John F. Kennedy

Indeed, from Asia it is clear that the Vietnam war will be important
in history mostly for what it did, internally, to the United States,
not what difference it made in Indochina.
—James Fallows

Fantasy and sensationalism shape the mind in ways beyond measure,
undoubtedly a great deal more than most scholarship does.
—John Dower

For thirty years, "Vietnam" has, for most Americans, been the
name of a war. That war has occupied a central position in American political and cultural discussion. The political positions that
were laid out during the war along the spectrum from conservative to liberal, pro- and anti-involvement, have become entrenched in American cultural reworkings of the war. Few voices in the ongoing U.S. discourse
on the subject acknowledge that Viet Nam is the name of a country.

New voices have appeared—the voices of Vietnamese exile writers, publishing in English and attempting to reach an American audience. These voices, however, have not been heard. Vietnamese exile writers face a dilemma of audience: writing in English, they are interested in communicating with a Euro-American audience that has largely ignored them, while the still-large reactionary element in the Vietnamese exile community reject them because they do not take a hard-line anti-Communist stance.

Most U.S. discourse about "Vietnam" the war is enmeshed in the history of stereotypical representations of Asians that make it almost impossible for that discourse to break from the idea of "Vietnam" the war in order to consider the participation in that war of Viet Nam the country.[1]

It has been said that normally the winners of a war write the history and the losers live with it. In the case of the Second Indochina War,[2] the United States and the Republic of Viet Nam (RVN)[3] are the losers, yet, on a worldwide scale, it is Americans who are writing the history of the war. The United States has steadfastly ignored any document published in English by the victors,[4] but it also steadfastly ignores any writings by Vietnamese refugee writers who are, also, among the losers of this war.

Ethnocentrism and nationalism have marked U.S. discourse about the war in Viet Nam, causing America to turn hermetically around and around about itself so that the same notes—a few notes from the Left, a few notes from the Right—are sounded repeatedly and no new understandings can be reached. These polarized positions share an ethnocentrism that conceives of the war as an American "experience."

The American "Vietnam experience" has been mythologized. This mythologizing has taken place from the beginning of the war, with many soldiers using John Wayne movies as paradigms through which to understand their personal experiences. In addition, the American cultural mythology that emphasizes individualism and the primacy of personal experience has caused U.S. mythologizing of the war to focus narrowly on soldiers' private experiences, thereby depoliticizing representations of the war and excluding Vietnamese "experience" of the war, because, for most American soldiers, any Vietnamese experience was almost by definition outside of their experience. The war was conducted in such a way as to ensure the separation between most American soldiers and most Vietnamese. By continuing to focus on individual experience, representations of the war reinforce, rather than critique, this ethnocentrism. Literary criticism of representations of the war has also participated in this mythologizing and valorizing of personal experience.

This mythologizing has also been present from the beginning of political discourse about the war. Globalist thinking—casting the world in cold war terms—made it unnecessary to look closely at Viet Nam, because it was simply a "domino." Because of the entrenched nature of anticommunism in U.S. politics and culture, the ethnocentrism of globalist thinking has not been immediately obvious. The mythic patterns predispose Americans to focus solely on the United States, to the exclusion of Viet Nam, and this exclusion is one of the reasons so little has changed in the ongoing discourse about the war. This mythology is part of the American cultural fabric, and few individuals have been able to transcend that mythology to challenge the ethnocentrism of the discourse.

The mythologizing, of course, fits the purposes of Americans across the political spectrum. The Right accuses the government of betraying the military, and the Left accuses the military-industrial complex of betraying the country. Both positions share basic assumptions: the assumption of betrayal and the assumption of American responsibility to the exclusion of any consideration of Viet Nam, Vietnamese politics, Vietnamese persons, or Vietnamese war-making capabilities or goals. When Americans are looking for somebody to blame for America's defeat, nobody thinks of blaming the Democratic Republic of Viet Nam (DRV) and the National Liberation Front (NLF) for defeating the United States. America's "Americanizing" of the war serves broad purposes and fits into historic attitudes Americans have about themselves and about the United States and the world, and into our institutionalized political discourse. It serves the perennial circular exchange between Left and Right. Thus, for the most part, America turns a deaf ear to any dissident voices, from within or without. A scene from the movie *Platoon* illustrates the way this totalizing mythology erases any fact or perception that runs counter to the myths.

Platoon's protagonist, Chris Taylor, has been wounded during the climactic battle between the U.S. Army and the People's Army of Viet Nam (PAVN).[5] After the battle he kills Sergeant Barnes, then is discovered in the forest by a relief column and is carried to the medevac helicopters. As the medevac carries Chris above the scene of the battle, he says in the voiceover, "We did not fight the enemy; we fought ourselves, and the enemy was in us."

While it is true that the United States was divided against itself, and Chris Taylor's comment is an accurate and heartfelt recognition of that division, his characterization of that division as the real and only war is at the very least an understatement. The editing of this scene makes it much more than an understatement, however, because Chris's remark is juxtaposed with a series of shots that draw direct attention to dead Vietnamese soldiers. Rah, one of Taylor's platoon mates, bends over a dead PAVN soldier and takes a packet of cigarettes from his pocket. Then Taylor's stretcher is carried past a bomb crater which is being used as a mass grave.[6] First we see a bulldozer pushing bodies into the crater, then we see a slow-motion shot of two American soldiers—one black, one white—throwing in a PAVN corpse. We hear a report being called in on the radio that five hundred "Victor Charlies" are said to be killed in action (these are not actually Viet Cong, but uniformed PAVN regulars; this is one of the few authenticity errors in the film).

Following the series of shots of Vietnamese corpses, when Chris Taylor actually speaks the line on the voiceover, he has just looked down from the helicopter at the mass grave around which PAVN bodies are strewn in grotesque positions. The callousness of the burial—the bodies being bull-dozed and the slow-motion shot of Americans tossing a dead Vietnamese into the grave—coupled with the ethnocentrism and the literal blindness of Chris Taylor's sentiment about the war, illustrate perfectly the dominant American attitude.[7]

The real war in *Platoon* and in American culture is not the historical war fought on the battlefields, but rather the ongoing meta-war, which attempts to erase Vietnamese from their own reality and make them part of American reality. The United States lost the shooting war, but so far it is winning this meta-war. U.S. discourse about the war seems most comfortable when it can center exclusively on American issues and abstract "Vietnam" the war from Viet Nam the country, or when it can discuss the war solely as a U.S. political conflict, rather than as a political and shooting war in the country of Viet Nam. In fact, for many years America seemed to regard a soldier's having been to Viet Nam as a kind of contamination: witness the genre of books, films, television shows, and feature articles portraying, almost as a stock character, the crazy veteran, who had brought the war home with him.

In a 1975 article, psychologist Robert Jay Lifton wrote about "the postwar war," a war of consciousness, "the struggle over the residual meaning of the Vietnam War as perceived by antagonistic groups in American society" ("Postwar" 181). He looked at the "contending expressions of survival" of two groups—antiwar veterans and former POWs, identifying them as two political poles who defined themselves in terms of either resistance or patriotism. These poles make up the postwar war—a war among Americans, the successful meta-war that finally succeeds in erasing the Vietnamese in a way that was never quite possible during the shooting phase of the American war in Viet Nam.

Susan Jeffords, in *The Remasculinization of America*, describes the way this meta-war has proceeded:

[Peter Goldman and Tony Fuller's] collection, *Charlie Company*, is subtitled, "What Vietnam Did To Us." In addition to participating in the establishment of the veteran-as-victim mythology, their subtitle now locates the blame for veterans' suffering in "Vietnam." Throughout the book, Vietnam takes the confused shape of the war itself, of the untrustworthy nature of the Vietnamese allies, of the enemy's strategies and deceptions, even of the unfamiliar terrain. . . . But in spite of the move toward identifying Vietnam as itself at fault, the phrase, "What Vietnam Did To Us," still focuses on the war as an interpersonal relationship in which the soldier has been victimized by the war and its circumstances. (145–46)

By identifying Viet Nam, the country, with the war in Viet Nam, U.S. representations collapse all distinctions between enemy and ally and among Vietnamese individuals, leaving only one distinction: "The World" of the West, being desirable, homey, and "good," versus "Vietnam," an entity composed of country and war together where only evil resides.

Paul Fussell, in *The Great War and Modern Memory*, contends that the supposed inadequacy of language to describe the experience of warfare is "less a problem of 'linguistics' than of rhetoric" (170). Writers addressing World War I had to draw on old-fashioned rhetoric, which seemed inadequate to describe the new form of warfare. Likewise, Americans going to war in Viet Nam had available to them only old-fashioned rhetoric, rhetoric derived from and most appropriate to World War II. As we will see in chapter 3, the 1940s rhetoric of the race war in the Pacific is often dropped whole onto the war in Viet Nam, contributing to the obscuring of the specific realities of Viet Nam by replacing them with a generic U.S. racism directed toward all Asians.

The American paradigm for warfare remains, for the most part, however, World War II in Europe, making the war in Viet Nam seem anomalous. Yet it is actually World War II in Europe, with its clear victory rather than a negotiated settlement, that is the anomaly. As Fussell points out in *Wartime*, his examination of behavior in World War II, our latter-day belief that soldiers in that war fought for clear ideals, that their battle experience somehow made sense to them, is another myth. But that is the myth against which most Euro-American Viet Nam War writers measure their own experience.

The American mythology of the war in Viet Nam is bonded to the idea of "experience." This "experience" is something that happens to a (traditionally male) individual, who uses the perceptual framework supplied to him by his culture to construct a narrative of it. This overriding faith in the validity of individual experience causes us to read Viet Nam narratives as historical documents rather than as literature. The relationship to reality is assumed to be unmediated. Thus, a mythology around the war has become the sum of American cultural understanding. Americans experienced only what their culture prepared them to experience. The majority of U.S. soldiers who have written novels and narratives cast the war in familiar terms—the Americans are the good guys in a cowboy mode, and the Vietnamese are evil "Japs" or little brown brothers. Viet Nam becomes the heart of darkness, seen exclusively in terms of jungle (though Viet Nam also contains plains and delta and cities).[8] "Vietnam" the war becomes a personal experience, devoid of political content and devoid of sense. The repeated American complaint is that the war did not make any sense; however, it is precisely the mythological framework in which Americans view that war that robs it of its sense.

As Lynne Hanley puts it in *Writing War: Fiction, Gender, and Memory*,

The soldier's story, rooted as it is in a particular man's expeirence of a particular war, tends not only to sentimentalize, but also to dehistoricize our apprehension of war. Vietnam is not seen as one in a series of wars whose repetitions reveal a pattern in our relations with the peoples and cultures of the Third World. . . . the clash of cultures and of political and commercial interests is mythologized and psychologized . . . as an isolated and personal encounter. (106)

By focusing on narrow personal experience, or the "grunt's eye view," the larger framework of U.S. history and its neo-imperialism and of Vietnamese politics—overviews that would provide "sense"—are erased from the parameters of the narrative.

For example, many U.S. narratives complain of the supposed "impossibility" of telling the enemy from the civilians. Individual soldiers, tied into a cultural framework that says Asians are "different," "sneaky," and "not to be trusted," see Vietnamese who are farmers by day and guerrillas by night, and interpret this dual role as Asian duplicity. Therefore, the American soldiers do not see the Vietnamese farmer/guerrillas may be honest men fighting for independence against a dictatorial and unwanted government that is cynically backed as a "democracy" by the U.S. government. Instead, the Americans' cultural framework has trained them to see themselves as atomized individuals devoid of history and politics, and to perceive others in the same light, so they see, and represent, themselves as well-meaning good guys senselessly betrayed by racially inferior peasants who do not recognize good intentions in the Americans. When Philip Caputo, in *A Rumor of War*, wants a Vietnamese woman whose home he has just searched to recognize that "[w]e're all-American good-guy GI Joes" (84), he is demonstrating exactly this attitude.

Another article of faith of the mythology is that the experience of war in "Vietnam" is unlike any previous American war.[9] The true "uniqueness" of this war lies in the American defeat, and even that is not without precedent (the South in the Civil War). It is telling that all previous U.S. wars have names that identify them as wars, rather than countries: the Mexican War, the Spanish-American War, and so on. Korea is halfway between: if one says "Korea" in the United States it is ambiguous as to whether the word refers to the war or to the country; "Korean War" is still the more common reference. But "Vietnam" in common usage refers unambiguously to the war rather than the country. Perhaps, as part of the meta-war, U.S. usage has colonized the name of the country as a stand-in for the name of the war. In this light it is also interesting to note that the losers of the American Civil War often call it by a different name—the War Between the States. Perhaps that is a name they can own, as Americans try to own the war in Viet Nam by colonizing the country's name.

One problem of the American emphasis on experience is that it is the experience of teenagers, with their adolescent moral visions, that is being written by adults. It is by now a commonplace that the average age of the American soldier in Viet Nam was nineteen, whereas in World War II it was twenty-six. (The Republic of Viet Nam refused to draft men younger than twenty, a policy the U.S. government consistently pressured the RVN to change.) Rather than expanding into more mature political, historical, or cross-cultural understandings, the discourse about the war has remained focused on the experiences of very young men and has resisted later reinterpretation. That reinterpretation of those experiences might result in transgressions against the dominant mythology about the war.

The literature is much more conservative in terms of such reevaluations than the actual lives of most veterans seem to be. Ellen Frey-Wouters and Robert S. Laufer report that only 31 percent of veterans surveyed "harbor negative feelings toward the Vietnamese" (135). Psychologist Robert Jay Lifton reports that an important phase in the readjustment of veterans he worked with after the war was ridding themselves of the "gook syndrome"— coming to see the humanity of the Vietnamese and exposing "previously untapped sources of guilt" ("Postwar" 188). That guilt arose from the actions taken by morally immature young men; as more mature older veterans, these men had to reevaluate their actions and attitudes. No reevaluation comparable to this private one has taken place in the public representation of the war.[10] One reason for this failure is the way canonization shapes publishing practice; the little evidence available suggests that writings by women and people of color might transgress the dominant mythologizing about the war. Very little material has been published, although lack of publication does not imply any lack of manuscripts.

One manuscript that suggests the ways in which "experiences" differing from the dominant mythology might transgress and challenge parts of that mythology is an autobiography written as a senior thesis by UCSC student Juan Ramirez. In this unpublished document Ramirez details the ways U.S. soldiers could be nonracist towards the Vietnamese.

As the column of Vietnamese people passed on in single file, some of our guys were pushing and kicking people along, sometimes jabbing the muzzle of their rifles into the people's ribs or up their rear ends. . . .

It was while I was standing guard over this line of people that I felt more like a Nazi or S.S. than a warrior. Images of Nazi troops herding Jewish people down streets where they had lived, pushing and kicking them as they passed, kept entering my mind. I tried to shake it, but I could not. (36)

In another incident, Ramirez unties a teenage prisoner and gives him a can of C ration peaches, for which his corporal rebukes him. "Are you retarded or something?!" the corporal screams (40).

Ramirez describes one incident which served as a breakthrough in understanding. His squad had finally defeated two PAVN soldiers who had been firing from a bunker, shooting down two helicopters, pinning down two hundred marines, killing eight and wounding eleven. When Ramirez entered the bunker he saw how the PAVN soldier, knowing he was dying, had laid out pictures of his family in a kind of altar. Ramirez threw out another American, who was playing with the stuff: "I used to think my life must have changed the most the day my grandmother died. But this day, I would have to say, was that day. I lost almost everything I knew and believed in. I lost my innocence, I lost my religion, I lost my own family, I lost my patriotism and national pride, and I lost what little self-respect I had left" (52). In seeing the PAVN soldier's preparation for his own death, Ramirez recognized him as a person with values similar to his own, and thus transcended any residual racism he might have felt toward the Vietnamese.

Ramirez's understanding of the Vietnamese was of practical use. He warned his squad that when they harass villagers, the Viet Cong take reprisals. Members of his squad ignored Ramirez and attempted to rape a village girl. That night, grenades were thrown at the squad's listening post, after more than three weeks of no contact. After the attack, Ramirez confronted the sergeant and the corpsman who had been involved in the attempted rape.

"You stupid motherfuckers! You're responsible for this. . . ."
The sergeant and corpsman were embarrassed. They both apologized, but I saw no real remorse from the sergeant, who kept reminding me who was in charge and for me to be careful with my temper. The corpsman was very affected by this incident. Some of it had to do with him having to treat one of our guys because of something he had done. He really felt guilty about the whole thing. For the remainder of our time together, he became more serious and professional. But more importantly, he became more human toward the Vietnamese. (96)

Ramirez is also one of the few writers on the war who recognizes the Vietnamese role in the outcome of the war—many better educated, so-called experts manage to forget that the United States was fighting against someone. He notes that the United States has been "retelling the history of the Vietnam War in a way that *discounts* the will and determination of the Vietnamese people and the arrogance and stupidity of our own leaders as the reasons for losing an unjust and immoral act of war, with great losses to the Vietnamese as well as nearly 60,000 men and women of our own" (21). Ramirez's position derives not from political analysis, but from empathy. His attitude toward the Vietnamese is also partially shaped by his own experience as a victim of racism. It is also important to note that Ramirez's account is an unpublished one; Americans of color are terribly underrepresented in the literature on the war, so any insights they might have are left uncommunicated.[11]

Other assumptions follow from the adherence to the idea of experience: only those who were "there" can really understand the experience. This qualification gives the participant writer greater "authority" and sets him (it is usually "him," since few books have been written by women veterans) at the center of the discussion. Viet Nam War narratives tend to be judged first on the basis of their "authenticity," rather than their literary merit, popularity, moral value, or political vision; in a circular argument, "authenticity" is construed as authenticity of *experience*. Trinh Minh-ha addresses the question of authenticity in terms of Third World writers:

They [First-World readers], like their anthropologists whose speciality is to detect all the layers of my falseness and truthfulness, are in a position to decide what/who is "authentic" and what/who is not. No uprooted person is invited to participate in this "special" [third world] wo/man's issue unless s/he "makes up" her/his mind and paints her/himself thick with authenticity. Eager not to disappoint, i try my best to offer my benefactors and benefactresses what they most anxiously yearn for: the possibility of a difference, yet a difference or an otherness that will not go so far as to question the foundation of their beings and makings. (88)

Minh-ha's insight into the politics of authenticity can be applied to writings about the Viet Nam War, as well. The readership has sought after difference and authenticity from the writers of these narratives, but a difference "that will not go so far as to question the foundation of their beings." Consequently, the highest value has been placed on narrowly defined works.

We can, in fact, watch as these narrowly defined works set the bounds of canon-formation in the area of Viet Nam War literature. If we look at what is being taught in college classes, at topics in critical journals and at conferences, there seem to be five books at the center of the emerging canon: Philip Caputo's *A Rumor of War*, Tim O'Brien's *Going after Cacciato*, Michael Herr's *Dispatches*, John Del Vecchio's *The Thirteenth Valley*, and Ron Kovic's *Born on the Fourth of July*.[12] This central canon is exclusively male and Euro-American, and consists entirely of participants (veterans or journalists) and, with one exception (Kovic), middle-class college graduates. Around the center of the canon revolve other works, including some works by women, but the standards for the central canon are maintained throughout. Although the political positions of the canonical and semicanonical authors differ somewhat (from conservatively liberal to liberally conservative, with O'Brien and James Webb at the respective poles), they are culturally homogeneous, strongly suggesting the privileging of a particular point of view. Some works by women, people of color, working-class writers, and nonparticipants have been published, but they have often been issued by small presses, distributed poorly, and gone out of print quickly, and have been generally ignored by critics.[13] The most stunning absence from this forming canon is that of Vietnamese American writers, an absence which, as I discuss in chapter 2, is itself related to questions of canon and literary categorization, as well as politics and American mythologizing. As Timothy Lomperis succinctly puts it, "Most of the literature on the Vietnam War is an exercise in American cultural narcissism" (63). I will propose a counter-canon, comprised of works that, in Trinh Minh-ha's words, have "no end that leaves the mind at rest" (142).

The literary criticism of Viet Nam War literature participates in this canon-formation process and also replicates the ethnocentrism that marks both canonical and noncanonical Viet Nam War literature. Book-length critical works have tended to define a narrow analytic framework, then to select a range of works that fits their particular paradigm, and exclude all other works. The Vietnamese exile writers' works have so far not been selected, because they do not fit any of the analytic paradigms.

Philip Beidler explores the American literature of the Viet Nam War in terms of American myth and myth making. In his first, pioneering book, *American Literature and the Experience of Vietnam*, he writes that American literature of the war, "even as it projects itself forward into new forms of imaginative invention that seem to challenge traditional modes of mythic understanding, proves often in retrospect to have shaped itself greatly in their prophetic image as well" (26). In Beidler's analysis, American literary renderings of the war fulfill American mythology, although he does not view what he has described as entrapment. If this analysis is valid, then American literature of the war is doomed to repeat endlessly its history of ethnocentrism, immaturity, and apolitical reliance on "experience."

Beidler is concerned with literary quality: he attempts to find the "important" writers on the war, claiming that the novelists he includes have produced "more than twenty-five works of major importance" (4). His judgments are based largely on whether an author gets the war "right," and his criteria for getting it right seem to be based mainly on whether the veteran or journalist authors' versions of their experience match his own conception of the "Vietnam experience"—a tangled "mixup" of "American mythic consciousness and realized experiential fact" that cannot be sorted out (31). Beidler does not define what "experiential fact" consists of; for him, memory and the re-creation of experience in narrative are relatively unproblematic. He judges novels on their truth value, and even calls William Eastlake's surreal novel *The Bamboo Bed* "art-truth."

Beidler is a veteran of the war, and his first book, especially in the opening chapters, is an oblique working out of his own experience through literary criticism rather than personal narrative. His first chapter is called "Situation Report." In a later chapter he writes, "It is a line, like some others . . . that in its way can crystallize the whole experience of the war for anyone who carries its memory" (97–98). Despite the lack of first-person pronoun in that sentence, it is clearly Beidler's own memory that is crystallized.

There is nothing intrinsically wrong with Beidler's choice of literary criticism for his own textual working out of the war. However, the analytic criteria that he chooses have many problems. He judges all works in terms of experience. Antiwar poets are good, for him, only when they "bring the experience home." Nothing that is abstract, philosophical, or polemical has value for him. He praises Frances Fitzgerald's study of the history and politics of the war, *Fire in the Lake*, but he can include it in his framework only by seeing it as being essentially about "experience"—a serious misreading, in my view, of Fitzgerald's historical/political analysis.

As a result, Beidler's analysis focuses on and valorizes an extremely narrow selection of works about the war. Because it is only American experience in which he is interested, works by non-Americans are excluded, as are works by nonparticipants (he does include work by journalists who were there—he is especially fond of Michael Herr's *Dispatches*). Thus the works Beidler deals with, and the analytic framework in which he discusses them, are necessarily ethnocentric and are almost exclusively either personal narratives or autobiographical novels. Further, they are restricted to the points of view of very young men.

The limitations of Beidler's definitions of American literature of the war become clearer in his second, more ambitious, book, *Rewriting America: Vietnam Authors in Their Generation* (the title is slightly misleading: Beidler does not compare "Vietnam authors" to other writers of their generation; rather, he compares them to one another). In this work, Beidler participates enthusiastically in the process of canon formation. He addresses the works of twenty-two writers, twenty of whom are men and twenty-one of whom are white. Sixteen of his writers are veterans, at least eight of whom were college graduates before going to the war; five were officers. While all of these writers represent important and interesting points of view, there are many other, unrepresented viewpoints, equally valid and important. The emerging canon of American Viet Nam War literature, however, has formed itself around the points of view Beidler focuses on, and he does not challenge these points of view in any fundamental way.

Beidler's selection process has been even more exact: he has chosen writers who have produced second and third works that, in some way, address the "experience" of the war; Beidler examines each author's oeuvre of Viet Nam War–related works. This approach gives depth and substance to his discussion of each author.

He works hard to place Viet Nam War authors within American literary traition and to find their forebears—for O'Brien it is Hemingway and Melville, for Caputo, Hemingway, Cooper, and Crane, for Winston Groom, James Jones. He looks at the ways in which his authors take American literary traditions and recast them to fit their experiences of the Viet Nam War, "that past reinscribing itself as mythic present" (45), and he makes a convincing argument about this reinscription. But once again, his argument preselected his sample: he has chosen works that do fit within these traditions and avoided any other works. (That Beidler has read more widely in the literature of the war than either of his two books indicate is clearly shown by his article in the January 1992 number of *College English*, in which he discusses Danielle Steel, Franklin Allen Leib, and Kurt Vonnegut.)

Nonetheless, Beidler does work across a wide generic range. He discusses the novelists Tim O'Brien, Philip Caputo, Robert Olen Butler, James Webb, Winston Groom, and Larry Heinemann in one chapter, the playwright David Rabe, the poets John Balaban, W. D. Ehrhart, David Huddle, Yusef Komunyakaa, Walter McDonald, and Bruce Weigl, and in the final chapter, "The Literature of Witness," the journalists Gloria Emerson, Frances Fitzgerald, Robert Stone, and Michael Herr.

His "Rewriting America" entails the reinscription of American cultural mythology into postmodern, "post-Vietnam" literature. Beidler claims that the most important achievement of the writers he examines is their desire to "reconstitute [American] mythoogy as a medium both of historical self-reconsideration and, in the same moment, of historical self-renewal and even self-reinvention." (5). It turns out that he means by this opaque prose that the Viet Nam War authors he writes about are finding ways to reintegrate their previously marginalized experience into the mainstream of American literary and cultural tradition. Although he mentions "a rewriting of major archetypal forms of American consciousness into new dimensions of imaginative possibility" (38), he never explains what it is that is new.

Beidler adopts Michael Herr's conceit that "there was no country here but the war" and refers repeatedly to "the country that was the war" and "a place that was the war," making clear that the experience and the memory that his American authors (and he himself) are addressing are the American mythic memory of a war that it considers to be its own, rather than a war fought in a country called Viet Nam, a war shared by Americans and Vietnamese of various political positions. He insists that the "best" narratives take place in "the country called the war." For Beidler, "best" means the most exclusively, Americanly ethnocentric. He therefore describes the 1968 Tet Offensive, as portrayed in Gustav Hasford's *The Short-Timers*, as "a Disneyland of megadeth called Vietnam" (280).

As in his first book, Beidler is still focused on "experience." He writes of his authors that "[t]heir sense of profound experiential authority in the same moment allows them to make their largest meanings through the bold embrace of new strategies of imaginative invention; and thus, precisely, in the inscription of memory into art, they become in the fullest sense the creators of cultural myth for new times and other" (2). In the same paragraph he writes that the Viet Nam generation had "the belief in acts of imagination, often conceived in some new, unmediated relationship with experience itself, that could do nothing less than change the world" (2). Beidler seems to share this belief in the possibility of art in an "unmediated" relationship with experience and its possibility to change the world. Yet, oddly, he claims that the war in Viet Nam "settled virtually nothing" (3), despite the clear victory by the NLF and PAVN that put in place the contemporary government of the Socialist Republic of Viet Nam. Clearly he means that it did not settle anything for Americans, but his ethnocentrism will not allow him to phrase it in that way. Indeed, Beidler's stress on "experience" is an affirmation of a major American mythopoeic metaphor.

Beidler's framework causes him to make contradictory arguments. He contends that the conservative James Webb, in *Fields of Fire* and subsequent novels, is writing propaganda and revisionist history, "reshaping the terms of Vietnam" (74), while Caputo and other more liberal writers are reinscribing older cultural myths in postmodern, "post-Vietnam" terms, and thus are doing a good thing. He does not recognize that all these writers are engaged in revisionist history, the liberals as well as the conservatives, that the act of turning memory into narrative is itself revision. Rather than openly saying that he is sympathetic to Caputo's politics and not to Webb's, Beidler makes a contradictory and insupportable argument about the nature of their narratives. Furthermore, he makes untenable aesthetic judgments to support his covert political judgment: he calls Webb's writing "popular stereotype and cliche . . . unintentionally parodic" (72) and condemns his portrayals of women. Yet he describes Caputo's novels as "post-Vietnam mythic fictions" (52) and fails to note Caputo's dismal portrait of June, the main female character of *Indian Country*, a novel Beidler unreservedly admires.

Beidler praises new, postmodern styles, as opposed to traditional "epic" war novels. Winston Groom, he writes, is "exemplary of the new and imaginatively inventive sense making, often resulting in new levels of insight and acceptance, achieved in second and third novels" (86), and of Heinemann's two novels he writes that they are a "paradigm to date of the Vietnam author in his generation and of his continued rewriting of the literary memory of the war into an ongoing revisionary encounter with the sundry mythologies of the national culture" (90). Although second and third novels by these authors may indeed display more "acceptance" of the experience, few of them extend larger political or philosophical musings. Although the writers gain distance and perspective, they do not seem to gain maturity. Rather, the genre they are working in requires them to re-present and rearticulate the understandings of the very young men they were when they were at war, and Beidler's criticism affirms this practice. As mature writers, these authors, including Beidler himself, simply reexplore those immature understandings.

Moreover, from his first book to his second, Beidler has moved from being a rather unsophisticated critic of personal experience to a hypersophisticated one sounding the syntax of postmodernism, writing in a grammar inaccessible to any but the initiated—thus Beidler himself seeks to join the canon of contemporary literary criticism. Ultimately, Beidler wants to have it both ways: he wants "postmodern" writing to be simultaneously about experience and about nothing but writing itself. It is not possible to have it both ways, and the only part of his argument that allows him to try is his unquestioning privileging of the term "experience."

Like Beidler, Thomas Myers is interested in "experience" in his study, *Walking Point: American Narratives of Vietnam* (1988). Myers leans so heavily on experience as a category of analysis that he considers students of his class on the literature of the war to be "veterans" of the class. He also seems to confuse the act of writing a critical study of the literature with the condition of being a veteran of the war. He constantly uses "insider" terminology to refer not only to the war, but to his project: in his acknowledgments he thanks people by noting that "one always finds the most necessary point men if he asks for volunteers" (xi). He writes of the authors under consideration in his study that they are "the necessary FNGs who, as they enter new American terrain, pass a line of ghostly short-timers that includes Cooper and Melville. . . . Walking point, they share the interior artistic resolution, the deciphered historical riddle" (33). Myers overextends his metaphor and thus muddies his own analysis irrevocably. Like Beidler, he believes in the primacy of the experience of the veteran-writer, to the point where he considers the veteran's "testimony, imaginatively and symbolically rendered by the literary point man," to be "the most telling historical text" (30).

Myers warps Hayden White's idea that historical narrative is a form of representation by turning it around and claiming that, therefore, historical novels are history. If, as he claims, the narrow, experiential point of view of the single veteran author is the best historical view of the war, then American understandings of the war are necessarily constricted by a drastically narrow frame.

Myers does criticize U.S. conduct of the war itself by remarking that "failure to read Vietnamese cultural history, however, would prove fatal to the desire to avoid a quagmire" (28). He replicates the error he criticizes, though, by valorizing the experience of the American soldier as the major category through which to view the war. In his critique of American conduct of the war he describes the "peasant population" and the "villagers . . . buffeted continually by the shifting practices of Saigon and Washington" (27). Nowhere does he refer to Vietnamese as persons, only as "peasants" and "villagers"—in his view of the war, shaped by the narratives of the writers he canonizes, there are no urbanites, no "people," simply Asian ciphers characterized by the stereotypes called up in the images of "peasants" and "villagers." These are particularly passive stereotypes, leaving no room for images of active resistance, such as that posed by the NLF.

Despite his indication that the roots of U.S. involvement can be traced at least as far back as Ho Chi Minh's overtures to Woodrow Wilson at the Versailles Conference at the end of World War I, Myers insists on seeing the war as "a dark monument to the powers of American imagination" (4), as if the war were the sole creation of the United States. For Myers, the war is "the extension and evolution of a number of deeply rooted American traditions, a crucial national experience requiring both text and context" (5), again as if it were a one-sided dance, without presence or participation by any Vietnamese party.

Myers's main claim is that war novelists are "walking point" because they break new ground in historical representation. He identifies writers who, he believes, counter the trends of both popular culture and governmental myth making: "To respond adequately to the leveling process of popular myth and official reification, the novelist must light out for new aesthetic territory and begin anew" (13). Myers's use of an overfamiliar line in his call for the new is perhaps telling, since that is precisely what the writers he studies do not do; instead they remain implicated in the old cultural paradigms that produce stereotypical representations of Asians.

Myers also tends to be self-contradictory. After claiming that the war is an outgrowth or extension of American tradition, he then sees it, oddly, as "a cultural disturbance of a new kind, the end point . . . of a number of long-standing components of national myth" (24). Aside from his inability to decide whether the war is a new thing in American culture or not, the war was clearly not the "end point" of anything, since history did not stop in 1975; the Republic of Viet Nam ceased to exist, but the United States continued. Myers's teleological view of history blinds him to America's participation as, in many ways, imperialist business as usual.

One of Myers's main assertions is that

the fullest and most self-conscious works redefine the American complexes of innocence and experience, guilt and expiation, taking into account not only the price paid by the Vietnamese in human life, material waste, and cultural fragmentation, but also the admission that any assertion of American victimization or loss must be accompanied by a recognition of the national capacity for excess and destruction. (26)

But most of the writers he studies, including Del Vecchio, O'Brien, Caputo, and Herr, do not take much account at all of "the price paid by the Vietnamese," in any more than superficial observations. He goes on to say that the "finest literary point men of Vietnam share a key narrative project—to re-create fully and imaginatively how the American soldier became both agent and victim of the narrow interpretive spectrum by which the conflict was illuminated" (26). It is true that many U.S. narratives of the war portray U.S. soldiers as both agents and victims, and rightly so. But Myers's vision is clouded by his own interpretive muddiness again: the experiential focus of the veteran writer of a novel or personal narrative centered in the daily experience of war sheds no light on the dynamics that create the agent/victim position. U.S. soldiers at the time usually could not see their way out of that position; recreating their experience through narrative also does not do so. Only by broadening one's cultural and historical and political frameworks can one illuminate the full dynamics of that position, and of all positions experienced by participants in the war. Myers organizes his study around "particular aesthetic" strategies, using the "finest Vietnam prose narratives" (32) as exemplars of each. All of his writers are white, all either veterans or journalists: he stays well within the bounds of the canon.

The most disturbing aspect about Myers's work is that he is guilty of sloppy scholarship. He casually remarks that 40 percent of U.S. casualties were "Black and Hispanic," but he cites no source for that figure; for most of the war, "Hispanics" were not counted separately from whites, so no accurate figure for Latino casualties can be ascertained (estimates have been made based on surnames); African-American casualties comprised 12.6 percent of deaths in Viet Nam between 1965 and 1970.[14] While this one use of an imaginary statistic might be excusable, it reflects on the quality of the work as a whole.

John Hellmann, in *American Myth and the Legacy of Vietnam*, shifts the analytic emphasis from "experience" to the dimensions of American myth. In so doing, however, he makes the same solipsistic move that many novelists and memoirists make. Hellmann conceives of the war as a one-sided endeavor, an event perpetrated by the United States against itself. This attitude is reflected in his choice of phraseology.

Vietnam is an experience that has severely called into question American myth. Americans entered Vietnam with certain expectations that a story, a distinctly American story, would unfold. When the story of America in Vietnam turned into something unexpected, the true nature of the larger story of America itself became the subjet of intense cultural dispute. On the deepest level, the legacy of Vietnam is the disruption of our story, of our explanation of the past and vision of the future. (x)

It is typical of most U.S. discourse about the war that rather than seeing the war as a collision between the United States and Viet Nam in which the United States was not completely in control, Hellmann sees it as a revelation of a larger—but still exclusively American—truth.

This view leads him to conclude that, "America has yet to be conquered, but it has inflicted upon itself a failure so spiritually wounding that its citizens have been compelled, of their own will, to open the landscape of the nation's capital with a Vietnam memorial that is a symbolic grave" (224). Again, the solipsism of the idea that America "inflicted upon itself a failure" in Viet Nam makes about as much sense as a line uttered by the character Shang, in the film *Alamo Bay*, to his wife: "You got yourself knocked up so I'd marry you, then you knocked yourself up again." A clear illustration of American attitudes of superiority is that Hellmann sees the war not as a victory for the Democratic Republic of Viet Nam and the National Liberation Front—to do so would be to admit defeat by a foreign power—but as a "failure" (less humiliating than a "defeat"?) America inflicted "on itself." Like so many U.S. writers, Hellmann overstates both the importance and the uniqueness of the war in U.S. history. Perhaps because it is the war of our lifetimes, most of us seem to lack perspective.

Hellmann traces the place of Asia in American myth in an attempt to create a context, but he does not follow through in this effort. He cites the commonplace view that civilization started in Asia and spread west—with the U.S. reaching west, the circle would be completed. He fails to see the United States reaching across the Pacific as a fulfillment of its own "manifest destiny," its historically imperialist westward movement.

Nonetheless, many of Hellmann's insights into the American debate over the conduct of the war are illuminating and useful, such as his identification of *The Ugly American* as a jeremiad in the three-hundred-year-old tradition defined by Sacvan Bercovitch. As so many intelligent and insightful writers do, however, Hellman conflates American debate and America's conduct of its portion of the war with the whole of the war itself, thus moving the war exclusively into U.S. territory and writing the nation of Viet Nam out of its own history. He describes Indochina as a "symbolic landscape embodying the opposed mythic values of city and country" (30) in *The Ugly American*, and cites the book's view of Asia as "a projection of American fantasy, a painting of Indochina with a lovely future that is really a wished for American past" (32). This is an astute observation, but Hellmann remains distressingly uncritical of the phenomenon he accurately describes.

In his discussion of the mythology surrounding the Green Berets, Hellmann identifies frontier mythology as the origin of the conflicts between Americans and Europeans and "civilization" versus "savagery," thus neatly accounting for the bizarre representations of Green Berets that have nothing to do with the actual war in Southeast Asia, but he has little to say about the inherent ethnocentrism of these portrayals. Indeed, he seems resolutely blind to the root problem that he clearly identifies—the wholesale transplanting of American mythology into Vietnamese reality. In fact, he seems shockingly unaware of issues of racism.

He notes the view of Susan Sontag and Mary McCarthy toward the Vietnamese, and how they both overlay an American mythic landscape on Viet Nam, but he is uncritical of the Orientalist, ethnocentric, imperial vision that these two leftist writers appropriate and perpetuate. He quotes both authors referring to the Vietnamese as "childlike," yet he offers no commentary. Later, he says that the film *The Deer Hunter* is not guilty of racism because it has white villains and Asian victims, despite his observation that

the film does employ the imagery that has traditionally obsessed American popular culture and which was projected upon Vietnam in *The Ugly American*, the legend of the Green Berets, and in reverse fashion the rhetoric and writings of the antiwar movement: a violent confrontation between the conscious and unconscious, civilization and wilderness, played out in the white imagination as a struggle between light and dark. (175)

Hellmann's conception of racism seems woefully unsophisticated if he is able to think that imposing a Eurocentric vision of light and dark, good and evil, onto Asia is a nonracist act.

He allows the canon to capture most of his attention, which leads him to state that "few novels" (94) about the war were published in the sixties and early seventies (an assertion that is demonstrably untrue; the novels did not sell well, but they were published), and he states that Hollywood also shunned Viet Nam in this period, ignoring the huge number of "crazy-vet" films that brought the war home in exactly the mythic terms he describes.[15]

The biggest problem with Hellmann's conception is his ideology concerning American myth itself. He describes the narratives by Philip Caputo, Tim O'Brien, James Webb, Ron Kovic, and William Turner Hugget as "a nightmare version of the landscapes of previous American myth" (102) without examining the possibility that they are merely the unadorned continuation of the myth. The myth itself is the nightmare: the frontier is built on Indian blood, the American empire is built on slaughter.

Hellmann mistakenly reads American myth only for its contemporary value, thus reading out of history the struggles and contentions over elements that are now myth. He forgets that there were debates and national political controversy over westward expansion and the slaughter of the Indians, just as there were debates and national political controversy over the war in Viet Nam. He remembers only what the popular imagination remembers, thereby participating in the very process of myth building that he seeks to examine. For Hellmann, the war is "the anti-frontier which American history has reached in Vietnam" (166), yet it was not an antifrontier at all, but rather the continuity of the frontier in American history (as Richard Drinnon makes clear in *Facing West: The Metaphysics of Indian-Hating and Empire-Building*)—as I hope to show by concentrating on the particular aspect of racism that has been endemic to the American project and to American myth.

I attempt to take a different tack in discussing representations of the American war in Viet Nam. By first examining works by Vietnamese exile writers I hope to set a radically new agenda. From these works, I argue, there emerges a paradigm of biculturality. Because these authors are writing in exile, removed from their cultural contexts, they are forced to develop new ways to address culturally different audiences. Facing the lack of a shared frame of reference, these writers try to embed in their narratives a didactic purpose—they are bringing something new to their readers, trying to teach about Vietnamese culture and history as much as they are writing their experiences of the war. The process of moving from one culture to another makes these writers themselves bicultural; to varying degress, they also make their writings bicultural and bring a perspective to the U.S. discourse about the war that lies outside the accepted American mythic paradigms.

By beginning with the Vietnamese exile writers, I intend to decenter the interpretive framework usually employed to discuss representations of the war. Instead of reading Euro-American works representing the war against the American cultural mythology, I want to read them against the new paradigm of biculturality and communality constructed by the Vietnamese exile writers.

Before turning to the Euro-American works, I take a further step in reconstructing the analytic paradigm by examining the ways that Asians have historically been represented in American literature and popular culture as a result of U.S. wars in Asia. It is these representations that inform Euro-American works about the war in Viet Nam; chapter 3 explores the way in which the long history of stereotyping and ethnocentrism has created the lens through which most Euro-American works representing the war in Viet Nam view Vietnamese. Placing this history after an examination of self-representation by Vietnamese exile writers shows how the dominant U.S. representations of the Asian "other" have been impoverished and crippled by racism.

In a discussion of Euro-American narratives of the war, in chapter 4, I explore some of what has been absent from American discourse about the war, and how the historical representations of Asians in American literature have been employed wholesale in representations of the American war in Viet Nam. Coming full circle, I end with a discussion of Euro-American works that adopt the same kind of bicultural stance as the Vietnamese exile writers with which I begin, thus demonstrating that resistance amounting to transgressions against dominant American myths can create new, nonracist representations.

Most Euro-American works about the war rarely include any representations of Vietnamese at all, and when they do, those figures are usually presented as "inscrutable" Asians, unknowable in their "otherness." These particular representations arise directly from the larger cultural pattern of representation of Asians and Asian Americans in literature and film, that have been dominated by stereotypes as widely held as they have been narrow in their definition of the Asian and Asian American other. The dominance of these kinds of representations almost wholly closes off the possibility of other explorations of individuals and societies, by predetermining the way those individuals and societies are perceived by the members of this culture. The American men and women who participated in the Viet Nam War, and came home and wrote books about it, grew up in a culture shaped by more than a century of stereotypical representations of Asians and others. Americans who went to Viet Nam saw what their cultural worldview had prepared them to see. Much of the fiction written by veterans of the war can be seen as a working out of that experience, individual attempts to come to an understanding of it, an understanding that our culture as a whole has not provided. Robert Weimann writes: "The process of making certain things one's own becomes inseparable from making other things (and persons) alien, so the act of appropriation must be seen always already to involve not only self-projection and assimilation but alienation through reification and expropriation" (184). This process clearly occurs in representations of the Viet Nam War created by Euro-Americans, veterans and nonveterans alike, who, in fighting the meta-war that will make the war American rather than Vietnamese, have done so at the expense of portraying the Vietnamese in stereotypical, limited, and predetermined ways.

Preservation of a (mythical) American culture as it stands is foremost, without permitting change or influence from other cultures brought into contact with it through war or through immigration. The resistance to influence contrasts sharply with the works of Vietnamese exile writers, who by choice or by necessity are dealing with both cultures. The one theme common to all writings by Vietnamese exile writers is the process of becoming bicultural, a process that begins in Viet Nam and continues in the United States.

I address pulp novels and "literary" works of poetry, fiction and nonfiction, "films" and B movies. This noncanonical inclusiveness acts as a representation and critique of the fabric of American cultural mythology (rather than of individual authors), because all of these categories and genres are caught up in that mythology, which valorizes American experience in such a way that the American history of racism and imperialism is played out repeatedly.[16] Across "high" and "popular" culture and across genres, most of these works have certain root similarities in their worldviews, causing their portrayals of Vietnamese to be almost identical, despite their surface thematic and formal differences. They are all so enmeshed in American cultural mythology about Asians that the "high culture" works attempting a certain self-awareness of their cultural context fail to transcend the paradigms in which the "popular culture" works, too, are thoroughly entangled.

After examining the few Euro-American works that do transgress these paradigms, I turn in conclusion to a new phenomenon in the ongoing U.S. discourse about the war—the representations of return to Viet Nam, in which Euro-Americans discover Viet Nam the country, in place of "Vietnam" the war.

TWO

Vietnamese Exile Narratives

I could never understand Americans. First they came to Viet Nam,
they killed my family, injured my neck with a grenade—today I
carry a scar on my neck—my voice, the way it sounds [is] because
of that wound. After what they did, they tried desperately to save
my life, all the way from Viet Nam to San Francisco. Today I'm an
American, too. Does that make me crazy?
—Thanh Pham, PBS television documentary, "Thanh's War"

We were fighting for a just cause. All people want to be free and
independent and do what they like. . . . The U.S. government has a
responsibility to heal the wounds of war. We didn't make that war
and I deem it reasonable that the U.S. government reconsider its
policy and shake hands with Viet Nam. . . . There is no reason to be
enemies. The world should be in peace and we should enjoy our
lives.
—Nguyen Van Tung, quoted in the *Indochina Newsletter*

A Hundred Tongues

Born somewhere, scattered out to the four winds,
a hundred children speak a hundred tongues.
Tomorrow, if we all should go back home,
let's hope we'll speak the common speech of tears.
—Vien Linh, translated by Huynh Sanh Thong, in *Vietnam Forum* 1

Of the seven thousand or so books published by 1990 in the
United States that deal with the American war in Viet Nam a little
more than a dozen are by Vietnamese exile writers. Of those
Vietnamese exile writers who have been published, very few are
being read, either in the context of Asian American studies or in Viet Nam
War studies. (The sole exception is Le Ly Hayslip, whose autobiography
only recently has begun to make its way into both fields.) What are the

reasons for this exclusion? In the case of Asian American studies, these works do not fit the critical definitions of Asian American literature; perhaps these works do not fit U.S. definitions of "literature" at all. In the case of Viet Nam War studies, these works challenge fundamental American mythologies and overarching narrative strategies implicit throughout the field. Also, and this is both trivial and important, these works are not readily available, which is both a cause and an effect of the other reasons for their exclusion.[1]

Publishing and distribution practices have hindered Vietnamese exile writers' ability to reach a large audience. Although over a dozen novels, personal narratives, and books of poetry by Vietnamese exile writers have been published in English as of 1992, most of them have been small press or academic publications that have not received wide distribution, such as Tran Van Dinh's 1983 novel, *Blue Dragon, White Tiger*, published by TriAm, a very small press, or Tran Tri Vu's 1988 memoir, *Lost Years*, printed as a monograph by the Berkeley Institute of East Asian Studies. Even books that were presented by major publishers, such as Nguyen Ngoc Ngan's *The Will of Heaven* (1982, E. P. Dutton; currently out of print) or Truong Nhu Tang's *A Vietcong Memoir* (1985, Vintage), have been largely ignored. None of these was promoted extensively and none of them sold well. Although *A Vietcong Memoir* was reviewed in a few periodicals, the reviewers dealt with it almost exclusively in political terms—that is, valued or not valued for what it had to say about the evils of communism—but not considered formally as autobiography or cross-cultural representation.

Why have Asian American studies not been more interested in Vietnamese exile writers? At an Asian American literature conference, the critic Sau-Ling Wong said that "a writer may have to be read as an Asian American writer in order to be read at all," despite the fact that "Asian American" is an inadequate and misleading cover term that includes several disparate nationalities and ethnicities. Wong's comment suggests that Asian American writers must be shoehorned into the artificially constructed, overly broad, and too generic "Asian American" context, regardless of nationality or ethnicity, otherwise they have no place in American literature.

Vietnamese American literature diverges from the general traditions of Asian American literature (at least that literature published by mainstream presses and addressed by literary critics). Elaine Kim points out that "our literature is written primarily by American-born, American-educated Asians whose first language is English. . . . They cannot be expected to speak in the voices of the vast numbers of immigrants and refugees whose stories have never been well represented in our literature, past or present" ("Defining Asian American Realities" 88–89). The growing body of Vietnamese American literature is outside the mainstream of Asian American literature because it does represent those refugee voices which, according to Kim, have not previously appeared.

Vietnamese American authors, in the few instances when they are discussed at all, are being read as Vietnamese, as foreigners, rather than as Americans or Asian Americans (all the reviews of Le Ly Hayslip's book cited here, for example, refer to her as Vietnamese). Perhaps because it is almost impossible to squeeze Vietnamese American writers into the "Asian American" context that has been defined almost exclusively in terms of Chinese and Japanese immigrants, Vietnamese American writers are excluded from discussions of Asian American literature. They are further marginalized within an already marginalized "canon."[2]

Le Ly Hayslip's first book was not, for example, reviewed in *Amerasia Journal* (although a much less widely read book, Nguyễn Thị Thu-Lâm's[3] *Fallen Leaves*, was). As of August 1991, no article dealing with Vietnamese American literature had appeared in any critical journal indexed in the Modern Language Association bibliography.[4] Even King-Kok Cheung and Stan Yogi's *Asian American Literature: An Annotated Bibliography* (1988) listed only five book-length works of prose by Vietnamese American authors, although there had been at least nine published by the time the bibliography was issued.[5]

The reasons for Vietnamese exile writers being excluded from Viet Nam War studies are perhaps somewhat different from the reasons for their exclusion from Asian American studies. Kalí Tal, editor of the journal *Viet Nam Generation*, writes in her introduction to the journal's special issue titled "Southeast Asian-American Communities":

This slim volume has taken two years to assemble. . . .
The lack of scholarly response to our call for papers dealing with topics of importance to Southeast Asian-American communities is indicative of the reluctance of American scholars to take upon themselves the task of academic inquiry into the subject. American scholars are perhaps hesitant to venture into new and unfamiliar territory, and to undertake the intensive study and resarch necessary to explore and understand a foreign culture. Scholars who can write with ease and elegance of the effects of the Vietnam war on "American" culture may find Vietnamese-American, or Cambodian-American culture impenetrable. (3)

The essays that appeared in this volume were almost exclusively in the disciplines of the social sciences. Other special-topic issues of the journal are heavily weighted toward literature and film criticism. Tal's point that scholars in literature and cultural studies, in particular, are still hesitant to venture into new territory is well taken. In addition, I would suggest that academic inquiry into Vietnamese American culture is marginalized by Euro-American ethnocentricity.

The marginalization of Vietnamese exile writers within the U.S. discourse about the war is attributable to the nationalistic and ethnocentric definitions of American experience implicit in that discourse. Since Vietnamese exile writers are not seen as part of the representation of "the American experience of 'Vietnam,'" they are not considered within a discourse that focuses on that narrowly defined perspective. Rather, because Vietnamese exile writers seriously challenge the bases and scope of that perspective, they are ignored.

As I discussed in chapter 1, the developing canon of works representing the Viet Nam War excludes Vietnamese exile writers and instead emphasizes American homogeneity, rather than diversity. That canon would be threatened by the inclusion of radically "other" points of view. There is some indication that Hayslip's first book, *When Heaven and Earth Changed Places*, may be entering the secondary level of the Viet Nam War canon—it is being taught in college classes, and scholars have been delivering papers on it at academic conferences. As I explain later, however, Hayslip's books are exceptions to Vietnamese American literature in many ways, and, of all the books I discuss, do the least to challenge the notions inherent in the Viet Nam War canon; therefore, they become the exception that proves the rule.

A reading of Vietnamese exile writers reveals at least three reasons why the Viet Nam War canon should be reformulated to include them. First, the inclusion of these works will open up the debate on the war, putting an end to the circular and endless form it has taken in the United States since the 1960s, by presenting challenging viewpoints that have always been excluded from the U.S. view of the war. Second, these works are worth reading for their own sakes as literature and as history and politics. Third, these works form the newest contribution to Asian American literature and are strikingly different from the critically defined mainstream traditions of Asian American writers.

Including Vietnamese refugee works in the discourse will bring new insight into the cultures of both Viet Nam and the United States. Another benefit will be the creation of an understanding of the true parameters of the war, the full costs, as well as insight into the newest American immigrant group—a group that has already begun to make a major impact on American life.[6] One of the difficulties of bringing these works into the U.S. discourse is that they ask us to bring politics and history into the discussion of literature, and New Historicism as a mode of criticism has not, as yet, made inroads into the study of Viet Nam War literature. The politics of U.S. intervention are still quite contentious, and the critics' own politics invariably affect their valuation of the literature in unacknowledged ways (as in Philip Beidler's uneven treatment of Philip Caputo and James Webb, discussed in chapter 1).

Worse still, the majority of Americans, including critics of Viet Nam War representations, remain inadequately informed about the history and politics surrounding the war. A surprising number of critical articles are marred by errors of simple historical fact. Unlike the majority of U.S. works about the war, which draw on long-standing American mythologies of warfare and its narration, works by Vietnamese exile authors cannot be understood outside of politics and history, both global and domestic.

Patricia Limerick has written in *The Legacy of Conquest* that Americans tend to cheerfully hold on to the idea of American innocence despite plentiful evidence to the contrary; the knowledge of history and politics that Vietnamese exile works demand from their readers provide so much adverse evidence, however, that it is almost impossible to maintain that cheerful idea. Because the war happened within our own lifetimes—so that we cannot disavow it as "the awful past" in the way we might disavow slavery or genocide against the Native Americans—New Historicist methodology is perhaps not as attractive to critics of this more recent era. Most of the scholars studying the Viet Nam War belong to the generation that fought the war and are still caught up in the political positions and cultural perceptions of the sixties. To look at new material in new ways would mean to look anew at ourselves. As David Berman, arguing for the inclusion of Vietnamese sources in secondary education, writes, "Such an approach provides us with an alternative world view, a perspective based upon cultural relativism in contrast to a more traditional approach which often tends to have an ethnocentric bias" (30). Considering the history of anti-Asian laws and attitudes in the United States, Berman's gentle suggestion that our usual perspective on teaching the war tends toward an "ethnocentrist bias" is an understatement.

Bringing a nonethnocentric approach to Viet Nam War literature demands that we debunk some of the mythology to which we are most attached; in re-forming our views of the representation of the war, we must reform not only our views of history, but our very selves. For the Euro-American reader, the Vietnamese exile writers hold up a mirror, making Euro-American readers look at themselves at the same time they are looking at the exotic "other." This is not a comfortable position for most Euro-American readers; as a result, the process of canon formation resists the bicultural vision offered and required by the Vietnamese American (and a few Euro-American) writers.

One striking if not surprising contrast emerges from this comparative reading: most Euro-American representations are focused on America, whereas Vietnamese exile writers' representations are focused on cultural negotiations, on the process of becoming bicultural. This process is not the same as assimilating, which is to leave behind one's culture of origin. Biculturality is one of the important ways in which Vietnamese American literature differs from much of the tradition of Asian American literature. Vietnamese exile authors, while becoming "American," insist on remaining Vietnamese at the same time, whether or not they intend to return to Viet Nam. The struggle to remain bicultural, to bring Vietnamese culture to America, is a theme that runs through most Vietnamese American literature. Bharati Mukherjee refers to this process of becoming bicultural as "transnational cultural fusion," a phrase that suggests the process of culture transcending national boundaries.

Anh K. Tran, reviewing John Balaban's *Ca Dao Việtnam: A Bilingual Anthology of Vietnamese Folk Poetry*, suggests that

little did Balaban realize that his work would not only serve to introduce "our American allies" to the Vietnamese culture but also acquaint Vietnamese youth with their own roots. Already the Vietnamese community in America has witnessed the rise in number of young Vietnamese who do not speak their parents' language. . . . In this book, Balaban succeeded in presenting this heretofore undiscovered gem *ca dao* [Vietnamese folk poetry], whose value once understood will bring forth the pillar of Vietnamese character and instill pride in the Vietnamese community in exile. And for this, generations of American-born Vietnamese shall be forever in his debt. (Tran 150)

That a Vietnamese reviewer could praise a Euro-American author for producing a book that will educate Vietnamese Americans about their cultural heritage shows the great degree of "transnational cultural fusion" that exists among Vietnamese American authors writing in English.[7]

Bicultural identity and cultural fusion are not easily or painlessly achieved. Andrew Lam writes in an article in *The Nation* of the experience of exile:

Sometimes I go to a Vietnamese restaurant in San Francisco's Tenderloin district. I sit and stare at two wooden clocks hanging on the wall. The left one is carved in the shape of the voluptuous S: the map of Vietnam. The one on the right is hewed in the shape of a deformed tooth: the map of America. Ticktock, ticktock. They run at different times. Ticktock, ticktock. I was born a Vietnamese. Ticktock, ticktock. I am reborn an American. Ticktock, ticktock. I am of one soul. Ticktock, ticktock. Two hearts. (726)

Lam's "one soul . . . two hearts" might serve as a description of biculturality; his phrase echoes W. E. B. DuBois's description of African Americans feeling "twoness . . . two warring ideals in one dark body" (215). Lam's metaphor for the shapes of the two clocks/countries reveals that his affection still lies with Viet Nam and that he is uneasy in America.

One result of the bicultural stance and the lingering nostalgia for home is that Vietnamese American authors tend to write more about life in Viet Nam than about their experience of the assimilation process in America. They are interested in bringing their culture of origin into the American context. Exile is a common phenomenon in the twentieth century, and the exile author is an increasingly common figure. Edward Said calls our era "the age of the refugee, the displaced person, mass immigration" (quoted in Kaplan 30). The exodus of Vietnamese after April 1975 is one of the largest of recent migrations. The position of Vietnamese in the United States (and in France, Canada, and Australia) is perhaps comparable only to that of the European Jewish refugees in America during World War II.

The question of literature in exile is one that is at issue in the Vietnamese-language exile press. Whether to term the Vietnamese-language literature produced by refugee writers "exile literature" is a topic of contention. Writers whose main focus is anticommunism dislike the term *exile literature* because it sounds sad and "pitiful." They prefer to constitute themselves as the "authentic" contemporary Vietnamese literature and to call the Communist writers in the Socialist Republic of Viet Nam (SRV) the "exile" writers. In an article that appeared in translation in the Australian *Journal of Vietnamese Studies*, Nguyen Hung Quoc dismisses this rather absurd claim, but seeks to define what exile literature is:

Living abroad and writing do not make a writer someone in exile: the pro-communist writers who are living abroad are not writers in exile. The feeling of being astray in his own country, by itself, is not enough to make a writer an author in exile. . . . It may be necessary to distinguish a writer in exile from a literature in exile. We may have writers in exile but not a literature in exile.

When we speak of a literature in exile we envisage an activity which includes many aspects: authors and readers in exile, and their relationships through the media in their country of asylum. . . . We can extract three conditions in the making of a literature in exile: (i) there must be authors in exile; (ii) there must be readers in exile; and (iii) they must be able to create a literary activity of their own, independent of the current literature in their country of origin. (26)

The Vietnamese-language exile writers are creating such a literature as Quoc describes. The English-language exile writers are not only writers in exile as Quoc defines, but also writers attempting to bridge the gap between their pasts, their current lives as exiles, and the English-language readers of their countries of refuge. They stand in perhaps an even more lonely place by so doing, but they also prefigure future generations, whose first language will be English and who may think of themselves as exiles politically, but will be at home in the West culturally. In the meantime, the current generation of exile writers, no matter which language they choose to publish in, are focused on Viet Nam and the war.

The exiles' focus on Viet Nam is illustrated in an article on Vietnamese refugee scholars by Dr. Nguyen Manh Hung, director of the Indochina Institute at George Mason University:

Being refugees rather than immigrants, the overwhelming majority of Vietnamese living in the United States still have strong emotional ties with Vietnam, and think of themselves as Vietnamese rather than as Vietnamese Americans. It is therefore not surprising that refugee scholars because of their emotional ties, intimate knowledge of Vietnam, and unfamiliarity with ethnic studies in the United States have been more attracted to studies of Vietnam than ethnic studies. . . . Vietnamese American studies will be an outgrowth of studies on Vietnam rather than . . . a product of Asian American studies. (90)

Dr. Hung's description of the work done by Vietnamese refugee scholars also fits, to a large degree, the work done by Vietnamese refugee fiction writers and memoirists. Their focus remains on Viet Nam and the war, rather than on the immigration experience. They express, as Dr. Hung writes, "strong emotional ties" with Viet Nam and tend toward a reexamination of their experiences before exile as the subject of their writings. Dr. Hung also notes that, because of their status as refugees rather than immigrants, when Vietnamese refugee scholars turn to studying Vietnamese Americans instead of Viet Nam, that discipline will be an outgrowth of their work focusing on

Viet Nam. In this way, Vietnamese exile scholars are part of the larger context of Vietnamese exile writing.

Nguyen Hung Quoc writes that, in exile literature,

consciousness may ultimately be the most important element. Literature in exile is an expression of the exile's consciousness. The exile did not flee with only a body longing for material comforts; on his fragile boat, facing stormy weather, he carried with him the shame of leaving his fatherland, and also a treasure of memories and affections to help him endure his future fate of a miserable wanderer in a foreign country. Mai Thao, in the first issue of [the exile literary journal] *Van* [Letters], considered this consciousness as a precondition for the realisation of literature in exile: "Consciousness will be associated permanently with one's native land, with the calamity in one's country." (29)

Quoc is writing of exile literature written in Vietnamese, which differs from that written in English in that the former is not necessarily bicultural, but the quality of consciousness that Quoc defines is shared by both forms of Vietnamese exile literature.

Marguerite Bouvard, in her preface to the anthology *Landscape and Exile*, identifies the unique value of the refugee writer:

The very word exile conjures up a state of anguish. However, the shock of change can also awaken insight. The writer, as an outsider, has a clear vision of his own native land and also his new society. The price may be a high one, but she or he gains a perspective on life unavailable to those on the inside. Often it is when we journey that we see the most clearly, both the places we have left, and the new and strange places of arrival. Moving between these visions, the writer experiences a unique sense of freedom. (x)

The Vietnamese refugee writers, whatever their political situation, have all experienced the kind of shift in perception Bouvard mentions. By writing about their own perspective shifts, they foster smaller perspective shifts in receptive readers. Freedom, in a literal sense as well as the metaphoric one Bouvard invokes, is an important issue for the Vietnamese refugee writers, since they have left their homeland as political and/or economic refugees, seeking greater freedom outside Viet Nam. They are the losers of the long series of wars fought in Viet Nam, in several ways. Some of the writers discussed here were on the side of the Republic of Viet Nam, and some were with the National Liberation Front but later felt betrayed for political reasons and felt themselves, as southerners, to be losers despite the NLF/PAVN victory.

Andrew Gurr, writing about exile authors, notes:

In consequence of this separation from home in space as well as time, the writer characteristically centers his attention not so much on his sense of his history . . . as on his sense of home as a unit in space and time together . . . the search for identity and the construction of a vision of home amount to the same thing. Typically the home is set in the past . . . the home of memory, which is the only basis for a sense of identity which the exiled writer can maintain. (11)

Gurr is writing about voluntary exiles, such as James Joyce, V. S. Naipaul, and Ngugi wa Thiong'o, but his formulation applies equally well to Vietnamese refugee writers. They construct their sense of home and locate it in a Viet Nam that exists only in the remembered past and that has no political continuity with the contemporary Viet Nam.

Gurr's study addresses writers who have gone into exile at least in part to foster their writing. In the case of the Vietnamese refugees, it is often the experience of exile itself which makes them into writers. With the exceptions of Tran Van Dinh and Vo Phien, the writers examined here were not writers before they were refugees. Their desires to write their identities, to write their versions of history, arise from their status as refugees. The terms "refugee" and "exile" might be used interchangeably, although the conditions of "refuge" and "exile" vary from writer to writer—some fled out of (perceived) life-or-death necessity, believing they would be killed by the Communists; some left more or less voluntarily, seeking a better life, mostly in economic terms. One useful distinction between "refugee" and "exile" is that exiles, voluntary or not, embrace the perspectival shift they experience; refugees, voluntary or not, have it forced on them.

Gurr describes his exile writers as trying to awaken from the nightmare of history, like Joyce's Stephen Dedalus. The Vietnamese refugee writers have a different project, however—not to separate themselves from their history, but to make that history as real for American readers as it is for them, and thus alter the American historical narrative.

Vietnamese exile writers' desire to keep their pasts alive in the present is exemplified in a poem by Tran Mong Tu published in *Vietnam Forum*, a bilingual cultural and scholarly journal. This poem appeared in the first issue of that journal as part of a group of poems translated by Huynh Sanh Thong, published under the collective title "Songs of Exile."

A New Year's Wish for a Little Refugee

Let me send you some words, a simple wish.
It's New Year's Eve—black night shrouds skies and seas.
A miracle saved your life, O little child!
Aboard that boat, all perished, but you.

Let me send you some words, a simple wish.
New Year's should be a day for love and joy.
But where are both your parents, little child?
You're pouring tears, enough to fill the sea.

Let me send you some words, a simple wish.
This New Year's Day, alone on foreign soil,
you'll feel just like a seaweed washed ashore—
you won't know what the future holds for you.

No lack of kindly hands that will grab you
and take you home to change what's now your name.
They'll turn you into some new human breed
that thinks your yellow skin is cause for shame.

They will send you to school where you'll be taught
their land's own history, modern ways of life.
You will grow up denying what you are—
you'll never hear your forbears spoken of.

Let me send you some words, a simple wish
for this new year, for scores of years to come.
O little child, may you keep it intact,
your past of sorrows, all your world of griefs.

The child's lack of parents symbolizes the loss of family that refugees experience. In Vietnamese culture, what Westerners call "ancestor worship" provides a familial and cultural structure that organizes Vietnamese society. Ancestor worship actually constitutes respect for the dead, and therefore the family, and it defines who one is related to through the patriline (*ancestor respect* might be a better term). The central place in an ancestor shrine is occupied by a man's paternal great-grandfather. Everyone to whom he is related, in the male line, through this great-grandfather, constitutes his family. A young child learns his or her family relations in this way. Thus ancestor worship defines a social group—the family—that was the main social group of the traditional peasant society. A Vietnamese proverb says, "Birds have nests; men have ancestors" (Clifford and Balaban 68). Loss of that familial structure means the loss of one's place in society. The child's lack of parents leaves that child without a cultural location, without knowledge of his or her place in society. This cultural rootlessness leaves the child vulnerable to the "education" the poet fears the new country will give him or her. The poet prefers that the sorrow and grief be kept alive—prefers active suffering to loss of cultural identity and heritage.

Shirley Geok-lin Lim writes that in Asian American literature, a "major motif is the urge to find a usable past; specifically, for writers to come to terms with the immigrant experiences of their race" (57). For Vietnamese American writers, the first circumstance in the past they must consider is the past of Viet Nam, which means the wars—for most of them, depending on their dates of birth and departure, both the French war and the American war—and the unfinished business (social, familial, political) that their flight as refugees forced them to leave behind. For them, that unfinished business on Vietnamese soil, and the interconnectedness of that business with America, makes more compelling subject matter than their experiences as new arrivals in America. This orientation aligns their writing with the exile literature that Gurr defines, even while it sets them outside the Asian American literary tradition as Lim defines it.

Lim does, however, describe Asian American writers as sharing "a concern with sociological texture in their attempts to rewrite the past; as such they exhibit in different degrees a burden of referentiality in which the texts demand to be read for their relevance to an outside historical meaning" (57). The Vietnamese American works do fit this pattern, and I will read them for their "relevance to an outside historical meaning." The "outside historical meaning" that these works attempt to rewrite contests the dominant Euro-American construction of the shared past of the war. By pointing out to their American audiences that what Americans call the Vietnam War is also known as the American War, some Vietnamese refugee writers attempt to alter Euro-American perspectives on "historical meaning." Trinh Minh-ha claims that "writing as a social function—as differentiated from the ideal of art for art's sake—is the aim that Third World writers, in defining their roles, highly esteem and claim" (10).

One way Vietnamese refugee works attempt this project is in their insistence on the intertwining of the shared past and shared future destinies of Viet Nam and America. While Euro-Americans tend to see the Viet Nam

War as being "about" America, Vietnamese refugee writers show it to be "about" both Viet Nam and America, together. This idea is alien to the U.S. Viet Nam War discourse, and we need ways to approach this new stance.

Myra Jehlen has proposed that neither universality nor radical otherness explains contemporary reality. As she says, "If difference ever existed, it is long lost." In other words, shared particular, historical experience overcomes otherness. Jehlen's term for this is *communality*. I take her point to be that colonizers and colonized (the example she bases her argument on is the Spanish conquest of the Aztecs), both being present in the colonizing experience, share that reality. Even if the two peoples approach the experience from different, unshared realities, the shared historical experience is a place to begin talking.

Vietnamese American works assert this communality.[8] Their goal is to explain the shared history to a U.S. audience from the point of view of the Vietnamese. So far, the U.S. audience has not been very good at listening; even Hayslip seems to be misread, in that the U.S. audience appears to be rejecting the possibility of communality. This position is evident in the cultural productions of Euro-Americans, whether film or literature, which continue to focus solely on the United States, without considering Viet Nam or the Vietnamese. Perhaps rather than rejecting communality, the U.S. audience does not even seem to recognize the possibility of communality, the possibility that the Viet Nam War is also the American War, a possibility spread out richly in all the Vietnamese American works about the war, yet so absent in the overwhelming majority of Euro-American works.[9] Caren Kaplan approaches the same problem with different terminology:

The western reader or critic has the products of an expanding concept of the world at their disposal, yet they do not necessarily feel emotionally connected to a geography or a people at any distance from themselves. We have not yet learned how to "feel global" in the West, I shall argue, because that literature apparently most relevant to such a feeling—travel and exile literature—relies on distance and separation. (3)

Vietnamese refugee writers have experienced "distance and separation," and from their experiences of displacement have learned to "feel global."

Hayslip, in a prologue to her narrative, addresses both U.S. veterans of the war and U.S. civilians who did not go to the war, with a message not just of reconciliation, but, more important, of the need to learn *mutually* from the experience of the war and to move forward together.

The least you [veterans] did—the least any of us did—was our duty. For that we must be proud. The most that any of us did—or saw—was another face of destiny or luck or god. Children and soldiers have always known it to be terrible. If you have not yet found peace at the end of your war, I hope you will find it here. We have important new roles to play. . . .

If you are a person who knows the Vietnam war, or any war, only by stories and pictures, this book is written for you too. . . . The special gift of that suffering, I have learned, is how to be strong while we are weak, how to be brave when we are afraid, how to be wise in the midst of confusion, and how to let go of that which we can no longer hold. In this way, anger can teach forgiveness, hate can teach us love, and war can teach us peace. (xv)

The "here" that Hayslip refers to is her book, which is not intended to be just "literature"; like the organization she founded, the East Meets West Foundation, the narration is intended as activism. She seeks, through the book and the organization, to change U.S. thinking about the war. She does not want readers to be the same people they were before they picked up her book.

The final sentence of the quoted Hayslip passage, with its reconciliation of opposites, might be dismissed as just so much Oriental mysticism by readers seeking to reject her suggestion of communality. However, the whole of her narrative goes on to support the assertion made in that sentence, that there are positive values to be learned from the horrifying experiences of war. The United States as a whole has yet to learn any of these positive values, as reflected by the government's current policies and the broad public support for them. The U.S. has certainly not learned forgiveness or love from its anger and hate: it has been unable to forgive the Socialist Republic of Viet Nam for defeating the United States in war. After the reunification of Viet Nam in 1975, the United States continued to wage the war by refusing to recognize the SRV government and by enforcing a trade embargo (until 1994) that helps keep contemporary Viet Nam one of the poorest countries in the world.

Furthermore, the United States has not learned peace. Despite slogans like "El Salvador is Spanish for Viet Nam," the United States has maintained a military presence in the form of advisors and arms supplies in Central America. It also waged a full-scale, if brief, war in the Persian Gulf. The public supported President Bush's military intervention despite being as ignorant of politics in the Arab world as it was of politics in Southeast Asia twenty-five years earlier.

Tran Van Dinh, in his novel *Blue Dragon, White Tiger*, goes even further than Hayslip in his demand for recognition of communality. He asserts that the destinies of the United States and Viet Nam are interlinked, and his novel is designed to foster recognition of that linked destiny in U.S. readers. Dinh stresses not only the connected present and future of the two nations and two peoples, but also their interlocked past, a past not recognized by a Western-centered worldview.

The main character of the novel is Minh, a professor who returns to Viet Nam in 1967 after teaching in the United States for several years. He plans to lecture his students at the University of Hue on "such concepts as 'life, liberty, and the pursuit of happiness'; the influences of Confucianism on French philosophers like Voltaire, Montesquieu, and Diderot, who in turn had influence on American revolutionaries like Thomas Jefferson; and the role of Thomas Paine in the 1776 revolution" (124). Dinh asserts that the communality between the two nations stretches far back into both of their pasts—that East and West have long influenced each other, and that the direction of influence has not flowed one way only. By tracing a line of thought from Confucianism through the French philosophers to Jefferson, author of the American Declaration of Independence, Dinh also points to the next step in the linkage. In 1945 Ho Chi Minh modeled the Vietnamese Declaration of Independence on the American declaration, and on the writings of the French revolution:

"All men are created equal. They are endowed by their Creator with certain unalienable Rights; among these are Life, Liberty and the pursuit of Happiness."
This immortal statement appeared in the Declaration of Independence of the United States of America in 1776. In a broader sense, it means: All the peoples on the earth are equal from birth, all the peoples have a right to live and to be happy and free.
The Declaration of the Rights of Man and the Citizen, made at the time of the French Revolution, in 1791, also states: "All men are born free and with equal rights, and must always remain free and have equal rights."
These are undeniable truths. (Ho, 53)

Students in my American studies class on the Viet Nam War in American popular culture are always astonished to discover that this is the Vietnamese Declaration of Independence. If we incorporated *Blue Dragon, White Tiger* or other Vietnamese American works into our curricula on the war, or our curricula on Asian American literature, or popular culture, or history, or politics, students might be quite a bit less astonished and might also become less parochial and politically naive in global terms.

Truong Nhu Tang, in *A Vietcong Memoir*, makes the same demand of his U.S. readers that Hayslip and Dinh do. Tang writes in his foreword: "It is only through understanding the Vietnamese who fought on the other side that Americans will have anything like a complete portrait of a war upon which they have been reflecting so deeply—the only war they have ever lost" (xiv).

How can we discuss these works that lie so far outside the familiar discourse? Actually, they are not difficult books, because they do much of the work themselves: designed by their authors to communicate with American audiences, they go far more than halfway in building the bridges. In the following pages I offer readings of several important Vietnamese refugee texts, including Tran Van Dinh's *Blue Dragon, White Tiger*, Truong Nhu Tang's *A Vietcong Memoir*, Nguyen Ngoc Ngan's *The Will of Heaven*, Le Ly Hayslip's *When Heaven and Earth Changed Places* and *Child of War, Woman of Peace*, Nguyễn Thị Thu-Lâm's *Fallen Leaves*, Minh Duc Hoai Trinh's *This Side, the Other Side*, and Vo Phien's *Intact* and short stories. My readings explore these works' bicultural stances, their self-representations, and the ways they challenge U.S. discourse about the war. I give detailed readings of each book, in order to trace the ways these Vietnamese refugee writers seek to enter the U.S. discourse about the war, and the ways they put forward their claim to the communality of experience gained by Americans and Vietnamese in that war, as well as to examine the authors' political, class, regional, and gender positions.

There is, of course, no single "Vietnamese refugee" position. These works represent a variety of political, class, regional, and gender positions. Dinh,[10] Tang, and Hayslip all worked with the Viet Cong/NLF. The RVN is represented by Thu-Lâm, Trinh, and Ngan, who was a soldier in the Army of the Republic of Viet Nam (ARVN). Diinh, Tang, Ngan, and Phien are men, Hayslip, Thu-Lâm, and Trinh are women. Hayslip is from peasant origins, Ngan, Thu-Lâm, Trinh, and Phien are middle class, and Dinh and Tang are upper class. Dinh and Hayslip are from Central Viet Nam, Thu-Lâm is a displaced Northerner, and the rest are Southerners. The texts by Dinh, Phien, and Trinh are fiction, those by Tang, Ngan, Hayslip, and Thu-Lâm are nonfiction narratives. These various positionings affect each writer's view of the war, of the experience of exile, and his or her construction of identity.

Blue Dragon, White Tiger

"The Harmonization of *Tinh*, feeling, and *Ly*, reason"

Blue Dragon, White Tiger: A Tet Story, by Tran Van Dinh (1983), is a novel about biculturality and identity, about the penetration of Western culture into Viet Nam, about one Vietnamese man negotiating his own identity and his country's and finding that, ironically, he can be "truly Vietnamese" only in exile in the West.

One review said of the novel, "Unlike many of the popular war novels, wherein the action is fast and the world is black and white, Tran Van Dinh's work leaves much room for reflection while telling his story against the background of the war, and, what is more important, within the texture of Vietnamese culture. It is a story that challenges the intellect and the imagination" (Crown 160). The "intellect and the imagination," although depersonified by this reviewer, are certainly the Euro-American intellect and imagination, and they are challenged precisely because Dinh's novel does not, as the reviewer notes, fit easily into the U.S. discourse about the war. The book is slower paced and places less emphasis on action than do Euro-American war novels, both because the author is writing in a Vietnamese novelistic tradition (although he writes in English) and because he is writing a "high culture" rather than a popular text. These factors place him outside the mainstream of U.S. discourse about the war.

Shirley Goek-lin Lim writes,

According to Irving Howe, "What usually shapes a new literary movement is less a common future than a common rejection of the recently dominant past." It is clear in Asian-American writing that those literary works which most embrace and exploit the dominant stereotypes of their racial history, are less powerfully works of imagination. . . . The strongest Asian-American writing offers alternate self-images to the ethnic commonplaces. (74)

Offering an alternate self-image that counters Western Orientalist images of Vietnamese is Dinh's project. He presents Viet Nam and Vietnamese culture unmediated by Western stereotypical perceptions; even while he is striving to translate that culture for a Western audience, he refuses to alter or adulterate his own perceptions of his beloved homeland.

Blue Dragon, White Tiger does not appeal to Orientalist views of Asia: the

41

characters contradict themselves and each other, and their lives are too consumed with the very conflicts of East versus West—in the form of trying to adapt marxism to their Confucian society—for them to be seen as stereotypical inscrutable Asians. The characters populating the novel are far too multidimensional to be so reduced.

From the very beginning it is clear that the negotiating of two cultures is the subject matter of this book. The epigraphs are a traditional Vietnamese cosmology, a Vietnamese folk song, and a quotation from General Westmoreland:

The Thanh Long, Blue Dragon, designates the eastern quadrant of the Uranosphere, the Bach Ho, White Tiger, its western section. The Blue Dragon represents spring and tenderness, the White Tiger, winter and force. All beings and all things on earth are affected by the constant struggle between the Blue Dragon and the White Tiger.

Traditional Vietnamese Belief

The first month of the year is for eating Tet at home. The second month is for gambling. And the third month is for going to the festivals.

Vietnamese Folk Song

The minds of the Vietnamese in Saigon and the other cities were preoccupied with the approaching Tet holiday, and our efforts to change this state of mind were only partially effective.

Gen. William Westmoreland, 1968

The novel uses the Vietnamese Tet (New Year's celebration) as one of its symbols for Viet Nam and Vietnamese identity. Westmoreland's attempt to "change this state of mind" does become effective in the novel as American culture changes Viet Nam, much to the disgust of the novel's main character, Professor Tran Van Minh. (The main character's name differs from the author's by only one character, suggesting that the novel is highly autobiographical, which Dinh almost—but not quite—admits in the novel's preface.)

Minh is suspended between two cultures. As the novel opens in 1967, he is a Vietnamese living in the United States, teaching at a progressive college in Massachusetts. He has been away from Viet Nam for most of his adult life and is comfortable in the United States. He has written antiwar articles for American magazines and newspapers. He has continued, as well, to write in

Vietnamese and publish novels and poetry in Viet Nam, under the pseudo-nym Co Tung, which means "Lone Pine Tree." Minh's choice of pseudo-nym emphasizes the isolation he feels as a result of being between cultures, of being unreconciled with either culture in its entirety.

By the end of the novel, Minh has participated in the National Liberation Front's struggle for liberation and its triumph in 1975, but he has become disillusioned, deciding that "only with freedom can I be a Vietnamese, can I appreciate the Vietnamese culture, wherever I may be" (310). He turns the revolution against itself with his decision to leave, saying, "I shall remain independent and free, according to your advice, respected Uncle Ho" (305). He appropriates Ho's slogan to justify his Western-style individualism.

His decision represents his biculturality: only by returning to the West can he continue to live by his own definition of what it means to be Vietnamese. He is an internationalist, appreciating bits of various cultures that he finds admirable, from the Swede Dag Hammarskjöld's book *Markings*, to the American Revolution, to Vietnamese cuisine. But his internationalism makes him lonely and isolated. He says to his friend Loc, a staunch Party member, "I need all the personal freeedoms that make me creative as a writer and an individual. You're part of a country, a Party; I'm all by myself" (307). He returns to the position he held at the beginning of the novel, that "even if poetry and politics blend, poetry and communism certainly cannot" (44).

Minh works with polar opposites throughout the novel—polarities are what drive both his character and the plot. In Viet Nam the Communist Party, which has grown rigid, demands that Minh adhere monoculturally to its ideology. He rejects this demand and moves toward greater freedom back in the United States, where he can be both an American and a Vietnamese. Minh has created himself as a hyphenated American, desiring to live out both identities. Although he also does not wish to submit to the Communist party in Viet Nam, he also does not want to assimilate to American culture. He remains an individualist, a concept he has adopted from America, but he intends to use that individualism to maintain his Vietnamese culture and identity, thus making of himself a permanent paradox.

The novel attempts to bring the experience of biculturality to its American readers by constantly juxtaposing elements of the two cultures. The narrative includes quotations from traditional Vietnamese poetry and literature and incorporates passages explaining Vietnamese culture to the American reader in an attempt to make both sides of Minh's character accessible. These passages, while part of the story, also perform a didactic function:

On important festive days, especially Tet, Vietnamese homes, rich and poor, are decorated with two lines of poetry or prose written on red cloth or rice paper. When he was only six Minh was initiated into the complicated art of calligraphy. (63)

As in all Vietnamese homes, the Ancestors' Altar occupied the central place, hidden from the living room by a silk curtain embroidered with figures of dragons and phoenixes. The beautifully prepared dinner lay spread about the altar. Brass candleholders in the shape of cranes on turtles' back were set on the altar on opposite sides of a porcelain incense burner. Behind a vase of lotus flowers, in an inlaid pearl frame, was a photograph of Minh's mother. (65)

Minh participates in Viet Nam's quest to fit marxism into the national culture. In one of the novel's most important passages, Minh's friend Loc, a Party member, explains how Viet Nam can appropriate marxism, using the traditional concepts of

Tinh, feeling, and Ly, reason. At the present time, our Tinh is grounded in our culture and our Ly is rooted in our just struggle for independence and freedom, and socialism. Ly helps us clarify our Tinh . . . Tinh, in turn, humanizes our Ly . . . Tinh and Ly form the unbroken circle in which our national communication operates.

In Marxist terminology, Tinh represents the "superstructure" and Ly, the "economic base." . . . Looking back at our history, we can see that from our original culture we've drawn the necessary strength to absorb and Vietnamize Confucianism, Taoism, and Buddhism. There's no reason to suppose that we can't Vietnamize Marxism as well. (96)

For Minh, however, marxism fails to become Vietnamized. The Party never develops sufficient Tinh, but is rather overwhelmed by Lý, and therefore fails to complete the "unbroken circle" which would Vietnamize the Western ideology of marxism. Tinh and Lý form two poles that Minh travels between in the course of the novel. He can never reconcile the two in terms of marxism. He has worked with the Party for years without being a member. When he is invited to join, he must "accept reform or . . . undergo transformation. To reform was to give up one's reason; to transform was to deny one's feeling" (304). He decides that, ironically, the only way he can maintain Tinh and Lý, the only way he can remain Vietnamese, is to leave Viet Nam, thus becoming an exile.

The novel thus sets up a structure of polar opposites and the attempt to reconcile them into an unbroken circle. Viet Nam and America are a pair that Minh eventually succeeds in reconciling for himself, although his reconciliation represents only his individual life and does not extend further to a reconciliation of the two nations. Minh's biculturality remains an individualist proposition.

The biculturality of the novel is also reflected in its structure, which combines the conventional narrative of a Western-style novel—a beginning, middle, and end, and a plot driven by cause and effect and character development—with a novel in the Vietnamese tradition, which is highly romantic, by American standards. Maurice Durand and Nguyen Tran Huan divide twentieth-century Vietnamese novels into three categories: the romantic, the socialist-realist, and the scholarly, this last "aimed at preserving Vietnam's ancient cultural heritage" (179). Dinh draws from all three of these traditions (the first two of which Vietnamese authors have adapted from French models) to produce his English-language refugee novel.

The Vietnamese-style plot in the novel turns on fate. Three women in the novel represent aspects of culture for Minh, and their appearances in the story are governed by fate.[11] The workings of fate might look like coincidence to the American reader, but they represent the influence of the Vietnamese romantic tradition on Dinh's writing. The novel's worldview makes Viet Nam and its war the center of the world, around which fate turns. Everything that happens to Minh happens for a reason controlled by fate. The women appear in the story whenever Minh needs them to teach him a lesson; they are not fully developed characters but plot devices, which Dinh manipulates to engineer Minh's development.

The first woman, Jennifer, represents America for Minh, who says to her,

"To me, New York City is America—dynamic, maybe brutal, but always aspiring toward the higher, the better, the impossible. One thing I'm sure of is that New York will always be a turbulent, ungovernable city. It will never be tamed or settled or grow stagnant. It will have no past, no history, because it will be changing all the time. Perhaps, someday, New York City will collapse under its own ambitions, its own dreams and excesses, but until then it will never stop creating, hoping, trying." Minh paused for a second. "It's a lot like you, Jennifer." (5)

Although Minh's description of New York is not altogether positive, Jennifer takes his comparison as a compliment and gives a reply that stresses "how alike we are" (6). While Minh sees in New York, and by extension in

45

Jennifer, an American capacity for self-destructiveness, created by America's lack of a sense of history, he also sees great potential for creativity and growth. It is this capacity, this energy of the younger civilization, that draws him to America, and to Jennifer, who, as his student, is significantly younger than he is.

With Jennifer in America Minh has attempted to walk the path of bicultural understanding. When he speaks with her, he quotes both Vietnamese poetry and Dag Hammarskjöld. He blends, in his person, the intellectual traditions of Europe and Asia, and his life reflects his biculturality—he is a Vietnamese in love with an American, a professor of politics who teaches about Third World revolutions at a U.S. college, and later, about the American Revolution at Hue University. Minh's survival depends on being able to span both cultures; when he is cut off from one or the other, he is not happy. He describes himself as an "internationalist," yet he finds he still has a "strong loyalty to his society" (47). He thinks of himself as "Americanized and Europeanized, what we call in Vietnamese Mat Goc, losing roots" (133).

Minh has left America with regret. Upon arrival in Viet Nam, he thinks of Jennifer constantly. Escorted by soldiers he believes are arresting him and taking him to his execution (in fact, they are not), he hopes he will have "several hours left to think of Jennifer, or perhaps, if he was allowed, to write her a poem" (21).

Working with the NLF, he eventually stops thinking about Jennifer. She comes to Viet Nam, however, with the American Friends Service Committee. Taken prisoner during the Uprising in Hue, she is brought to the tunnel complex where Minh works. They see each other briefly before she is released in a prisoner exchange. Minh is allowed to walk part way to the exchange point with her. After he has left her, American planes bomb the area. Minh is wounded; Jennifer and all the other prisoners, Vietnamese and American, are killed. Minh does not find out about her death until a year later in Paris, where he has been sent, partially in reward for his wounds, as part of the NLF delegation to the peace talks.

Jennifer reminds Minh of America just when he is becoming disillusioned with his work for the NLF. Living in the tunnels, "he wasn't even sure he was in Vietnam at all" (214). Jennifer's death represents for Minh the necessity of stopping the war between Viet Nam and America, which mirrors the war in his soul. When he decides to return to America at the end of the novel, he believes he is doing what Jennifer would have wanted. In his return to America he reasserts his love for Jennifer, his symbol of biculturality.

The second woman, Xuan, is one of Minh's students at Hue University.

She is his younger brother Phong's girlfriend, and she is suspected by the police of being Viet Cong. Xuan disappears, then reappears at the end of the novel, when Minh is escaping from Viet Nam by boat. Fatefully, Xuan is on the same boat. She tells Minh that she is going to integrate into the U.S. Vietnamese community as a Party spy. She also tells him the story of her involvement with the Party: "In 1964, when I was a young girl in Hue, I was raped right in my living room by two army officers, one American and one Vietnamese. . . . Yet I didn't fall, I recovered, thanks to the care of the Party. The Party was the only place where I could regain and maintain my self-esteem. It was the warm womb from which I was reborn" (327). Xuan's story can be seen as the story of Viet Nam—raped both by the corrupt Saigon regime and by the Americans, the Communist revolution was the only way for the nation to be reborn. Xuan's fate, like Viet Nam's, is tragic. Her service to the Party causes her death. Minh tells the captain that she is a spy. Minh betrays her without any soul searching—he has burned his bridges, his ties to the Party. He feels no connection to Xuan because he sees her as a symbol of the Party, not as a person. But fate saves Minh from the guilt of his betrayal. The captain plans to kill Xuan in the night, but that day Thai pirates board the boat, rape and kill her, and throw her body overboard.

In terms of Minh's fate, Xuan represents a path that Minh has not chosen—that of monocultural adherence to the Vietnamese Communist party, as opposed to his cosmopolitanism and more fluid and mutable politics. Her death at the hands of Thai pirates, in an ironic repeat of the experience that originally drove her into the Party, confirms Minh's decision to embrace biculturality and the assumption that the Communist party cannot provide the "home" that Xuan and he have sought.

The third woman who comes to Minh as a messenger from fate is Thai, his high school love, now working as an NLF cadre. While Minh is in the NLF tunnels, preparing for the 1968 Tet Uprising, he encounters Thai, who is now a political commissar. She is cold to him and shows no sign of recognition. Her attitude symbolizes the part of Vietnamese communism that eventually causes Minh to leave Viet Nam—he sees her as all *Lý*, with no *Tình*, no heart. Later, when Minh is asked to join the NLF negotiating team in Paris, Thai becomes head of the delegation. He is attracted to her because she is the only link he has with the past that means so much to him, and from which he is so cut off. When he writes her a letter asking for recognition of their old love and for friendship, she denounces him to the delegation for his "bourgeois nostalgia." He decides, then, that "in order to exist, he must resist" (258). He continues to work for the Party, but the *Tình* has gone out

47

of it for him. Thai's rejection symbolizes for Minh the cost of adhering to the Party: it means rejecting the Vietnamese culture of his youth, which he loves so much. Fate has sent Thai to teach him this lesson.

One narrative result of the construction of the three women in the plot is that national loyalties are symbolically displaced onto the bodies of women, who as a result do not exist in themselves as characters.[12] As such, this novel can be read as a misogynist text, which uses women to embody Minh's anxieties of identity without granting the women independent identities. Nothing displays Minh's (and perhaps the author's) attitudes so clearly as the way in which Minh finds out about Jennifer's death. At the time of the bombing raid it never occurs to him that she might have been injured or killed—he is focused solely on his own experience.

Throughout the novel Minh wavers, unable to find his way through the complexities of his situation. Bewilderment is a predicament favored in Vietnamese fiction; it is a major component of the national epic, the *Truyện Kiều* (a nineteenth-century verse epic by Nguyễn Du). Minh constantly wants to take action, but is unable to; he waits for fate to bring events to him. The only actions he takes of his own initiative are his decision at the beginning to leave the United States to return to Viet Nam and his decision at the end to leave Viet Nam to return to the United States. Thus, at the beginning and ending of the novel, Minh takes action like a Western-style character; in the middle, he is controlled by his responses to fate, like a Vietnamese-style character. The novel blends the two traditions to create a form that is unique, as its main character is unique.

Unlike many American works entrenched in monoculturalism, *Blue Dragon, White Tiger* asserts that bicultural understanding is a real possibility. Minh has no trouble understanding either Vietnamese or Americans. Upon meeting the American vice-consul in Hue, Minh thinks, "There's something phony about the man" (58). American faces are not inscrutable to him. Likewise, some of the American characters are able to read Vietnamese characters. Minh, mistakenly arrested by ARVN soldiers, is rescued by an American lieutenant who recognizes Minh's innocence (he has not yet joined the NLF at this point in the text). The lieutenant says, "A black man in America learns to tell truth-tellers from liars. By the way you speak, your conduct, I know you're not a liar, professor" (84).

Minh's quest throughout the novel is a quest for identity. His identity is always multiple, which is the essence of biculturality. He is Professor Tran Van Minh in both America and Viet Nam, but he is also the poet Co Tung, who writes against the war from a non-Communist position. As Co Tung, he is anonymous; even his own cousin does not know his identity. In Saigon, he is serenaded by one of his poems set to music at a dinner party. Even in "a city without secrets" (29), Minh can remain an enigma. When he first arrives in Viet Nam, his identity as Co Tung is mentioned frequently, making it clear that he is an outsider in his own culture, as the "Lone Tree Pine" he has become because he embraces the West.

When he joins the NLF, his identity as Tran Van Minh and Co Tung is taken from him. When he takes the path to the liberated zones, his guide asks him to "leave everything behind" (204). He is given a new name, Phan Viet Dieu, which he keeps until he goes to Paris, where "he noted immediately that his name had been changed once more, this time to Tran Van Thong" (240). All his years in exile, first in the tunnels and then in Paris, are lived under false names.

He gets his old name, Tran Van Minh, back upon his return from Paris to Hanoi. Still his other identity, Co Tung, haunts him. When he meets a famous novelist in Hanoi she mentions Co Tung's works (269), but Minh is not ready to reclaim that part of his identity yet. He does not tell her that he is Co Tung. In effect, at this point in his story, he is not Co Tung; he has not been Co Tung since he left his identity behind to join the NLF. When he returns to Saigon, he is again known as Co Tung. His new superior says to him, "I've read your books and poems, so I feel as if I know you already" (281). Almost without Minh's will, Co Tung is coming to reclaim Minh.

Minh takes on one last identity in his escape from Viet Nam. His code name with his contact is Chuong. "The code signal was taken from the name of Vu Hoang Chuong, a well-known Vietnamese poet rumored to have died in a re-education camp after the liberation" (305). Minh leaves Viet Nam so that Co Tung will be reborn and will not die like Vu Hoang Chuong. Co Tung represents Minh's bicultural personality. As Co Tung he is a Vietnamese poet, but one who writes his Vietnamese poetry from his position as an American university professor. The multiple naming represents the transitions that Minh goes through as he tries on various identities. In the end his identity remains multiple: Tran Van Minh/Co Tung. For a person who becomes a refugee and insists on preserving his old culture while simultaneously adopting his new culture, only a multiple identity is possible.

Although Minh respects and admires his adopted American culture, he is not uncritical of it; Minh is anything but naive. The novel is critical of some aspects of America, of Viet Nam, and of communism, yet it also embraces other aspects of each. In this respect, it is much more sophisticated than the majority of Euro-American books about the war.

While he is in Viet Nam, Minh begins to see how American culture, in which he has been so at home, has affected Viet Nam. He meets a woman at a party who has had her nose "corrected" and who complains that she does not have enough money to have her eyes "broadened like Sophia Loren's" (28). American culture has colonized Vietnamese women's bodies, creating in them the internalized oppression that causes them to want to alter their looks to fit the standard of the dominant culture of America and Europe, which has been exported to Viet Nam. Minh is disgusted. He is capable of recognizing American colonization of female Vietnamese bodies, even if he is not able to recognize his own symbolic colonization of Vietnamese and American women in the way he plays out his anxieties through his relationships to them.

The American war is also literally and metaphorically poisoning Viet Nam. Minh's father tells him that they can no longer put lotus stamens in their tea because "the water in the moats and ponds has become so polluted with poisonous chemicals it's dangerous to use them" (61). Minh's two teenage cousins are rude and disrespectful, and spend their time watching "I Love Lucy" on Armed Forces television. Vietnamese culture is in danger of being erased, as his father says when Minh tells him that a radio report has not given the name of the Buddhist nun who has immolated herself in protest: "No name! The Vietnamese have no name any more. The whole of Vietnam ceases to have a name. We are a battlefield, pawns for the greedy and the powerful" (140).

Minh cannot, however, free himself from Western culture entirely; it is part of his being, part of his self. Visiting the Buddhist patriarch of the Thien Mu pagoda, "Minh listened attentively to the Patriarch's every word. A few rays of sunlight passed through the window and shone on his clean-shaven head. An aureole seemed to surround his body, like those Minh had seen in paintings of Christian saints" (78). Even while in a Buddhist pagoda, part of his native culture, he brings the perceptions of his adopted culture: he sees both a Buddhist Patriarch and a Christian saint.

One of the cultural elements Minh works to negotiate is that of family. He is tied to Viet Nam by his family, and it is at his father's request that he returns to Viet Nam from the United States. His father is a traditional Buddhist, a scholar, a descendant of an old and noble family of Hue. He preserves his serenity by isolating himself from visitors and the outside world. Minh's mother is dead, but he is close to his father's minor wife, his "auntie," who is the mother of his two half-brothers, both of whom are in the ARVN. Although An and Phong have taken their ARVN positions partially to protect their father, the old man disapproves of the Saigon government. Because

An is a soldier of the corrupt Republic of Viet Nam, his father warns him not to disgrace the family. This passage shows the many double binds of the war: An has joined the ARVN to protect his family, but his father does not count that protection as worth much since it jeopardizes the family's honor.

Minh's father sympathizes with the NLF. He tells Minh the true story of the death of Minh's mother, which had been previously concealed from Minh. She was killed by the French while working with the Viet Minh. His father tells the story in order to persuade Minh, the oldest son, to join the right side in the current war. Minh's father demands of Minh that he reject America entirely: "Remember, it's the American wood that sets the Vietnamese house on fire" (66). Ultimately, however, Minh decides that he cannot live as his father lived. When Minh returns to Viet Nam from Paris in 1973, he longs to return to "a normal Vietnam" (259), but he has not learned the lessons that have been given to him by fate—that there is no more "normal Vietnam." When he lands in Hanoi, he feels "colder at the Vietnamese airport than he had [in Paris]" (262). Minh has been changed by his experiences and it is not possible for him to live the life his father had envisioned for him.

After liberation Minh finds out that his family has been killed. His family ties, which had brought him home in the first place, are dead. Nonetheless, Minh stays on in Viet Nam for three years. When he does decide to leave, part of what he tries to recapture in his escape is a sense of family. The group he escapes with refer to themselves as family; the captain of the boat calls them "our boat family" (323). Minh has never found this sense of family among the Party members he has worked with for the last several years. He must define himself, along with his boat family, against the Party in order to constitute himself as part of the boat family. The reason he betrays Xuan so easily is because she is not a member of the boat family; she is still a member of the rival Party family. Minh is taking his place among the "family" of refugees, and as such, will live as part of the Vietnamese exile community in the United States, seeking to reconstitute his Vietnamese family, and thus maintain his ties to the part of his native culture that he loves and respects, though living in America.

Minh returns to the United States via Thailand. In Bangkok he notices that "the noise, the dirt, the smell, the chaotic traffic on the crowded narrow streets didn't bother or annoy him as they had the last time he was here. He even liked them now. They were, he believed, part of the necessary, insignificant price one had to pay for individual liberty" (331). Minh has learned in the course of the novel that in order to live by the Western definition of freedom that he has chosen, one must accept the destructive elements of

Western culture as well, the choice that Bangkok symbolizes. In exile, Minh will preserve his heritage, "but it would be henceforward the spirit of the historic Vietnam that he held in his heart, not the political one—the mystic Vietnam, not the vulgar and brutal one" (334).

By the end of the novel Minh has come full circle, and in that circle he finds a reconciliation with himself: "I've lost everything, but at the same time, I'm gaining everything back. I'm reclaiming myself. Thank you, Jennifer, and you too, Xuan and Loc. Thank you, Vietnam, thank you, Vietnam Communist Party. Thank you all. I've lost you all in different ways and in different circumstances, but I've gained everything. I've regained myself" (332). Maxine Hong Kingston writes in *The Woman Warrior*, "I learned to make my mind large, as the universe is large, so that there is room for paradoxes" (35). The self that Minh has built by the end of the novel has room for paradoxes, so that losing all can also be gaining all. He lives the paradoxical life of the exile.

Dinh's novel is the only book in this group of works that could be defined as "elite" or "high" culture. It is a highly constructed novel marked by self-conscious narrative technique. Its author is a university professor. The other works discussed here would fit more comfortably into most definitions of "popular" rather than "elite" culture. Dinh's book is also the one most closely focused on questions of selfhood and identity; it is the most introspective and the one that most privileges Western-style individualism. Minh's life experience and the history he passes through are the catalysts through which he finds himself.

In this respect, Dinh's novel contrasts strongly with Hayslip's autobiography, which is more openly concerned with the redemption of two cultures— Viet Nam and America—and their political and moral resolution. Her focus is outward, while Dinh's is inward. Dinh's novel has many of the trappings of biculturality, and the novel's end promises redemption only for the individual, whereas Hayslip's narrative, as I discuss later, asks for—demands—redemption for whole peoples.

A Vietcong Memoir

"These—the survivors—now have a chance to reflect on the trajectories their lives have taken. My own seems to have described a kind of circle."

Each Vietnamese American work published in the United States seems to be hailed as the first and only one of its kind. Douglas Pike's review of *A*

Vietcong Memoir in the *New Republic* begins: "We have here a singular work—a Vietcong turncoat's account of wartime life in the enemy camp. . . . No such book has ever been published before" (33). Pike's opening sentence employs confusing syntax—Truong Nhu Tang did not spend the war in an "enemy camp"—he spent the war working with the NLF, first in Saigon, then at the Provisional Revolutionary Government headquarters on the Cambodian border. What Pike means is that Tang spent the war in the camp of *our* enemy, "us" being the United States. His syntax shows that he takes it for granted that his readers consider the Viet Cong to have been their enemy, therefore they will not find his sentence confusing.

The larger problem, though, is that even Pike, the director of the Indochina Studies program at the University of California, Berkeley at the time he wrote the review, is not paying attention. He specifically means that no nonfiction account by a former NLF official who has defected has been published. *Blue Dragon, White Tiger*, a novel nearly conceded by the author to being autobiographical, is written from a point of view similar to that of *A Vietcong Memoir*—that of a man who worked with the NLF during the war, then defected. Furthermore, a series of books by Dr. Nguyen Khac Vien, including *Tradition and Revolution in Vietnam* (1974), show the war from the "other side."[13] Van Tien Dung's *Our Great Spring Victory* (1977) and Vo Nguyen Giap's *How We Won the War* (1976) show the war from the point of view of the PAVN. Nonetheless, Pike's review deals with *A Vietcong Memoir* as if it were the only book in English by a Vietnamese.

Pike critiques Tang's book almost entirely in terms of its truth claims. The review begins by undercutting Tang's presentation of himself as an important leader. But in doing so, Pike does a curious thing—Tang does not claim to have held an official NLF position—rather, he was in the Provisional Revolutionary Government (PRG), a separate entity. Pike asserts, however, that Tang came to the revolution late: "Our knowledge of virtually all of the NLF leaders, presumably Tang's associates, was voluminous at a time when he was unknown" (34). Does Pike fail to make the distinction between NLF and PRG because he thinks American readers will not follow? Pike, who paints himself as an expert, says that living in Viet Nam for fifteen years made him "as socially suspicious and cynical as is the average Vietnamese" (34). He takes the interesting tack of trying to discredit Tang by making himself a sort of surrogate Vietnamese.[14]

Pike's reasons for wanting to discredit Tang's truth claims are clearly political. He takes Tang and his contemporaries to task for not choosing President Diem over the NLF, even though Pike admits Diem "was not a leader capable of mobilizing the South Vietnamese and defeating the Hanoi threat"

(34). He also chastises Tang for being "Francophile"—though, as we will see, Tang's position in relation to France is much too complex and contradictory to be described with the simplistic term *Francophile.*

When Pike discusses Tang's role with the PRG, he does so to belittle the organization. He describes it as not a government, but a group of " 'cabinet officials' hiding out in the jungle, fleeing at the first sign of an advancing ARVN . . . military sweep" (35). He is evidently referring to a passage in which Tang describes an attack on PRG headquarters by ARVN troops airlifted in by American helicopters:

Hour followed hour as the firing surged, died down, then flared up again. All day long I hunkered down in the shelter, my two bodyguards watching the fighting closely, occasionally letting off a volley from the AK47s through the embrasures. Squirming around on my stomach, I gathered together the most important papers, knowing, whatever the cost, we would have to break through the en-circlement when night came. . . . Meanwhile, the 9th Division threw up a screen against the ARVN drive, while the 5th moved to block the Cambodians on our left. Along the corridor between them the headquarters and government per-sonnel fled, closely shielded by units from the 7th. . . . We were not sure whether the forces trying to head us off were aware of exactly who or what they were after, and to this day I do not know whether American or Saigon government military analysts realized how close they were to annihilating or capturing the core of the Southern resistance. (179–80)

What the review fails to mention is that before this ARVN incursion, the PRG headquarters was subjected to repeated B-52 attacks. Rather than characterizing his disagreements with Tang as a political opposition, Pike is playing a game of undercutting and belittling in order to depict himself as the greater expert. Characterizing the scene as "fleeing at the first sign of an advancing ARVN" strikes me as cheating in this game.

Much worse is a review in *Commentary* by Arch Puddington, which paints Tang as an unwitting dupe of the Communists, a member of a "special class of people whose experiences have been uniquely tragic" (60). Puddington says such people exist "even today in nations like El Salvador which face the threat of a Marxist takeover" (60). He reveals the typical American view of both Viet Nam and communism in this statement: "While today the NLF and PRG are but dimly recollected, during the war they were crucial ex-hibits supporting the argument that the American government was wrong to identify the Vietnam conflict as fundamentally a struggle against Communism" (60). Dimly recollected by whom? By Puddington and Americans like him? Clearly Tang recalls them vividly. Further, the NLF and PRG were never "exhibits"—they were always political entities created by living persons. Puddington's reductionism is ethnocentric, politically naive, and a bizarre rhetorical stance.

Puddington further reveals his ignorance of Viet Nam and the Vietnamese by mixing up the naming conventions—he refers to the author as "Truong." (Pike, of course, gets that detail right. My quarrel with Pike is not that he's ignorant—he's not—but that he's willing to misrepresent Tang's narrative to make political points.) Puddington draws from Tang's book the message that "there is something far worse than corruption and excessive American influence—a brutal totalitarianism which provides neither social justice, freedom, nor genuine independence" (62). Puddington has been so busy arguing against the worldwide spread of communism that he has missed important elements of Tang's book, including the fact that Tang does not ascribe the failure of the revolution entirely to communism, but rather to regional prejudice. He wants the (Communist) NLF to have power in the postwar government, but sees it being dismantled and absorbed by northerners. Tang's reviewers have been too occupied beating the anti-Communist horse to pause to take a close look at what Tang has to say.

Tang's memoir describes the effects of colonialism on bright, young, upper-class Vietnamese like himself. He also shows us the intricacies of politics in postcolonial Viet Nam. Even if Pike is correct in his accusation that Tang is guilty of self-aggrandizement and turns out not to have been as important a personage as he presents himself, his story is still of interest to American audiences because it shows how differently the author negotiated the course of his life from the way so many young American men made decisions about their participation in the war. For example, the stories that Tim O'Brien (in *If I Die in a Combat Zone*) and William Broyles (in *Brothers in Arms*) tell about how they decided to approach their military service differ enormously from Tang's presentation of his developing politics, in that the decision-making process of O'Brien and Broyles is characterized by American individualism. Broyles, already in the marines, decides to desert on the eve of being shipped to Viet Nam:

And so an idea began to build in my mind. I would do what [Siegfried] Sassoon had done. I would refuse to go. A Marine lieutenant refusing to board the plane to Vietnam because he was against the war—it would be a great gesture. Unlike my going to Vietnam, which was a moral gesture that would most likely go unnoticed and which could leave me dead, this gesture would definitely be noticed—and I would live. (74).

Talked out of this plan by a friend, Broyles changes his mind: "Jan was right about one thing. I did compose that statement to conceal a simple fact: I was afraid. Worse, I had tried to conceal my fear behind morality and principle. If I were going to take a stand against the war, I should have done it long before" (76). O'Brien was drafted after graduating from college. After considering the alternatives of evading or being inducted, he decides to submit to the draft. He writes:

It was an intellectual and physical stand-off, and I did not have the energy to see it to an end. I did not want to be a soldier, not even an observer to war. But neither did I want to upset a peculiar balance between the order I knew, the people I knew, and my own private world. It was not just that I valued that order. I also feared its opposite—inevitable chaos, censure, embarrassment, the end of everything that had happened in my life, the end of it all. (31)

Both O'Brien and Broyles focus on the self; their experiences are described in terms that place the personal at the center of the discussion—their inner discussions in deciding what to do, and their recounting of those discussions to their readers.

Tang's decision processes are different, focused more on his place within his family and society, on political and historical movements. He talks of his "initiation into the mysteries of colonialism" (5) and of how his "heart had embraced the patriotic fire, and my soul was winging its way toward the empyrean of national liberation" (22). I am not suggesting that either cultural style is better than the other—rather that American readers are much more used to the kind of personalism represented by Broyles and O'Brien than the style represented by Tang.

Truong Nhu Tang was the son of a wealthy Saigon family, who became politically active while he was a university student in Paris. He returned to Viet Nam and helped found the NLF. He worked undercover in Saigon for several years, was arrested and tortured, then released in a secret exchange of prisoners. He joined the Provisional Revolutionary Government as minister of justice and lived at PRG headquarters in the jungle near the Cambodian border, enduring American B-52 bombing attacks for several more years before being transferred to Hanoi as a liaison. After the liberation he became disillusioned over the northern, Communist domination of the new unified government (despite his activities with the NLF and PRG, he was not a Party member). He eventually settled in Paris.

Tang's memoir is aimed at unsettling its American readers' complacency by providing them with a view that will shake their thinking out of its provincialism. He announces his intentions in his foreword: "These memoirs are the story of my life as a revolutionary. There is little in them about some of the Vietnam War's events best remembered in the West: the clash of arms at Khe Sanh, the surprise offensive of Tet Mau Than, the POWs, or the last American helicopters darting from the embassy roof as Saigon fell to the North Vietnamese army" (xii). He is declaring, here, that there is more to the war than the familiar images that have become the icons of the war in America, that there are ways of thinking about the war that will be new to Americans. He delineates one of the differences between Americans and Vietnamese (to which he will later attribute America's "loss" of the war) by comparing America's interest solely in military action with Viet Nam's interest in political action: "But there was another side of the war as well, one that the Vietnamese revolutionaries considered primary—the political side. My own direct involvement, over almost two decades, was on this front. . . . The West knows, I think, extraordinarily little about the Vietcong: its plans, its difficulties—especially its inner conflicts" (xii–xiv). The project of Tang's book is to fill in some of this missing knowledge. As such, it presents itself as a historical document, equipped with maps, index, glossary of names, and an appendix contining several documents of the NLF. The volume also contains many pictures which seem to act as authentication. Many of the pictures show Tang with other prominent revolutionary figures.

This book is not, however, a personal narrative in the usual Western sense. Although it does narrate Tang's life story, the focus is not primarily on Tang's personal life, but on his participation in revolutionary politics. Political maneuvering and historic events always take center stage. For example, during the years that Tang lived at PRG headquarters in the jungle, he was separated from his family, yet no mention is made of any attempts to communicate with them or of missing them. When he returns to Saigon after the liberation, he discovers that his wife has divorced him and left the country, and that one of his children is living in France, the other in the United States. Even this personal information is offered more as an illustration of the disruption that returning cadres found in Saigon than as part of a detailed personal account. Tang has five brothers, all of whom were on the other side—two as

ARVN officers, one as a government official, two as businessmen. Despite this rift in his family, he mentions them only once, in the context of reunion after the liberation.

The marketing of the book is oriented toward sensationalism and is quite inappropriate to its actual tone and content. The title is "A *Vietcong* Memoir," although Tang consistently uses the term *NLF* (except once in his foreword) and was not a guerrilla fighter, the image that a reference to Viet Cong most readily evokes in America. The cover proclaims the book to be an "inside account," which it is, but, in combination with the other aspects of the cover, that description is rather lurid in its suggestiveness. The cover photograph of the trade paperback edition is the most sensationalist marketing device. It shows a peasant in black pajamas (the Viet Cong "uniform" to American eyes), wearing a snail hat, and looking like the stereotypical image of what Americans tend to see as "sneaky Asians," because you cannot tell which side they are on. But the figure is photographed from behind fronds of vegetation that look like bars. The cover proclaims, Look, here are the enemy's own words, but safe, encapsulated. Instead of the sensational war story promised by the cover, however, the reader gets an extended and sophisticated political narrative.

Part of the didactic message of the book is to show the United States and the West in general the ways in which they were not sophisticated enough in their appraisal of Viet Nam and Vietnamese politics, making it inevitable that the United States would enter into a no-win situation. Tang takes it as a given that, for all the power of the United States, Viet Nam was never a "helpless" subordinate. For him, Vietnamese internal politics always take primacy over American policies. In his assessment of what will happen after the Geneva Convention temporarily divides Viet Nam as part of the settlement after the French withdrawal, Tang ponders President Diem: "Similarly, United States objectives were one thing, but so far it was impossible to tell to what extent Ngo Dinh Diem might merely be using the Americans as a stepping-stone to help him build a viable South Vietnamese government, or to what extent he truly shared the American vision of Viet Nam" (34). American readers, used to seeing the world in the globalist terms of the cold war and the United States as the center around which the world turns, should be surprised and shaken out of their geopolitical complacency by such a dismissal from a citizen of a client state.

Tang unwaveringly equates America's role in Viet Nam with that of the French colonialists. He sees all Western intervention in Viet Nam as being cut from the same cloth. "The United States was thus blithely assuming for itself the mantle of the newly departed French colonialists—in a country whose simmering xenophobia had just exploded in an eight-year-long revolution. Diem's inability to conceive of himself as a popular leader meant that he would have to put his regime in permanent thrall to American aid and protection" (39). Tang refers to the United States as "France's successor" (73), and generalizes the attitudes of both France and America to criticize the West's attitude toward Asia:

France and the West had helped shape much of our political thinking, but it was a bitter paradox that France and the West had given us nothing to go along with it, no hope and no help toward adapting their own values to our society. To all appearances, it had never occurred to Western leaders to try to accommodate Vietnamese aspirations for independence, decent government, and economic progress within their policies. On the contrary, the French had given up control only inch by bloody inch. And the Americans regarded the country as a pawn of strategy, turning a blind and ignorant eye to the motivations of its people, infusing strength into dictators, and nurturing the former officers of French colonialism. (191)

Tang is taking France and the United States—bastions of Western democracy and promulgators of revolutionary ideology—to task for their refusal to extend their own principles of democracy and freedom to Asians. He exposes the hypocrisy of both countries, while laying bare the paradox of his own politics—he has learned to love democratic ideals he has imbibed in Paris, only to learn that the French and American revolutionary slogans "liberte, egalite, fraternite" and "all men are created equal" do not include Asians in that brotherhood of equality. It is a hard pill for him and his compatriots to swallow. In this respect Tang is similar to Tran Van Dinh, who also adopts Western democratic ideals and demonstrates that Westerners do not extend those ideals to Asians. Tang takes the long view about the involvement of the West in Viet Nam: it is not the most important aspect of Vietnamese history or politics. "How to manage China was the classic Vietnamese dilemma, and it would become so again as soon as the Western presence in our country was permanently ended" (248).

Tang also shows that the political strategy of the NLF made a distinction between the American people and the American government. "We would simultaneously confront our enemy in the field, mobilize our domestic support while undermining Diem's, and gather allies internationally—not forgetting the American people themselves" (86–87). Tang overestimates the amount of resistance to government policy that existed among the American people and in the U.S. Congress. The NLF was too hopeful about the antiwar movement. Nonetheless, his analysis of the executive branch is fairly acute. In describing the strategy of the NLF, he writes:

The Americans seemed never to appreciate fully this strategic perspective, which among ourselves we most often simply called *Danh va dam, dam va danh* ("fighting and talking, talking and fighting"). It was, after all, a traditional Vietnamese approach to warfare, a technique refined over centuries of confrontation with invaders more powerful than ourselves. (87)

Tang is holding up a mirror for his American readers to examine their own ethnocentrism and political naïveté. He is particularly critical of Richard Nixon and Henry Kissinger (whose memoirs he has read). He describes them both as suffering "from a fundamental inability to enter into the mental world of their enemy" (209), resulting in their defeat at the Paris bargaining table: their "ignorance of Vietnamese political geography led them into an ambush that Le Duc Tho had carefully prepared" (213).

Tang has little to say about America's conduct of the war itself; commentary appears only in two places, both of them critical of American technological brutality. He describes the conduct of the ground war: "The Americans were subjecting their enemies (and anyone else who got in the way) to state-of-the-art methods of extermination" (134). Later he describes the unrelenting B-52 attacks that the PRG headquarters is subjected to: "The first few times I experienced a B-52 attack it seemed, as I strained to press myself into the bunker floor, that I had been caught in the Apocalypse" (168). Some Americans continue to claim that the United States could have won by stepped up bombing—"bombing them into the Stone Age," the saying goes. But Tang's descriptions of B-52 raids, and the PRG leadership's continuation anyway, point out how wrong that attitude is. Any group of people willing to endure the hardships Tang describes, for a period of several years, could not be defeated except by total genocide.

Tang is equally critical of the brutality of the Saigon government, whose cruelty was inflicted not at long range through technology, but rather person to person through old-fashioned torture. When in prison, he was subjected to treatment that permanently destroyed his health, including having soapy water forced down his throat and being kept in a pitch-black cell for months at a time with little relief.

In contrast to the picture of a too naive, too provincial America that Tang paints, he presents himself as a sophisticated cosmopolite, a world citizen, a child of privilege who capitalizes on the opportunities he is afforded by that privilege. When he visits Algeria as a diplomat in the days just before the war's end, he feels "almost at home with the residual French culture that marked this one-time sister colony" (244), and when he meets Enver Hoxha in Albania, he comments on Hoxha's "excellent French" (249). When he is escaping from Viet Nam, he worries about being captured and suffering a fate similar to Tran Duc Thao, "the great Vietnamese philosopher, who had been Sartre's classmate and friend" (299) and who had been forced into a sort of internal exile in Hanoi in 1956 during a Communist campaign of repression of intellectuals. Tang sees himself as being in the same category as Thao. As the epigraph of this section of my book shows, Tang considers himself to have traveled a circular journey through his Vietnamese nationalism that begins and ends in Paris. He sees no contradiction in this view. His attitude is similar to that of Tran Van Dinh—he wants to take whatever aspects he finds attractive from all the cultures available to him, and remold the parts into an internationalist, cosmopolitan perspective.

Tang's upbringing prepared him for this perspective. His grandfather imbued him with Confucian tradition: "He would talk about the five cardinal ethical principles: *nhon, nghia, le, tri, tin* ('benevolence, duty, propriety, conscience, and faithfulness')" (3). His father had been raised with a French education, "less severe than the native Vietnamese variety, [which] encouraged him to forgo the corporal punishment and dictatorial manner inflicted by most fathers on their children" (2). His mother's side of the family were Cao Daists. "Cao Dai is a syncretic religion, combining elements of Buddhism, Christianity, Islam, and Confucianism with heavy overtones of Vietnamese nationalism" (4). These early, mixed, influences, along with his French university education, formed him into a transnational cosmopolite; at the same time, he is a Vietnamese nationalist.

This mixture of influences is shown clearly in the author's description of his meeting with Ho Chi Minh in Paris in 1945. Ho's appeal is familial—"Almost immediately I found myself thinking of my grandfather" (12)—but simultaneously world historical: "I sat next to him, already infusing this remarkable person . . . with the schoolboy reverence I had felt toward the personal heroes adopted from my reading of history: Gandhi, Sun Yat-sen, and especially Abraham Lincoln" (12).

Hearing Ho Chi Minh compared to Abraham Lincoln might be shocking for many American readers. Yet it seems perfectly natural to Tang, who, as a young stuent, had not yet discovered the hypocrisy of the West, and who will always be able to contain paradoxes because of the transnational cultural influences of his upbringing.[15] Because he has not yet discovered the hypocrisy of the colonial West, he sees no contradiction when he says, "Already in love with French culture, I was now utterly fascinated by the spirit and vitality of French political life. . . . Meanwhile, I decided to join the movement for Vietnamese independence that was beginning to percolate in the Paris streets and debating halls" (19). Rather, he makes an international synthesis, writing that he "began to envision a radical westernization of Vietnam along the lines of Japan's miraculous industrialization of the late nineteenth and early twentieth centuries. . . . [Vietnam could] adopt the best from the world's political and economic cultures: the American approach to economics, the German scientific spirit, the French fervor for democracy" (20).

Like Tran Van Dinh, Tang is interested in the ways Vietnamese culture can absorb and transform marxism (another Western invention). He describes the early formation of the NLF and the division of its membership into "cells": "This cell structure is sometimes thought of as a communist innovation, but for the Vietnamese, with their long history of secret societies, it is practically second nature" (70).

Tang explains the ways people with political differences—members of the NLF who were and were not Communists—could work together. "Although Vietnamese are often suspicious and inconstant in their feelings toward organizations and institutions, they place great value on personal loyalties and trust" (135). He goes on to describe the intricacies of their "debts and obligations": "Indeed the war was replete with instances of friends and relatives protecting each other, even though they were fighting on opposite sides. . . . General Tran Van Trung, [President] Thieu's chief of psychological warfare, hid in his own house a sister-in-law who was the Vietcong cadre in charge of the Hue People's Uprising Committee" (136). Examples like this show how inadequate was the typical American attitude of "you can't tell who's VC." Americans' refusal to consider the complexity of the situation, both political and personal, for the Vietnamese, led to much needless brutality (an issue discussed in depth in chapter 4).

The politics of the war, as Tang describes them, were tremendously complex. Ironically, Tang himself seems to have been a member of a faction that the United States had been looking for all along—the "third force" that would steer a course between Communist domination and RVN dictatorship. Even more ironically, it was the American presence that created that force, but the Americans never recognized it as a solution, or its existence at all: "The Alliance of National, Democratic, and Peace Forces was an organization that had become necessary as a result of the American intervention that began in 1965. . . . It was now past time for a strong effort to reestablish the image of the South's revolution as a broad-based movement that included Southern nationalists of every stripe" (131). Tang maintained the opinion (perhaps a dubious one) that South Viet Nam could remain a nation and negotiate with the DRV. He believed strongly in the reconciliation of all southern factions. Although he seems to have been exactly what the United States was supposedly looking for in South Vietnamese leadership, the United States saw the NLF as monolithically Communist, and therefore out of bounds for any sort of negotiation. Douglas Pike maintains that belief so strongly that he calls Tang's description of the coalition "naive." Tang hoped, before the end of the war, that "the Southern nationalists [could] carve out a distinct role for themselves, as a swing or third force operating between the Party and the American-Thieu forces" (192).

But, with the American withdrawal, the war ultimately ended in a military victory for the PAVN. Shortly after the victory, Tang began to feel disillusioned and betrayed by the revolution he had spent his adult life working for. He saw the South taken over by northerners, and his fond hope for reconciliation of all factions thwarted by the Lao-Đông's reeducation camps. Part of the problem was the class status of Tang and his PRG compatriots, which they were unwilling to renounce. Tang saw the NLF and the PRG as coalitions, not Communist party organizations. But the Lao-Đông, the North Vietnamese Communist party, moved to consolidate, which it accomplished easily because of the losses inflicted on the Viet Cong during Tet of 1968.

Tang's disillusionment is symbolized by the victory parade, which he watches from the reviewing stand after the liberation of Saigon. Unit after unit of the PAVN marches by. "At last, when our patience had almost broken, the Vietcong units finally appeared. They came marching down the street, several straggling companies, looking unkempt and ragtag after the display that had preceded them. Above their heads flew a red flag with a single yellow star—the flag of the Democratic Republic of North Vietnam" (264). But he is most disconcerted over the methods of reunification that the North pursues.

As the reconciliation policy expired in the reeducation camps and prisons, another of the revolution's ideals was also in its death throes: a careful approach to the unification problem. "Haste never breeds success," runs the old Confucian adage. But a year after our Great Spring Victory, whatever relevance this pro-verbial wisdom might have had for Vietnam's unification had long since been a dead letter. So had the PRG and Alliance formulas for eventual confedera-tion. . . . Ho Chi Minh had written that "Vietnam is one, the Vietnamese people are one. Though the rivers may run dry and the mountains crumble, this verity is eternal." Whatever the reality of Ho's words, there is another reality equally pro-found. And that is the political, psychological, moral, and economic differences between the North and the South and among Vietnam's various peoples. (282)

Bitter over the betrayal of his revolution, Tang first retired to a farm in the country with his new wife, then became a "boat person," making his way through a refugee camp to Paris.

Tang is also bitter toward the new Vietnamese government: "Ho Chi Minh's successors have given us a country devouring its own and beholden once again to foreigners, though now it is the Soviets rather than the Ameri-cans" (310). He is resentful as well toward France and the United States. This book is his "talking back" to the United States, telling the nation what he thinks it should have known.

There are many similarities between Tang and Tran Van Dinh. They are from a similar class background, although Tang was much wealthier; they both joined the NLF and left in disillusionment after 1975. The two con-tinue to respect and admire the person of Ho Chi Minh and to believe that his writings are true and correct while his followers have led Viet Nam into a government that betrays the revolution that Ho led. Both take a cosmopoli-tan, internationalist view of culture and politics. Tang and Dinh are a type of Third World exile intellectuals of which the second half of the twentieth century has produced many. The First World would do well to learn the lessons that writers like Tang and Dinh are trying to teach.

The Will of Heaven

"I had not really been released from prison. . . . I had been merely transferred to a much larger one."

Nguyen Ngoc Ngan was a high school literature teacher from a middle-class Catholic family. He was drafted into the ARVN and served as a lieuten-ant. He spent three years in a reeducation camp after the war, then became a "boat person," fleeing to Malaysia, where his boat was denied port and sank in a storm; his wife and son drowned.

Ngan's narrative is firmly rooted in his bourgeois attitudes. He devotes the bulk of his book to his time in the reeducation camp, although he spent an equal amount of time fighting in the delta with the ARVN. He focuses on the corruption of the Communists and consistently portrays himself as pro-American from his high school days onward.

As an ARVN officer he is critical of his captain's anti-American attitude. Ngan admires the American advisor, Captain Johnson, more than his own captain: "The young American was always cheerful, and in his relationship with Captain Tu he was discreet and tactful" (35). Ngan describes a scene that reveals misunderstandings between Vietnamese and Americans in the war. Johnson is talking to Tu about Tu's troops stealing chickens from villagers:

"But about the small matter of the chickens," Captain Tu added, leaning forward and trying to smile in an offhand manner, "I'm sure those were Viet Cong chickens."

"Perhaps," responded Captain Johnson, smiling broadly to show that he appreciated Tu's rare attempt at humor.

I knew that Tu was not trying to be humorous. Indeed, he could not have been more serious. (38)

Despite his pro-American sentiments, Ngan feels betrayed by the Paris peace accords. He finds it difficult to believe that the Americans have abandoned Viet Nam; the two nations have misunderstood each other just as Johnson and Tu have.

Ngan's attitude toward peasants reveals obvious class bias:

It seemed that Tu's troops went out of their way to alienate the peasants, whose goodwill it was, after all, their responsibility to win. The peasants in the South have an inborn hostility toward Saigon and the authority emanating from there. To them the ARVN soldier was symbolic of Saigon and that oppressive authority. The Southern peasant knew nothing about politics and cared even less. He asked only to be left alone to pursue his simple life and to draw a relatively easy living from the rich, productive soil. (36)

Ngan wants to have it both ways—he criticizes the ARVN soldiers who "alienate" the peasants, because that friction helps the other side in the war, and yet he wants to use the peasants in the same way he accuses the Viet Cong of using them. He wants their support, but how can a man with such a condescending attitude, who portrays peasants as lazy and willfully ignorant, gain their trust?

Indeed, he shows his full ignorance of the peasantry when he declares that the NLF is "more of a Northern import than the spontaneous result of Southern Vietnamese dissatisfaction" (90). He steadfastly sticks to the notion that communism is a northern phenomenon: he calls Hoan and Dinh, who are Communist administrators at Ngan's school, "our Northern conquerors" (90) because they are Party members, despite the fact that the men were both born in the South. Ironically, Ngan's own family is northern Catholic and migrated to the South in 1954.

After the PAVN has entered Saigon, Ngan reveals equal prejudice toward the northern peasant soldiers. He relates a story about a soldier who is burned by a hot water tap, and who declares that the former owner has left a trap behind to kill him. "There were other stories of how naive Northern soldiers first used the toilet bowls to wash their vegetables and their subsequent surprise when the vegetables were suddenly flushed out of sight. . . . Many other tales were too farfetched to be taken even half-seriously, but they made us all laugh at a time when there was nothing else to laugh about" (84). Ngan clearly prefers peasants who like the class system the way it stands. In one episode a Communist administrator named Khai, who takes over the high school where Ngan teaches, includes the gatekeeper and charwoman on the staff "patriotic committee." Later all the members of the committee desert Khai.

A moment later, the old gatekeeper glanced uncertainly at the charwoman, and then they both got up and followed the headmaster. All their lives these two old working people had served in a well-ordered society of classes that gave the highest honor and respect to the intellectual. Because of their Confucian heritage, they accepted this system unquestioningly. For many years their respect had been given to the former headmaster. But since they had been appointed to the committee, they had been confused and embarrassed by Khai's obvious disdain for this ancient tradition. Now, thinking they saw a chance to return to the old ways, they rebelled. (86)

These loyal servants who do not challenge Ngan's own position at the top of the hierarchy win his approval. He displays no hesitation in reading their minds and supplying them with motivations, although he had not even known the gatekeeper's name before the committee was formed. Ngan's smugness leaves a reader wondering what the story might be like if told by the gatekeeper or the charwoman.

When Ngan is released from reeducation camp, he rides a pedicab through the streets of Saigon. The driver tells him the houses of the rich are being confiscated.

No doubt it seemed to him [the driver] that there was a kind of retributive justice in what was happening in Saigon. All his life the fine homes and villas of the rich had been a deadening reminder to him of his own grinding poverty and the wide gulf existing between the classes in the old, clearly defined social structure of Saigon. How often he must have compared his hand-to-mouth existence with the sheltered ease and luxury of the lives of the wealthy! He had probably often seen those privileged people in their fine clothes and expensive cars go and come from their luxurious homes while he pedaled through the Saigon streets looking for just one more fare, enough to buy a thin bowl of soup at a sidewalk kiosk. How he must have envied even the secure lives of those well-dressed chauffeurs who sat so smugly at the wheels of those beautiful cars. (296)

Despite Ngan's ability to colorfully imagine a poor worker's life, Ngan finds no irony, no responsibility on his own part for the poverty of the driver's life, because he does not consider himself to be wealthy, despite the fact that he owns a house, that he and his wife still possess enough gold (three years after he has been interned) to buy three unsuccessful escape attempts, that his wife has been able to live without working or any visible means of support while he is away, and that finding a way to make a living is not his first concern upon arriving home. The pedicab driver earns Ngan's approval when he declares that he does not like the Communist regime because nothing has changed—he does not own his pedicab: "The only difference is that now I must rent it from a transportation cooperative instead of a businessman" (297). The driver says, "I'm still poor." Ngan replies, "We all are" (297). Clearly, his conception of poverty differs greatly from that of the pedicab driver, but he is unwilling or unable to see that difference.

In addition to classism, Ngan exhibits racism. He is moved to a new reeducation camp near a Montagnard village. He refers to them as *moi*, a word that literally means "savage" or "barbarian." (There is no polite term in general use to refer to the hill-dwelling ethnic groups in Viet Nam, so the French term *Montagnard* is now commonly used.) Ngan portrays them as rude and exotic savages who are childlike in their simplicity. He describes a Montagnard man who "laughed with childish glee" (287). Despite his disdain, he has a prurient sexual interest in the Montagnard women.

Ngan has little use for peasants or Montagnards, and no use whatever for the revolution. He sees in the revolution only corruption and injustice. Khai,

67

the new school administrator, is unjustly deprived of his house and belong-
ings (confiscated as "abandoned" when Khai has zealously spent night and
day at the school). Ngan is shocked by the revolution's betrayal of one of its
own. Later he discovers that Khai, too, is corrupt—he has been sleeping with
his female student assistants. Ngan cannot imagine a Communist who is not
corrupt. When Private Lam, a guard at the reeducation camp, asks Ngan to
tell him about corruption among the other guards and camp officials, so Lam
can report it to their superiors (as he has twice already done), Ngan decides
Lam is just jealous because he is not in on the take. He decides, "The less I
had to do with Lam, I decided, the better it would be for me" (280).

Conditions at the reeducation camp really are horrendous. The PAVN
inflicts various forms of revenge on the former servants of the "puppet
regime," who are considered to be traitors to Viet Nam for having col-
laborated with the neocolonialist Americans. The southerners are forced
to clear an old ARVN minefield. The few who refuse to denounce their
former loyalties are beaten and shot. Although a reader might wish for a
less self-pitying rendition of camp conditions, one cannot dismiss Ngan's
sufferings.

Ngan differs from other refugee writers in that he does not spend much
time in a didactic mode, teaching his readers about Vietnamese culture; the
little he does present along those lines he relegates to footnotes.[16] His focus
instead, is on anticommunism. This book most closely resembles U.S. POW
narratives like those of Jeremiah Denton and James Stockdale, which deal
with the problem of physical, mental, and spiritual survival in hostile cap-
tivity. Ngan himself points to this parallel. A guard says to a prisoner, "If we
could reeducate the American prisoners, we can certainly reeducate you"
(141). On an expedition from the camp to collect firewood, a column of
prisoners and guards passes through a nearby town. As they approach the
town, Ngan "recalled [the guard] Than's stories of the hostility the American
prisoners in the North had encountered from the populace whenever they
appeared in public. . . . The communist guards were placed in the strange
position of having to protect their American captives" (211–12). This is one
of the many ways Ngan positions himself in alignment with the Americans
and in opposition to the Communists.

A man whose wife writes to him in reeducation camp that she has had to
become a prostitute to support their children says, "The fact that my wife
chose to become a prostitute is not really important. . . . But the thing that
fills me with shame and outrage is the fact that she's sleeping with the
goddam communists!" (134). This story seems to embody Ngan's own ideas:

he does not mind if Viet Nam prostitutes itself to America, or even to France. (He is capable of a little nostalgia for the French, if they are responsible for providing luxuries he likes: "The coffee was terrible. Since the takeover, most of the best coffee from the fine former French plantations of Ban Me Thuot has been diverted to Hanoi" [311].) What he does mind is if Viet Nam is sleeping with Communists.

The most disturbing aspect of this book is Ngan's unintentional self-revelation. He shows himself to be almost completely lacking in integrity. In reeducation camp he accepts positions, like that of deputy of the Cultural Activities Committee, from the camp commanders, then wonders why his fellow prisoners cease to trust him. His closest friend in camp, Dr. Van, escapes with a companion to Cambodia, where the latter is killed. After his companion's death, Dr. Van returns to camp. He is hiding in the jungle (the prisoners—or students, as the Communists refer to them—are at this point engaged in slash-and-burn agriculture in the jungle) when Ngan finds him. Ngan promises to get a sympathetic guard to bring him in, so he will not be shot. It takes Ngan awhile to make contact with the guard, and before the guard can leave to get Dr. Van, Ngan sees two other guards heading into the jungle where Dr. Van is hiding. Ngan watches them go and does nothing, although it seems he might have found a way to distract the guards. Dr. Van is shot in the leg by one of the guards, but he survives.

When a prisoner's wife is raped on the road home after a visit to the camp, and the prisoner asks Ngan to report it to the guards for him, Ngan initially says he can do nothing. "He had come to me for help, and it no doubt seemed to him that it was I who was giving him the very double talk of which I spoke" (276). Ngan is unwilling to admit that it not only *seems* that way—it *is* that way. By accepting favors from the guards, he has violated the prisoners' code of ethics. He believes he is trying to help and protect the prisoners, but in fact he is a collaborator.

It seems that Ngan has written the story that most Americans would expect to hear. He is constantly decrying the Communists as "robots" and reminding the reader of his own pro-American stance. He is a musician and likes to play American songs. His portrayal of stupid Communists versus superior pro-Americans appears in this scene:

[The camp commander asks Ngan's fellow musician,] "What is your favorite song?"
"Sir, I especially like a song called 'The Sounds of Silence.'"
The camp leader looked perplexed. "What does it mean?"

Toan translated the title again into Vietnamese. The camp leader's perplexity seemed to deepen and then turn to mild irritation.

"Are you trying to make fun of me?" he growled. "Silence means 'no sound,' so how can you say 'sounds of silence'?"

"It's just the name of the song, sir," Toan said uncertainly. "The composer was perhaps trying to make an interesting statement of paradox."

"That's true, sir," I hurriedly interrupted. "It's very difficult to explain."

Camp Leader Thien looked mildly at me a moment and seemed inclined to pursue the matter no further. Suddenly he frowned again and said, as if to himself, "Who would be stupid enough to compose a song called 'The Sounds of Silence'?" (189)

Ngan affirms what he sees as the superiority of American culture by announcing to the camp leader that the metaphysics of Simon and Garfunkel's song title is "very difficult to explain." He is clearly implying to his American audience, which he knows understands the song title perfectly, as do he and Toan, that he is a member of an in-group, along with his American readers, and that the camp leader is a member of an out-group, the Communists.

Because of this attempt to meet the expectations of the American audience and curry American favor through his doctrinaire anticommunism and cloying pro-Americanism, Ngan's book stands apart from the others. Having internalized the ideals of the culture that has dominated him in Viet Nam and in his new home in North America, Ngan displays the same shortsightedness of the majority of Euro-American writers, rather than the complex biculturality of other exile writers. Still, episodes like the discussion of the Simon and Garfunkel title do show Ngan negotiating two cultures much more than is evident in most Euro-American narratives.

When Heaven and Earth Changed Places and Child of War, Woman of Peace

"If you have not yet found peace at the end of your war, I hope you will find it here."

"There is an official version of the war and its aftermath," Le Ly Hayslip writes in her autobiography, When Heaven and Earth Changed Places (60). The story she tells is designed to amend that offical version. This effort aligns Hayslip with the other writers discussed here (except perhaps Ngan, who tends to endorse the "official view").

Hayslip, however, occupies a unique position from which to write. She is an outcast in Viet Nam because of her political history, her class status (she is the only peasant in this group of writers), and her dealings with Americans; she is an outsider in America because of her status as an immigrant from a country that the United States would like to forget and ignore. Hayslip takes that outsider positon and uses it to become a storyteller, communicating to her readers a story that none of them has heard before, because she speaks from a position that is systematically erased from the discourse on both sides of the ocean. Hayslip is a peasant, a woman, and a victim of both of the warring sides—the Viet Cong and the U.S.–RVN alliance. Through her book, and her life, she turns that victimization into a force for healing and reconciliation.

When Heaven and Earth Changed Places reveals the hidden class structure of the war; it identifies the alliance of the governing-class Vietnamese with the governing-class Americans against the Vietnamese peasants. It is important to distinguish American officialdom from American soldiers, as Hayslip does, since, in one of the many ironies this book points to, the American soldiers are often poor people, like Hayslip herself, who are likewise victims of the hierarchy. She discovers the powerlessness of the individual Americans against the American and Vietnamese power structures through the individual men with whom she becomes involved. When she and Ed Munro want to get married, Munro cannot simply wave his hand and make the Vietnamese and American bureaucracies go away, any more than Le Ly can.

The book reveals this class alliance of transnational governing classes against transnational underclasses covertly—the revelations come as subtext. Hayslip does not make any sort of overt analysis—she simply tells stories. She does this in part because her goal is reconciliation of all sides, but also, perhaps, because she wants to draw in rather than to alienate her readers, many of whom might think that peasants are uninteresting drudges, and that the poor suffer what they must, anyway. Hayslip is aware that on both sides of the ocean her audience will be middle-class readers who might not immediately identify with her story, both because of her position as a peasant and because of her sympathy, at least in the beginning, for the Viet Cong. She works against this obstacle by simultaneously insisting on the dignity, worth, and rootedness in tradition of the peasants and downplaying her sympathies for the Viet Cong.

She accomplishes the goals of the book by setting *Tình* (feeling) against *Lý* (reason), the terms used by Tran Van Dinh, to remove the "otherness" of her ethnicity (for Euro-American readers) and her class (for both Euro-American and Vietnamese American readers). She enlists the readers' empathy and invites her audience to identify with her and her family members, therefore

71

making herself and her family familiar rather than exotic, understandable rather than inscrutable.

Hayslip uses *Tình*, making an implicit claim for the place of the peasants as the center and source of Vietnamese culture, even while they are exploited, abused, and killed by the higher classes, in order to work her way narratively into the *Lý* of her readers. In other words, she is making an appeal to their hearts and minds, using the heart as the means to the mind. This can be seen as a traditionally feminine narrative strategy. She tells emotion-charged stories, eliciting the reader's attention and sympathies for her family and herself. She exposes the harsh truths of Vietnamese peasant life, deromanticizing any notions that middle-class Vietnamese or Americans might have about happy, unaware farmers leading their water buffalo through the pleasant rice fields (attitudes clearly expressed by Ngan). At the same time, however, she asserts the dignity and decency of the peasants, thus arguing, through her storytelling, for their right to be alive. She accomplishes this partially through humor, as in her description of how she learned to weed the rice paddies with her mother: "I copied my mother's stance in the muddy water, planting my feet like a woman warrior. Her strong back swiveled easily at the hips. Her arms churned like a tireless machine. Together we hurled the defeated weeds into shallow baskets—slain soldiers for a funeral pyre. . . . Being a woman warrior was harder work than I expected, so I rested on my basket" (11–12). Even with the humor, images of war are always present.

The key to a full, cross-cultural reading of this book is to understand that Hayslip's family, on whom her story centers, is part of the doubly oppressed underclass: their choices are limited both by the structure of their own society and by the war. In other words, the peasants are already oppressed by the social structures of Vietnamese culture, and the war, rather than overturning those structures, magnifies them, because the war is fought mostly in the countryside, mostly by peasants, and mostly on their land. After Le Ly and her mother have both been condemned by the Viet Cong for supposed betrayals, they go to Saigon, where Hai, Hayslip's eldest sister, works as a maid. Hayslip's father is unable to join them in the city, because if he leaves the land, the family will lose it. Hayslip and her mother find being poor in the city even more difficult than being poor in the country. Her mother expects Hai to give them jobs, but as Hai tells her, "I'm just a cook—a maidservant. I'm not even allowed in my boss's living quarters" (119).

Through the wide eyes of a naive country girl, Hayslip discovers the truth about the distribution of wealth when she goes to work for an affluent family:

There was a cleaning girl for every floor, a cook and scullery maid, a handyman, and two chauffeurs: one for the master's limousine and one for the mistress's Mercedes, which was kept parked in a garage below the house. . . . When our old clothes wore out, replacements were furnished by the master, along with two hearty meals each day, in addition to which we received a small monthly stipend that my mother began hoarding immediately to send to my father in Ky La. (122)

Young Le Ly is quite dazzled by all this splendor. She is eventually seduced by the master of the house and cast out, pregnant, by the master's wife. Yet her message, twenty years later, is one of forgiveness and reconciliation even for her former employers. Anh, the father of her first child, now employed by the state to run the business he used to own, becomes her guide on her first trip back to Viet Nam. He is her first contact, her road back to her homeland. Hayslip views this scenario not with irony but instead as confirmation that forgiveness, not vengeance, is the road to survival and peace.

Even as a youth, however, Hayslip was not so dazzled by the big city that she was unaware of the structural inequalities of the system. After being forced out of Saigon, the young Le Ly and her mother go to Da Nang, which is close to their home village. Le Ly stays with her sister Lan, who has become a bar girl. Le Ly herself works as a maid, then a street vendor, and eventually secures a job as a nurse's aide in a hospital. Of that job she says, "In contrast to the hustlers I dealt with in the black market, these were educated people dedicated to helping others—not exploiting them. In contrast to the overseers I had worked for as a housekeeper, they were kind and considerate employers. And to be paid a living wage on top of that was too much to believe" (275). She quickly loses this job as a result of sexual harrassment by a Vietnamese sergeant, which leads her to accept the "protection" of an American. He persuades her to transform herself from a peasant girl into a "beauty"—to wear "sexy" clothes and makeup, get a beehive hairdo, and go to work in a bar, all in order to boost his self-esteem by having a desirable Vietnamese girlfriend. After her brief rise to the decent situation in the hospital, Hayslip is again lowered into a world of exploitation, this time the sexist and colonialist exploitation of Vietnamese women by the American military establishment.

By telling these stories, Hayslip quietly debunks the American mythology that the United States was fighting to save Viet Nam from communism, that the United States was fighting for freedom for Vietnamese citizens. She shows a Viet Nam in which the poor are exploited by the rich, and shows that the Americans join the rich, not the poor, when they arrive. Hayslip realizes that her own attempts to use the capitalist system make her into a "capitalist running dog." Her awareness of this positions puts her into an uneasy relationship with her beloved family. Driven by the necessity to survive, she still recognizes that she is violating her gender and class positions.

The Americans did bring a lot of money to Hayslip, her sister Lan, and other poor Vietnamese, but the price for that temporary prosperity was the figurative soul and the literal body. Hayslip is a member of the underclass by reason not ony of social class, but also of gender. The book begins like so many women's books—with an attempt to silence the author. " 'Suffocate her!' the midwife told my mother when I came into the world" (1). Le Ly is a victim of sexual oppression by both Vietnamese and Americans. As a fifteen-year-old village girl, she is raped by the corrupt Viet Cong cadre who are sent to execute her after she is unjustly accused of betraying the Viet Cong cause. The rapists, perhaps out of guilt and shame, allow her to live, but Le Ly feels her life has been destroyed, because her marriageability has been destroyed. She keeps the rape secret, so as not to disgrace her family. Later, when she is seduced and made pregnant by her employer in Saigon, and she and her mother are forced to move to Da Nang, Hayslip survives by acquiring a series of American boyfriends, by one act of literal prostitution, and by eventually marrying an American who brings her to the United States. Before she finds her husband, she is mistreated, abused, and abandoned by several American men; as one woman tells her, "Let's face it, to most American men, we're *thay ao*, eh?—shirts they change when it suits them" (324).

This city world of corruption, which Hayslip contrasts sharply with the solid tradition of the prewar village, undermines her sense of self—from the way her American boyfriend makes her transform her looks to the moral dilemma she faces over money for survival versus selling her body:

I stared at the cash the way a thirsty prisoner stares at water. Four hundred dollars would support my mother, me, and [my son] for over a year—a year I could use finding a better job and making connections. . . . What could they do to me that hadn't been done already? Maybe it was time some men paid me back for what other men had taken—. . . . To tell [my mother] what had actually happened was unthinkable. Even if I hadn't been too ashamed to do so, the mere suggestion that her baby daughter had sold herself as a prostitute would have killed her—or at least the part of her that loved me, and that's something I would never risk. Love, like money, was in too short a supply to risk on peacetime honesty. (259–61)

Despite the oppression she suffers as a woman, despite her move to the city and later to the United States, Hayslip's strongest identity remains that of a peasant. She says of herself on her first return to Viet Nam after the war, "I pull off my shoes and dig my toes into the moist grass—for an international diplomat, I will always make a better farm girl!" (272).

Although Hayslip recognizes the ways she is oppressed because of her gender, this is not a feminist book. Hayslip respects and preserves the paternalistic tradition in which she was raised: when she meets Per, a Norwegian United Nations emissary, in Bangkok, she looks to him for guidance and behaves toward him exactly as a dutiful daughter would. She first enlists his aid by a calculated display of "feminine" need for help with the authorities, then continues to follow his advice and to reward him with her daughterly loyalty and respect.

This book does not, then, critique the patriarchal system. In fact, it is written as a gesture of remembrance for Hayslip's father, who died in an attempt to protect her. Hayslip sets her father up as the righteous patriarch, the good man who embodies traditional values and who tries to fulfill his role in a world where traditional values have been violently disrupted. The book is written in fulfillment of her role as the dutiful daughter: "I have promised my father's spirit that I will tell everything that I have learened to my family, my people, and the world" (60). Her stance as a dutiful daughter is key to her identity as a Vietnamese. As Leslie Bow writes, "As her relationship to her family and her loyalty to Vietnam become posed as a question of her sexual allegiances, her text reinscribes her present American citizenship as the fulfillment of a Vietnamese daughter's duty" (2).

Hayslip does critique both Ho and Diem, and all their followers, along with the Americans, for not being good patriarchs to the Vietnamese people. She is critiquing not the system but the holders of power within that system, who betrayed the best interests of the people; thus she puts nationalism before feminism. I would argue that as a consequence she misses the root of the problem, that such a system is inherently unjust and will always work against the interests of those not in power; nonetheless, her portrayal of both sides' oppression and destruction of the peasants is unassailable.

Hayslip shows how the war and the American intervention rocked the selfhood of Viet Nam. Not only was her personal selfhood undermined, but her family was torn apart: one brother in Hanoi, one brother drafted by the Republic but killed on his way to join the Viet Cong, one sister coerced into marrying a Republican policeman, their village destroyed by the war, her father dead by suicide, taking his own life to protect her from sacrificing her

75

life, as the local Viet Cong have requested that he ask her to do. Hayslip's book reveals the war for what it was—a civil war, in which the ordinary farmers were the losers, caught between both sides.

In showing the effects of the corruption of both sides so strongly, Hayslip throws the political notions of both the American mainstream and the American antiwar left into disarray. The Republic of Viet Nam is clearly nothing but a dictatorship that employs terror and torture as its means of retaining rule. Although most of the farmers support the Viet Cong, who are familiar and come from the same villages, and who fight to throw out first the corrupt Republicans and later the invading Americans, the farmers also suffer at the hands of the Viet Cong. Hayslip says of her portrayal of the Viet Cong, "Both sides in a war will behave like they are at war." As Hayslip shows, it is not the politics of communism or democracy but rather the war itself that threatens to destroy her country, because it is fought as a war of the affluent against the poor.

Her distrust of government extends to the Communist government of the Socialist Republic of Viet Nam in 1986, the Republican government during the war, and the U.S. government always. For peasants, power, no matter whose, is distant, removed, and repressive. Hayslip's portrait of peasants contradicts Ngan's picture of peasants who "knew nothing about politics and cared even less." Hayslip's peasants do not discuss competing political theories, but they have a very clear picture of their relationship to power. Looking at a picture of Ho Chi Minh, Hayslip writes, "The religious aura of the picture only reminds me of the awesome power of the state compared with puny individuals like me" (159). She characterizes the peasants collectively in the same way: "For the next few days, the Republicans and Americans poured troops and firepower into the jungle around Ky La—a raging elephant stomping on red ants too far down in their holes now to feel the blows" (68). Although the peasants experienced the effects of the conduct of the war, they felt like they had little influence over it—"we defined 'politics' as something other people did someplace else" (xiii).

When she begins to have dealings with American soldiers as well as Vietnamese during the war, Hayslip notes that oppression is not limited to one side or the other. Sometimes Americans protected her, sometimes they exploited her, as was true with the Vietnamese. "The dividing line between friends and enemies—spiritual kinsmen and barbarian invaders—gradually became a blur" (190). From that blur Hayslip began developing a perspective that would champion the cause of the weak over the strong, the victim over the oppressor, regardless of race or national origin.

The underclass Hayslip describes needs a defense against its oppressors. Playing dumb is a survival skill for the underclass and a motif throughout the book. Hayslip has been taught by her mother: "If you're too smart or too dumb, you'll die—so play stupid, eh? That shouldn't be too hard for a silly girl who lets herself get caught! Act like you don't know anything because you are young and stupid. That goes for either side, no matter who's asking the questions. Play stupid, eh? Stupid, stupid child!" (49). She employs this strategy successfully when captured and tortured by the Republicans, after being accused of working with the Viet Cong. She also employs the strategy against the Viet Cong when they try to recruit her in Saigon: "For once, it was smarter to stay bumbling peasants than to play liberation heroes and they left us alone" (128).

Hayslip reveals that what the Americans saw, and what the Vietnamese overclass saw as stupidity in the peasants was in fact intelligence—their ability to play the system to insure survival. The peasants, as Hayslip's mother makes clear with her lesson on how to play dumb, not only adopt this stance, but are consciously aware of doing so—of putting one over on the oppressors.

Hayslip also speaks directly to Euro-American literature about the war that so often characterizes the peasants as primitive. Many U.S. novels and personal narratives of the war have made issue of rice paddies fertilized with human excrement. Hayslip, in her characteristically understated fashion, sets the record straight on this point:

When the planting was done, the ground had to be watered every other day and, because each parcel had supported our village for centuries, fertilized as well. Unless a family was very wealthy, it could not buy chemicals for this purpose, so we had to shovel manure from the animal pens and carry it in baskets to the fields where we would cast it evenly onto the growing plants. When animals became scarce later in the war, we sometimes had to add human waste collected from the latrines outside the village. (7)

This passage reveals one of the paradoxes of colonialism: the dominant power creates a situation in the subordinate nation that observers from the dominant power are then horrified by, but because they have not seen the previous state of the colonized, they attribute the situation to the "primitivism" of the "natives," rather than to the depredations inflicted by the dominant power.[17]

Another recurring theme in Euro-American works is the frustration of American soldiers looking for Viet Cong bodies to count. The Viet Cong practice of quickly removing the dead and wounded from the site of a battle

77

is sometimes described as if that were an aberration. Hayslip again supplies a corrective: "I didn't see any Republican or American casualties—there must have been many—but it was their custom to remove their dead and wounded as soon as possible, even in the middle of a fight" (67).[18]

While Hayslip accuses both the Vietnamese Communists and the Republicans of betraying the people, she gives a mixed review of the Americans. She praises the aspects of the United States that she appreciates. When an American job counselor in an employment office on a base in Da Nang tries to force her to have sex with him, she calls the police, and they arrest him: "That the Americans could take the side of a poor Vietnamese girl over one of their own made that curious nation of barbarian-saints even more wondrous in my eyes. Perhaps, someplace in this cruel and dangerous world, justice *was* the order of the day, and not just the exception" (310). When she writes "poor Vietnamese girl," she means coming from poverty, *not* poor in the sense of pitiful; up to this point, she has seen "justice" available to the rich but denied to the poor. Hayslip also criticizes Americans for what she perceives as their shortcomings. When she marries Ed Munro, a friend tells her, "Americans are *thu vo thuy vo chung*—they have no beginning and no end. They don't care about their ancestors. Because they don't know what reincarnation is, they think they're free to do any cruel thing they want in this life—no matter how much it hurts others" (348). In this passage Hayslip is contrasting the tradition-bound, patriarchal system's strengths with the American culture's weaknesses. Ultimately, however, her message is one of transcendence over class, culture, and racial difference. After she was cheated by several Americans with whom she made black market deals, she "began to see the value of looking into the face of another race the same way I studied the faces of my own" (189). Her book invites its Euro-American readers to do the same.

Hayslip invites readers to do even more; this book is intended as a work of activism. She represents contemporary Viet Nam as a sort of underclass country in comparison with the United States as an overclass country. This difference is symbolized by the two embassies in Bangkok:

The Vietnamese embassy had looked like a middle-class Thai house. . . . Only the Communist flag and brass nameplate outside the door let you know you were in a government building and not some second-rate Asian insurance company.

The American embassy, on the other hand, was majestic and imposing. . . . A wrought-iron fence, concrete terrorist barriers, and young marines in tapered shirts guarded the entrance. (55)

She continually contrasts contemporary Viet Nam's poverty with America's wealth. She situates some of the blame for Viet Nam's situation on the inefficient and corrupt Communist government, but primarily she is asking the United States to recognize its responsibility for the poverty of Viet Nam, and asking not for guilt or remorse but for action: for the United States to normalize relations with Viet Nam and begin sending the humanitarian aid, mostly in the form of medicine, which the country so desperately needs. She is making an appeal to individuals apart from their governments and nations. In so doing, she dodges some of the harder questions of the war in much the same way as most Euro-American texts do.

Hayslip is trying to get across the necessity of reconciliation. At the end of the book, she reunites with her family in Viet Nam. The family reunion includes Le Ly's "Hanoi" brother who now works for the government of the Socialist Republic of Viet Nam, Le Ly's sister and her husband, a policeman under the old republic who spent several years in a reeducation camp, Le Ly's mother, who still lives in their home village and tends their ancestors' graves, and Le Ly herself, now an American citizen. This family reunion serves as a metaphor for the reconciliation that Hayslip wishes to bring about through her book—a reconciliation among all the Vietnamese factions, in Viet Nam and abroad, and between the nations of Viet Nam and the United States. She writes of the family reunion: "With their feelings out in the open but not trampled on, they seem able to find peace with each other" (355). Finding peace has been the goal of both her journey and her writing.

About her journey back to Viet Nam Hayslip notes, "Coming back always sets things straight" (24). The book is structured to juxtapose the stories of her life in Viet Nam with her return journey in 1986, after an absence of sixteen years. Thus the stories of separation and reconciliation evolve side by side, and as she describes the events that drove her from Viet Nam, she also recounts her return. By weaving these two stories together rather than narrating them chronologically, she demonstrates the principle that she preaches.

One measure of the unwillingness of American audiences to listen to a Vietnamese point of view before Hayslip's book was published is that Doubleday cut one-third of the manuscript before agreeing to publish it. Hayslip says that Doubleday thought her story was "repetitive," since she worked as a maid more than once and was raped more than once.[19] She reports Doubleday also said that readers were not interested in anything "so awful." The effect of this editorial position has been to water down the book's critical messages.

Nonetheless, against the odds, *When Heaven and Earth Changed Places* has been a commercial success, and unlike other Vietnamese refugee writers, Hayslip has gained a large American audience. The book went through three printings in hardback, multiple paperback printings, and it has been made into a film by Oliver Stone. It is read in college courses and was reviewed on the front page of the *New York Times Book Review.*

That review, however, reveals the way the book is being misread by American audiences. In his review, titled "A Child's Tour of Duty," David Shipler praises the author for managing "so gracefully to transcend politics, keeping her humaneness as the focus." He thus points to Hayslip's narrative strategy of emphasizing *Tình,* what he calls "humaneness," over *Lý,* which would include politics. Shipler quotes a passage in which Hayslip describes playing war games as a child:

When I played a Republican [an ARVN soldier] I always imagined that the laughing face at the end of my stick-rifle was my brother Bon Nghe, who had gone to Hanoi and who might one day come back to fight around Ky La. . . . When I played a Viet Cong, I could think only of my sister Ba in Danang, who, being married to a policeman, locked her door every night out of fear of "those terrorists."

Shipler misses the point by declaring that the book "transcends politics" and focusing on Hayslip's "humaneness." It is precisely the politics of civil war, of class conflict, that this passage, indeed the whole book, describes. The civil war has divided Hayslip's family, so that the child Le Ly cannot take either side in the war "game" without seeing the faces of her family members positioned across from her as the enemy .

Shipler also emphasizes the section that covers Hayslip's childhood, barely mentioning the later parts of the book: "But the most touching and illuminating sections of the book are those set in her lovingly described home village, for there is nothing more anguishing to read than portrayals of a war through a child's eyes." This statement romanticizes the peasants, in the manner of Ngan. By focusing on Hayslip's childhood, Shipler displays the usual paternalistic attitude that Americans take toward Third World peoples, and allies himself with the paternalism of the Vietnamese overclass. Most reviewers, like Shipler, tend to concentrate on descriptions of Hayslip's childhood, although these sections occupy far less than half of her book (see, for example, Mary Warren Marien's *Christian Science Monitor* review, half of which recounts Hayslip's childhood).

Other reviews, while praising the book, have been equally bound by American ignorance and ethnocentrism, the very attitudes the book seeks to resist. Lynne Bundesen's review in the *Los Angeles Times* faults Hayslip for not giving details like "such and such a date, in a town of so many people, at a spot x meters from the edge of town." Bundesen complains that although she can picture Hayslip signaling the Viet Cong, she cannot sort out what is happening when "the endless wars and invasions became merely the backdrop of [Hayslip's] personal life." Bundesen thus puts the burden of educating ignorant Americans on Hayslip's shoulders. In fact, Hayslip constantly gives reminders of historical events in the American war throughout her narrative. However, if American readers do not have a rudimentary grasp of the history of America's involvement in the war, then they will miss the clues, as Bundesen obviously did. American ignorance about the war should stand as an indictment of American education, not of Hayslip's book.

Arnold R. Isaacs's review in the *Washington Post* illustrates how the American focus on the war's effects on the United States creates ignorance like Bundesen's: the first three paragraphs of his review focus on his own experience as a war correspondent in Viet Nam, rather than on the book he is reviewing. From that inauspicious beginning, his review nonetheless develops into the best one written about the book, showing a political and cultural understanding, and concluding that "it should not be missed by anyone—especially anyone who still thinks there is anything noble or glorious about war."

Why, then, are American readers interested in this book in a way they have been interested in no other Vietnamese refugee book? One reason may be timing. In 1986, for the first time since 1975, talk started about normalization of relations; perhaps Americans were beginning to separate Viet Nam from the Viet Nam War, and in so doing freeing themselves to be interested in a Vietnamese refugee writer.

But there is more at work than just timing. To read any of the works by Vietnamese authors, or any of the oral histories of Vietnamese refugees, is to realize the unmitigated wrongness and ill conception of U.S. participation in the war. Hayslip's book is no exception, but the author lets her Euro-American readers feel no guilt, because her message is one of forgiveness and reconciliation. She dedicates the book "to all those who fought for their country, wherever it may be. It is dedicated, too, to those who did not fight—but suffered, wept, raged, bled, and died just the same. We all did what we had to do. By mingling our blood and tears on the earth, god has made us brothers and sisters" (xiv). In this dedication she brings together

Vietnamese who fought for the Republic and who fought for the Communists, Americans who fought the war and who protested the war. No previous writer has brought together all these groups, and no one has suggested forgiving and reconciling all of them, rather than singling out one or more groups for blame and recrimination. Hayslip means what she says about brothers and sisters quite literally. It is only by recognizing, she insists, that the destinies of our two countries are linked by the experience of the war which they shared that they can create a viable future.

In her preface Hayslip addresses U.S. veterans directly: "The least you did—the least any of us did—was our duty. For that we must be proud. The most that any of us did—or saw—was another face of destiny or luck or god. Children and soldiers have always known [war] to be terrible. If you have not yet found peace at the end of your war, I hope you will find it here. We have important new roles to play" (xv). The important new roles Hayslip envisions involve rebuilding on both sides of the ocean. Her East Meets West Foundation has sent groups of U.S. veterans back to Viet Nam to build medical clinics, providing material aid to Viet Nam and spiritual aid to the veterans. The blend of material and spiritual aid is also an important part of Hayslip's message—the book shows that she believes both spiritual and material well-being are necessary aspects for a life. *Tình* and *Lý* must be blended.

Hayslip also seeks reconciliation for the Vietnamese community in the United States, which is perhaps the most daunting task. How have Vietnamese American audiences responded to the book? She says that she has been roundly criticized in Vietnamese-language newspapers in California for her book, for her politics. In the Vietnamese American community there are groups that work to build a campaign to return to Viet Nam and overthrow the Communist government, to replace it with a new Republic. Hayslip has once again aligned herself—the small against the mighty—to argue for a different solution, one that embraces peace rather than war.

Hayslip's second book, *Child of War, Woman of Peace*, does not succeed in the same terms as her first book. Although the second volume carries on the themes of forgiveness and reconciliation that the first book emphasizes, a large proportion of it is a fairly standard immigration autobiography that concentrates on material acquisition and success. The title of the first chapter, "Yearning to Breathe Free," and that of part two, "Finding the American Dream," place the book in the celebratory immigrant autobiography genre. In the middle of the narrative Hayslip falls into immigrant consciousness, calling her attempt at cultural melding "crazy" and monocultural Americans "normal" (107). Despite her troubles with two American husbands and their racist and greedy families, she tends during the first two-thirds of the narrative to characterize the United States as a sort of paradise. After describing how she has increased the value of her house by $25,000, she writes, "This was the America we had dreamed about in Vietnam" (205).

When her sister Lan and her children arrive in the United States, Hayslip notes that the "boys looked neglected and underfed, which was understandable, but nothing America couldn't cure" (131). She celebrates her Americanization, such as in the contrast between her style of raising her three sons (two of them half Caucasian) and her sister's Vietnamese-style "son-coddling," which to Hayslip, the new American, seems "archaic and more than a little useless. In fact, this was the first of many instances in which my own Americanization—much further along than I had dreamed—was magnified by my sister's example" (134). She does maintain the bicultural stance set forth so strongly in the first book—"I felt these changes made me a better person—a woman with two cultures instead of one" (134), but for stretches the narrative loses sight of biculturality when she describes her accumulation of wealth.

The strongest assertion of biculturality throughout most of the narrative comes through Hayslip's attitude toward religion. Her view embraces religious tolerance, and a sort of syncretic stance in which she accepts the wisdom of all religious traditions. For her it is no contradiction to burn incense at the spirit altar she has constructed in her San Diego home and to also engage in Bible study with someone from her husband's church. Her husband does see this as a contradiction, however, and it causes serious problems in their marriage.

Although Hayslip retains her consistently forgiving tone, this book is a devastating portrayal of U.S. racism, both deliberate and unconscious forms. Hayslip describes the experiences of her own and her sister's sons: "Not everybody appreciated this mix of cultures. Jimmy and Tommy had gotten used to turning their backs on catcalls of 'chink' and 'gook' and so forth—but Eddie and Robert had not. More than once they came back from a neighborhood 'day of play' with black eyes and bloody noses" (135). Hayslip's encouragement of her sons Jimmy and Tommy to simply turn their backs reflects her religious attitude that to engage in violence or hatred, no matter what the provocation, incurs "soul debt" that one must work out in this life or the next. This attitude causes her to stay with her viciously abusive second husband, Dennis Hayslip, and to forgive the other two men, Dan DeParma and Cliff Parry, who abandon her and swindle her.

But she is not immune from the effects of U.S. racism. Early in her stay in the United States she suffers from internalized oppression after having to shop for clothes in the children's department because she is so much smaller than most Americans. She writes, "I hated my hair for being Oriental black, not European brown or blond or silver. I hated my body for being Vietnamese puny and not Polish plump or German hardy or big-boobed and long-legged like the glossy American girls Ed ogled on the sidewalk" (27). U.S. racism appears everywhere in the early part of the narrative. After her first husband's death, her sister-in-law gives her advice, which Hayslip represents as well meaning, about not waiting for the American lover she last saw in Viet Nam: "The Major was just another American who got lonely in a foreign land and decided to take up with a local ding-a-ling" (106).

The racism of Ed Munro's family is nothing compared with that of Hayslip's second husband, Dennis, who believes that there is a vast Vietnamese conspiracy against Americans and who accuses Le Ly of plotting against him. Dennis would make remarks like "Why don't you go back to Vietnam and swing from the trees and eat bananas?" (162). In keeping with her themes of reconciliation, however, she forgives and thanks these very people in her acknowledgments section.

One odd feature of this book is that, unlike the first book, it is marked by disturbing errors that may simply be the result of memory lapse and poor editing, but nonetheless do not help its credibility. Some errors are as simple as misspelled place names: Qoc Lo for Quoc Lo (63), Fleuku for Pleiku (70). The name of the one of the Viet Cong cadres who raped Hayslip appears differently from in the first book—where it was Mau, here it is Tau (357). There is a historical error, in which Hayslip describes withdrawing U.S. units in An Khe as being replaced by ARVN units, when, in fact, they were not (63). The oddest inconsistency is in the story of Dennis Hayslip's trip to Viet Nam in 1975 to rescue Le Ly's sister Lan and her children. Hayslip writes that she received a telegram on 19 April 1975 from Lan. Then she writes, "Almost three weeks after Dennis left and a week after the south had fallen," Dennis and Lan arrived at her house in San Diego (130). Since the South fell on 30 April, however, that would mean that Dennis had left about 16 April, which was before Lan's telegram arrived. This cannot be a discrepancy of just a few days, because Hayslip has described a time-consuming process of trying other avenues before Dennis volunteered to go, and after he volunteered, it took more days to put that plan into place. The mistake might be as simple as an editing error; the date of the telegram might have been 19 March. These inconsistencies make one wish the book had been edited more closely.

As in her first book, her real theme is of achieving peace, which is announced early on: "Lasting victories are won in the heart, not on this soil or that. Happiness is not a place called America or Vietnam. It is a state of grace. Someone may rescue you, but only you can save yourself" (86). Not until after the sections on Hayslip's relationships with men and her American success story, though, does she return to this theme and describe the founding of her East Meets West Foundation and its relief efforts in Viet Nam. Hayslip realizes she "had become *danh loi*, a slave to my wealth" (251), and turns again toward her larger lifework.

In this section she continues one of the themes of the first book: that of bringing together Viet Nam and America. She compares the FBI agent who questions her after her first trip back to Viet Nam to the "village 'watchers' " back in Viet Nam (247), and she points out that the United States, while not nearly as repressive as Communist Viet Nam, is also not as free as she had once believed.

Hayslip ends her narrative with a description of the first health clinic built by the East Meets West Foundation—in her home village of Ky La. Through a bit of narrative sleight of hand she emphasizes her message of bringing the two nations together by describing the first patient at the clinic. He has metal fragments in his hand, and "government doctors who had last examined him thought the operation too minor to consume their valuable time." After recounting the successful removal of the fragments, she reveals the identity of the former soldier as "Louis Block, U.S. Viet Nam Veteran from Plummer, ID, USA" (362).

One major contribution the second book makes to the ongoing discussion of the first book is an extended description of how Hayslip wrote the earlier volume. She started writing down her memories, in Vietnamese, while married to Dennis Hayslip. This writing "became a lifeline to my past, and, I also realized, to my future as well. Even if nothing came of it, the project kept my head above the water whenever Dennis tried to push me under" (163). She put the manuscript aside for several years; when she went back to it, she had an "unexpected ally" in Jimmy, her teenage son, who transcribed her notes into his computer and later typed as she dictated. After Dennis Hayslip's death, she

worked even harder on my family's history, although now that I approached the story of my own teenage years, the memories brought cold sweats, cramps, and tears, like a mother's hard labor. Because putting the manuscript aside for even a day was much easier than going on, I began to doubt my will to finish it. Yet I persevered. How could I not? I had a million lost souls behind me: pushing, wailing, singing a joyful chorus at every completed page. (209)

By 1985, before her first trip back to Viet Nam, she and Jimmy had completed three hundred pages. Hayslip tried to publish this manuscript, but met with no success. She decided that she needed a professional writer as a collaborator and carried out an unsuccessful first search for one. Eventually she found an agent, and then found Jay Wurts.

Although simply saying "I was terrified" or "I was sad" was enough to reawaken those feelings in me, it did not always do so for others. The feedback I had gotten from publishers only confirmed that living through a harrowing story is a different challenge from communicating it to readers.

I had been working with different writers to express my story in a way that was close to how I felt it—but without much luck. I finally found such a writer in Jay Wurts, a man about my age but with a very "old soul"—a person who, in my opinion at least, had seen enough karmic cycles to understand what my story was about, feel what I had felt, and live those feelings on paper. (300)

Here Hayslip directly confronts the question of whose book it is and also names the significance of both her books: "People like Mom Munro and Erma and Dennis's sister and the cashier at Safeway and anybody else who could read—would now have access to a hidden side of their own national experience. My paddy had become the printed page. I had sowed thoughts and feelings like rice and in return reaped words to nourish my readers' spirit" (304). All of us who read and write about the American war in Viet Nam should remember that no matter what the conditions of writing of both of her books, the stories are certainly hers, and her work to put them in front of the American reading public is pioneering and will remain important.

Fallen Leaves

"I am a child of war; I am a child of Vietnam."

Nguyễn Thị Thu-Lâm's memoir, *Fallen Leaves* (1989), tells the story of an upper middle-class Catholic woman and her family from World War II through the French war and the American war, to their eventual immigration to America. This is a cosmopolitan text, incorporating French and Vietnamese dialogue as well as English. Thu-Lâm's class and culture easily adopt what they like of foreign cultures, while resisting foreign domination. Earl Jackson, in a discussion of Japan, calls this phenomenon "cultural cross-fertilization" (256) and says that in Japan "the adaptation of Western concepts was not unequivocal" (269). So, too, with the Vietnamese class and culture portrayed by Thu-Lâm (as well as by Truong Nhu Tang).

The narrative establishes the family's resistance to French colonialism in the first chapter, in which Thu-Lâm describes an incident that took place in 1944, when she was a child. Her father, Mr. Quốc, instructs his chauffeur to pass a car ahead of them on the road. That car passes them again and blocks the road. An irate Frenchman slaps Mr. Quốc's chauffeur. Mr. Quốc in turn slaps the Frenchman. "In later years, from the way my sister Lan retold the story, I knew that Father had done something brave" (8). Thu-Lâm's family continues to resist the French, joining in the Viet Minh revolution. Later, however, her father leaves the revolution, because he is pro-nationalist, but anti-communist.

Thu-Lâm's narrative reveals the contradictory position of her family members. Although they want independence, they do not want the redistribution of wealth that the revolution seeks. Thu-Lâm's father is arrested by the Viet Minh; when her mother protests the soldiers carrying away the family's goods, a soldier replies, "You're too rich. You should be helping fight in the North, not sitting here getting rich" (32). They do go north to join the revolution, but when it becomes clear that fighting against the French means joining the Communists, and therefore joining a system that will not let the family keep its wealth, Thu-Lâm's father turns against the revolution. "What right do those ignorant peasants have to terrorize those wealthier than they?" he asks (65).

A statement by Long, Thu-Lâm's cousin—who would eventually become an ARVN colonel and die by his own hand after the fall of Saigon in 1975— makes it clear that the revolution will be a class war as well as a war for independence:

I couldn't hide my feelings any longer, fighting side by side with ignorant, uneducated men who use the revolution as an excuse to get even with those better than they are! I fought alongside them because I believed that was the only way to drive the French out. Now that the French are gone and the Việt Minh are turning North Vietnam into a communist state, I want to get the hell out! (91)

Long's unabashed statement that he is better than the peasants reveals his class attitude and the nature of the conflict that would tear Viet Nam apart in civil war. But, of course, it is more complicated than even Long's statement indicates. Civil wars also tear families apart over matters of principle. Long's brother would stay in the North and be unable, even with his position among the victors, to save Long at war's end.

Anh-Đào, Thu-Lâm's older sister, joins the Viet Minh in an act of re-bellion against her family, much like Truong Nhu Tang's response. Unlike Tang, Anh-Đào becomes convinced that her family's wealth is wrong. In her case, however, gender roles overpower revolutionary fervor, and Anh-Đào is coerced back into the family by her father. Anh-Đào's mother and the younger children are separated from her father and the older children during the trip north, and it is many months before they are reunited. Anh-Đào has traveled north independently and joined the Viet Minh on her own. Her father persuades her to leave them to take her mother's place with the family until they are reunited (47).

Thu-Lâm's father leaves the revolution and goes to work as a civil engi-neer for the French-backed government. The circumstances that allow him to leave the revolution further illustrate the conflicts and contradictions that encircle the family like a web. They are fleeing Hanoi to go to a safer place that will also be out of reach of the Viet Minh. They are stopped by a French officer who has several Viet Minh prisoners in tow. Anh-Đào speaks to him in French when his soldiers throw her father to the ground. The officer is so taken with her that he not only apologizes, but ends up helping the family relocate, and helps Mr. Quốc get a job with the French-backed Vietnamese government. The family's privileged and educated status allows them to form a personal alliance with the French officer and to leave the revolution safely, while secretly still hoping for independence.

The family will not let Anh-Đào marry the Frenchman, although he courts her. They felt that her marriage to him would have negated all that they had spent years of their life fighting for—Vietnamese independence. Yet they liked and respected him. He had everything they would want for their daughter—a kind and gentle nature, good breeding, education: everything but Vietnamese blood. (75)

The Quốc family would like to establish a cosmopolitan but independent Viet Nam that would allow them to remain affluent and to enjoy the French material goods their position allows them. At a wedding feast for Thu-Lâm's sister, the guests bring "boxes of French biscuits and bottles of champagne beautifully wrapped in red paper, substituting for the traditional rice cakes and wine" (101). This desire for independence built on the poverty of their countrymen does not appear to the family to be a problem or a contradiction. After the partition of Viet Nam in 1954, Thu-Lâm and her family return south and work to help elect Ngo Dinh Diem. They are soon disillusioned by the corruption of his regime, however, and by the time of the American war, they have withdrawn completely from politics, in despair.

While Thu-Lâm's narrative supplies some political analysis of the effects of colonialism on Viet Nam, she seems at the same time stunningly unaware of some of its effects: "I was . . . the only curly-headed one in our family; I was spoiled and petted and able to get away with things the others couldn't. . . . There was a French ad for a brand of soap popular at that time, Savon Cadum, and I looked like the brown-eyed, curly-haired girl on the box. Mother loved to comb my hair like that little girl and call me her petite 'Savon Cadum'" (27). She presents this passage without analysis or comment, to be taken at face value. But it is clear that she receives privileges in her family because she looks like the ideal of the colonial culture. Despite the revolution and the fight for independence her family is engaged in, this internalized oppression remains invisible to her and her family.

Thu-Lâm is blinded to some extent by the privilege with which she has grown up. Despite being a refugee, having relocated to the North, then back to the South again, and living relatively poorly for a few years, she has absorbed her family's worldview, part of which is to do charity work for the poor. In 1954, as a fourteen-year-old newly arrived in the South and restored to her previous affluence, Thu-Lâm and a friend, Khánh, unofficially adopt a poor girl, Kim, whom they meet in a park, selling peanuts. They give her money and food, in effect supporting her, for two years. Then Thu-Lâm's family moves, and Thu-Lâm writes, "The lessons I had learned as a child of the war stayed with me. When it came time to leave Mỹ Tho, I never asked either Khánh or Kim for their addresses" (99). She is focused only on her own sense of loss and rootlessness; the material devastation that her departure will bring to Kim does not appear to occur to her.

When Thu-Lâm's parents turn against Diem, one of the reasons is because "Diem struck down all political opponents, not only former supporters of the Viet Minh but many other political foes as well" (101). While Diem is "striking down" Communists, that is all right with the family. Only when he applies the same tactics to others does the family perceive it as a problem. Again, they are caught in a net of contradictions.

When Thu-Lâm becomes an adult, the focus of her narrative shifts to her life and her accommodations to the Americans. Gender constraints drive her first into a bad marriage (she agrees to marry only because her mother constantly finds fault with her) and then into doing business with the Americans (because her husband's low earnings force her to live with her in-laws, a situation that quickly becomes intolerable to her).

Her experiences are revealing about the position of women in upper middle-class Vietnamese society during the 1950s and 1960s. Her familial position of dutiful daughter and dutiful daughter-in-law is difficult because of personal conflicts with her mother and religious conflicts with her in-laws (they are Buddhists, and tend to blame Thu-Lâm, a Catholic, for the repressions the Catholic Diem regime is inflicting on Buddhists). She escapes from these difficulties by becoming an entrepreneur, an avenue her society has no barricades against. Thu-Lâm turns out to be a fantastically successful businesswoman, at one point employing five hundred workers. She and her first, Vietnamese, husband have no conflict over her being in business, and although they are estranged he works with her, managing a branch of their business. This situation is very different from that with her second, American, husband, who resents her because she makes more money than he does and abuses her brutally for making business decisions on her own.

The picture of Americans in Viet Nam that emerges from this book is not flattering. When Thu-Lâm starts her various businesses—first a laundry, then a tailoring service, a gift shop, a restaurant, and finally a steam bath, on the base of the 25th Infantry Division at Cũ Chi—she is subjected to almost constant sexual harassment by Americans. She mostly escapes serious consequences of this harassment because of her position as a successful entrepreneur and because she knows how to go over the harassers' heads and talk to their superiors, but she devotes one chapter to the story of Bạch-Nga, a woman who is coerced and tricked into sleeping with her boss, and then blackmailed by him to continue. Although she refuses to continue, her life is ruined, and she loses her husband. Thu-Lâm holds the example of Bạch-Nga before her, and although she has relationships with two Americans, those relationships are consensual and not the result of Thu-Lâm submitting to sexual harassment.

In relation to the Americans, Thu-Lâm is again caught in contradictions. Although it is through Americans that she is able to earn her fortune and her freedom from her first husband and in-laws, "I became my business and my business became me" (127), she is also aware of the damage the American presence is inflicting on her country. The contradiction is the same that her parents' generation faced with the French, only this time it is worse. "The higher cost of living and the 25% inflation rate made it impossible for most people in the south to live like they had before. More and more they turned themselves over to the Americans, one way or another" (129). The Americans are destroying what they came to save, by their mere presence. Thu-Lâm believes they are more destructive than the French, under whom "the traditional ways were threatened and compromised, but they survived. With the Americans, the old ways were uprooted altogether" (167). Thu-Lâm's is a belated and reluctant recognition of what Hayslip sees clearly as soon as she has dealing with the Americans. The two women's narratives show how class positions led them into making different sorts of compromises.

Thu-Lâm's narrative speaks directly to the many narratives written by American veterans describing their experiences in Viet Nam:

The Americans were arrogant and rude towards the Vietnamese, even the officials and the military. Many of them didn't know why they were in Vietnam. When they were looking for a few Việt Công, they would lay waste a whole village with its men, women, children, old people . . . the denigrating way Americans handled Vietnamese troops and civilians alike made many Vietnamese feel that they were not fighting to prevent the Communists from conquering Vietnam, but to prevent the Communists from conquering the Americans in Vietnam. (166)

In this passage Thu-Lâm exposes the arrogance and ethnocentrism of both the American presence in Viet Nam and the subsequent narratives about that presence. American narratives repeatedly point to the American inability to distinguish among Vietnamese; Thu-Lâm's passage points out that the result was to destroy the alliance in the hearts and minds of the South Vietnamese. Complaints about the ARVN are numerous in American narratives; Thu-Lâm shows that those who were bad fighters were so because they perceived themselves as fighting for someone else, rather than for themselves, which is more than disheartening after the successful revolution against the French in order to gain independence.

She also subtly shows how the Vietnamese thought of Americans as barbarians, describing Paul, an American soldier who went AWOL to live in Saigon with one of the girls from Thu-Lâm's steam bath, and who learned from kids how to curse in Vietnamese:

A little white-beared old man would call the neighbors together. "Come one and all, the show begins!," he would trumpet. Then bowing before the assembled citizens of the slum, he would introduce Paul who would emerge from the old man's hovel dressed in black pajamas and a conical peasant hat. Then Paul would perform his tricks—eating with chopsticks, squatting, talking, and the *piece de resistance*, swearing like a Vietnamese. By this time, his audience would be rolling on the ground, holding their sides and laughing. (153)

The audience is laughing because Paul is something like a trained ape—a barbarian performing the same acts that civilized people perform.

Perhaps the most interesting aspect of *Fallen Leaves* is its narrative structure. The narrative opens with a prologue, written in the third person, in which Thu-Lâm shows her American readers a Vietnamese as Americans are accustomed, from Euro-American narratives of the war, to seeing them.

At the gate of the military camp, the young woman hesitates. . . . After a few minutes, an American captain walks toward her.

"Mrs. Nguyen, I see you're right on time," he says, jutting out his hand.

"Yes, Captain. My appointment not til nine o'clock, but I get up five. That way, I not late."

"Here, this is for you." The captain holds out several sheets of paper.

"What for?"

"You must sign each one of these. These are the contracts allowing you to open the laundry we spoke about." (3)

The young woman seems the American stereotype of the Vietnamese—speaking in pidgin English, overanxious and nervous about her contact with Americans, mystified by American paperwork. The prologue concludes in the first person: "The year was 1964 and I was the young Vietnamese woman who so timidly approached a captain in the United States Army. . . . My name is Thu-Lâm, 'The Forest in Autumn,' and this is my story" (4). The second part of the prologue removes the veil from the stereotype that it begins with, promising to show readers the person who exists on the other side of that stereotype. By asserting the "I," Thu-Lâm undercuts the third-person perspective with which she begins, inviting American readers to identify with her and to enter into her account of her experience. The prologue ends with her giving her name and translating it. The gesture of translating her name stands as a figure for the narrative as a whole—the author is translating her experience for an American audience to try to foster an understanding of her participation in the shared history of the two nations.

The narrative structure of most of the chapters continues this process of translation and education. Thu-Lâm usually begins with a few paragraphs explaining a piece of Vietnamese history or politics. Then the rest of the chapter narrates an experience of her own, or of someone in her family, that results from the particular historical or political situation she has described. The narrative thus shows its desire to educate American readers sufficiently that they can enter into her story and understand her experiences and those of her family.

Another interesting aspect of the narrative is that although Thu-Lâm does stand at the center, almost as much space is devoted to events that happened to, or were witnessed by, other members of her family as is devoted to her own story. Further, as with most Vietnamese American narratives, the book concentrates on the story of Viet Nam rather than on the author's assimilation experiences in America. Even in the last few chapters, when Thu-Lâm has moved to Hawaii with her American husband, she focuses on her trips back to Viet Nam to buy goods for her import business, not on her assimilation troubles or difficulties with her husband, which were considerable. The author tells us only enough about her marriage and her problems in the United States for us to know that her husband was severely abusing her and that they were planning to divorce. When the fall of Saigon in 1975 prevents her from returning to Viet Nam, the narrative focuses on the stories of the rest of her family and their various escapes to the United States and France, and on the fates of family members who were unable or unwilling to leave Viet Nam.

In the preface Thu-Lâm recounts that while she was writing the book she was a student in California and that she was quite poor, but one line explains the narrative's main focus: "At the time it was written it served a a lifeline not only to the past, but to a hoped-for happier future" (vii). In the epilogue Thu-Lâm makes clear the kind of future she envisions as a blending of cultures, represented in the story of her niece's wedding to a Euro-American. In the ceremony, performed in a Catholic church, "Tom promises not only to love and cherish Quyên, but to let her be her own woman. Quyên repeats a phrase from the traditional Vietnamese wedding ceremony" (205). The wedding reception brings together the families of both newlyweds. Quyên wears an American-style wedding dress at the ceremony; at the reception she has changed into a traditional Vietnamese wedding dress, a symbol of the possibility of biculturality.

Thu-Lâm ends her memoir with these words:

I try once more to exorcise the ghosts of the past, to shut out the obsessive litany of bygone voices. "You are no longer in Vietnam," I keep telling myself. It is 1982 and I have just witnessed the union of two people and two peoples. Born of different cultures, both Quyên and Tom have grown up in a common one— America. Perhaps the shared experience of this new generation which they represent will accomplish what no politician or soldier ever could. . . .

As for me and the Vietnamese of my generation, there will always be memories of another time and place, another life. I will forever remain an immigrant here. And even when I am happiest, I will remember my beloved Vietnam and the fate of my people.

I am a child of war; I am a child of Vietnam. (206)

Thu-Lâm renders her version of the exile experience by describing herself as haunted even in her happiest moments. She describes herself as a witness to, rather than a participant in, the possibility of "transnational cultural fusion" that is represented by Quyên and Tom's wedding. Her exile experiences hold her separate and apart, forever haunted by the ghosts of Viet Nam.

This Side, the Other Side

This Side, the Other Side, by Minh Duc Hoai Trinh, is another work in English by a Vietnamese refugee writer living in France (like Truong Nhu Tang). Trinh's novel displaces the political conflicts of the war onto familial conflicts and reconciliations.

According to the biographical information appended to the novel, Trinh is the daughter of a mandarin. She was born in Hue. After involvement in the war against the French, she went to France in 1953 to study journalism. In 1964 she returned to Viet Nam as a journalist, eventually going to Paris to cover the peace negotiations from 1968 to 1974. In 1974 she became a professor at the Buddhist University Van Hanh. She currently lives in exile in Paris, and was once president of the P.E.N. Center of Vietnamese Writers Abroad.

Trinh's class attitudes inform her writing, as is the case for all the writers I discuss here. The main character, Bui, is a peasant from a village near Hue who is seduced by a middle-class man who takes her to Hue and educates her, then leaves her, but provides for her by sending her to a friend, the widow of an ARVN general, in Saigon. Bui becomes a bar girl (but not a prostitute), and with her earnings is able to bring her family to Saigon. On a trip back to Hue to exhume the remains of Bui's father, Bui's mother and younger brother are killed during the Tết Offensive of 1968. Although Trinh has made the main characters of her novel peasants, she presents their opportunity to move into the middle class as a positive event that almost makes the war worthwhile. Trinh's novel is a romance; her notion of peasants and peasant life, although much more positive than Ngan's, is still a romantic one, as can be seen in a scene in which Bui and her mother and other peasants work to empty a fish pond for a wealthy woman. Whereas Hayslip shows how hard agricultural labor is, Trinh paints a picture of strong, tireless peasants working cheerfully.

A parallel plot to Bui's story is that of her brother, Thuong, who has been drafted by "the other side." Thuong, the peasant, is the Communists' ideal man, but his friend Loc, a son of the middle class, while devoid of socialist fervor, is the humanitarian who takes care of Thuong when he suffers bouts of malaria (58). It is Loc who, after Thuong's death in the Tết Offensive, eventually meets Bui and her surviving siblings, and takes Thuong's place as their older brother and protector.

While Thuong starts out pure, his ardor becomes tainted when he is manipulated by Thanh-Thanh, the revolutionary theater actress who says her ideal man would "be able to put Uncle Ho before all" (172). Thuong puts Thanh-Thanh, not Uncle Ho, before all. Loc suspects many youth are motivated by Thanh-Thanh and women like her, rather than by ardor for the cause. He, the middle-class sophisticate, is able to see through her in a way that Thuong, the peasant, cannot.

Thuong dies and Loc is wounded in the Tết Offensive. Loc becomes a Hồi Chánh (defector). When he joins the Republican side, he philosophizes about his old side and his new side:

> To say that on the other side people hadn't the right to happiness, like the propaganda from this side said, was false. Happiness was personal, each one conceived of it in his own way. Beings like Thuong, like Thanh-Thanh or like Comrade Dung were happy. In that atmosphere they were like fish in water. . . .
> What others found inhuman and monstrous, was just and reasonable to them. . . .
> More than ever Loc wanted to be like everyone else. He wanted to go to the movies, to the popular theater. (193–94)

His conclusion suggests that middle-class people cannot be happy under communism, although dedicated peasants might be. Loc feels like he belongs to neither side.

> Why wasn't he like them, the people from here. And on the other hand, why wasn't he like Thuong?
> If the other side had maintained this heroic spirit admired by so many people which succeeded in forcing the people to sacrifice their goods and their lives, it was because it was cut off from the world. Not a single new current could penetrate. (198)

He feels a sense of belonging only when he meets Thuong's now bourgeois family in Saigon. Loc has unsuccessfully tried to become a peasant; Thuong's sister Bui and her family have successfully made the transition to the middle class. Trinh clearly sees upward mobility as the only possible direction, and, in her analysis, this makes communism an impossible system for Viet Nam.

Bui and her family have been completely transformed: Bui has changed from the ignorant but beautiful peasant into the cultured, educated "Kim Lan" (her assumed name in Saigon); the peasant Thuong has been replaced by the bourgeois Loc; the elderly parents (who presumably could not have been transformed) are dead; and Madame Lam, a general's widow, has become Bui's substitute mother.

In addition to being pro-bourgeois, the novel is pro-Western. Bui benefits from her relationship with Jim, an American assigned to JUSPAO (Joint United States Public Affairs Office). Jim, however, is not a typically coarse American like the others described in the novel—he speaks Vietnamese and is interested in Vietnamese culture. Trinh idealizes cultural exchange at a national and a personal level. The novel valorizes the personal over the political—Bui has gained elegance, refinement, and bourgeois charm; the more adaptable Loc survives while the doctrinaire Thuong dies. This side and the other side are united over their political differences through familial relationship, with the promise of removing Thuong's body from the mass grave in which it was buried during the offensive, and giving it a proper familial burial, thus overcoming the wounds inflicted on the country by the war and achieving reconciliation on all sides, achieving continuity between this side and the other side. But we know it is a fantasy—the novel ends in 1969. Bui and Loc will have to flee in 1975, becoming refugees.

Another way the novel stresses the personal over the political is in the almost spiritual slant it gives to the political division. The RVN and the

Communists are referred to only as "this side" and "the other side," never by any other name. "The other side" becomes ghostly: "Later, when the country had been divided into North and South, these people [the Viet Minh] retreated to the other side. Then they had come back from time to time, appearing and disappearing like ghosts" (21). This novel, like other Vietnamese works, is populated by ghosts:

Some people believed that those who died before they were destined to did not know where to lodge and as nobody made offerings to them they would be condemned to this wandering life until the next incarnation. Ghosts of various races and nationalities, former French colonials, Moroccan and Algerian soldiers, Americans and their allies . . . they and their souls were there and would never be able to return to their countries. (6–7)

Judged by Western standards, *This Side, the Other Side* is not a very compelling novel. The characters are flat, point of view shifts appear from nowhere, and the writing seems simplistic. It definitely belongs to the Vietnamese novelistic tradition that Durand and Huan label romantic. Nonetheless, it is interesting for the apolitical way it addresses the subject of the war—in this way it is an exception to the usual, politicized, method Vietnamese exile authors use to describe their subjects.

Vo Phien's Intact *and Short Stories: The Metaphysics of Exile*

Vo Phien was a professor of literature and a publisher in Viet Nam, a prolific author and the winner of the Vietnamese National Literary Prize. He came to the United States in 1975 and is the founder and editor of *Van Hoc Nghe Thuat*, a literary journal published in Vietnamese. His novel, *Intact*, was translated from Vietnamese by James Banerian and published in Australia in 1990. Three of his stories, translated by Huynh San Thong, Phan Phan, and Vo-Dinh Mai, appear in the collection *Landscape and Exile*, edited by Marguerite Bouvard.

Intact tells a story of the effects of the war on Viet Nam and the effects of exile on the refugees through the romantic story of a young girl named Dung (pronounced "Zoong"). Phien uses the story of Dung's disrupted romance to stand for the national agony of his country.

The first of the four sections of the novel takes place in Dung's home village in Viet Nam in 1974. This section focuses on normal life, largely on

97

relationships between the sexes. Phien celebrates Vietnamese culture by describing at length several relationships: Dung's engagement to Trieu; Nguyen (Dung's best friend) and her engagement to Thu, Dung's brother; Dung's encounter with Professor Tung; and her father's affairs, which broke up his first marriage. Phien creates an atmosphere of normality in this hiatus in the war. The war intrudes only on the periphery of the story, such as when Dung sees a soldier on a ferry flirting with a girl, and when Nguyen's marriage is postponed because of her fiancé's military service. Nguyen says of her engagement, "Who knows when it will be official? As long as the war goes on, this thing drags on . . . semi-officially" (36).

Phien also stresses family relationships, especially those between Dung and her parents and aunt, as well as her brother, as a way of showing how much the heart and soul of Vietnamese culture lie within family relationships. Later sections identify the tragedy of exile as the disruption of normal family relationships. As with many exile writers, Phien also puts a lot of nostalgic emphasis on food. At one point Nguyen says to Dung, "If you want to enjoy good food you have to practice. Anything requires effort—it doesn't just come to you. You have to learn how to bend to the taste of the food, not make the food bend to your likes" (33). Phien could as easily be speaking of culture as of food here.

Politics also finds its way into the novel, especially in a long discussion between Dung and her father, ARVN Lieutenant Colonel Du, who compares the war between the United States and the Vietnamese Communists to the conflict between the ancient Vietnamese and the kingdom of Champa (51). He is an ardent anti-Communist, but he is a realist who knows that the Communists are on the verge of victory; therefore, he makes plans to evacuate his family.

Balancing Du's political opinion is that of Professor Tung, an opponent of the RVN government who has a romantic interest in Dung. She remains positioned in the middle, however, clinging to her apolitical stance. Phien portrays traditional Vietnamese culture, embodied in Dung, as torn between political forces.

In the second section of the novel, the war comes to the foreground with the news of an ambush on Thu's boat and with the arrival of Aunt Thuc, a refugee from Dalat. All the characters cling to the ideas of normalcy and permanence as long as possible. They are not denying the coming collapse, they simply seem to lack recognition of it, because of its unbelievable enormity. But the war has begun to disrupt normal life in undeniable ways. With the refugees staying at her house, Dung can no longer find a way to be alone with Trieu, her fiancé, an activity to which the first section devoted considerable time and emphasis. Trieu is perhaps the only character who truly realizes what is about to happen. He says to Dung,

"I want you with me. From now on we must always be together. When we leave, we leave together. I'm afraid if we should become separated and an emergency arose, I might not make it back here in time to get you out."
"You mean out of the country? To America?"
There was a pause.
"I don't know where. I don't want to go to America. But there's no question we have to leave the country." (74)

Dung is "stunned" by this announcement, but her life becomes centered around plans for escape, and the disruption that threatens her selfhood begins.

People's thoughts begin to turn to loss. Uncle Chat thinks of loss of material wealth. And, since Chat had a seat on the city council, he had close contacts with the other side. His business in the surrounding forests also gave him ample opportunity to meet with the cadres. He had paid their taxes and at times added a little something extra in return for which he received some duty or function that had no danger in it. He calculated in order to survive and prosper under any system. . . . He knew that under the Communists he could only hope to earn a modest living without being able to hold onto his big property. (85)

Nguyen worries about losing Dung and how that would affect her connection to her culture: "Losing Dung would mean losing so much of her life as a student, as a young woman" (88).

One of the costs of the coming collapse is that the social order goes to hell. After Dung's family leaves their house, it is looted by their neighbors. They have taken "the Mitsubishi sewing machine that had been in the family for twenty years, even the mattress from grandfather's bed" (102). The lost items symbolize the loss of tradition, culture, and social values.

Dung is torn from her traditional role within her family as dutiful daughter when she must be independent and responsible and deal with escape arrangements herself. She ends up separated from her family and her fiancé, who had been the center of her life; in exile, her life is robbed of a center. With the escalation of the war, people do not make coherent decisions but are pushed by events. Phien depicts the exiles as victims, rather than agents, of the fate of their country.

The third section focuses on the immediacy of exile and how the strains of prolonged time in transit affect everyone. The biggest strain is the effort to reunite families and thus knit the culture back together. But exile has turned the culture upside down. Children are now responsible for parents. Lan, a friend Dung makes in exile, says, "Back in Saigon, my parents could get along by themselves. Over here in America it'll be different. They don't know the language or anything. And my mother is driving me up a wall. You know . . . I mean, because she doesn't think straight" (117). Exile has caused her mother's thinking to go crooked. There has also been great social dislocation: "Now, a successful man was no different from a man who had nothing" (120).

Dung is overwhelmed with feelings of alienation. She marvels over how long the evenings are in North America and how cold a stream is. She feels "like a leaf picked up and thrown about by the wind" (137), feels orphaned and alone. The exiles "got coughs, sore throats and chapped lips, and it came to them that the future was full of unforeseeable things" (153). Once, after overhearing a couple making love and being overwhelmed by missing Trieu, "from the sleepy recesses of her mind, one word appeared, vividly, with bold intensity: 'belong' " (154). It is a sense of belonging that exile has taken from her.

Dung and the other exiles respond to this alienation with nostalgia for Viet Nam. Dung listens to a fellow exile, an old man who had been part of President Diem's bugle corps, and who had "set foot in nearly every province in South Vietnam. This was especially meaningful to someone who now had no hope of ever returning to his homeland" (126). She listens to another old couple describe "every detail of their village and the old times" (133).

In section four Dung settles into her exile. She is still overwhelmed by feelings of alienation and nostalgia, although she has managed to join her family in Minnesota. Trieu, however, remains in Viet Nam, and so Dung still feels lost and hopeless.

The other refugees begin making accommodations to their new home.
The refugees' initial attempts to understand their new friends usually led to their making extreme judgments abut Americans. . . . One side claimed Americans are "khai" (kind) while the other side said they are "bet" (bad). (167)

Much of the feelings of alienation are expressed through the exiles' discomfort with the Minnesota winter, an issue Phien also addresses in his short stories.

Dung's broken engagement stands as a metaphor for exile:

Yet she had lost not only her home, but also her first love. For a girl, that first love is something of a home—a home of the heart. . . . And in her heart, in her senses, even in her unconscious gestures, there would always be reminders of that past love. Like the memories of a displaced person thinking about the old country. If those who had lost their homeland were already tormented, how much more she, who had lost her home twice? (175)

Dung has become "like a bodiless soul" (177). She begins to be reembodied when a potential romance with Nghia, a fellow refugee, enters her life. Although she is open to the possibility—"Life would draw her. Surely it would draw her. And who knew where it would take her?" (195)—she is still connected to Trieu and thus to the homeland. The novel ends with her exclamation of how much she misses him.

The possibility that Trieu might eventually leave Viet Nam and join Dung in exile never arises. There is no discussion of the political realities that might underlie that possibility or the lack of it. This omission is best seen not as part of the novel's realism, but rather as part of the novel's metaphoric structure, with the romance between Dung and Trieu representing the unity of Viet Nam as a nation and as a culture.

Vo Phien's short stories also paint pictures of exile and the ultimate price of the war in cultural more than political terms. "A Spring of Quiet and Peace" addresses the issue of adjusting to the new climate—literal and figurative—of America. The story begins with a nostalgic scene portraying the "peanut-husking bee" at Tết "back home" (1). A second section describes the narrator's current situation—living in Minnesota, with "half a meter of snow on my front steps and a cold of some twenty-five degrees C. below zero" (2). He explains how the physical landscape of America disrupts his cultural landscape: "It simply would not do to have no Tet. I had just left my country: how could I forget one of its old customs? But if I was to celebrate Nguyen-dan amidst the dismal gloom of winter, amidst the death and decay of all vegetation beneath that bleak sky, would I not be mocking the idea of renewal, of fresh start, that this one national holiday implies?" (3). The narrator constructs the alien landscape of America as a barrier to the preservation of his traditional customs. This sentiment is typical of Vietnamese exile literature—this narrator wishes to preserve his culture and adapt it to his new landscape, rather than to shed it like an old skin and assimilate to a new culture.

He experiences further cultural dislocations when spring finally comes, and young women sunbathe nude or nearly nude "in positions that no Vietnamese girl could get away with in public" (5). The narrator recalls an incident in which an "American" visitor to his home had mistaken his "*ba-ba* suit" for pajamas and been uncomfortable. "Indoors, you hermetically dress yourself from neck to foot and may thus commit a breach of etiquette; in public, you nearly reveal your all and fulfill the rules of decorum. In those wrangles over differences between cultures, there are some weird paradoxes" (6).

There are also painful paradoxes:

As I was growing up in my homeland, was there ever any time like this year when I was allowed to hail spring without a worry about offensives and counter-offensives, plans and programs. . . . Now I am absolutely . . . safe!

From now on, spring will no longer have anything to do with peanuts, nor with policies, plans, high points. What will it mean? Johnny-jump-ups? Sunbathing? Crab apple blossoms? I don't know. At least, all these things will bring on no tragedy, no grief. (9)

But it is grief that this story expresses most clearly—grief for all that was lost in exile, things that the wonders of the new land cannot compensate for, and, most of all, grief over the damage inflicted on the human soul by a feeling of rootlessness: "Life abruptly turns into a yawning void. . . . Of a sudden, there is nothing left that your eyes can look forward to: you stand utterly outside the circle of all cares and concerns" (9). To be in exile is, for this narrator, to be no longer a member of his old culture and not yet a member of the new. Phien's characterization of this experience is similar to Tran Van Dinh's description of exile in an essay called "The Tale of Kieu: Joy and Sadness in the Life of Vietnamese in the United States": "Because Vietnamese are romantic people extremely sensitive to poetic communication, the realization of the difference between U.S. and Vietnam, between comfort and security 'over here' and privations and uncertainty 'over there,' becomes the major source of a deepening sadness" (87). Phien's story expresses just that "deepening sadness."

"The Key" is a wrenching story that speaks of the ties that continue to bind the exiles to their home country, and the regrets that the refugees will carry with them for life, a position similar to that of Thu-Lâm. Arriving in Guam on a refugee ship of nine thousand people, the narrator first notices the showers at the refugee camp.

In my country, there is an expression, "rubbing off the dirt." In honor of a friend or relative who just returned from a trip, we might have a party or a dinner "to rub the dirt off from the long journey." The word "dirt" is, of course, used figuratively. And so, I compared the rubbing-off-the-dirt feast in my country with the way people rub off the dirt with soap and water here and could not help but worry for the vast differences between the two cultures. (12)

Yet, in another paradox, the American showers provide an opportunity for the narrator to hear a story from a usually withdrawn man. While using the shower facility together one night, the narrator and the shy man talk. The shy man tells of his family's decision to leave behind his senile ninety-three-year-old father. The father has left money and valuables locked in a wardrobe; any family member who does not get out will use this wealth to care for the old man, or if all family members escape, neighbors will be given the wealth and asked to care for him. When the shy man is on his escape boat out at sea, however, he discovers that he has mistakenly taken the key to the wardrobe with him. Those left behind will have to smash the wardrobe, which will disturb and upset his elderly father.

The shy man is tortured by worry for his father. He feels that God has punished him for being stupid. The narrator and the shy man never get an opportunity to speak again, but the narrator reveals his own burden:

Yes, I had a key, kept in my pocket, from a situation similar to that of the old man. (In fact, isn't it true that most of the refugees brought a key along? I mean, who did not feel sorry for a certain mistake, a certain shortcoming he had made to his relatives and close friends who were left behind, something he would feel sorry for the rest of his wandering life?). (19)

The key becomes a symbol for the regrets the refugees carry. Because the refugees cannot return home, they have no second chances. All their actions are locked into permanence, irrevocable, unmalleable. The key, rather than symbolizing the possibility of openings and new beginnings, symbolizes for the exiles the closing and locking up of their past. The past has become unreachable except in memory. The refugees can replay their scenes of regret in memory, but cannot reach back through the locked door of exile to right what they perceive to be the wrongs they have done. This discontinuity between the past and the present creates the psychic disturbance, the feeling of being in a void, that Phien describes in "A Spring of Quiet and Peace."

Despite the fact that Phien writes in Vietnamese and publishes in Vietnamese-language magazines in the United States, his stories are marked by phrases such as "in my country." Like the Vietnamese exile writers who publish in English, Phien seems to be trying to reach a Euro-American audience and educate them about the place that he still considers to be "my country"—Viet Nam. The fact that he has reached beyond an audience literate in Vietnamese, by publishing in translation in Bouvard's anthology, as well as in *Vietnam Forum*, supports this proposition.[20] Phien, like many other exile writers from many countries, is isolated from his native language.

The Land I Lost: *Common Elements, Common Themes*

As these readings of Vietnamese refugee texts have shown, certain elements occur in the majority of Vietnamese refugee writers' stories, across boundaries of gender, class, and political stance. These elements are so strongly present that they are even evident in a children's book, *The Land I Lost*, by Huynh Quong Nhuong.

Nhuong was an ARVN soldier who was paralyzed by a gunshot wound in 1969 and subsequently came to live in the United States. His book is characterized most strongly by nostalgia, as the title indicates. He presents a cosmopolitan picture of the central highlands hamlet where he grew up, and the book is infused with war metaphors.

Nostalgia is also apparent in Nhuong's preface: "I always planned to return to my hamlet to live the rest of my life there. But war disrupted my dreams. The land I love was lost to me forever. These stories are my memories . . ." (xi; ellipsis in original). The entire book is designed to educate readers about rural life in a hamlet in the central highlands (a different geographical perspective from any other represented in this study). His stories teach about domestic and wild animals, holidays, family structure, weddings, folklore (although some of it reads like tall tales, especially some of the animal stories).

Nhuong portrays his isolated rural hamlet as having some cultural cosmopolitanism. His father is a farmer but has a college education and serves as the local schoolteacher. The best illustration of cosmopolitanism is Nhuong's cousin teaching pet birds to sing "The Blue Danube" and "The Bridge over the River Kwai."

The Land I Lost is actually an odd book—although it is a children's book, most of the stories Nhuong tells have to do with death and violence. He includes only two references to war (he was a child during the First Indochina War), but the citizens of his hamlet are constantly terrorized by wild animals. War metaphors seem to be part of the fabric of life. Nhuong's family names their favorite water buffalo Tank, "because when he hit another male during a fight, he struck as heavily as a tank" (3). When they capture a string of monkeys to train, they "march them home like prisoners of war" (93). The impact of war on Nhuong's childhood becomes clear only at the end of the book, in a chapter entitled simply "Sorrow," in which his beloved water buffalo, Tank, is killed by a stray bullet from a nearby battle. It is clear from taking a look at this children's book that the themes common to Vietnamese refugee writers inform that literature across genres, and thus form a sort of narrative core of these works.

Conclusion

One result of American readers and critics taking notice of works by Vietnamese refugee writers is that the way will be opened for more of these books to be published. Reviewers, critics, and teachers can affect the politics of publishing by writing reviews, critical studies,[21] and teaching guides and by ordering Vietnamese refugee texts for classses, thus helping to keep them in print.

There is also another issue: a generation of young Vietnamese American writers is coming of age, writers who have grown up in America but who carry the heritage of the Vietnamese experience of the war. Elizabeth Gordon, Lucille Hanh Clark, and Truong Tran are three of these young writers.

Elizabeth Gordon is the daughter of a Vietnamese mother and a GI father. She was born in Saigon and grew up in Tennessee. Her story "On the Other Side of War" appears in Sylvia Watanabe and Elizabeth Bruchac's anthology *Home to Stay: Asian American Women's Fiction.* Gordon's story focuses on the question of American racial identity and is told in five brief sections. All of the sections use a sort of sarcastic humor, seemingly as a distancing device from the pain that the story seeks to represent. The first describes the narrator's father calling his parents to tell them he's bringing home an orphan. They see through him immediately, and tell him to marry his girlfriend and bring her and their baby home with him. The second section describes the cultural dislocation of the narrator's mother in terms like those used by Vo Phien. The narrator's mother cries for cows standing out in the snow, because she thinks they are cold: "My mother was in the trailer with me, crying and crying for the cows" (50). The focus of the story is really the narrator's quest for identity, and this scene situates the daughter as a participant in her mother's uneasiness and cultural dislocations.

The third section describes the problems of the parents' cross-cultural marriage in terms of food. The narrator's mother confuses pancakes and hamburgers because they are both "round, flat, and fried in a pan" (50). The fourth section describes a photograph, taken in 1965, of a typical American scene—a suburban street with a Chevy, and a mother and child.

But something in the photograph seems not quite right. Strangers often tilt their heads when looking at it, as if it is uncomfortable to view straight up and down. Possibly, it's the incomparable blackness of the woman's hair, the way it seems forced into a wave it can barely hold. Or maybe it has something to do with the baby's eyes which, though blue, are shaped exactly like the woman's: round at the center, narrow at the corners, and heavy lidded.

What are eyes like that doing among frame houses and a shiny Chevrolet? It seems a reasonable thing to ask. (51)

In passages like this the indirection and incompleteness of Gordon's writing is most clear. Who are the strangers looking at the photograph? To whom does it seem reasonable to ask the question? The passage emphasizes the narrator's feeling of displacement, her search for an American identity. Nothing in this passage, or the story as a whole, however, differentiates Gordon's framing of identity from that of other Asian Americans. She frames her difference as that of generic Asian—black hair and epicanthal folds—rather than specifically Vietnamese. The fifth and final section of the story describes the narrator's difficulty in picking a blank to fill in on a school questionnaire asking her to name her race. Her father solves the problem by telling her mother "to put an 'H' in that blank. 'For human race,' he said" (51).

"On the Other Side of the War" is a slight story, although clearly the product of a talented young writer. If Gordon continues to write, she may produce an interesting body of work. She is the only mixed-race Vietnamese American writer whose work has appeared in a national forum thus far, making her an important pioneer.

Lucille Hanh Clark was born in Viet Nam, to Vietnamese parents, but raised in America from the age of five by her Vietnamese mother and American stepfather. Clark is a fiction writer, poet, and photographer whose work has appeared in *Giao Điểm / Crosspoint*, the bilingual publication of the Vietnamese Student Association of the University of California, Santa Cruz. She is interested in both assimilation and cultural preservation. One of her most striking images is a photograph of a young Vietnamese woman wearing a snail hat and standing in a field, as if she were a peasant in Viet Nam; however, she is wearing American-style clothes and has a U.S. flag wrapped around her like a shawl. In this image, Clark encapsulates difference/assimilation. In her creative writing senior thesis, "Dowry of Myths," Clark writes that the thesis is the kernel of the novel she hopes to write "about a girl whose family has taught her to carry on, to survive the world with stories and myths, intertwined from Viet Nam and the United States" (ii). Clark addresses the difficulties of bicultural writing in her story "What Do You Do with a White Man's Ignorance: Creative Writing Class":

A man who tells you that you are writing for a white audience, for him. He, being white, himself, can't understand what a Vietnamese family is like, so you should explain, should give the phonetic pronunciations of Vietnamese names, because he'll skip over Le, Hanh, Dung, Tam, Bao anyway. A man who insists that there aren't any white people in your story? Does he not see Don, the Irish American from Watertown, New York, one of the central characters in your story? No, a white man, he says. A white man. No alcoholic, tit grabbing, gook loving janitor. A white man. He wants. (18)

Clark's autobiographical story captures both the resistance of the audience to bicultural work and her continued willingness to work to bridge that gap. Her answer to the question, "What do you do" is: "You don't yell. You remember. You write and write, working hard, learning your languages, English and Vietnamese, your cultures, Vietnamese and American, as well" (18).

In other autobiographical stories Clark examines the cultural tangle of growing up in San Francisco's Tenderloin district with a Vietnamese mother who shaved her head to show her Buddhist devotion and an Irish American stepfather who was the closest parent to Clark and her two sisters. Clark, like Gordon, will be another interesting writer to watch in the future.

Truong Tran is a young poet who also represents the possible future of second-generation Vietnamese American writers. One of his literary models is Octavio Paz (as the poem "The Day I Ran into Octavio Paz" describes). Tran represents the possibilities of America: a refugee writer from Viet Nam who has made America his home, and who looks for literary inspiration to a Latin American author. Assimilation has not been easy for Tran, as his poem "Ode to a Fruit Salad" shows:

They refuse
to put
papayas
mangos
or lychees
in the
fruit salad.
It's just
not American.
So instead
I am stuck
with this
sour apple
that sticks
between
my teeth.

Like other Vietnamese American writers, Tran wants assimilation to be a two-way street. He wants elements of Vietnamese culture (papayas, mangos, lychees) to be incorporated into American culture, just as he is assimilated into America.

Gordon, Clark, and Tran, although all born in Viet Nam, came to America when they were very young. They do not suffer the language barriers the older generation of immigrants face, but their hold on their culture of origin is more tenuous than that of their elders. The ways in which they and other Vietnamese refugee writers of their generation write about their cultural negotiations should make a fascinating contribution to American literature.

Hue-Thanh Bergevin, a refugee who entered the United States as an adult, also writes of the situation of younger Vietnamese losing their heritage, but working to preserve it through connection to the older generation. In her short story, "Uncle Vy," she presents the story of two young women, cousins, who visit an elderly man. Ha-Truc, the narrator, is impatient with Vietnamese customs. She is thirsty and dismayed at the small cups Uncle Vy sets before his guests. " 'Do you know that drinking tea is an art, too?' Uncle Vy starts the conversation. I looked at the little cups and admitted, 'Yeah, I think so' " (38). Ha-Truc is suspended between her new, American, persona and a half-remembered Vietnamese persona who knows that drinking tea is also an art.

Ha-Truc violates rules of politeness by not paying attention to Uncle Vy, and is embarrassed at being caught at it. Mai, her cousin, also suffers a moment of embarrassment when she fails to remember a Vietnamese poem Uncle Vy mentions. But both young women are returned to their Vietnamese roots when Uncle Vy plays music on traditional Vietnamese instruments for them.

The story begins and ends with descriptions of the old man. In the beginning the narrator says, "Uncle Vy is just like thousands of other elderly Vietnamese who left Vietnam when Saigon fell. . . . Unknowingly, they chose to enter the fast-moving life that is America, and have had to adjust as best they can" (38). At the end the narrator observes, "Uncle Vy walked us to our car. He stood on the pavement watching our car pull away from the curb. I waved to him. He looked so small and lonely on the concrete sidewalk" (40). While the narrator's concern for Uncle Vy frames the story, at its center is what Uncle Vy represents for her and her cousin: a link to and a reimmersion in a culture they are in danger of losing in the fast-moving life of America.

This examination of Vietnamese refugee writers raises many questions. The idea of "transnational cultural fusion," which I have borrowed from Mukherjee as a model for the way in which Vietnamese refugee writers attempt to work, suggests one model of cultural pluralism. In that model, the immigrant is transformed by America and at the same time transforms America. While this model may stand as an ideal, and certainly describes the project of the Vietnamese refugee writers, it is not an adequate explanation of what is happening in contemporary America. One problem with this model is that it minimizes the power of the dominant ideologies that control the discourse about the war.[22]

How much power do these marginalized texts have to change the dominant discourse? Since they have been largely ignored both by the reading public and by scholars, are they trees falling in the forest with no one to hear? For the most part, unfortunately, I think they are. But I have also observed a surprising and striking occurrence. In an introductory course for first-year students called Social Change in the Third World, I have seen students' attitudes almost completely transformed by reading Hayslip's autobiography. In class discussions after reading the book (and after a lecture given by Hayslip herself), students expressed new attitudes. Several members of the class who had remained stuck in entrenched ignorance about the Third World and Third World cultures and peoples for much of the term came to class after reading *When Heaven and Earth Changed Places* with an attitude of having had the scales lifted from their eyes. Many students made comments indicating that they now had a very different picture of the war in Viet Nam from the one they had entered the class with—formed mostly by movies, television, and high school history texts.

In an upper division course about the representation of the Viet Nam War in American popular culture, a similar transformation took place in some students' attitudes. Despite extended discussions about the racism against Vietnamese that informs most of the Euro-American works that students read and viewed in this class, there were several students who failed to "see" where the Euro-American texts were racist. These students remained locked in the framework of the dominant American discourse. After reading Hayslip's narrative toward the end of the course, however, most of the students who previously failed to "see" could then "see" quite clearly. Again, reading the Vietnamese refugee point of view became a transformative experience for these students in the context of discussions of the war.

Although I believe that these texts, if they can gain an audience, do possess some power, I also believe that the dominant U.S. discourse wields great power. In the next chapter, I examine both the power of the dominant discourse and the possibilities for transformative perspective and new vision.

U.S. Wars in Asia and the Representation of Asians

Whoever has emerged victorious participates to this day in the
triumphal procession in which present rulers step over those who
are lying prostrate. According to traditional practice, the spoils
are carried along in the procession. They are called cultural
treasures. . . . There is no document of civilization which is not at
the same time a document of barbarism.
—Walter Benjamin, *Illuminations*

Britain and France were the pioneer nations in the Orient and in
Oriental studies . . . these vanguard positions were held by virtue of
the two greatest colonial networks in pre-twentieth-century
history; the American Oriental position since World War II has
fit . . . in the places excavated by the two earlier European powers.
—Edward Said, *Orientalism*

This chapter is partially about imperialism and the damage that
imperialism does not only to Third-World peoples, but also to
peoples of the First World countries that perpetrate imperialism.
The chapter also discusses representations and the complicated
interaction between representation (in the various discourses and media) and
perception (by the members of our culture) that results in widely held cultural stereotypes, including the inability to see possibilities outside the dominant cultural framework. The only way to surmount the hegemonic nature
of these cultural stereotypes is to make what Frances Fitzgerald has called a
"leap in perspective." Such a leap would allow one to see a wider view than
that mandated by the hegemonic paradigm.

The legacy of imperialism left to us from the last one hundred and fifty
years or so is still widespread. Writing about Joseph Conrad's *Nostromo*,
Edward Said points out the insidiousness of the legacy of imperialism by noting that even works such as Conrad's (and Graham Greene's and V.S. Naipaul's), which take anti-imperialist positions, "invariably locate the source of

all significant action and life in the West, whose representatives seem at liberty to visit their fantasies and philanthropies upon a mind-deadened Third World. Without the West, the outlying regions of the world have no life, history, or culture to speak of, no independence or integrity *worth representing*" ("Through Gringo Eyes" 72; emphasis added). One of the legacies of imperialism is this divided, us/them, West-centered perspective which is so much a part of the Euro-American dominant culture that it requires a wrenching effort to tear oneself away from it, to shift the matrix of one's point of view. Said describes Conrad as a writer "in whom a *Western* view of the *non*-Western world is so deeply ingrained that it blinds him to other histories, other cultures, other aspirations" ("Through Gringo Eyes" 70). Western writers who do not examine the framework within which they write, but instead accept as a given the cultural perceptions that lie all about us, will also be victims of that deeply ingrained worldview. The majority of Euro-Americans writing about the war in Viet Nam are just such victims.

My aim here is to uncover some of the ways these cultural perceptions have caused American popular representations of Asians and Asian Americans[1] to follow a set of unreexamined stereotypes since the middle of the nineteenth century, a set of stereotypes based on this Western-centered worldview that Said describes as being "capable of warping the perspectives of reader and author equally" ("Through Gringo Eyes" 72).

Sander L. Gilman, in *Difference and Pathology*, defines stereotypes as "images of things we fear or glorify. These images never remain abstractions: we understand them as real-world entities. We assign them labels that serve to set them apart from ourselves. We create 'stereotypes' " (15). The most important part of Gilman's definition is the assertion that we understand stereotypes as "real-world entities." The literary and popular culture images of Asians and Asian Americans that have prevailed since the nineteenth century have become, for many Americans, real-world entities.

Gilman then describes stereotyping as a function of the normal process of individuation: "Our own sense of self and the world is built upon the illusionary image of the world divided into two camps, 'us' and 'them' " (17). We will see in the history examined here that a permanent us/them nexus is set up between Euro-Americans and Asians. Yet Gilman describes this process as only a phase in the development of a normal individual, which is replaced "early in development by the illusion of integration" (17). He further states that stereotypes are not "random or personal. . . . Every social group has a set vocabulary of images for this externalized Other. These images are the product of history and of a culture that perpetuates them.

None is random; none is isolated from the historical context" (20). As discussed in this chapter, the stereotypes of Asians used by individual Euro-American authors are not individual or random, but adhere to broad and predictable patterns.

Gilman also suggests that "stereotypes arise when self-integration is threatened. They are therefore part of our way of dealing with the instabilities of our perception of the world. . . . We can and must make the distinction between pathological stereotyping and the stereotyping all of us need to do to preserve our illusion of control over the self and the world" (18). The case of the stereotyping of Asians by the dominant Euro-American culture has been of the pathological sort. This history is one of hysteria, xenophobia, and destruction.

I do not mean to suggest that stereotyping is a uniquely American phenomenon. John Dower makes clear in his study of the race war in the Pacific in World War II that the Japanese and the Americans were playing at the same deadly game in terms of the stereotypical images each culture produced of the other. As I showed in chapter 2, Vietnamese have stereotypical ideas of Americans, as well (far more of these stereotypes can be seen by reading Vietnamese, rather than Vietnamese exile, literature). However, the focus of this chapter is on Euro-American literature and culture.

In order to recognize the cultural stereotypes that Euro-Americans took to Viet Nam, we need to examine the ways Asians and Asian Americans have been represented in American popular culture[2] and the ways these representations, which are limited and to a great extent predetermined by what has gone before, are both based on and perpetuate perceptions that Westerners have of Asians.

The process is cyclical: society and representations influence and determine each other. Stephen Greenblatt calls for the development of "terms to describe the ways in which material—here official documents, private papers, newspaper clippings, and so forth—is transferred from one discursive sphere to another and becomes aesthetic property" (12). It is productive to examine the coincidence of certain types of representations of Asians in the aesthetic sphere with certain types of historical events. Representations influence how people in a culture are willing to perceive the objects of those representations,[3] and the perceptions of people in a culture influence historical events in a reciprocal structure. The representations and perceptions of Asians in American culture have been limiting and inflexible, and therefore oppressive to both the perceived and the perceivers, who are locked into the dualistic structure of us and them.

There are three periods in the history of the representation of Asians and Asian Americans in U.S. culture, during which significant and discernible patterns in the representations emerge that are relevant to the Euro-American portrayal of Vietnamese. The first is the period of Chinese and Japanese immigration into the United States, the passage of the Asian Exclusion acts, and American imperialist incursions into the Philippines, an era stretching from 1848 to 1941. The second period is World War II, and the third is the period of American involvement in Viet Nam.

This particular history of representation has closed off any possibilities for perceptions that lie outside the sphere of the traditional representations, except for a shift of perception that takes one outside the mainstream of one's cultural context and puts one into, if not opposition, at least tension, with one's own culture and allows one to see the "others" on their own terms.

Frances Fitzgerald, in *Fire in the Lake*, describes this shift in perception:

In going to Vietnam the United States was entering a country where the victory of one of the great world ideologies occasionally depended on the price of tea in a certain village or the outcome of a football game. For the Americans in Vietnam it would be too difficult to make this leap of perspective, difficult to understand that while they saw themselves as building world order, many Vietnamese saw them merely as the producers of garbage from which they could build houses. The effort of translation was too great. (5–6)

The "effort of translation" has, indeed, in most cases, proved to be too great, although it is clearly not impossible. Some Americans, including to some extent Fitzgerald herself, have clearly managed to make it. Another who has made the effort of translation is photographer Geoffrey Clifford, whom John Balaban describes as having "seen Vietnam as if he were a Vietnamese" (Clifford and Balaban 16)

To make such a leap, Americans must learn to think in greater time spans than we are usually encouraged to. Roger Daniels and Harry Kitano, in *American Racism*, write that political domination of the world by Europe has now come to an end: "The Indian historian K.M. Pannikar, understanding this, has written of a Vasco de Gama epoch, dating from 1498 to 1945, as being the only period in Asian history in which that continent's destiny was controlled by non-Asians" (3). Americans tend to think of history beginning when America enters it. Thus, in the cultural imagination, there is no Japan before Commodore Perry, no Viet Nam before the Office of Strategic Services (OSS) parachuted in during the end of World War II. (It may be even worse—there may be no Japan before Pearl Harbor and no Viet Nam before the Gulf of Tonkin incident.) The United States does not like to see itself in ways that diminish its importance in the world; as a result, it is almost impossible for U.S. discourse on the war in Viet Nam to acknowledge that U.S. involvement was a brief interlude in Vietnamese history. Many in the United States cannot see it as the "American War" as well as the "Viet Nam War."

Another issue that makes the leap of perspective difficult is the massed history of the representation of Asians and Asian Americans that must be divested by anyone desiring to make the effort of translation. Anyone attempting to make this leap must find a way to see beyond the culturally constructed paradigm that limits the range of ways one can understand Asian countries and Asian people.

My major contention is that the dominance of certain kinds of representations closes off the possibility of other explorations of individuals and societies, by predetermining the way those individuals and societies are perceived by the members of a culture. Edward Said makes a similar point in *Orientalism*, where he writes, "I believe no one writing, thinking, or acting on the Orient could do so without taking account of the limitations on thought and action imposed by Orientalism," which he defines, in this instance, as the Western "corporate institution for dealing with the Orient" (3). Echoing Sander Gilman on stereotypes as nonpersonal, Said further points out that someone from Europe or the United States

comes up against the Orient as a European or American first, as an individual second. And to be a European or an American in such a situation is by no means an inert act. It meant and means being aware, however dimly, that one belongs to a power with definite interests in the Orient, and more important, that one belongs to a part of the earth with a definite history of involvement in the Orient. (11)

This chapter traces, in part, the ways the United States has manifested its involvement as an imperial power in the "Orient," the ways it has reacted to immigration from Asia, and how, in turn, these cultural manifestations shaped the American individuals who have written about the American war in Viet Nam. Said notes that "saturating hegemonic systems like culture['s] . . . internal constraints on writers and thinkers were *productive*, not unilaterally inhibiting" (14). It is with this frame of reference that I proceed.

Said deals mostly with "high culture" products in his analysis. Orientalism, however, is pervasive throughout all aspects of culture—popular as well as political. This predetermining of attitudes is discussed by Elaine Kim when she writes:

Probably more Americans know Fu Manchu and Charlie Chan than know Asian or Asian-American human beings. Even the elite culture shares the popular stereotypes. Contemporary Chinese American playwright Frank Chin notes that New York critics of his play, "Chickencoop Chinaman," complained in the early 1970s that his characters did not speak, dress, or act "like Orientals." (*Asian American Literature* xv)

Since Euro-Americans' perceptions of Asians would then be more likely to be formed by the representations of Fu Manchu and Charlie Chan than by personal acquaintances, when and if a Euro-American individual came into contact with an Asian or Asian American, that Euro-American's (at least initial) perceptions of that Asian would be filtered through that individual's knowledge of the stereotypical representations to a greater or lesser degree, depending somewhat on the good faith of the individual. The individual's perceptions may change, may undergo the "leap of perspective" to be wrenched out of the Western cultural framework, or they may not.

Kim further points out that there is a "vast numerical superiority of books by Anglo-Americans about Asians to those written by Asian Americans, who found less acceptance among publishers and readers" (27). In much of the fiction examined here, those Euro-American writers have a polemical purpose and deliberately use negative stereotypes of Asian characters. But with the narrowed range of perceptions fostered by this widespread stereotyping, even writers trying to represent Asians favorably usually fall back on the common stereotypes Euro-Americans have held about Asians.

In the majority of representations in Euro-American literature, Asians appear as either "good" or "bad" Asians. The only good Asian is a "sidekick" or ally, under the control of, and always inferior to, the Euro-Americans (a dead Asian may also be a "good" Asian). The rest are "sinister Orientals" of inscrutable and cunning nature. Good or bad, they are always alien others, never human beings on equal footing with Euro-American human beings. Sometimes they are America's "model minority,"[4] sometimes they are the enemy Yellow hordes (whether in the late nineteenth-century fantasies of Chinese invasion, or the World War II fears of Japanese spies on California farms, or the falling dominoes that would endanger U.S. security, or the invasion of transistor radios and Toyotas). According to Kim, "The power-hungry despot, the helpless heathen, the sensuous dragon lady, the comical loyal servant, and the pudgy, de-sexed detective who talks about Confucius are all part of the standard American image of the Asian" (ibid. 3). These stereotypes, as she points out, derive from widely read pulp novels, such as the Mr. Moto series by John P. Marquand (winner of the 1938 Pulitzer Prize for a more "serious" work, *The Late George Apley*), the Fu Manchu series by Sax Rohmer (the alias for A. S. Ward, a British, not an American, writer, who was read widely in America), and the Charlie Chan series by Earl Derr Biggers. These series were turned into films, as well. All these representations are related to earlier representations from the nineteenth century, which are in turn related to eighteenth- and early nineteenth-century representations by missionaries. This history of stereotyping has proved to be a self-perpetuating system.

William Wu contends, correctly I believe, that the Yellow Peril theme is overwhelmingly dominant in American fiction about Chinese Americans between 1850 and 1940, and that "a realistic character portrayal of a Chinese American in an accurate historical context could not sustain the vision of a Yellow Peril" (5). The very attempt to portray sympathetically Asian charac-ters in their accurate historical context has often been thwarted by the dominance of the Western-centered worldview which makes us all its vic-tims, unless we create a new vision. As a step toward that new vision, let us trace the history of the old vision.

Asian Immigration and Exclusion and the Philippine War, 1848 to 1941

> I co-wrote one movie called *The Challenge*, and the director said,
> "Well, I know they're all Chinese in the script, but let's make them
> all Japanese because I can get Toshiro Mifune and who knows the
> difference anyway?"
> —John Sayles, quoted in *American Film*, April 1988

Chinese immigration into the American west began around 1848. By that time, traders and missionaries in China had already presented a negative portrait of the Chinese as cheating, drug-abusing heathens. Missionaries had portrayed Asians as poor, abject, and helpless in order to win sympathy for their mission (Kim, *Asian American Literature* 16).

As early as 1839 . . . Samuel George Morton, whose pioneer work in the measurement of crania became a central prop for theories of biological determinism, wrote of the Chinese that "they have been compared to the monkey race, whose attention is perpetually changing from one object to another" . . . Diplomats, missionaries, and traders [wrote that] the Chinese were "depraved and vicious," and "on a level with the rudest tribes of mankind." They were "pagan savages," "idolatrous savages," and "almond-eyed heathens"; a nation of "children or idiots" who lived in an "imbecile world"; "a poor, miserable, dwarfish race of inferior beings." (Dower 155)

These stereotypes stayed with Western representations of Asians for the next century and a half.

Before 1849 the Chinese were welcomed in California as servants and "coolies," but when they started mining in competition with Euro-American miners, a foreign miners' tax was instituted, requiring them to pay 50 percent of their income to the state (Lucas 42). Despite this punitive taxation, Chinese immigrants continued to be welcomed during the 1860s, while the transcontinental railroad still needed them as laborers.

Euro-American miners objected in absolute terms to the competition of Chinese immigrants. An 1852 resolution of the Columbia mining district, banning mining by "Asiatic or South Sea Islander" in Tuolumne county, makes this clear:

Be it resolved: That it is the duty of the miners to take the matter into their own hands . . . to erect such barriers as shall be sufficient to check this Asiatic inundation. . . . That the Capitalists, ship-owners and merchants and others who are encouraging or engaged in the importation of these burlesques on humanity would crowd their ships with the long-tailed, horned and cloven-hoofed inhabitants of the infernal regions [if they could make a profit on it]. (quoted in Daniels and Kitano 36)

The Chinese immigrants are described as an "inundation"—this is an early use of the imagery of flooding that came to be common in the description of immigrants, especially those from Asia. Another rhetorical strategy that would become common is the representation of Asians as heathens, and sometimes as devils.

Asians had been defined as "other" from the beginnings of the United States. The Naturalization Law of 1790 allowed only "whites" to become naturalized citizens (Takaki 82).[5] In 1854 the California Supreme Court ruled that Chinese could not testify in court against whites. The chief justice's opinion again displays the sort of rhetoric often used in discussing the Chinese:

The anomalous spectacle of a distinct people, living in our community . . . whose mendacity is proverbial; a race of people whom nature has marked as inferior, and who are incapable of progress or intellectual development beyond a certain point, as their history has shown; differing in language, opinion, color, and physical conformation; between whom and ourselves nature has placed an impassable difference, is now presented and for them is claimed, not only the right to swear away the life of a citizen, but the further privilege of participating with us in administering the affairs of our Government. (quoted in Daniels and Kitano 37)

The chief justice sets out an us/them dichotomy, placing the Chinese on the "them" side. This court decision added Chinese to the list of "Black, or Mulatto person, or Indian," set by an 1850 statute, who could not testify against whites in court. The 1854 decision basically determined whether Chinese were to be regarded as "white" or "colored." The chief justice uses the markers of "language, opinion, color, and physical conformation" to mark Chinese as "colored." By this criteria, a community must share similarity not only of physical features, but of opinion and language. By this definition, of course, many Europeans would fail, by reason of not speaking English, by reason of not agreeing with the justice, and by reason of color. Most southern Europeans are far darker-skinned than most Chinese, yet they were not barred from the rights of citizenship.

What is being reflected and codified here are guidelines not only for law, but for perception, These early declarations are shaping the grounds for the perception that Europeans as diverse as Swedes and Italians may count as Americans, but Chinese never can. Daniels and Kitano point out that in California, where Chinese comprised as much as 10 percent of the population in the mid-nineteenth century. "The color question almost automatically promoted all white men and tended to blur lines of [European] ethnic demarcation more rapidly than they were blurred elsewhere in the United States" (38).

Also established is the perception of the relations between Americans and Asians as that of struggle, competition, and warfare. Asians arriving in the United States are seen not as immigrants, but as "invaders." California governor Leland Stanford's inaugural address of 1862 employed typical anti-Chinese rhetoric:

To my mind it is clear that the settlement among us of an inferior race is to be discouraged by every legitimate means. Asia, with her numberless millions, sends to our shores the dregs of her population. Large numbers of this class are already here; and, unless we do something early to check their immigration, the question which of the two tides of immigration meeting upon the shores of the Pacific shall be turned back will be forced upon our consideration. . . . There can be no doubt but that the presence of numbers among us of a degraded and distinct people must exercise a deleterious influence upon the superior race, and, to a certain extent, repel desirable immigration. (quoted in Cheng-Tsu Wu 109)

Stanford is appealing to the rhetoric of the hordes, and of the unassimilability of the Chinese. He also invents the striking image of two tides of immigration meeting each other, and one turning the other away, rather than mingling and coexisting. His stance clearly partakes of the us–them dichotomy and of the rhetoric of warfare.

In the 1870s the Workingmen's Party of California brought the "problem" of Chinese immigration to national attention. An editorial in the *New York Times* claimed that "with Oriental blood will necessarily come Oriental thoughts and the attempt at Oriental social habits" (quoted in Cheng-Tsu Wu 109). This is an early statement of a feeling that would be restated repeatedly in American literature—that the Oriental was irredeemably, genetically, alien and unassimilable. Anti-Chinese propaganda carried a hysterical tone: a *New York World* editorial proclaimed that the Western states were "degenerating into Chinese colonies" (Lucas 45). Such attitudes reflect the misinterpretations and misuses of Darwinism that were common at the end of the nineteenth century.[6] This presumption of character traits being transmitted by "blood" represents the same kind of pseudoscience used to justify oppression of American blacks by measuring their crania and declaring them inferior.[7]

Because of the nationwide depression during the 1870s, anti-Chinese agitation in California rose to a high pitch. California passed laws intended to harass the Chinese, including a "Queue Ordinance, which placed a tax on pigtails" (Daniels and Kitano 40). This ordinance required that every Chinese in jail would have his hair cut to within an inch of his scalp. In 1876 a federal investigating committee came to San Francisco to look into the Chinese question. The testimony centered on economic issues: big business, including the railroader Charles Crocker, testified as to the usefulness of Chinese labor, while opponents to Chinese immigration testified that they drove down wages for whites. One witness echoed the theme of Chinese as devils: "I have never found a strong advocate of Chinese immigration who was not actuated by fanaticism or selfishness. . . . I have seen men . . . American born, who certainly would, if I may use a strong expression, employ devils from Hell if the devils would work for 25 cents less than a white man" (quoted in Daniels and Kitano 43). Another common complaint about Chinese laborers was that they posed a threat to Euro-American laborers because they were willing to work harder and for less. The American virtue of hard work becomes a vice when practiced by a non-European race. This same complaint is voiced about Vietnamese fishermen in the 1985 film *Alamo Bay*, demonstrating the staying power of such rhetoric.

In 1882, after more than a decade of riots, lynching, and agitation against the Chinese, primarily in California, Congress passed the Chinese Exclusion Act, which was the first immigration restriction against any specific nationality. In 1888 it was amended by the Scott Act, which widened the definition of "Chinese" to mean anyone of Chinese ancestry, no matter how many generations a person's ancestors might have lived outside China. No other nationality was ever defined in this way (W. Wu 30).[8]

Anti-Asian bias was by no means limited to popular culture or to working-class organizations. Henry Adams traveled in Asia and found it to be childlike and primitive. He wrote in a letter to John Jay:

The only moral of Japan is that the children's story books were good history. This is a child's country. Men, women, and children are taken out of the fairy books. The whole show is of the nursery. Nothing is serious; nothing is taken seriously. All is toy; sometimes, as with the women, badly made and repulsive; sometimes laughable, as with the houses, gardens and children. (quoted in Dower 343)

Adams's inability to take Japan seriously reflects a widespread strain in Western thinking about Asia that echoes through the decades right up to the American war in Viet Nam.

Just sixteen years after the Chinese Exclusion Act, the United States embarked on its first colonial war: the conquest of the Philippines, from 1898 to 1901. The anti-Filipino rhetoric resembled the anti-Chinese rhetoric of the previous decade. It also stands as a precursor of the U.S. rhetoric involving Viet Nam seventy-five years later. John Dower writes that

a U.S. general, vexed by the difficulty of separating enemy soldiers from the native population as the war dragged on, wrote in 1901 that "the problem here is more difficult on account of the inbred treachery of these people, their great number, and the impossibility of recognizing the actively bad from the only passively so. . . . Theodore Roosevelt expressed a popular sentiment when he characterized the U.S. victory in the Philippines as a triumph of civilization over 'the black chaos of savagery and barbarism.' " (151)

The term *gook* has its origins in this war in the Philippines; the Filipinos were referred to as "goo-goos." As Richard Drinnon reports, to U.S. soldiers, even black U.S. soldiers, "all goos-goos look alike" (313). Drinnon quotes testimony given before a congressional committee investigating the conduct of the war in the Philippines:

Colonel Wagner: If the town were notoriously a nest of ladrones ["bandits"], if it was impossible to get the rest of the people to yield them up, it would be justifiable and proper to destroy the town, even though we destroyed the property of some innocent people. The Almighty destroyed Sodom, notwithstanding the fact that there were a few just people in that community—less than ten. (319)

Substitute "VC" for "ladrones" in the colonel's statement, and he could easily have been talking about a village in Viet Nam. After the success of this war, in which 70,000 U.S. troops were deployed, taking 4,000 casualties while killing 20,000 Filipino insurgents and perhaps 200,000 civilians (Dower 151), the United States possessed an Asian colony. It is ironic that popular rhetoric accused both China and Japan of trying to colonize California, while the United States was in reality colonizing the Philippines.

Japanese farm workers began arriving in California in the 1890s, after Chinese immigration had been outlawed. In 1900 there were 10,000 Japanese in a total state population of 1.5 million (Daniels and Kitano 46). The movement to expel them followed the pattern of the anti-Chinese movement, although the Japanese immigration pattern was different from that of the Chinese. Unlike the largely male Chinese population, many of whom were sojourners, Japanese families came and settled into farming, intending to stay. By 1918, Japanese immigrants owned 1 percent of the farming land in California and produced "ten percent of the dollar value of the state's crops" (ibid. 50).

The rhetoric of the anti-Chinese campaign was applied directly to the Japanese. Daniels and Kitano quote several headlines from the *San Francisco Chronicle* of 1905:

JAPANESE A MENACE TO AMERICAN WOMEN
BROWN MEN AS AN EVIL IN PUBLIC SCHOOLS
ADULT JAPANESE CROWD OUT CHILDREN
THE YELLOW PERIL—HOW JAPANESE CROWD OUT THE WHITE RACE
BROWN PERIL ASSUMES NATIONAL PROPORTIONS
BROWN ARTISANS STEAL BRAINS OF WHITES. (47)

The focus is again on displacement of whites by Asian immigrants. The *Chronicle* and other newspapers, according to Daniels and Kitano, consistently painted the Japanese as "hordes," although before 1925 they never made up more than a tiny percentage of the population of California (47). Notice also in the headlines quoted here the portrayal of Japanese immigrants as a sexual threat—a theme that would be revived during World War II in anti-Japanese propaganda.

V.S. McClatchy, a California newspaper publisher, wrote about the Japanese:

The Japanese are less assimilable and more dangerous as residents of this country than any other of the peoples ineligible under our laws . . . They come here specifically and professedly for the purpose of colonizing and establishing here permanently [their] race. They never cease being Japanese . . . In pursuit of their intent to colonize this country with that race they seek to secure land and to found large families . . . They have greater energy, greater determination, and greater ambition than the other yellow and brown races [and] the same low standards of living. (quoted in Daniels and Kitano 52; ellipses and brackets in original)

Perhaps most bizarre is McClatchy's criticizing the Japanese immigrants for having exactly those qualities so valued in Americans—energy, determination, and ambition—characteristics usually attributed as positive qualities to Euro-American pioneers moving westward. As in the rhetoric used against the Chinese, the Japanese are declared unassimilable, and consequently undesirable and inferior aliens. Yet the Japanese, learning from the treatment of the Chinese, attempted to "Westernize" early on in their immigration. The ideology behind the formation of the United States is an ideology not only of conformity but of homogeneity. Both the *Chronicle* and McClatchy are unable to decide whether the Japanese are "yellow" or "brown"; Asian Indian and Filipino naturalization cases also posed problems in racial identification. Racial identity obviously obsessed America to the point of over-shadowing any other consideration.

In 1922 the Supreme Court decided in *Ozawa vs. U.S.* that Japanese immigrants could not be granted citizenship because the founders of the United States were white and had intended for only "more of their kind to come" (Lucas 49). In 1924 a new quota law was passed to exclude all aliens ineligible for citizenship, namely Asians. Interracial marriages between Asian immigrants and Euro-American women were also forbidden by this law. (Other laws forbidding interracial marriages among Asians and Euro-Americans had arisen as early as 1880.)

Filipinos faced a different situation. When all other Asians were banned from immigration, labor contractors turned to the Philippines (Ignacio 5). When Filipinos began to immigrate in the 1920s, they could not be excluded under the statutes applied to Japanese and Chinese, because Filipinos carried U.S. passports. When their labor was no longer needed during the Depression, however, Philippines independence was authorized by Congress in 1934 (though not actually granted until 1946). The 1934 act that authorized independence also set an immigration quota of fifty persons per year (Daniels and Kitano 66).

California's miscegenation statute was ruled not to include Filipinos, who, the courts concluded, were not Negroes, Mongolians, or mulattoes—they were Malayans. The legislature subsequently amended the statute to include Malayans in the list of people banned from marrying whites (ibid. 67–68). As with first the Chinese and then the Japanese, a legal racial status for Filipinos had to be adjudicated.

In the years of debate over immigration from Asia and elsewhere, a definition of "American" became clear. An American was white, of northern European descent, and Protestant, in that order of importance. "This culturally relative perspective," says Valerie Lucas, "constitutes the Chinese and Japanese immigrant in terms of lack: he is an alien other whose barbarous ways must be reformed or who poses a threat to the dominant culture" (41). Teddy Roosevelt expressed his faith in the juggernaut-like ability of that dominant culture to absorb outsiders and eradicate their differences when he said, "We have room for but one language here, and that is the English Language, for we intend to see that the crucible turns people out as Americans."[9]

We can see several of the important issues of Asian "otherness" in these debates over immigration. Physical appearance, language, and supposedly biologically determined cultural patterns were perceived as making Asians not only other, but dangerous and incomprehensible. In nineteenth-century representations, Chinese always speak a heavy pidgin. "You wantee debbil? All lightee: me catchee him," says Ah Ri, a character in Bret Harte's "Wan Lee, the Pagan" (Inability to speak proper English is a trait of all stereotypically represented ethnic groups. Native Americans who speak like Tonto, the Lone Ranger's monosyllabic, ungrammatical sidekick, blacks who cannot speak properly because of their "thick lips," Irish who speak nothing resembling English as we know it, along with working-class people who know no grammar, keep company in this respect with the Chinese. These representations of speech are hard to read—one has to decipher the Chinese character's speech, rather than read it—which keeps that character distant, alien, different from the reader. Later, in the 1920s and 1930s, Charlie Chan spoke grammatical English, but in a flowery style peppered with Confucianstyle sayings that marked him as different. Fu Manchu's ability to speak perfect English, on the other hand, was seen as a threat by Anglo characters. In Viet Nam War novels, the Vietnamese characters were back to speaking pidgin.

Appearance, also, is important in these nineteenth-century representations. The main objects seized upon here are the epicanthal folds in Asians' eyelids, and the queue worn by Chinese males to show their loyalty to the Manchu emperors. Charlie Chan, in 1925, was the first Chinese character to appear without a queue, although the Manchu dynasty fell in 1911, and Chinese in China and overseas cut their queues at that time. Chinese immigrants' "strange" clothing also made them appear alien in Euro-American eyes. Chinese are usually described as small and therefore insignificant. Eyes, body size, and the queue are all present in this passage from Joaquin Miller: "The moon-eyed little man tried to get back into the house, but the great big giant had been too long a patient and uncomplaining sufferer to let him escape now, and he reached for his queue, and drew him forth as a showman does a black snake from a cage" (*First Fam'lies of the Sierras* 41). Notice the contrast, in this passage, between the small Chinese and the "great big giant" Euro-American. The contrast is so important that the Euro-American is described with hyperbole that sounds almost ridiculous. Notice also how powerless the Chinese is once the Euro-American decides to act. The final application of the standard anti-Chinese rhetoric in this passage is the comparison of the Chinese to an animal, in this case, a snake.

William Wu points out that some of the earliest American fiction about Chinese immigrants attempted to portray them in a favorable light. These attempts, however, are not always successful. Bret Harte portrayed the Chinese as good Asians—loyal and skillful servants. In three stories, "Wan Lee, the Pagan," "See Yup," and "Three Vagabonds of Trinidad," he uses Asians to show the failings of the Euro-American characters. Wan Lee is killed by a rioting mob; the reader's sympathy is clearly meant to lie with Wan Lee, not the mob. See Yup dupes the stupid Euro-Americans out of the foreign miners' tax by taking advantage of their inability to tell one Chinese from another. Here the Euro-Americans are the butt of the joke. The "Three Vagabonds" are a Chinese, an Indian, and a dog who are exiled to the woods, then hunted down and killed. This is an early example of a phenomenon I return to later, that of attempting to humanize and individualize an Asian character only to use him to show the evil of Euro-American characters.

In "Three Vagabonds," Mr. Parkin Skinner, "a prominent citizen," says, "The nigger of every description—yeller, brown or black, call him 'Chinese,' 'Injin,' or 'Kanaka,' or what you like—hez to clear off of God's footstool when the Anglo-Saxon gets started!" (*Tales* 221). Harte portrays Skinner negatively, diverting sympathy away from him and his cohorts. However, Li Tee, the Chinese of the story, while presented as a person deserving a right to life, is still seen as a stereotyped, alien, "Chinee," with whom the reader cannot identify. His speech is the stereotypical pidgin: "Allee same Li Tee; me no changee. Me no ollee China boy" (211). Harte's narrator says of See Yup, "In our confidential intercourse, I never seemed to really get nearer to him" (99). As these portraits of Chinese characters show, Harte was not able to make the perceptual shift to step outside of his Western framework and see these characters as knowable.

Between 1878 and 1911, a time when anti-Chinese agitation was high (when, ironically, the United States was taking over the Philippines and other former Spanish colonies), several novels and stories about a Chinese takeover of the United States were published and widely read. Atwell Whitney's *Almond-Eyed: The Great Agitator* (1878), Pierton W. Dooner's *Last Days of the Republic* (1880), Robert Woltor's *A Short and Truthful History of the Taking of Oregon and California by the Chinese in the Year A.D. 1899* (1882), Oto Mundo's *The Recovered Continent: A Tale of the Chinese Invasion* (1898), and four stories published in the *Overland Monthly*[10] portray the menace of the Yellow Peril to Euro-American "civilization." These works speak of and to the Euro-American hysteria and terror of the "alien" Chinese, and conceptualize the relationship between the two groups as warfare. They portray the Chinese never as individuals, but as hordes, who seem to act in unison without leadership that the Euro-American eye can discern. The Chinese are presented as indifferent to pain, as willing to take enormous casualties to win battles. William Wu says that these works depict the behavior of the Chinese as "due to their race and not to free will. . . . The Chinese cannot be dealt with on a rational basis as humans, but can only be confronted and opposed as an irrational force" (40). This theme reappears in portrayals of Chinese Communists during the Korean War and again in portrayals of the Viet Cong in Viet Nam War narratives.

"The Year 1899" is a bizarre, white supremacist fantasy in which an unholy league of Chinese, Indians, and blacks revolts against the U.S. government. No individuals of these groups are portrayed. The Chinese troops are presented as inhuman in their attacks. They are shown not as brave, but as fanatical: "Death seemed to have no terrors for them" (586). In contrast, the black troops all run away when the white cavalry arrives. The Chinese are portrayed as a flood: "Now that the human inundation from the East has become a thing of the past, we can see the influences that gave it its immense power. But Asiatic strength was less important than European weakness. The warning we have had is plain and clear" (589). This story is obviously meant as a cautionary tale, that "whites" should keep "coloreds" in their place.

Representation by absence appears again in "The Sacking of Grubbville." No Chinese actually appear in the story at all. They are an off-stage threat used as a plot device to effect the reconciliation of two Euro-American characters, when one of them perpetrates a hoax, claiming that Chinese have taken over San Francisco and are on their way to Grubbville (a fictional peninsula town). Again, the Chinese are likened to odious animals. The citizens of Grubbville are keeping watch on a waterway: "Perhaps they expected to see it black with the heads of their enemy swimming in upon them, as the rats came upon the wicked bishop of Bingen" (575).

The cover of *Almond-Eyed* shows a Chinese man smoking an opium pipe. A long queue is pulled forward over his shoulder. His face is elongated, his ears huge, the top of his head bald, the eyes exaggerated, tilted, so that he looks like a fairytale dwarf. When the Anglo citizens of Yarbtown rise against the Chinese immigrants, the queue, as the symbol of Chinese difference and alienness, becomes the object of their battle cry. " 'Cut off their pigtails' shouted the crowd" (139). The Chinese are again characterized as a pack of animals: "There had been small inducement offered to the mongrel herd of Chinese who flooded even fairer portions of the State" (8). The Chinese are frightening by their very numerousness: "Not a doorway, not a window did he see, but that a grinning Chinaman occupied it" (106). As in the more benign works, the unknowability of the Chinese is mentioned:

A Chinaman, like the redskin, never forgets either a real or a fancied injury. Revenge is strongly ingrafted in their nature. Their revenge is usually as mean and treacherous as that of the meanest Digger Indian. They can smile in your face while they pour poison into your cup. . . . Whether his dreams of revenge consisted of plans for the use of the silent knife, or whether he simply meditated upon the plan of requesting Ling Yung, the washman, to cut off the shirt buttons of all the friends of Job, would be a difficult thing for a white man to decide. (42)

In both the propagandistic works agitating for Chinese exclusion by portraying a military invasion of the United States by Chinese forces and the more sympathetic works by writers such as Harte and Miller, the stereotypical representations of the Chinese take form, reflecting the political rhetoric of the anti-Chinese agitation. When the Chinese are good, they are passive and malleable, and when bad they are sinister, powerful devils, "hordes" and "floods" threatening to invade and conquer America. As these representations flourished in political rhetoric, popular culture, and the literature of the West, the parameters within which the national imagination viewed Chinese immigrants were set.

After 1924, all mainland Asian immigration into the United States was barred. Meanwhile Japan had become a rising military power at the turn of the century, after the first Sino-Japanese War (1894–95). With the Russo-Japanese War of 1904–5, a European power was defeated by an Asian power for the first time in the modern era. In 1931 Japan invaded Manchuria and in 1937 occupied Shanghai and controlled strategic spots in China until the end of World War II. With China seeming weak and relatively helpless all during the first part of the twentieth century, and Japan increasingly strong, Euro-American fears were transferred somewhat from the Chinese to the Japanese.

Two novels appeared in 1921 which were similar to the nineteenth-century Chinese invasion novels, only with the invaders being Japanese. Wallace Irwin's *Seed of the Sun* and Gene Stratton-Porter's *Her Father's Daughter* make use of all the stereotypes developed about the Chinese and apply them to the Japanese. In *Seed of the Sun*, the Japanese immigrants have been sent to California by the emperor to take over all the farmland and marry Euro-American women in order to promote their race. The Asians are still unassimilable: the halfbreed offspring of these infiltrators will nevertheless be Japanese: "Even unto the tenth generation, Japanese with blond skins and blue eyes will still be Japanese" (233).

The opening of *Seed of the Sun* is laden with symbolism and is worth quoting at length, as it exemplifies the typical patterns of the invasion novels:

Early spring air was gorgeous with flying kites and flying clouds over the little short town with the little short name—a name, by the way, which the Japanese inhabitants could not pronounce because the letter *l* will always be an obstacle to the fluent tongues of Nippon. The younger and more progressive referred to it as "Bry"; the conservative ones adhered to the Japanese name which they had given it when first they decided that the region around the old Bly tract was worthy of attention. . . . But to the slanting black eyes of its inhabitants Bly was, at best, a barbarian word. Indeed, as a settlement for Californians, the town of Bly had long since ceased to exist. (9)

The Japanese inhabitants of the town are defined as permanent outsiders, through their inability to pronounce the town's Anglo-Saxon name. They are quickly described in terms of their eyes. This paragraph also serves to rouse xenophobic feelings in readers by declaring that the Japanese inhabitants have given the town their own name (significantly not supplied, leaving a bit of mystery) and find the Anglo-Saxon name barbaric. Immediate hostility is set up. Further, the Japanese are "Japanese"—despite the fact that they live in California, they are not defined, in this paragraph, as "Californians." At the end of the novel the transformation of the town will be complete: "All the signs on the stores were now in Japanese" (351).

The alienness of the Japanese is reinforced as the text continues:

Bow-legged little women, dressed in hand-me-down American clothes, were assembled on the porch of Mr. Sago's establishment, a respectful distance removed from the conference of their lords. Their large, broad faces bobbing and smiling above their undersized bodies gave them more than ever the appearance of quaint toys cheaply outfitted in the style of the day. (9–10)

Here the Japanese women are not only non-American, by the end of the paragraph, they are nonhuman "toys." Their smallness is also emphasized. The relative size of Euro-Americans and Asians is always a factor in the description of Asians as other.

Later in the first section the fear that this novel will play on is hinted at when the farmers are described as having "abundant offspring." The section ends, however, with a reinforcement of Euro-American supremacy: "Now this is but a passing snapshot of the town whose name, defying race and color, remains so stubbornly Anglo-Saxon" (11).

Anna, a widow, has inherited a California farm, which has been leased to Japanese farmers. She decides to move there and enter a sharecropping deal, rather than simply collect rent. Anna and her sister Zudie are acquainted with Japanese, because their father was a military man who had been in Japan. Baron Tazumi is the family's old friend. They will be driven out of business, however, by the Japanese plot—ordered by the emperor—to take over part of the world: "The Japanese were moving in America, just as they were moving in Manchuria and Siberia, to gain control of the land that was to make them a great people upon earth" (348).

Japan is presented as a frightening power that is encroaching everywhere. The little boys of Bly fly kites which all have the legend "Nippon ichi" on them, which Henry Johnson translates as "Japan uber alles" (279). A white farmer explains what he thinks the Japanese are up to: "Peaceful war. The conquest of the world by agriculture, commerce, immigration, secret treaties, counterfeit labels, soft words, hard bargains and the Japanese genius for teamwork" (144). Notice again how old-fashioned American values like teamwork become sinister in the hands of another culture.

At the beginning of the novel Baron Tazumi, an old family friend of Anna and Zudie, is described as "a figure of a very noble gentleman. His skin was paler, his eyes rounder than the average of his race. With his tightly twisted little mustache he appeared more like a Frenchman than an Oriental" (35). The quality that makes him admirable to American eyes is his resemblance to a European rather than an Asian. He will turn out to be the "inscrutable Oriental," after all, when he is revealed to be K. Sato, the mysterious proprietor of the Natural Energy Fruit and Land Company, which is carrying out the emperor's plot to take over the Sacramento Valley.

Miscegenation appears early in the novel, in the person of a philosophy-spouting window cleaner named Henry Johnson:

He was quite different from anything she had seen in New York's parade of undesirable aliens. In costume he recalled a figure out of La Boheme, but the greasy Windsor tie and the suit that flapped loosely over his tall, bony form somehow suggested the Bowery. The face under a thatch of long wiry black hair was grotesque as it was pathetic. It was as though two incomplete faces had been joined rather clumsily and made to serve as one. (43)

Miscegenation produces monstrosity. Henry is akin to the "tragic mulatto" figure so prevalent in late nineteenth-century fiction. He is loyal to Anna and Zudie when he becomes their servant, but he eventually shambles off to a "shabby fate" in Japan. His own explanation for his misery is that "nature rebels against bad mixtures of breed just as much in the human species as in the case of sheep or cattle" (333). When he finally tells the story of his mother's unhappy marriage to his father, the reader is supposed to infer that Baron Tazumi is Henry's father. Henry's mother has married him because she is the daughter of abolitionists who had "filled her with romance about the dark-skinned races" (330).

Nonetheless the Japanese in the novel are interested in marrying white women. Henry explains to Anna that they "want to borrow your stature" (234). Baron Tazumi has asked Anna to marry him, and in a moment of "weakness," in despair over the prospect of losing her farm, she has almost said yes. The reader is supposed to be relieved at her deliverance into the hands of a neighboring white farmer, Dunc, a rabid anti-Japanese. The novel employs the technique of trying to convert the reader to its point of view along with the main character, in this case Anna, who begins as a defender of the Japanese and ends up despising them as much as the other characters of the book do.

The greatest objection to the Japanese is their overindustriousness. "The American's an eight-hour man, the Jap's a sixteen-hour man" (100) complains a white farmer. Anna and Zudie—still, at this point, respectful of the Japanese—think that the farmer is "as Bolshevik as [he] can get" (101). In fact, the reason the whites are losing their land to the Japanese is lack of industriousness—caused by the I.W.W. White laborers are unwilling to work. Zudie declares: "Out round Lodi the I.W.W. delegates were nailing up signs demanding five dollars a day for an eight-hour day and seventy-five cents an hour for overtime. Work seems to have gone out of fashion. What's happening to our country, Ann?" (281). Irwin's message is clearly that whites should work harder to avoid being driven out by the industrious Japanese through their "peaceful war." As always, the only imaginable relationship between the United States and Asia is warfare and invasion.

Her Father's Daughter is a run-of-the-mill romance about a tomboy orphan who finds love, but it contains a subplot driven by virulent hatred of the Japanese and paranoia about Japanese world dominance, in alliance with other peoples of color: "A vision of his country threatened on one side by the red menace of the Bolshevik, on the other by the yellow menace of the Jap, and yet on another by the treachery of the Mexican and the slowly uprising might of the black man" (247). Stratton-Porter later adds,

If California does not wake up very shortly and very thoroughly she is going to pay an awful price for the luxury she is experiencing while she pampers herself with the service of the Japanese, just as the South has pampered herself with the service of the negroes. When the negroes learn what there is to know, then the day of retribution will be at hand. . . . Keep your eyes wide open for Japs. (375)

These sentiments are put into the mouths of Linda, the heroine, and her love interest, Peter, a journalist who writes white supremacist articles. Linda's proposed remedy is white reproduction: "If every home in Lilac Valley had at least six sturdy boys and girls growing up in it with the proper love of country and the proper realization of the white man's right to supremacy, and if all the world now occupied by white men could make an equal record, where would be the talk of the yellow peril? There wouldn't be any yellow peril" (149). Linda and Peter both view the world in terms of race war, with the white race embattled by the "inferior" colored races. While this may seem like a weird imposition on the romance story, it is actually integral to it: their attraction to one another is built on their race attitudes.

Linda is a high school junior who forms a friendship with Donald, a senior, who is in second place in his class, behind Oka Sayye, a Japanese. Linda encourages Donald to "beat the Jap":

Well, you can't beat him calling him names. There is only one way on god's footstool that you can beat him. You can't beat him legislating against him. You can't beat him boycotting him. You can't beat him with any tricks. He is as sly as a cat and he has got a whole bag full of tricks of his own, and he has proved right here in Los Angeles that he has got a brain that is hard to beat. All you can do, and be a man commendable to your own soul, is to take his subject and put your brain on it to such purpose that you cut pigeon wings around him. . . . There is just one way in all this world that we can beat Eastern civilization and all that it intends to do to us eventually. The white man has dominated by his colour so far in the history of the world, but it is written in the Books that when the men of colour acquire our culture and combine it with their own methods of living and rate of production, they are going to bring forth greater numbers, better equipped for the battle of life, than we are. (115)

Linda believes that the colored races are "imitative" and that "they are not creating one single thing" (116); therefore, the white races can beat them by creativity. She advises Donald to beat Oka Sayye by being more original than he is.

It turns out that Oka Sayye is a man in his thirties who has graduated from a university in Japan and come to an American high school to unfairly expropriate American knowledge. Further, all the Japanese in Los Angeles form some sort of secret and dangerous network. When Donald starts to get ahead of Oka Sayye, various Japanese start menacing Donald and Linda, sabotaging his car, sneaking around Linda's garage, offering their services to her housekeeper with intent of doing her some sabotage.

Eventually, when Donald and Linda are on a picnic with her housekeeper, Katy, Oka Sayye himself tries to kill Donald by rolling a boulder over a cliff. Linda and Katy kill Oka Sayye. After Katy has chopped off the tree limb he's clinging to, sending him down a thousand-foot embankment, Linda's response is: " 'Get him?' she asked tersely, as if she were speaking of a rat or a rattlesnake" (442).

Both *Seed of the Sun* and *Her Father's Daughter* construct Japanese as powerful and dangerous enemies, but enemies who can be defeated by American ingenuity. In this way, they prefigure some American attitudes toward the Japanese enemy in World War II. Asians remain alien and either servile or wicked. There are almost no other options in the popular culture representations, until Pearl Buck's *The Good Earth* (1931), which won the Pulitzer Prize in 1932 and stayed on the best-seller list for two years. Buck won the Nobel Prize in 1938 for her China novels. The daughter of missionaries, she lived in China from 1892 to 1934.

The Good Earth attempts to redeem the image of the Chinese by showing them as hard working, upwardly mobile, striving people, just like Americans. Wang Lung, the peasant main character, through the urging of his industrious and self-effacing wife, O-lan, acquires land and becomes a rich man, eventually moving into the House of Hwang, the dwelling of the former richest family of the village. This upward mobility has something of a Horatio Alger cast to it, although the cycle of prosperity that has caused the House of Hwang to fall will also cause the downfall of the House of Wang: Wang Lung's sons will sell the land after his death, thus losing their source of wealth.

Although Buck's characterization of Wang Lung might be seen as a positive stereotype, it remains a stereotype. He is a hard working and responsible peasant who becomes dissolute and pleasure seeking when he gains wealth. There is nothing unpredictable about Wang Lung. The two major female characters of the book embody the Christian madonna/whore dichotomy: O-lan is the stoic, virtuous, self-sacrificing mother, while Cuckoo, Wang Lung's concubine, is a hedonist who totters on bound feet and demands an endless supply of sweets.

When Wang Lung takes his family south during a great famine, they live for a while in a large city. Buck, in portraying the effects of poverty and oppression on poor peasants, makes buffoons of them:

Their faces were like the face of O-lan, inarticulate, dumb. . . . They themselves had no idea what manner of men they were. One of them once, seeing himself in a mirror that passed on a van of household goods, had cried out, "There is an ugly fellow!" And when others laughed at him loudly he smiled painfully, never knowing at what they laughed, and looking about hastily to see if he had offended someone. (81)

In her attempt to gain sympathy for the Chinese, Buck seems to have succeeded, but what she gained was indeed sympathy, or pity, rather than empathy. Her characters remain closed, flat, "inscrutable," and inferior.

Why did *The Good Earth* become so popular during the decade of the 1930s? In the United States, anti-Asian racism and fears of invasion had been allayed by the total ban on immigration from Asia, and international fears had settled on Japan's expansionism. In the 1930s China had been named as an ally of the United States against the axis forces, so the U.S. propaganda machine had to work to reverse at least some of the negative view of China. Buck's novel portrays not Chinese immigrants, but Chinese in China—safely removed from an American context. Her Chinese peasants are nonthreatening (similar to the way Charlie Chan was nonthreatening). Although sometimes cunning and clever, they are never smart. They are stolid, dependable. They are at the mercy of the seasons, and, in the cliché that Americans of good intention later applied to Vietnamese peasants, all they want to do is grow their rice and vegetables and be left alone by authorities, governments, and bandits. They appear to be simple, harmless folk who would make an excellent flock for missionary work.

Another factor may have been at work in the popularity of *The Good Earth*. During the Depression many novels and narratives concerning "ordinary" people were published. Buck's novel fits into that mold, but even while her people are "ordinary," their story is romanticized. It is easy to see in the films of the 1930s, as well as the literature, that romantic, "escapist" themes were popular. (The bestselling books of the decade were *The Good Earth*, *Anthony Adverse*, a romance about early European immigrants to America, *Gone with the Wind*, a romanticization of the Civil War, and *The Grapes of Wrath*, which, despite its serious political content, is a romanticization of "Okies.")

Buck's novel may have altered the stereotypes of Chinese toward the "positive" somewhat, but it did not change into a nonstereotypical representation of Chinese. The "positive" stereotypes put forth in *The Good Earth*, are, in the final analysis, not so positive. By portraying the peasants as rooted in their poverty, in their ignorance (the only characters who become educated also become venal), and in their gender stereotypes (which Buck imported from Western culture, in the form of the madonna/whore dichotomy), she furthered the portrayal of Asians as backward, primitive, inscrutable, and obtuse. It is impossible to imagine Buck's peasants desiring tractors, for example. (During the war in Viet Nam, some antiwar activists would stubbornly argue that Vietnamese peasants preferred the backbreaking manual labor that underdevelopment and poverty force them into, because it is "traditional.") In this way, Buck resembles Harte and Miller of the previous century, who, while writing in defense of the Chinese, failed to truly humanize them. Although the hysterically xenophobic portrayals of Asians of the nineteenth century gave way, in the first part of the twentieth, to more moderated portrayals, no "leap of perspective" was made.[11]

World War II

Between 1941 and 1991, the United States fought four wars against Asian people: World War II, the Korean War, the war in Viet Nam, and the war against Iraq. In each of these wars, some Asians have been enemies and some allies. In World War II, the Japanese were enemies, while the Chinese and Indians were allies; in the Korean War, North Koreans and Chinese were enemies, while South Koreans were allies; in the war in Viet Nam, the Democratic Republic of Viet Nam and the National Liberation Front were enemies, while the Republic of Viet Nam and the Republic of Korea were allies; in the war against Iraq, Iraqis were enemies, while Kuwaitis and Saudis were allies.

This seesawing between different enemies and allies could be confusing, but it has been culturally managed through the maintenance of stable stereotypical images, which are applied in turn to the appropriate group. Of course there are long-standing traditions of creating dehumanizing portraits of the enemy, but the astonishing point about American dealings with Asia is that not only are the enemies dehumanized, but so are the allies. A survey by Frey-Wouters and Laufer of men who were of draft age during the Viet Nam war (some of whom served and some of whom did not) showed that "feelings of mutuality with the allies were dramatically absent. Indeed, despite an evident hostility toward the enemy, sentiments expressed toward them . . . show more respect than is accorded the allies" (108).

When the United States has Asian allies, they are, in the resentful words of Deong, in the film version of *The Ugly American*, "little brown brothers"—

the image descended through Pearl Buck's Chinese peasants, Charlie Chan, and the loyal servants portrayed by Harte and Miller. This sidekick role was transferred to the Japanese (MacArthur's "children") after World War II and to the ARVN and Vietnamese peasants during the war in Viet Nam.

When the United States has Asian enemies, they are, as Dower writes about representations of the Japanese, either "subhuman," represented as apes and vermin, or "superhuman, possessed of uncanny discipline and fighting skills. Subhuman, inhuman, lesser human, superhuman—all that was lacking in the perception of the Japanese enemy was a human like oneself" (9). Representations of Asian enemies are descended through Fu Manchu and Almond-Eyed, from the Chinese invasion novel of that name. The PAVN and NLF were assigned this image during the war in Viet Nam.

After the end of World War II, the racist patterns of thinking that had characterized American attitudes toward Japan were, in Dower's words, "transferred laterally." After 1949, our former ally, China, again became demonized, assigned the devil image which usually carries with it the idea of "hordes"—imagery clearly applied to the Chinese army that "poured" across the border to defeat the U.S. army at Inchon, Korea. During the post–World War II years, Japan, our former enemy, became our ally and friend. Through all these transformations, the rhetoric remains the same, merely "transferred laterally," over and over again.

Another shift appears to be under way. Since the end of World War II, Japan has been "little brown brother" to the United States, and China has been the cap-with-red-star, steely-eyed Communist devil. For the last few years, however, images seem to have been shifting. The dominant image of China now is that of a man standing before a tank in Tiananmen square. This image has moved from the news media into popular culture. It has appeared on T-shirts, posters, and in a popular song. While this is a heroic image, I doubt that it alone is enough to alter completely the image of the Chinese—if they are becoming the "good guys," they will become "little brown brothers." The image of Japan, on the other hand, is shifting toward that of economic imperialists—superhuman, ultradisciplined hordes whose children outscore American children on math tests and who threaten U.S. prosperity.

Viet Nam may be undergoing an image shift, as well. From 1979 until recently the dominant image of Viet Nam has been militarism (cast in terms of its occupation of Cambodia) and the police state. Recently, newspapers and television have featured the image of the poor Vietnamese peasant, and images of underdevelopment have been posed in sympathy-generating ways. Perhaps Viet Nam is again being cast in the role of "little brown brother"—a brother who shares in the United States' dislike of Japan and is ready to welcome American business interests. The stories of U.S. veterans returning to Viet Nam all emphasize how friendly Vietnamese are to Americans and how much they dislike Japanese and, especially, Russian tourists. The depiction of Asian enemies and allies throughout these recent wars has its roots in imagery circulated during World War II (and the depiction of Japanese and Chinese in World War II has its roots in the older history of the representation of Asians in American culture examined in the previous section). To understand the source of some of the depictions of Vietnamese, it is necessary to examine the way America perceived Japanese during World War II, because that is the model on which much of the American view of Vietnamese is built. In fact, some representations of Vietnamese appear to be World War II propaganda with only a change of names.

Daniels and Kitano point out the contradiction of the U.S. role in World War II: "On the one hand the United States was at war with the most viciously racist government of all time—Nazi Germany—and was committed to the destruction of that government and all it represented; on the other hand the United States was itself an officially racist country with a tradition of discrimination more than three centuries old" (61). John Dower, in his illuminating study of racism in the war in the Pacific, *War without Mercy*, writes about the ways this contradiction affected the participants in the war:

The Germans pointed to the status of blacks in America as proof of the validity of their dogma as well as the hollowness of Allied attacks on Nazi beliefs. The Japanese, acutely sensitive to "color" issues from an entirely different perspective, exploited every display of racial conflict in the United States in their appeals to other Asians. . . . Although only a few [American] individuals spoke up on behalf of the persecuted Japanese-Americans, both the oppression of blacks and the exclusion of Asian immigrants became political issues in wartime America. Blacks raised questions about "fighting for the white folk," and called for "double victory" at home and abroad. Asians, especially Chinese and Indians, decried the humiliation of being allied to a country which deemed them unfit for citizenship; and for a full year in the midst of the war, the U.S. Congress debated the issue of revising the suddenly notorious Oriental exclusion laws. (5)

During the war in Viet Nam, the issue of racism at home would be raised again, in much the same way. Black soldiers in the U.S. army would ask the same questions as had black soldiers in World War II, although during the war in Viet Nam the U.S. Army was integrated. Antiwar activists in the

United States, and others in countries critical of American policy, would see the American war in Viet Nam as an extension of racist policies at home.

U.S. racism led to an especially brutal war against Japan and to the internment of not only Japanese immigrants, but also American-born citizens of Japanese ancestry. In August 1945, the United States became the first and only country to use atomic weapons against another nation. When asked why the United States carried out these two actions—internment and bombing—some Euro-Americans give as answers stereotypes about Asians: "You can't tell if a Jap is a spy or not"; "We had to use the bomb because the Japanese have no regard for human life."[12]

With this treatment of the Japanese and Japanese Americans, it became, for the first time, a good thing to be Chinese in California. Chinese American writer Pardee Lowe published his *Father and Glorious Descendant* in 1943. The publishers used Lowe's enlistment in the U.S. Army as a promotional strategy for the book, proclaiming that he belonged to "one of America's loyal minorities" (Kim, *Asian American Literature* xvi). During the war Chinese shopkeepers in California put signs in their windows proclaiming "We are Chinese," the import being, of course, that they were not Japanese. China had been invaded by Japan in 1936, and when the United States entered the war, China became an American ally. The image of the Chinese therefore needed some revamping. The 1944 film *Thirty Seconds over Tokyo* shows an American pilot, shot down in China and helped by Chinese peasants, enthusiastic about what great people the Chinese are, and how he wants to come back and fight side by side with them. *The Battle of China*, a 1944 documentary, is, in the words of John Dower, "an epic paean to the resistance of the Chinese people against Japan's aggression" (17).

The new status of Chinese as allies was not enough to correct decades of negative images, as Cheng-Tsu Wu reports in "*Chink!*":

In Harold Isaacs' survey, conducted during the 1940s, one still found the following prejudiced image of the Chinese: "A Congressman said he had an idea of the Chinese as a 'savage people' from the comic strip, 'The Gumps,' and, a public opinion specialist thought that the Chinese might be 'untrustworthy in business' because he had heard repeatedly in his boyhood that one should 'Never trust a Chink!'" (6)

A congressman basing his racial views on a comic strip illustrates the power of popular culture in shaping people's images and attitudes, and through those attitudes, laws and policies.

The historic racism against the Japanese became elevated to new levels after 7 December 1941. The dominant attitude toward Japanese and Japanese Americans was clearly stated by Culbert Olson, governor of California: "You know, when I look out at a group of Americans of German or Italian descent, I can tell whether they are loyal or not. I can tell how they think . . . but it is impossible for me to do that with inscrutable Orientals, particularly the Japanese" (quoted in Lucas 51). What is extraordinary about this passsage is not Olson's claim that he cannot tell what Japanese persons are thinking, but that he can tell what Euro-Americans are thinking. He is making a strong claim that similarity of national origin creates a bond which allows unspoken communication to take place among individuals. This constitution of a mystical European racial bond puts the Asian forever outside of that bond, alien and apart, dangerous because of the Euro-Americans' supposed lack of access to the Asian's "inscrutable" thoughts.

Olson was not alone. The mayor of Los Angeles declared, "Blood will tell," and General John DeWitt, architect of the internment, said, "A Jap is a Jap." Congressman John Rankin of Mississippi said, "Once a Jap, always a Jap. You can't any more regenerate a Jap than you can reverse the laws of nature" (quoted in Dower 80–81). Following the historic pattern of U.S. racism, these statements refer to the supposed unassimilability of the Japanese in the United States.

Dower describes *Prelude to War*, one of the documentary films in Frank Capra's series "Why We Fight," commissioned by the U.S. Army. In this film, a scene "actually depicted 'the conquering Jap army' marching down Pennsylvania Avenue in Washington, D.C. 'You will see what they did to the men and women of Nanking, Hong Kong, and Manila,' viewers were warned. 'Imagine the field day they'd enjoy if they marched through the streets of Washington'" (17). The similarity of this scene to the Chinese invasion novels and stories of the nineteenth century and the Japanese invasion novels of the 1920s is obvious. This is a brilliant propaganda tactic—instilling fear in the American public by showing the imaginary consequences of a Japanese invasion. One of the interesting points about this scene is that it is set in the nation's capital, although fear of Japanese invasion was largely a West Coast phenomenon.[13] As with the agitation for Chinese exclusion at the end of the nineteenth century, a regional fear is made national. In addition, the voiceover, as reported by Dower, aligns Washington with "Nanking, Hong Kong, and Manila," which are Asian cities. This link serves a dual propaganda purpose by inspiring hatred and fear of the Asian enemy and evoking identification and sympathy with the Asian allies.

Another propaganda piece that attempted the same ploy was a *Time* article called "How to Tell Your Friends Apart from the Japs," which included a chart to distinguish supposed Japanese facial characteristics from supposed Chinese ones; it turned out to show that Chinese look friendly and happy while Japanese look sneaky and evil.

Another of Capra's films, *Know Your Enemy—Japan*, reinforced the image of Japanese as a people "devoid of individual identity" (Dower 19). Capra's device was to use footage from captured Japanese newsreels and samurai movies of the 1930s. "The narrative referred to 'an obedient mass with but a single mind'." (ibid. 19–20).

Dower points out how deep the hatred of the Japanese enemy ran in America. He quotes Adm. William Halsey as saying that "by the end of the war Japanese would be spoken only in hell" (36), and cites a 1943 U.S. Army poll showing that half of all GIs "believed that it would be necessary to kill all Japanese before peace could be achieved" (53). Japanese Americans were sometimes included in these sentiments, as when the governor of Idaho proposed that "a good solution to the Jap problem would be to send them all back to Japan, then sink the island" (92).[14] By 1945, 25 percent of U.S. combatants in the Pacific saw their aim as "not to help bring about Japan's surrender, but simply to kill as many Japanese as possible" (53), which became the goal of U.S. soldiers in Viet Nam, where enemy "body counts" were the main measure of military success.

Dower cites stories from several personal narratives of American soldiers which indicate that Japanese prisoners and wounded Japanese were often killed. As I note in the next chapter, especially in the discussion of Larry Heinemann's *Close Quarters*, the same was true in Viet Nam. Dower also examines the practice of souvenir hunting in the form of ears, bones, and skulls. He quotes one marine who wrote, "The other night . . . Stanley emptied his pockets of 'souvenirs'—eleven ears from dead Japs. It was not disgusting, as it would be from the civilian point of view. None of us could get emotional over it" (65). Dower also cites a 1944 *Life* magazine photograph of an American woman posing with the skull of a Japanese sent to her by her soldier fiancé. While there is no account I know of that describes Americans taking Vietnamese skulls for trophies, references in personal narratives and novels to taking ears and teeth are numerous. Many of these stories may be apocryphal, but the idea is constantly present in American narratives of the war in Viet Nam.

Dower goes on to point out, correctly, I believe, that "it is virtually inconceivable, however, that teeth, ears, and skulls could have been collected from German or Italian war dead and publicized in the Anglo-American countries without provoking an uproar; and in this we have yet another inkling of the racial dimensions of the war" (66). There is no other enemy in the war in Viet Nam equivalent to the Germans and Italians, so a similar comparison cannot be made, yet it is clear that the racial dimension of the Viet Nam War is in part a continuation of the racial dimension of World War II—that dimension which allowed for savagery such as the taking of body parts as souvenirs.

Dower notes that the common wartime phraseology called the enemies "Nazis" and "Japs." Americans could conceive of individual "good Germans," but the only good "Jap" was a "dead Jap" (78 and passim). For many Americans in Viet Nam, the only good "gook" was a "dead gook." Although some writers make a distinction between "gooks" (the enemy) and Vietnamese, for many that distinction was a hard one to maintain, resulting in the adage, "If it's dead and Vietnamese it's VC." Other World War II racial terminology defined all Asians by eye shape: " 'slant-eye,' 'slants,' 'squint eyes,' and 'almond eye.' 'Slopey' or 'slopie' was GI jargon for the Chinese (a Chinese woman was a 'slopie gal')" (ibid. 162). In Viet Nam, the most common epithets, after "gook," were "slope," "slant," "dink," and "zip."

In another rhetorical move that was echoed in the war in Viet Nam, Americans often referred to Japanese in terms of animals and insects. Dower reports that the most common epithets were "mad dogs" and "yellow dogs," and that Japanese were frequently described in terms of anthills and beehives (82–83). The most common likeness of Japanese, however, was as monkeys or apes. The depiction of Japanese as monkeys and apes in wartime cartoons was extensive (87). Dower draws this conclusion about the practice: "What we are concerned with there is . . . the attachment of stupid, bestial, even pestilential subhuman caricatures on the enemy, and the manner in which this blocked seeing the foe as rational or even human, and facilitated mass killing" (89). The comparison of Asians to animals is a historic one, and its use in World War II emerges directly out of that history.[15]

Another image of the Japanese in World War II also derives from the history of American representations of race: that of Japanese as both subhumans and superhumans. The subhuman image was the most common before Pearl Harbor. The Japanese were widely regarded as militarily incompetent. Fletcher Pratt, a military commentator, explained in 1939 that Japan was full of military weaknesses. One of these was a decided inferiority in aviation. One of Pratt's explanations for this was that "the Japanese, even more than the Germans, are a people of combination. 'Nothing is much stupider than one Japanese, and nothing much brighter than two.' But the aviator is peculiarly alone, and the Japanese, poor individualists, are thus poor aviators" (Dower 103). Another of Pratt's explanations was that Japanese children did not receive enough mechanical toys.[16]

After Pearl Harbor, the fall of Singapore, and Japan's spectacular military victories in Southeast Asia, including the sinking of the British ships *Prince of Wales* and *Repulse* in the South China Sea, a different image emerged—that of the superman. Dower quotes an article in *Fortune* magazine which chronicled the switch in the characterization of the Japanese:

The Honorable Enemy has shown himself to be much more complicated than our casual impressions had painted him—a bowing, smirking, bespectacled, bandy-legged little man who leaves his shoes on the porch and wears his hat in the temple; who has a passion for arranging flowers and constructing thirty-one syllable poems; who never invented anything important of his own, but copied everything he saw, complete with leaky fuel lines and broken glass; who couldn't shoot or fly straight and whose flashy warships were all top-heavy, underarmored, and undergunned. (110).

Yank magazine called the Japanese "a 'born' jungle and night fighter" (an illogical concept, since there are no jungles in Japan). General William Slim called them "superbogeymen of the jungle" (Dower 112). Col. Archie Roosevelt, son of Theodore, wrote to the undersecretary of war to complain that "the Japanese soldier 'has been built up, officially and unofficially, as a sort of superman-superdevil, in ability, ferocity, and training. This resulted in U.S.-trained soldiers coming into battle with an inferiority complex." The *New York Times Magazine* ran an article in 1942 titled "Japanese Superman: That Too Is a Fallacy" (Dower 115). The image of the kamikaze pilot combines the image of superman with that of fanatic (as in the Chinese and Japanese "invasion" novels of earlier in the century).

This same subhuman/superhuman status would later be assigned to the Vietnamese. While they were seen as subhuman "gooks," the PAVN and Viet Cong were simultaneously seen by U.S. soldiers as supersoldiers who could appear almost by magic and could survive incredible expenditure of U.S. firepower, artillery, and bombing. Dower says of the coexistence of the subhuman and superhuman perceptions: "Subhuman and superhuman were not mutually exclusive, as might be expected, but complementary. The visual images associated with each might appear or recede in accordance with fortunes on the battlefield, but the Japanese ape and the Japanese giant went through the war together in the imagination of their Anglo-American enemies" (116). The subhuman/superhuman split was more complicated in Viet Nam. While the Viet Cong/PAVN might be perceived as simultaneously subhuman and superhuman, the split also had a different, and particularly destructive,[17] political dimension. While the Viet Cong/PAVN were often perceived as superhuman, the United States' allies, the ARVN, were almost always perceived as subhuman (or, if not subhuman, at least disastrously incompetent). The Vietnamese peasants, the people in whose interests the United States was supposed to be fighting the war, were also often regarded as subhuman, thus sticking to the American pattern of dehumanizing both enemies and allies in Asia.

The effects of World War II's representation of Japanese are still with us today in America. Daniels and Kitano report a study in which "children in Georgia were recently asked their opinions about Japanese. The majority who had never seen a Japanese before used the adjective 'sneaky,' no doubt strongly influenced by old Hollywood movies recently shown on TV about World War II" (108). In many ways, World War II was the model war for the generation that was involved in the American war in Viet Nam. An entire book could be written about the influence of John Wayne and Audie Murphy on the young men who have written about their experiences as soldiers in Viet Nam. For many of them, World War II was their fathers' war. It was the good war, the glory war. They wanted to go to the war in Viet Nam and do what their fathers had done before.[18] The great tragedy is, of course, that they did exactly that.

The American Era in Viet Nam

The U.S. Soldiers

Robert Jay Lifton titles one chapter of his landmark study, *Home from the War: Vietnam Veterans: Neither Victims nor Executioners*, "Gooks and Men." In this chapter he discusses the attitudes of some veterans toward the Vietnamese. He quotes one veteran as saying, "There was a hell of a difference between Vietnamese and American bodies. With Vietnamese bodies you just didn't feel a thing. But with American bodies—well, that was different" (192). Lifton cites this quotation in a footnote and maintains that it was not the majority attitude, and I agree with him. However, the attitude of the veteran quoted is that reflected in the vast majority of literature and film about the war. Why? I believe that in translating their experience into literature, veteran writers fall into the only narrative paradigms available, the paradigms I have just described at length.

Lifton describes a slide show by a veteran which contained moving images of Vietnamese people. He uses this slide show as a way to talk about the experience of veterans:

The veteran who showed the slide sequence spoke of having himself lived on two levels in Vietnam: the one, of marked desensitization or numbing in which he, like everyone else, killed without feeling; but the other, of awareness of the humanity of the Vietnamese, attested to by the sensitive photographs he took during trips about the country. Everyone else in the group quickly emphasized that everything in Vietnam worked psychologically against the second level, against maintaining an awareness of Vietnamese humanity. (192)

Again, I agree with Lifton, but he leaves out the racial dimension of the war. U.S. soldiers would suffer desensitization and numbing if they were fighting a war in Europe, as well, but there would not be accumulated cultural baggage telling them that the people they were fighting were not fully equal human beings.

Lifton describes the healing process the veterans he counseled had to undergo: "The transformation involved is from gooks to men: from the gooks they had created to the Vietnamese men and women they were beginning to experience, and from the gook in themselves (the numbed and brutalized portions of their psyches) responsible for this victimization to the men they were struggling to become" (193). This transformation is not one our culture as a whole has undergone. Further, Lifton errs by calling the numbed portion of the veterans' psyches the "gook in themselves," since again he is overlooking the racial dimension of the imagery. He quotes a veteran who "spoke critically of certain officers who had condemned the Vietnamese for stealing, dishonesty, and fighting with one another for garbage scraps, 'as if we should be amazed that [in a] barnyard of starving chickens, [when you] throw in a few kernels of corn, the chickens fight over them'" (195). While Lifton analyzes this statement as a "vicious circle" of victimization, it also fits neatly into the pattern of describing Asians in terms of animals. Rather than seeing suffering human beings, this veteran has been conditioned to see the Vietnamese as animals.

Lifton quotes a participant in the massacre at My Lai: "I hate the gooks . . . so, wow! I killed 121 of them. That means I hate them worse than anybody does. . . . And of course the only way you could determine who hated them the most was how many times you beat them or killed them or raped them or something like that" (201). Although this man is a criminal and psychologically aberrant, he has merely taken American racism to its ultimate, Conradian conclusion: "Exterminate the brutes." The My Lai participant echoed the sentiments of some American World War II soldiers toward the Japanese: "The Indian idea . . . the only good gook is a dead gook" (47). While the My Lai participant might be seen as an outlaw to society, the ideas he expresses are rooted firmly in the World War II race-war paradigm. Lifton also quotes another veteran—not involved in the My Lai incident but someone Lifton describes as "hawkish"—as saying, "We should have killed all the gooks" (213). Some Americans had trouble distinguishing allies from enemies—disrespect for the ARVN was widespread, but the United States had also been allied with Korean troops. The same "hawkish" man recalled, "Koreans and Vietnamese, as far as they were concerned, there wasn't very much of a line. . . . They called them gooks over there" (205).

Lifton reproduces a passage from a pamphlet written by a veteran:

There is a large gap of feeling and understanding between the American soldier and the Vietnamese. Most fighting men don't trust them because of the way they live and the language they speak. They don't respect the Vietnamese people because they do our laundry, clean our buildings, fill our sandbags, polish our boots, wash our dishes, and women sacrifice their bodies, all for the Almighty American Dollar. Vietnamese people are commonly referred to as Dinks or Gooks by the large majority of American personnel. Would you lay down your life for the freedom of a Gook?

The people whose freedom we're fighting for have become our servants. (196)

This passage points out the class dimensions of American disrespect for Vietnamese—but this, too, draws on a long tradition of representation. As William Wu notes of nineteenth-century fiction, the most common role in which to find an Asian was that of servant. It was consistent with the cultural paradigm laid down by more than a hundred years of representations for Americans to see Vietnamese living off the boom economy created by the American occupation not as displaced persons, but as fulfilling a "natural" role as servants.

Lifton quotes some veterans whose reactions to Vietnamese were quite the opposite, such as a man who said, "The atrocity that was there in daily life . . . [American vehicles] going through the village at forty miles an hour, kicking up a cloud of dust when the mama-san just got through sweeping off the front porch" (210). Lifton analyzes this observation as standing for "the overall abuse of weak and helpless Vietnamese by blindly rampaging and numbed American power." Lifton's own racism surfaces here—he can envision the Vietnamese as only weak and helpless. This American attitude persists among analysts of the war on both the Left and the Right, despite the fact that the Vietnamese were the opposite of weak and helpless—they were strong and powerful enough to win wars against the French, Americans, and Chinese. Orientalism demands, however, that Americans see Vietnamese, especially poor Vietnamese, as weak and helpless.[19]

Lifton also cites a few veterans who did break the paradigm. One sergeant remembered:

I could tell my troops till they were blue in the face, punish them when I caught them doing it [calling the Vietnamese gooks or otherwise brutalizing them], and yet the whole military establishment was contrary to what I was doing . . . supporting the [idea] that it was gooks. The colonels called them gooks, the captain called them gooks, the staff all called them gooks. They were dinks, you know, subhuman. They used to deal with them in this way, so they took the cue from that and they considered me some kind of weird freak. (202)

A former navy man reported that he watched artillery fire on the outskirts of Saigon and said to a friend, "There are *people* out there" (209; emphasis in original).

What about Asian American veterans? Can their experiences serve as an analytical paradigm? Lifton quotes a Hawaiian veteran, who, subsequent to the war, became involved in the Hawaiian nationalist movement: "Like all the GIs I just killed everyone—they were all gooks to us. . . . But when I came back and looked at all the faces in the shopping center . . . they looked just like all the people I killed. I felt very strange and very bad" (215). This particular Asian American veteran experienced a revelation that removed him from the dominant paradigms under which he had operated, but those models had been sufficiently strong that it was only after his war experience that he made this reorientation.

Almost nothing is in print by or about Asian Americans and the Viet Nam War. There were Asian American soldiers in the war (one of the dead from my hometown, as listed on the California Vietnam Veterans Memorial, was Japanese American) and Asian Americans in the war protests. The position of Asian American soldiers during the war was a difficult one. Of all the underrepresented groups in the literature, Asian American veterans are perhaps the most seriously underrepresented; I am aware of only one book-length work by an Asian American veteran.[20]

G. Akito Maehara remembers his marine drill instructor standing him in front of his unit and saying, " 'This is what the enemy looks like! We kill people who look like him.' From that time until I left the service I was always being referred to as a friendly gook, Charlie Chan's cousin, Slant Eye, Yellow Belly and Zipper Head. It was as though my name and identity had been lost in the deep cesspool of racism which affected everyone in the military, now and then" (124). Maehara's experience is especially clear in illustrating the problems of Asian Americans involved in a war against Asians.

Sam Choy told the story of his army service in an interview with a New York Chinatown newspaper, *Getting Together.* The interview was reprinted in *Third World News.*

What kind of treatment did you receive?
Well, a couple of days after [his arrival in Viet Nam], the Viet Cong started shelling us. Then the other GIs started making comments about me looking like the Viet Cong.
How did you react?
I didn't do nothing. I was just doing a job. This went on and got worse. They asked me what I was doing on their side; I told them I was just doing a job. I didn't have any political awareness.
When was this harassment the worst?
Right after the GIs got back from patrol. They really gave it to me. They started asking me where I was born, where my parents were born, if I was a Communist. They even asked me what I thought about China. They thought I could turn traitor any time.

Choy served as a cook. After racial harassment by the mess sergeant, Choy got into a fight with the mess sergeant and a staff sergeant, during which he shot at them: "By this time I was near the perimeter of the base and was thinking of joining the Viet Cong; at least they would trust me" (quoted in Cheng-Tsu Wu 268). Choy's story illustrates the tendency of some Euro-Americans to refuse to make distinctions among Asians and Americans of Asian descent. Lily Lee Adams, an American nurse who served in Viet Nam, experienced similar harassment: "As far as the issue about my looking Asian, when I was in civilian clothes and walking around the compound with a guy, the other guys would just assume I was a whore. . . . It made me very angry.

Only it wasn't a personal thing; I was more angry because I was thinking, 'So that's how you treat Vietnamese women' " (quoted in Marshall 222).

Adams also had contact with Vietnamese who expected her to be able to speak their language. Paradoxically, Adams had gone to the war as a fired-up follower of the John F. Kennedy rhetoric of "to bear any burden" and had been a gung-ho soldier in the American cause. But her identification with the Vietnamese eventually changed her attitude.

I did have Vietnamese interpreters talk to me about how much they hated Americans. They'd tell me we were destroying their country and that we weren't doing what we were supposed to be doing. And I understood that. I really understood that.

Another time I was in triage and an old lady came in . . . the doctor yells at her to pull her pants down, and in my mind he was talking to a grandma—that was the day I really think I came out of the racist trance. I yell back at the doctor, "How can you do that to an old lady?" . . . Yeah, from that day on I stopped being a gook-hater and started to appreciate the Vietnamese. (ibid.)

Adams's identification switched from a focus on a nonethnic American identity to acknowledging a racial, if not national, similarity with the Vietnamese. This shift in identity focus led to a change in her politics and turned her against the war.

Sam Tagatac, a Filipino American writer who is not a veteran of the war, writes in his experimental short story, "The New Anak": "Ai anako, Roman says to his son when Nam is created for his children and they leave to seek their ancestry" (166); the war exists, in this story, for the Asian American character to fulfill his destiny. Elpidio, the character who is a soldier in Viet Nam, ends the story with a vision of barbed wire which fuses Viet Nam and America: ". . . dear francisco I've touched the barb wire again . . . how red the rust falls each day now . . . each day now I've twisted the line of the fence taut, this barb which surrounds our hearts, the land. The knife flash. I remember each morning the pet rooster you set against . . . the knife flash . . ." (168). In Elpidio's vision, the barbed wire around his position in Viet Nam fuses with the barbed wire of the farm at home, just as the visions of death that the barbed wire represents in both locations fuse for him.

Janice Mirikitani, another nonveteran writer, also explores the identification of Asian Americans with Vietnamese in her poem "Loving from Vietnam to Zimbabwe," in which a Japanese American woman's lover is an African American veteran of the war:

You never saw them alive
but knew they looked like me
And you got sick a lot
wondering what color
their blood. (215)

Mirikitani's poem attempts to build bridges among all oppressed peoples of color—the African American soldier, the Vietnamese enemy, the Japanese American woman.

Ashley Sheun Dunn's story "No Man's Land" builds no bridges, but rather chronicles rifts and separations. The narrator's brother, Stuart, is a newly returned veteran who tells stories of his experiences with Sam, a fellow soldier who is a recent immigrant from Hong Kong. Both the white and black soldiers had identified Sam and Stuart with the Vietnamese—to harass them, the other soldiers have left black pajamas sitting on their bunks, suggesting that they are akin to the Viet Cong.

Stuart is disturbed by how much he identifies with Sam, who barely speaks English—Stuart thinks of himself as American, and disrespects Sam even as he identifies with him. Stuart is also disturbed by how much he identifies with Vietnamese: "It's a funny thing, there you are in a place where everybody around you looked just like you, only you couldn't understand a word they say, everything they do is strange. I mean it made you feel lonely as hell" (118). At home, Stuart sees the residents of Chinatown as disturbingly similar to the Vietnamese.

Stuart remains haunted by one story he tells his brother, about how he and Sam tried to steal a duck from a farmer and got caught. Sam returned the next week to take the farmer a present and apologize. Sam continued to visit the farmer. Once he was unable to visit and convinced Stuart to go in his place. Stuart took a ring as his gift, which the farmer interpreted to mean Stuart wanted to marry his daughter. When Sam and Stuart visited together the next week, the marriage ceremony was waiting for Stuart. He ran out, pulling Sam with him, humiliating the farmer and his family. Sam insisted he go back and apologize, telling Stuart that the farmer would understand, even though they could not really talk to each other. Stuart eventually did go back, but the farmer came after him with a cleaver and Stuart punched him, possibly killing him.

Stuart cannot free himself of this story, telling it repeatedly, in the form of dreams, to his brother. To heal from his post-traumatic stress, he must reconcile himself to a series of things: his identification with the Vietnamese, his identification with the immigrant Sam, and, ultimately, himself. Stuart suffers from internalized oppression, and he turns his rage outward, in the secret that he reveals to his brother: that he wanted Sam to die. The story ends with Stuart on his way to possible reconciliation, boarding a bus to take him to New York and Sam's family. This is a powerful story that takes the war in Viet Nam as an opportunity to explore the workings of internalized oppression in an assimilated Chinese American.

One section of Maxine Hong Kingston's *China Men* deals with her brother, who is in the navy and stationed in the South China Sea. The most striking aspect of "The Brother in Vietnam" is how much it holds its silence. Viet Nam barely appears, as it barely appears in most American narratives of the war. This is partially because the brother was on a ship and not really *in* Viet Nam, but this narrative follows the standard pattern of American narratives. The war is not about the Vietnamese, it is about the Americans, even if the Americans in question are Chinese Americans.

For example, the way the brother conceptualizes his problem in terms of complicity in the war, and his conclusion—that being in the navy is not really being any more complicit than living in the war economy—highlights (as do the thousands of American narratives in print) how much decisions about the war, and what one was going to do about it, were individual and profoundly personal rather than political.

But there are several things that are striking about this Chinese American narrative, in the context of other Viet Nam war narratives. First, the history of the older generation draft-dodging in World War II shows how much the idea of the "Good War" is a myth only of the dominant American culture. The majority of the literature of that war is about volunteering, not evading, but here we have a group caught in the irony of having come to America from China to avoid conscription, only to face conscription.

The brother's decision to join the navy is also a way to claim his Americanness: "The United States was the only country he had ever lived in. He would not be driven out" (283). His decision not to be driven out, however, puts his family in jeopardy. When he discovers his background has been investigated, his first thought is that his family might be deported. Instead, the unfathomable officialdom of the United States declares them to be "super-Americans, extraordinarily secure—Q Clearance Americans" (299). His serving in a war against an Asian nation has certified not only him, but his family. Another irony.

When he decides not to go to language school to become an interrogator, he decides because of words—"the important words the same in Chinese and

Vietnamese. Talking Chinese and Vietnamese and also French, he'd be a persuasive interrogator-torturer" (301–2). He imagines forcing a Vietnamese mother to choose between betraying her baby or her husband. On a metaphoric level, he is imagining doing to others what his family has had done to them; he decides against language school. He has learned something, perhaps, from oppression.

Vietnamese Immigration into the United States

During 1974, there were 3,192 immigrants into the United States from Viet Nam. In 1975, with the war lost by the RVN/United States, 130,000 Vietnamese and Cambodian refugees came to America (Ignacio 200). This influx of people was met with hostility:

Anti-refugee feelings swept the country and racist emotional outbursts ran rampant and high. A California politician complained that there were already too many "Orientals" in his district. The "yellow peril" era was revived. Many Americans felt that they were being overrun by the Indochinese evacuees. This sentiment was demonstrated by the slogans, "NOW OUR MONEY . . . NEXT OUR JOBS . . . THEN OUR COUNTRY!" and several others seen in several places throughout the United States. "GOOKS, go home!" declared a placard in Arkansas. (ibid.)

Since 1975, almost a million Southeast Asian refugees have entered the United States. They have sometimes been met with attitudes resembling those taken toward the Chinese at the end of the nineteenth century and the Japanese in the 1920s. Nguyen Dang Liem, in "Vietnamese-American Crosscultural Communication," quotes an article in *Time* that reported, "Ironically, many refugees have aroused indignation for working too hard, not too little" (10).

A 1982 study reported by Alden Roberts in an article titled "Racism Sent and Received: Americans and Vietnamese View One Another" showed that "one-fourth of the respondents agreed that 'America has too many Asians in its population'" (76), a response that echoes the "invasion," "hordes," and "flood" imagery of earlier times. In Roberts's own study, 77 percent of Americans surveyed "would disapprove of the marriage of an Indo-Chinese refugee into their family," and 65 percent would not want a refugee as a guest in their homes; 11 percent wanted to exclude Indo-Chinese refugees from the United States altogether (81). James W. Tollefson, in an article titled "Indochinese Refugees: A Challenge to America's Memory of Vietnam," writes that most Americans "continue to rely upon stereotypes formed during the war and its tragic aftermath. . . . During a generation of involvement with Indochina, Americans have seen Southeast Asians as creatures to be killed, pitied, or saved, but rarely as human beings" (262–63). He notes that in the debate over the war Americans did not recognize Southeast Asians as the "real victims of the war. . . . The assumption that Asians are different from Americans—despite the fact that descendents of people from Asia have been in the United States for 150 years—seemed to unite Americans who were otherwise divided by the war" (265).

As Tollefson implies, American attitudes toward Vietnamese refugees echo the century-old attitudes aimed at the exclusion of the Chinese and Japanese, although the anti-Vietnamese sentiments were certainly informed not only by the usual American racism against Asians and the economic recession of the 1970s and 1980s, but also by the frustration many Americans felt over losing the war. Many people irrationally blamed the refugees, and often people could not differentiate between the refugees—citizens of America's former ally country, the RVN—and the former enemy, the Viet Cong. This confusion is portrayed in Louis Malle's 1985 film, *Alamo Bay.*

Despite its shortcomings, *Alamo Bay* stands alone among American films in taking notice of the Vietnamese immigrant community in a serious and sympathetic way. The film was inspired by real events that took place on the Gulf coast of Texas between 1979 and 1981. A Vietnamese immigrant, Dinh, arrives in Port Alamo. He meets Glory, who helps her father run his wholesale shrimp business. Shang, a Viet Nam veteran, is about to have his new shrimping boat repossessed by the bank. Dinh, a "Saigon fancy boy," is taken in by the Vietnamese community and learns shrimping. There is tension between the Vietnamese American and Euro-American shrimpers. Louis, the one Mexican American who works for Glory's father, tells Dinh, "This is a gringo bay."

Shang's boat is repossessed, and he turns to crabbing from a skiff. Dinh is also crabbing. Shang, insisting the Bay belongs to whites, shoots at him and wrecks his boat. Armed patrols of boats with men in Ku Klux Klan robes and Confederate flags flying drive the Vietnamese fishermen from the bay. The Vietnamese, except Dinh and his partner, Ben, leave town. Dinh talks Glory into renting him a boat and staying in business. In a night raid, Shang and two other men burn the boat. Ben shoots one of Shang's boys; Shang shoots Ben. Glory returns just as Shang is beating Dinh to death; Glory picks up Dinh's gun and shoots Shang.

Alamo Bay is unique in that it tries to deal seriously with relations between

Vietnamese and Euro-Americans. Interestingly, it was made by a French director, although Malle made the film for an American studio. The film is devastating in its portrayal of deep American ignorance of politics. At a town meeting a woman mistakes the South Vietnamese refugees for their former enemies: "My boy fought the VC over there, and now they're right here in Texas taking the bread out of our mouths."

The film shows that the trouble stems from these immigrants being not too different from the Americans, but rather too similar—they are budding capitalists. Dinh's ambition is to own his own boat, run his own business. A minister at the town meeting suggests to the Vietnamese priest that perhaps the problems could be solved if only the Vietnamese would not work so hard. The film does contain eloquent scenes of people who do physical work; the scenes show both the dignity and the cost of that work. It also depicts a marked contrast between the working styles of the immigrants, who fish in groups, in dilapidated boats, hauling in the nets by hand, and the Euro-Americans, such as Shang, who works alone on a large, expensive boat, pulling in his nets with a hydraulic winch.

Shang is portrayed as a stereotypical redneck—complete with gunrack on his truck, baseball cap with a Confederate flag, and a tattoo on his arm—who says to his wife, "You got knocked up so I'd marry you, then you knocked yourself up again." It is hard to understand the now-urbanized Glory's attraction to him. The film depicts it as more than purely sexual—she confesses to Dinh that she has been obsessed with Shang for fifteen years, ever since high school. But Glory has been out of Port Alamo for several years, living in Corpus Christi, which she describes as a different world. Dinh is portrayed as trying to assimilate. He says "Howdy" and "Have a nice day," buys a cowboy hat, and teaches the Vietnamese kids how to play baseball.

Alamo Bay backs away from one of the most important tensions it sets up, the triangle among Shang, Glory, and Dinh. The film cannot quite transcend its own boundaries. Dinh is obviously attracted to Glory, and he names his boat after her. When Shang sees Glory talking to Dinh, he questions her. Glory says, "He's just some kid that works for me," denying any possible sexual attraction between them by emphasizing the age difference between them, although Dinh is clearly an adult, not a kid. Shang replies, "Do you go down on him, too?" revealing his sexual jealousy and his basic possessiveness: he does not want to share "his" bay or "his" woman with any Vietnamese. The film remains careful, however, not to let the Glory-Dinh side of the triangle develop. Glory's attitude toward Dinh remains akin to a female version of paternalism. When she shoots Shang at the end of the film, she is clearly not choosing Dinh over Shang as a romantic partner. Rather, the film offers the usual American rewriting of the situation, turning the conflict into Americans versus Americans, in the persons of Shang and Glory, and leaving the Vietnamese character powerless, marginal, and not part of his own fight. The film also fails to truly humanize the Vietnamese community. While Dinh is a major, and sympathetic, character, none of the other Vietnamese characters plays a significant role. The glimpses the film gives into the Vietnamese community keep the viewer at a distance, partially because the Vietnamese characters always speak in Vietnamese and no subtitles are provided. Context provides clues to the probable nature of their conversations, but we, as viewers, remain outsiders to their community, just as the Vietnamese and Euro-American communities in the film remain outsiders to one another.

Yet, as Tollefson points out, "Americans and Indochinese have in common . . . shared suffering in the war and its aftermath, and no two groups symbolize that shared suffering more than the Indochinese refugees and America's Vietnam veterans" (265). Tollefson traces the changing attitudes toward U.S. veterans and the eventual recognition that "the vets are us," but "for most Americans the refugees are not us" (276).

The Quiet American

Before turning to American works about the war in Viet Nam, I want to examine Graham Greene's novel *The Quiet American*. Although Greene is British, *The Quiet American* received extensive attention when it was published in the United States and has continued to serve as a sort of foundation document for American literature about the war (at least the "higher" culture literature). John Clark Pratt used York Harding, a character who is mentioned but never actually appears in *The Quiet American*, as a major character in his 1974 novel *The Laotian Fragments*. Michael Herr, in *Dispatches*, assumes his readers will understand the reference to Alden Pyle and *The Quiet American* when he writes,

Maybe it was already over for us in Indochina when Alden Pyle's body washed up under the bridge at Dakao, his lungs all full of mud; maybe it caved in with Dien Bien Phu. But the first happened in a novel, and while the second happened on the ground it happened to the French, and Washington gave it no more substance than if Graham Greene had made it up, too. (51)

William Broyles uses *The Quiet American* as a device to make meaning out of 1984 return journey to Viet Nam: "After breakfast we drove to Phat Diem. . . . A scene from Graham Greene's *The Quiet American* takes place there" (65). He goes on to describe the scene of Pyle coming to where Fowler is "trapped . . . during a Viet Minh raid," to declare his love for Fowler's girlfriend, Phuong. Broyles continues, " 'I never knew a man,' Fowler muses, in a line that would describe America's entire history in Vietnam, 'who had better motives for all the trouble he caused' " (65). Gloria Emerson writes that *The Quiet American* was the "first great warning against American involvement."[21]

These and other writers place *The Quiet American* in an almost sanctified place, as precursor and prophet, investing the novel with the almost mystical power to have predicted the entire course of the American war in Viet Nam. Richard Drinnon writes of Greene's book, "And of course it was hardly a decade later that Indochina was very nearly swamped by Pyles who streamed in by the hundreds of thousands. Only a novelist of genius could have caught so perceptively the inner meaning of their coming while they were still far beyond the horizon" (418). With so much American cultural history invested in this novel, it is worth looking at closely, particularly since, although it is praised highly by writers of the Center and the Left, it exhibits nothing but colonialist attitudes, especially in its depiction of the Vietnamese. If it is a model for post-facto thinking about American involvement in the war, it is also a model for an entire segment of Euro-American portrayals of the Vietnamese—that segment which I identify as attempts to break the stereotypes that nonetheless fail.

The Quiet American (first published in 1955; 1956 in the United States) is set in 1952, during the First Indochina War. It concerns two major characters: Fowler, the narrator, is a British journalist in Saigon, and Pyle, the quiet American, works for an aid organization that is a cover for the CIA. Both are in love with a Vietnamese woman, Phuong, who has been living with Fowler, a married man, until Pyle wins her away with the offer of marriage and life in the United States. Pyle is importing "plastics" into Viet Nam, which are, in reality, plastique explosive, which he supplies to General The. Pyle sees The as the leader of the "third force" he believes must rule Viet Nam—neither French nor Communist. He comes to this belief through books by a theorist, York Harding, who writes from the distance of his Harvard University sanctuary. After a bombing in a public square in Saigon in which women and children are killed, Fowler betrays Pyle to the Communists, who kill him. Fowler does this because, in the words of his Communist contact, Mr. Heng, "One has to take sides—if one is to remain human" (168).

The book was roundly criticized at its initial American publication for its anti-Americanism. As John Hellmann reports in *American Myth and the Legacy of Vietnam*: "Nathan A. Scott in *Christian Century* called it 'gross nonsense'. . . . and A.J. Liebling in the *New Yorker* dismissed it as an 'exercise in national projection' by a member of the British Empire history had passed by" (15). Richard Drinnon, in *Facing West*, also reports some of the negative reviews:

> American reviewers of *The Quiet American* could hardly believe "the malice toward the United States that controls the novel"—*Christian Century*, August 1, 1956. "Its two principal characters are so fantastic that one is half inclined to suspect that the whole thing has been devised as an elaborate leg-pulling"—*New York Herald Tribune*, March 11, 1956. "It is hard to know whether the author is presenting a thesis or a burlesque"—*Christian Science Monitor*, March 22, 1956. (417–18)

When it was made into an American movie (by Joseph Mankiewicz), the plot was changed from anti-American to anti-Communist. (In the film, Pyle is importing plastic, not plastique, and Fowler is a dupe of the Communists who betrays Pyle out of jealousy.)

Greene said in an interview that he "would go to almost any length to put my feeble twig in the spoke of American foreign policy."[22] *The Quiet American* is one of his "twigs," but his objections are based on an abstract and general sort of moral stance which does not require him to form a clear picture of Viet Nam itself.

Indeed, critics have concentrated on Greene's moral purpose rather than on his portrayal of Viet Nam and the Vietnamese. Miriam Allott writes that Greene "succeeds in reminding us that we need Pyle's courage and none of his ignorance, Fowler's moral intelligence and none of his indecisiveness, if we are to find a way out of the alarming difficulties which as nations and individuals we are most of us nowadays required to face" (206). Allott does not define the "alarming difficulties," and it is this very lack of definition which allows Greene to be seen as entirely moral.

Ray Snape writes that Greene's "novels do uniformly evidence a sympathy with the underdogs, the wronged, the exploited, the oppressed, and with those simply ignored . . . it's important to stress that this commitment to the underdog is not a sentimental but an angry one; and Greene's vituperative newsworthiness, which is a salient quality of the political fiction, is not to be despised" (74). Greene does clearly conceptualize the situation in Indochina as one in which he sets himself up as the spokesperson for the Vietnamese "underdogs." He shows no recognition that by presenting them as underdogs he has already done them a disservice. There is nothing in the novel which suggests that Greene favors a radical overthrow of colonialism. He prefers to keep the Vietnamese in a subordinate place—he simply does not like to see them wantonly slaughtered.

At least one critic seriously misreads the novel by focusing on Greene's moral stance to the exclusion of a recognition of the colonial dynamics that inform the book. A. A. DeVitis reduces *The Quiet American* to "the relationships that ultimately form the meaning of the novel" (110). He makes what I consider to be a vital misreading of a key incident in the novel. "Fowler and Pyle," he writes, "respect and discover a reciprocal appreciation of each other's basic integrity and goodness. . . . They come to an appreciation of one another as good men in the scene in which they are attacked by guerrillas as they shelter in a sentry hut on the outskirts of Phat-Diem" (111).

In the scene DeVitis refers to, Pyle and Fowler, on the way back to Saigon after attending a Cao Dai festival, run out of gasoline. The sentry hut DeVitis mentions is really a guard tower, one of many on the road to Saigon, built by the French and staffed by Vietnamese soldiers. Pyle and Fowler take refuge in the tower with two frightened Vietnamese soldiers with whom, lacking a common language, they cannot communicate. Enemy soldiers arrive with a megaphone and demand that the two Vietnamese in the tower turn Pyle and Fowler over. Pyle and Fowler flee, Fowler breaks his leg falling from the ladder, the tower is rocketed, Pyle carries Fowler to the safety of a rice paddy, then goes for help. Contrary to DeVitis's assumption, however, neither man comes to "the appreciation of one another as good men." Fowler says of Pyle, "We had spent what seemed to have been a week of nights together, but he could no more understand me than he could understand French" (104). When Pyle admits to saving Fowler for Phuong's sake, Fowler's jealousy speaks: "In love we are incapable of honor—the courageous act is no more than playing a part with an audience of two" (105). Finally, Fowler thinks of the Vietnamese soldier in the rocketed tower: "Poor devil, if we hadn't broken down outside *his* post, he could have surrendered as they nearly all surrendered" (105; italics in original). Earlier, Pyle, in possession of a Sten gun, had proposed shooting the guards, to which Fowler objected. There is no recognition of each other as "good men."

DeVitis has misinterpreted something else that Fowler says, elsewhere:

"Was I the only one who cared for Pyle?" (22). Yes, Fowler cared about Pyle, and perhaps saw him as a well-meaning man, but saw in his actions that he was an evil man. It is Pyle's actions that make him evil, no matter how good his intentions, and it is Fowler's recognition of that evil that motivates his actions. Pyle's effect on the world is the most important point for Fowler, and for Greene. This is the whole political stance of the novel. Pyle's actions had to be stopped, because he was doing moral (rather than political) wrong, whether or not he was a nice guy.

Note that Fowler does regard Pyle as an equal—as a formidable man capable of doing great evil, as a strong rival for Phuong's affections. But Fowler regards the Vietnamese soldier in the tower as a "poor devil"—an incapable, slight person whom Fowler can only regard with pity. Pity seems to be Fowler's main attitude toward the Vietnamese.

Robert Boyers, in *Atrocity and Amnesia: The Political Novel since 1945*, remarks on the similarity of the settings of Greene's political novels, regardless of the country in which they take place: "It little matters where these works are set, that for all their attention to particular detail, their true setting is a region of the mind, their object not the examination of political conflict or the testing of human possibilities but the striking of desirable attitudes or postures" (56). Although Boyers criticizes Greene for not presenting a clear picture of the "sides" available to be taken in the conflict, he concludes that *The Quiet American* is a "minor classic" because of its portrayal of destructive innocence in the person of Pyle.

But there is more that is destructive than Pyle's innocence. Greene's main representation of the Vietnamese centers on the woman Fowler and Pyle both desire. Phuong, whose name, as Fowler points out, means "phoenix," is made to symbolize her country. Through this symbolism we see how seductive the United States can be to "underdeveloped" countries (Phuong is portrayed throughout as innocent, childlike, and naive). The marriage that Pyle offers her is symbolic of the alliance that the United States offers client countries—it is inherently not a marriage of equals. Pyle expects that Phuong will come to live with him in Boston and suit herself to his culture. He makes no attempt to suit himself to hers. The two can barely communicate, because Pyle speaks neither French nor Vietnamese and Phuong's English is only rudimentary. In one scene, Fowler must translate Pyle's declaration of love and proposal of marriage into French for Phuong. (Note that although Fowler does speak French, he speaks no Vietnamese, but understands a little. The Asian must always accommodate herself to the superstrate power, never vice versa.)

This unequal marriage is one of the devices Greene uses to comment on the relationship between Viet Nam and the European and American powers, and is a sympathetic portrayal of Viet Nam, meant to mediate against Western interference. However, it is a belittling and condescending representation. The use of a woman as this symbol and the sexual nature of the relationship between Phuong and the men is endemic to American representations of Asians. The Asian woman is used to represent relative helplessness, naïveté, inferiority, and subservience.

Overall, Greene's critique is only of American involvement in Indochina—it is not a critique of colonialism as a whole, and it is not a representation of Viet Nam and Vietnamese as a fully developed culture and fully developed individuals.

Richard West performs a little debunking of *The Quiet American*'s status as an icon of the American Left. He points out that Fowler tends to side with the French, quoting what Fowler tells Pyle: "I'd rather be an exploiter who fights for what he exploits, and dies with it" (49); West also notes that Greene's own views, as reflected in his journalism, were "more pro-French and anti-Communist than those he attributes to Fowler" (49). West also attacks Greene's portrayal of Vigot, the sensitive and philosophical French policeman, as unbelievable: "The French police in Indochina systematically locked up, tortured, and even killed political suspects. Many were brutes who would not have read a Simenon story, let alone Pascal. French Indochina had been from the start a commercial racket, exploiting virtually forced labor to work in the paddy fields, mines, and rubber plantations" (50).

By pointing out Greene's romanticization of French colonialism, West opens the way for an important insight about how Greene viewed the Vietnamese. Greene's views of the Vietnamese were filtered through his admiration for the French. Greene's siding with the French is a clear theme in the book. The French "were, when all was said, fighting this war" (23). Fowler feels sympathy for a French colonel giving a briefing: "After all it was their war, not ours. We had no God-given right to information. We didn't have to fight Left-Wing deputies in Paris as well as the troops of Ho Chi Minh between the Red and the Black Rivers. We were not dying" (65). Fowler does not examine the worthiness of the war being fought, and although later he objects to Pyle's involvement in the killing of Vietnamese civilians, his sympathy in the quoted passage is all for the French soldiers who are dying, not for the Vietnamese.

West quotes the discussion between Fowler and Pyle when they are stranded in the roadside watchtower on the road to Saigon.

Fowler tells Pyle that the Vietnamese peasants are only concerned with getting their rice, to which Pyle says they want to think for themselves. "Thought's a luxury," Fowler replies. "Do you think the peasant sits and thinks of God and Democracy when he gets inside his mud hut at night?"

. . . Although I once spent three weeks making a film in a Delta village . . . I would not set myself up as an expert on [the peasants'] thinking. However, I found those I met interested in the outside world, and, like most Vietnamese peasants then and now, they were avid listeners to the BBC's broadcasts. (51)

West accurately analyses Fowler's attitude as one of colonialist condescension toward the Vietnamese peasantry. I would add that part of Fowler's motivation is projection—he would like his own life to be simpler; he imagines that the life of the peasantry is simpler, so he can admire and almost envy it from a distance. "From reading *The Quiet American*," West continues, "one would not guess that the Vietnamese had a civilization, literature, and national pride when 'our ancestors the Gauls' were still savages dressed in skins" (51).

Indeed, Greene is a meticulous observer of the surface of Viet Nam and the Vietnamese while remaining ignorant of their depths, as illustrated by the telltale errors he makes. He describes Phuong as "the daughter of a mandarin," then, on the same page, writes:

Phuong on the other hand was wonderfully ignorant; if Hitler had come into the conversation she would have interrupted to ask who he was. The explanation would be all the more difficult because she had never met a German or a Pole and had only the vaguest knowledge of European geography, though about Princess Margaret of course she knew more than I. (12)

Later Phuong thinks the Statue of Liberty is in London. The daughter of a mandarin would not be so "wonderfully ignorant." (Compare, for example, Greene's Phuong with Nguyỹen Thị Thu-Lâm, who is not even the daughter of a mandarin, but of a businessman.) Greene, through the voice of Fowler, is romanticizing and simplifying Phuong, just as he does the peasants. Fowler has had trouble with his wife and with a previous English lover; it is clear that he loves Phuong because he sees her as simple.

Greene reveals his ignorance of Vietnamese culture again when Phuong's sister, Miss Hei, whose main goal is to marry off Phuong to a Westerner, examines Pyle's marriageability. Pyle says his father is a professor, and Miss Hei responds negatively: "'A teacher?' she asked with a faint note of disappointment" (42). She had been hoping he was a businessman. But Vietnamese traditionally regard scholars—professors—as among the most honorable and respectable members of society; Miss Hei should be impressed, not disappointed, with the profession of Pyle's father.

Fowler freezes Asia within "tradition": "I'd bet . . . that in five hundred years there may be no New York or London, but they'll be growing paddy in these fields, they'll be carrying their produce to market on long poles wearing their pointed hats. The small boys will be sitting on buffaloes" (95). Fowler cannot imagine a future Viet Nam in which poverty, in the form of carry-poles and buffaloes, will have been replaced by Hondas and tractors. Viet Nam, to satisfy his own desire for "simplicity," must be forever frozen.

Pyle, too, holds a paternalistic attitude toward Viet Nam. When he declares to Fowler his love for Phuong he says, "I want to protect her" (132). In another conversation Pyle says,

". . . These people aren't complicated."
"Is that what you've learned in a few months? You'll be calling them childlike next."
"Well—in a way."

Fowler then criticizes Pyle's attitude, yet he has been displaying a similar stance throughout the novel. Fowler says to Pyle:

"She's no child. She's tougher than you'll ever be. Do you know the kind of polish that doesn't take scratches? That's Phuong. She can survive a dozen of us. She'll get old, that's all. She'll suffer from childbirth and hunger and cold and rheumatism, but she'll never suffer like we do from thoughts, obsessions—she won't scratch, she'll only decay." But even while I made my speech and watched her . . . I knew I was inventing a character just as much as Pyle was. One never knows another human being; for all I could tell, she was as scared as the rest of us; she didn't have the gift of expression, that was all. (133)

Fowler first constructs a picture of Phuong as the inscrutable Oriental, but then he repudiates it and recognizes that he is making her up even as he speaks. He comes to the conclusion that he cannot know what she is really thinking, however, because "she didn't have the gift of expression." Rather than seeing Phuong's reticence as a cultural difference, he sees her as lacking something that he sees both himself and Pyle, as Westerners, possessing. Thus, he pictures her whole culture as lacking a "gift" which he values.

In a pattern that will be repeated many times in Euro-American literature about Viet Nam, the narrative tends to describe Vietnamese in terms of plants and animals. Phuong "was indigenous like a herb" (14). To make the picture complete, Fowler even says of the Vietnamese, "They looked so much alike" (178).

Greene's success in seducing readers and critics has been large. Despite his Orientalist, procolonialist views, Greene is a persuasive writer. Philip Melling, a British critic, writes in his book *Vietnam in American Literature*: "Fowler tries to encounter the East through observation in order to appreciate the naturist mysticism of the country and the communal identity of the Vietnamese" (91). Yet Melling's own characterization of Viet Nam and the Vietnamese is Orientalist. Melling discusses in detail not Greene's book, but American critical reactions to it: "The critic Gordon Taylor sees *The Quiet American* as 'an established point of reference for those interested in problems of literary response to the war' (note the assumption that Greene is responding to the war rather than to the Vietnamese or to the conflict of values that might exist between those who live in Vietnam and those who merely visit it)" (91). While Melling properly critiques Taylor's view that later American narratives (especially those that place America and American personal experiences, rather than Viet Nam, at the center of their consciousness) have definitively replaced *The Quiet American*, Melling's implied characterization of Greene as a proper spokesperson for the Vietnamese is not viable. Melling declares: "The tragedy of indifference is the continuing tragedy of the war itself: the failure to recognize that the war in Vietnam belongs to the country, not the country to the war. For Graham Greene this was the problem that lay at the heart of the American dilemma in Indochina" (95). Although Melling is clearly right in his first assertion, he is off base in attributing such sentiments to Greene, who, as shown earlier, was concerned with the French position in the war, not the Vietnamese. For Greene, the war of which he wrote was not in Viet Nam at all; it was in French Indochina.

The critics and writers who see Greene as setting the agenda for American writing about the war are in part correct. If he has not clearly set the agenda for subsequent American writers, he has at least exemplified the cultural paradigm out of which most of them write.

In the next chapter I turn to Euro-American works about the war. Some of them are thoroughly caught up in the same Orientalist paradigms from which Greene writes; some attempt but fail to make the leap of perspective that would take them outside those paradigms. A few genuinely break out of the hegemonic American worldview and produce new insights that create biculturality in the same way the Vietnamese exile writings do; thus they create new perspectives on the American war in Viet Nam and its aftermath in the United States for both Americans and immigrants—perspectives that stress the idea of communality rather than the hegemonic, monocultural American worldview.

FOUR

Euro-American Representations
of the Vietnamese

This effort to make sense of the Vietnamese experience has
prompted an outpouring of creative writing. . . . This new
literature will shape how Americans view the Vietnam experience
and our relations with Vietnam and Asia.
                                        —Timothy Lomperis, *"Reading the Wind"*

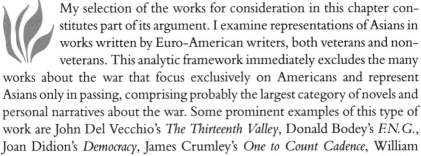 My selection of the works for consideration in this chapter con-
stitutes part of its argument. I examine representations of Asians in
works written by Euro-American writers, both veterans and nonveterans. This analytic framework immediately excludes the many
works about the war that focus exclusively on Americans and represent
Asians only in passing, comprising probably the largest category of novels and
personal narratives about the war. Some prominent examples of this type of
work are John Del Vecchio's *The Thirteenth Valley*, Donald Bodey's *F.N.G.*,
Joan Didion's *Democracy*, James Crumley's *One to Count Cadence*, William
Holland's *Let a Soldier Die*, Nicholas Proffitt's *Gardens of Stone*, Jayne Anne
Philips's *Machine Dreams*, Danielle Steel's *Message from Nam*, John Irving's *A
Prayer for Owen Meany*, Norman Mailer's *Why Are We in Vietnam?* and works
that take place in America after the war, such as Bobbie Ann Mason's *In
Country*, Philip Caputo's *Indian Country*, R. Lanny Hunter and Victor Hun-
ter's *Living Dogs and Dead Lions*, David Morrell's *First Blood*, and Newton
Thornburg's *Cutter and Bone*. The list could go on and on.

I have constructed this list both deliberately and randomly. It is a mixture
of the famous and the unknown, of enduring works and throwaway works,
of books by veterans, by antiwar activists, by nonveterans, by men, and by
women. The main commonality among these works, besides the bare fact of
being "about" the war in one way or another, is their focus on America and
Americans, to the near total exclusion of Viet Nam and Vietnamese. As far as
most of these works are concerned, the war might have taken place in

Arizona. The problem is not that many American works focus on America—certainly the effect of the war on the United States is a legitimate subject for representations. Neither is the problem that individual American writers are ethnocentric. The problem is that the American cultural paradigm erects a totalizing vision which demands an America-centric focus to the extent that almost all works about the war share it. Only a tiny fraction take a bicultural point of view, and none of those is within the canon.

The most obvious example of this common ethnocentric attitude is exemplified by one of the most famous works in my list: Mailer's *Why Are We in Vietnam?*, a novel that never sets foot in Viet Nam. It substitutes big-game hunting in Alaska for the war, in an effort to explore what it is about the American character that makes the United States go adventuring into foreign wars. While this is an interesting, perhaps even vital, inquiry, it is only part of the story. Nonetheless, it has been taken as a "true" portrait of the war in some circles. For example, Philip Beidler wrote that it "*is* Vietnam, summoned up at its very springs in the American soul" (*American Literature* 42).

Exploring the American reasons why America became involved in the war in Viet Nam may, someday, explain the motivation for post–World War II America to conduct its foreign policy as it did. But that exploration will never explain what happened after the United States committed its resources to backing its puppet government in Saigon in a war against communism (as the United States envisioned that war). To say that the progress of the war can be understood by understanding one side only is to deny the agency, the presence, of the Vietnamese on both sides of that war. In other words, it denies the possibility of communality by denying the significance of the existence of the Vietnamese. This point of view is a version of the us-them legacy of imperialism I examined in chapter 3.

Those American works that depart from the norm and provide extensive portrayals of Vietnamese can be divided into three categories, which are reflected in the three subsections of this chapter. The first section, "Same Old, Same Old," examines the category into which the largest number of works fall—those that replicate the history of stereotyping examined in chapter 3. This section defines the attitude of superiority that these works take toward Viet Nam and Vietnamese, first establishing the framework in which to understand these representations by examining passages from a variety of books. I then turn to a series of repetitive patterns in print media representations, including the image of Viet Nam as a "second rate" place, not worth fighting for, and the paternalistic representation of Vietnamese as "little brown brothers" and prostitutes. The section ends with an in-depth examination of three representative works—Lederer and Burdick's *The Ugly American*, Robin Moore's *The Green Berets*, and Larry Heinemann's *Close Quarters*—emphasizing the ways in which racist portrayals of Vietnamese persist across time, across political orientation, and across the experiential positioning of the author.

The second section, "Trying, but Failing, to Break the Mold," looks at Euro-American works that, even while they remain America-centered, attempt to counteract American stereotypes of Vietnamese, but fall back into the ethnocentric paradigms they attempt to transcend. This section addresses Philip Caputo's and Robert Mason's frustrated efforts, in their personal narratives, to understand the Vietnamese they encounter and takes as its major examples Tim Mahoney's *We're Not Here* and Tim O'Brien's *Going after Cacciato*, which attempt to critique American ignorance of Viet Nam through the use of central Vietnamese characters, who nonetheless remain stereotypes. I next discuss James Webb's *Fields of Fire*, which includes in its "melting-pot platoon" a Vietnamese scout who, although he becomes a sympathetic character, is cut from cardboard. Susan Fromberg Schaeffer's novel *Buffalo Afternoon* is one of the first attempts to tell part of the story from a Vietnamese point of view, but the Vietnamese character, Li, remains a creation of ethnocentric myth. I end the section with an account of John Casey's *Spartina*, a novel not about the war, which brings a Vietnamese immigrant character into its multiethnic milieu, but is marred by its treatment of that character.

The final section of this chapter, "Subtracting the Fear from the Landscape," examines an extraordinary set of Euro-American works which take as their starting point the assumption that the war is a shared experience of Americans and Vietnamese, and that only the sort of recognition of communality demanded by the Vietnamese exile writers can produce both personal healing and political/historical coherence. This section begins with a reading of the poetry of Bruce Weigl and the poetry and prose of W. D. Ehrhart and John Balaban, all of whom work through their writing to produce new, bicultural portrayals of Vietnamese. Lloyd Little's early novel, *Parthian Shot*, presents nonstereotyped Vietnamese characters. Wayne Karlin's *Lost Armies* is a stunning novel which insists that American and Vietnamese veterans are part of one another; the mystery plot of the novel depends on American and Vietnamese characters assuming one another's identities. Finally, I examine the work of Robert Olen Butler, the Euro-American veteran writer who has turned out the largest body of work that recognizes the communality of Americans and Vietnamese.

Same Old, Same Old

Vietnam . . . [was] a two-lane highway, one for the Vietnamese and
one for the Americans, with no intersections.
            —Bernard Kalb and Marvin Kalb, *The Last Ambassador*

The experience of the Vietnamese is closed to us . . . You are asking
people to evoke, in art, experiences which were in reality very
distant.
            —William Broyles, quoted in Lomperis, *"Reading the Wind"*

The impulse to leave the Other alone rejoins the impulse to
obliterate the Other on the ground they have in common: the
inability to describe something outside the self, to see, in Clifford
Geertz's words, "ourselves among others."
            —Christopher L. Miller, "Theories of Africans"

"This isn't civilization. This is Nam."
            —Tim O'Brien, "How to Tell a True War Story"

Timothy Lomperis writes of the representation of Vietnamese in Euro-
American literature about the war:

The images of Asians presented in the literature are so muted that there really are
no dominant images. Thus if any misperceptions of the Vietnamese have grown
out of the literature, they have come most fundamentally from the literature's
very lack of perceptions of the Vietnamese. In the literature to date, they are
either simple and childlike or devious and treacherous, which is to say mysterious—which is to say nothing. (74)

In other words, for most Euro-American works, the representation of Vietnamese differs not at all from the most common presentations of Asians
in the history of American literature that we have seen in the preceding
chapter. Edward Said puts it this way: "Every writer on the Orient . . .
assumes some Oriental precedent, some previous knowledge of the Orient,
to which he refers and on which he relies" (*Orientalism* 20). The previous
knowledge on which most Euro-American writers of the war rely is the
paradigm about "Orientals" that has informed American culture since the
nineteenth century.

American ignorance about Asia and Asians can be connected to the history of American imperialism, as Lomperis describes:

In recounting a roughly similar record of blindness in the American interaction in East Asia over two centuries, James C. Thomson, Jr., Peter Stanley, and John Perry conclude in their recent book that the recurring theme in this interaction, whether from the right or the left, is one of "virtually invincible ignorance" (1981, p. 309). This is in large part because, in the central contention of their book, American imperialism was not due to a bloodlust for territory or conquest, or, for that matter, for plunder or economic advantage; rather, for the Americans "their inexhaustible fuel was sentiment" (p. 311). Hence their title, *Sentimental Imperialists.* Unfortunately, sentiment requires only good intentions, not information. Indeed, too much information may be too confusing to these intentions.

It is sad to have to say that, with respect to Asia and the Vietnam War, literature, in the main, has only compounded this political ignorance. (105).

Indeed, some of the portrayals of Vietnamese most guilty of ignorance seem to be those most informed by the type of sentiment Thomson, Stanley, and Perry describe. Lederer and Burdick's *The Ugly American* and Robin Moore's *The Green Berets* are excellent examples of this sentiment—they are novels infused with a desire to "save" Viet Nam and equally infused with total ignorance of and blindness to Viet Nam. As Thomson, Stanley, and Perry argue, that ignorance seems to be invincible; I would add that it is, at times, also willful and self-righteous. As Lomperis suggests, literature, which might have served a transformative function, has largely failed to do so in terms of the American war in Viet Nam. As Edward Said writes, "Orientalism is . . . a considerable dimension of modern political-intellectual culture, and as such has less to do with the Orient than it does with 'our' world (*Orientalism* 12).

Lomperis attributes much of the attitude of invincible ignorance in the literature to existentialism:

Existentialism developed in the West, and there is the prosaic fact, then, that the people espousing this philosophy were from politically powerful and materially wealthy societies. As they scrutinized themselves, they ignored others. Perhaps it was not the same studied and racist ignorance of the classic imperial sahib, but they demeaned other people, including those of other societies, by viewing them, in philosophic and indeed in existential terms, as "non-persons." This "ignorance" received its most insensitive expression in Albert Camus's *The Stranger* (1954). (106)

Clearly, however, as shown in the preceding chapter, Americans' Orientalist and imperialist attitudes toward Asians long predate the development of existentialism. Although Lomperis's analysis may help to shed extra light on some of the elite-culture writers (especially Tim O'Brien), it is inadequate as a general analysis of the bulk of the Euro-American Viet Nam War literature.

Realism is not a cure for racism: some of the most grittily realist of narratives of the American war in Viet Nam are guiltiest of overtly racist portrayals. Veterans sometimes defend racist representations of Vietnamese with the phrase, "That's the way it was." I attempt to show here that what appears to be "realism" is conditioned by the cultural attitudes of the writers (and readers) of these texts. American service people brought their cultures with them to Viet Nam, and they viewed that country and its people through the lenses their culture had created for them. As Paul Fussell puts it, "One notices and remembers what one has been 'coded'—usually by literature or its popular equivalent—to notice and remember" (*Great War* 247). An American might not have noticed and remembered the same thing as a Vietnamese present at the same event would have, because the American and the Vietnamese brought different cultural codings with them.[1]

Further, because most Americans' historical and political knowledge is extremely limited, when they noticed and remembered something, they may not have understood how what they saw got to be the way it was. An excellent example of this "failure of seeing" is the passage mentioned earlier from Le Ly Hayslip's autobiography in which she explains why human waste was used to fertilize rice fields. Americans "really saw" this happening, but their understanding of it was conditioned by preconceived notions of how Asians are—primitive, childlike, barbaric—rather than by sufficient historical knowledge, which would have told them what Hayslip, twenty years after the war, tells them—that the practice arose because the American war killed all the animals that had previously supplied manure fertilizer.

Jon Forrest Glade addresses this failure of seeing in a poem:

> All these years later,
> I think the problem
> was not with our film,
> or our eyes, or our minds,
> but with our anticipations.
> We weren't looking for beauty in Vietnam
> and consequently couldn't see it. (79)

It is one of the tragedies of the war that most Americans did not see any beauty in Viet Nam, or any humanity; this blindness, in turn, intensified the war so that it replicated the racist conditions of the war in the Pacific.

Richard Drinnon, in his study of American racism and its fatal consequences, *Facing West: the Metaphysics of Indian-Hating and Empire-Building*,
draws a connection between America's eighteenth- and nineteenth-century
westward expansion and resulting treatment of the Indians, and America's
twentieth-century imperialism and treatment of Asians in the Philippines
and Viet Nam. He describes how perceptions of Asians were conflated with
perceptions of Indians, and how both were identified as primitive, savage,
Stone Age, and subhuman (and therefore available for extinction). Quoting
from both fictional representations and official U.S. government documents,
Drinnon shows how Americans perceived the Vietnamese. "Never for a
moment was the superiority of the norms of the West questioned," he
writes. "Natives existed to be manipulated and hoodwinked. . . . Feigned
concern for their culture helped mask the cold warriors' contempt for their
'Stone Age' existence (379). Drinnon notes how John Mecklin, in his book
Mission in Torment,

drew on the accumulated racial arrogance of three centuries to depict the illiter-
ate peasant as cut off from "civilization." He had an untrained mind that "atro-
phies like the shriveled leg of a polio victim. His vocabulary is limited to a few
hundred words. His power of reason, the greatest of nature's gifts to mankind,
develops only slightly beyond the level of an American six year-old, because it is
never trained." (449)

That is, never trained in American modes. Mecklin and Americans like him
would probably be shocked to consider that Vietnamese considered Americans equally uncivilized and untrained.

The army had in force the M.G.R.—the "Mere Gook Rule"—which,
according to Drinnon, systematized the Americans' assessment of natives as
less than full human beings. He finds this informal rule to have been codified
in the army's original indictment of Lieutenant Calley for the My Lai massacre, which stated that Calley had murdered at least 102 "Oriental human beings." Drinnon wonders, "How many 'Oriental human beings' were
equal to one real human being?" (455).

The attitudes described by Drinnon originate in the process of stereotyping Asians. Sander Gilman writes:

Since all of the images of the Other derive from the same deep structure, various
signs of difference can be linked without any recognition of inappropriateness,
contradictoriness, or even impossibility. Patterns of association are most com-

monly based, however, on a combination of real-life experience (as filtered through the models of perception) and the world of myth, and the two intertwine to form fabulous images, neither entirely of this world nor of the realm of myth. The analogizing essential to this process functions much like systems of metaphor. Since analogies are rooted in a habitual perception of the world, they are understood as an adequate representation of reality. The mental representation that results, of course, divides the world into categories in accordance with stereotypical perception. All experience can thus be measured against this "reality," and since this experience is structured through a system of mental representations in precisely the same way as was the overall structure of the world, the experience reifies the stereotypical image of the world. (21)

For many Americans, the experience of going to Viet Nam seems to have reified their preexisting, stereotypical, view of the world. Gilman's explanation of this phenomenon is useful in helping us understand the sorts of representations examined in this section.

The Americans who fought in the war in Viet Nam and came home and wrote books about it grew up in a culture permeated by the representation of Asians as lesser humans or as nonhumans. Since the Americans were immersed in this culture, it is not surprising that their writings usually represent Asians in terms of the limited stock of stereotypes the culture has made available. The canon-formation process also has an effect on the prevailing representation of Asians in that there are so few works by writers of color that have been published or widely circulated. A study reported by B. G. Fiman, J. F. Borus, and M. D. Stanton shows that "many whites viewed the Vietnamese as lazy, deceptive, cowardly, and subhuman. Blacks were reported to hold a less prejudiced and more respectful view of the Vietnamese" (42).[2]

Much of the writing by veterans of the war can be seen as a working out of their war experience in an attempt to come to an understanding of it on individual terms, an understanding that our culture as a whole has not provided. Robert Weimann writes: "The process of making certain things one's own becomes inseparable from making other things (and persons) alien, so that the act of appropriation must be seen always already to involve not only self-projection and assimilation but alienation through reification and expropriation" (184). We have seen this process in the prewar history of the representation of Asians. It happens again in representations of the American war in Viet Nam. Americans, veterans and nonveterans alike, in attempting to make that war their own, have done so at the expense of portraying the Vietnamese in stereotypical, limited, and predetermined ways. Weimann contends that representational art thrives on loss and that it may be about closure and recuperation. If America's representations of the war so far are "recuperation," then that process is, for the most part, at the expense of the Vietnamese, just as the war was fought at their expense, on their soil.

Americans were very confused by the Vietnamese and often seemingly unaware of the contradictory positions this confusion caused them to take. Richard Drinnon reports that Gen. Maxwell Taylor, ambassador to the Republic of Viet Nam, ascribed the South Vietnamese lack of unity to racial characteristics, "but then marvelled at the phoenix-like power of the VC to regroup" (369–70). Other contradictory positions, discussed later, include the American tendency simultaneously to see the Vietnamese as helpless, yet to fear them, to see Vietnamese women as dangerous yet alluring, and to discover the proximity of death and yet displace it onto the Vietnamese.

One way representations of the war draw the reader into a world of racism is through their collapsing of fact and fiction. Susan Jeffords writes:

The position of the reader/viewer/soldier in Vietnam narrative is constructed by the (con)fusion of the status of fact and fiction. The resulting paralysis of response can then be overlaid by the "new" "facts" of the narrative: "they" become "we," the viewers and participants slide together. There are three stages to this process: denying previous concepts of fact, offering the narrator/author as authority/guide for the new definitions of fact, and having the narrator/author predetermine and occupy the reader's position. All work toward positioning the reader in a kind of paralysis in relation to textual interpretation. (30)

Through that interpretive paralysis, many American readers have come to accept the virulent racism of the majority of U.S. works representing American experiences in the war. Because the veteran author is imbued with so much authority by virtue of having "been there," his perceptions must be accepted as accurate, including the racist bias of his representations of Vietnamese. Jeffords goes on to remark that the "very subject and method of Vietnam representation is difference. . . . The most obvious expression of difference in Vietnam representation, and often therefore apparently that of least notice, is gender" (49). While I agree substantially with Jeffords's analysis, I argue that an equally obvious expression of difference is racism. As Jeffords shows in *The Remasculinization of America*, the issue of race among Americans is deemphasized in Viet Nam War representations. However, racial difference between Americans and Vietnamese is foregrounded as an expression of difference so that it, like the issue of gender, is so obvious as to be invisible.[3]

The representation of Vietnamese as "gooks" who are not human runs throughout the literature. In "How to Tell a True War Story," a short story by Tim O'Brien that originally appeared in *Esquire* magazine, the narrator says of one of the characters, "The guy was a little crazy, for sure, but crazy in a good way, a real daredevil, because he liked the challenge of it, he liked testing himself, just man against gook" (208). The American character is a "man"; the Asian characters are something else, "gooks." In William Pelfrey's novel *The Big V*, the narrator says, "The MPs were frisking the gooks. . . . They were mostly young girls and old men, used as KPs, waitresses, and PX cashiers" (14). Pelfrey's narrator sees all Vietnamese, not just enemy soldiers, as "gooks."

Bill Crownover, an American who worked for a civilian contractor in Viet Nam, is quoted by Harry Maurer in *Strange Ground: Americans in Vietnam 1945–1975: An Oral History* as saying:

I think everybody was that way. I'm a fucking American and you're a goddam gook, so you've got no right to talk to me. Damn silly stupid geeks. Zips. Slopes. Of course, you're in this hazy world, drinking all the time, working all the time, running into the same people all the time. And to you personally as an American it seems the Orientals have their own way of thinking, which they do. They have their own culture, which isn't yours, and you realize, man, they just don't do it this way back in the real world. The terminology, too, will screw you up. "The real world," because you're out here in never-never land, and it doesn't matter what you do in never-never land because it doesn't affect the real world. You very rarely referred to the Vietnamese as Vietnamese. The zips, always the zips. Zips could mean zipper-heads, because someone unzipped his head and dumped all his brains out. Or it could mean zero, which means nothing, which is what they were. The zip mentality. Zip, zip, zip, zip, zip. It was a beautiful word. (497)

Crownover expresses an attitude widespread among Americans in Viet Nam, both soldier and civilian.

Such attitudes are not confined to Americans who traveled to Viet Nam during the war. *American Blood* is a novel by John Nichols, a nonveteran author who has a reputation for writing fine novels about the American southwest which contain nonracist portrayals of Chicano characters. He was not able, however, to create nonracist portrayals of Vietnamese in *American Blood*. Note, first, the title—as usual in American portrayals of the war, American blood is more central than Vietnamese blood.[4]

Nichols started out to write a novel called "American Blood" that would, indeed, be about America: "But what I intended to do was to do an historical novel based on the rise of industrial capitalism in the United States from 1870 to the present. . . . the central metaphor at the heart and the beginning of it was . . . something like the Sand Creek Massacre."[5] The book he ended up writing is about a veteran of the war in Viet Nam,

But *American Blood*'s no more a book about Vietnam than anything else. Vietnam's a handy metaphor. As far as I'm concerned Vietnam is sort of daily translated in our own culture, which didn't change because we left Vietnam because that's not where it had its genesis. If it had any genesis it was when the first pilgrim landed on Plymouth Rock and started heading west committing genocide on the Native American people. (interview transcript)

Superficially, Nichols's argument here seems similar to Richard Drinnon's, but Nichols's argument, as realized in the novel, is deeply implicated in exactly the problem he names and describes himself as writing against: by making the war in Viet Nam nothing but a metaphor, something translated into our culture, we continue to commit the crime.

An incident in the opening chapter of *American Blood* illustrates my point. An American platoon enters a village in a downpour. Everyone seeks shelter, "but this one Vietnamese kid wouldn't get out of the downpour. Maybe because there was a Yankee grunt in the doorway of almost every hooch. Maybe he was retarded. Maybe he was confused. Maybe he was part duck. He was five or six years old, scrawny like they all were, and he just stood in the middle of the muddy plaza" (6). This passage is all over the map. A feeble attempt to see the situation from the child's point of view (the recognition that there are soldiers in all the possible refuges) does not last—the immediate turn is to the suggestion that he might be retarded, and this descends into the sarcasm of the "part duck" remark. An American soldier shoots the little boy.

And there were gooks—'scuse me, Vietnamese human beings—huddled around, too, sheltering under whatever. Wrinkled papasans and mamasans, their arms folded, glaring out at the rain with those eyes they assumed whenever we showed up. Holy Moses, you were never dry over in the Nam. Surprised me sometimes those Asiatics didn't have moss and big green dripping bunches of weedy slop dangling off them, like creatures from a black lagoon. (7)

The narrator of this book, like so many of the central figures of Euro-American narratives of the war, is an average American corrupted by the horrors of war. The description quoted here reverts to the inscrutability of the Asians: "those eyes." In a surreal and horrific conclusion to this scene (which I believe Nichols has taken from a scene in the film *The Deer Hunter*, making this a representation of a representation), a pig eats the little boy's entrails.

Then poked its head forward, bumped into flesh, started slurping at the belly wound. The kid's hands fluttered against the big snout. The pig snorted, irritated, shaking off the hands. Weakening, the hands flapped against the dirt-blotched ears—no silk purses in the offing here. . . . Arms danced up a final time and flopped against the tough hide, the right leg jerked a bit; the left foot scooted out. . . . The pig kept on for a while, methodical, chewing carefully, making sure it devoured everything. Finally nosed in and chomped the heart, savored the delicacy, then shook its gruff head in satisfaction, glanced once around, and gulped it down. Still beating, the heart? Who knows? Sometimes, I swear, given the dumb courage of those feisty relics from the Stone Age up against our fully automated slaughtering machine—sometimes I swear their hearts just never stopped beating. (8–9)

Clichés abound in this passage. Asians are passive—the boy does nothing but flutter his hands in his own defense, and none of the villagers moves to his rescue. The Vietnamese are from the Stone Age. There is some sort of admiration because they are "feisty" and keep fighting against superior technology. The child is a symbol, again, not a full-fledged character. The immediate purpose of the child's horrible death is to rub American noses in guilt. Feeling guilty, however, does nothing toward improving human relations, which authentic and humanizing portraits of characters from other cultures might accomplish.

The larger symbolic import of the scene is that Viet Nam was that child, gut-shot by American technology. It is common for American literature to portray Asians as childlike, small, immature, inferior to the adult Americans.[6] The implications of Nichols's symbolism are equally offensive to the Vietnamese, portrayed as helpless children, and to the Americans, portrayed as superior beings who should know better than to slaughter children.

Moreover, it is absurd for Americans to portray Vietnamese repeatedly as simply victims, since the NLF and PAVN won the war. Portraying winners as victims is bizarre, but since Americans do not think of Vietnamese as the winners, the absurdity does not surface in the U.S. discourse about the war. This is not to deny that plenty of individual Vietnamese on both sides were victimized by Americans, and by Vietnamese governments, but the portrayal of the entire nation of Viet Nam as a victim is a gross oversimplification, and either a strategic denial of the reality of U.S. defeat or a product of American liberal guilt that is part of the mindset keeping Asians "helpless." History shows that the Vietnamese are not helpless, having defeated not one but three major powers (France, the United States, and China).

As there has always been, there is still, in Nichols's novel an inability or refusal to imagine the interior, unexpressed thoughts and feelings of the Vietnamese. In one scene in *American Blood* a female Viet Cong prisoner is raped in a helicopter. The narrator, who has been wounded, watches:

The woman just accepted it, I reckon, knowing that her ghost would flap off and enter the bodies of a hundred other women creeping toward other battles under that green canopy below. Who knows what a female dink thought at a time like this: *I wonder if the Rams will beat the Giants next Friday? Is my hair a little sloppy? Is this shade of polish on my fingernails really me?* (19)

Here it is clearly not the Asian character who has "no regard for human life" (the common stereotype of Asians) but rather the American narrator, who cannot conceive that this is a real and equal human being before him, enduring torture before being killed. He attributes some sort of "Oriental mysticism" to her, believing that she accepts her rape and death because she will be reincarnated to "[creep] toward other battles." This passage does not seem to be expressing the narrator's distancing mechanism, trying to shut out the horror of the event; instead, he appears to perceive the woman as an available target not only for rape and murder, but also for ridicule.

This novel offers no opportunity for the reader to see the Asian characters as persons. It is not a matter of the American characters seeing the Asian characters in a certain light—an attitude readers can then understand as limiting and harmful—but rather of the reader being inundated with stereotypical images of Asians as alien, passive, helpless, unattractive, unknowable.

Americans in these types of narratives always fear the Vietnamese, even while they are seen as helpless, which is the only possible way to react to people who have always been seen as, in William Wu's words, "humble and passive, but also sneaky and treacherous" (13). In the rape scene just quoted, the woman is in an American helicopter with a U.S. Army squad, she is tied, and the soldier holding a rifle to her head still finds it necessary to continually shout at her, "Don't you move, or I'll blow your fuckin' head off!" (19).

This confusion and denial is illustrated by the scene from *Platoon* (a film widely praised by veterans for its "realism") that I discussed in chapter 1. In that scene Chris Taylor's voiceover tells us, "We did not fight the enemy; we fought ourselves, and the enemy was in us," while the bodies of PAVN casualties are being bulldozed into a mass grave. Here, the film pulls off a double victory by showing the Vietnamese soldiers, who have been so terrifying up to this point, in the ultimate position of helplessness and powerlessness—death—while simultaneously writing their participation out of history through the meta-war conducted by Taylor's voiceover.

Platoon is also one of the best examples of portrayals of Vietnamese harkening back to World War II representations of Japanese. In battle scenes the PAVN always seriously outnumber the Americans—they are truly the "yellow hordes" of the old American nightmare. While we see on the screen only a few, individualized American soldiers, we see masses of mostly faceless, shadowy PAVN who scream as they run directly into the camera toward us.

In one notable scene, a sapper carrying a satchel charge runs into a bunker occupied by a U.S. captain (played by Oliver Stone, the film's director), carrying out a suicide attack. First we see the American captain in his bunker, talking on a radio telephone, trying to sort out the mess of the battle. The scene is designed to promote a double recognition: we are supposed to recognize the concerned, good officer as an American individual, then those viewers in the know are supposed to recognize the appearance of the director in his own film. Next there is a cut to an exterior scene, where we see the sapper, at a distance and from behind, run toward the bunker and throw himself into it. An explosion follows. The editing and perspective of the scene allow us to see it in no other way than as a classic "kamikaze" attack—an act which most Americans think of as fanatical. (Americans are so conditioned in their thinking about the kamikaze that it is almost impossible to go against the grain. In Stephen Spielberg's World War II film *Empire of the Sun*, a young kamikaze gets in his plane to carry out his attack, after the solemn religious ceremony to prepare him for it, and the plane will not start. The young man is devastated. The film plays this straight, but the theater audience laughs. Part of this laugh response comes from preconceived notions about fanatic Asians which prevent the audience from recognizing the commonality with portrayals of American suicide missions as heroic, in films like *The Dirty Dozen*.)

These two scenes do not begin to exhaust the ethnocentrism of *Platoon*. In the scene where Bunny, the homicidal maniac of the platoon, bashes in the skull of a young Vietnamese man, the man is seen as a grinning, cringing, alien being. He infuriates Bunny because he is smiling, and Bunny shoots at his feet to make him "dance," the cliché from old westerns. American audiences, with Bunny, cannot quite see that he is smiling to try to appease the American monster with an M-16 who has barged into his house. When Bunny smashes the young man's head we are meant to be sickened and to condemn Bunny, because he has killed a human being. Yet we are shown only an alien, "Oriental human being"; we are not shown a portrait of a young man who had a life before the war, who becomes a person to us, as Bunny does, no matter how sick we might think he is.[7] Platoon, for all its critical acclaim, merely participates in the semiotic that almost all U.S. filmic representations of Viet Nam have set up.[8]

Another typical set of American attitudes that defines Vietnamese as sneaky and treacherous is encoded in the Rambo films, which, unlike Platoon, have received no critical acclaim but are much more popular, not only in the United States but worldwide.[9]

The character John Rambo made his first film appearance in First Blood (1982).[10] In this film Rambo, a returned veteran, is hassled by a small-town sheriff and proceeds to claim revenge. The action, except for brief flashbacks, is confined to the United States, so no Vietnamese characters appear, but the Vietnamese are represented by implication in two stereotypical ways.

Rambo is arrested by the sheriff and has flashbacks to his time as a POW in Viet Nam as soon as he is in jail. The history of his experience in Viet Nam is written into his body—he has extensive scars covering his torso. One American image of the Vietnamese is encoded in Rambo's physique—the sadistic torturers.[11] The sadistic American jailer has no compassion for Rambo's scars. He hits Rambo with a nightstick and hoses him down with a firehose. A more compassionate cop asks, "Can't you see he's crazy?" Although Rambo has grown increasingly silent since his arrest, the audience is shown that he is not crazy through flashbacks that show the Vietnamese torturers who gave him his scars.

The second representation of Vietnamese appears in a story Rambo tells in a long monologue at the end of the film, after he has surrendered. In it, we hear the famous apocryphal story of the killer/sacrificial Vietnamese child:

Remember Joe Forrest? . . . We were in this bar in Saigon and this kid comes up, carrying a shoeshine box . . . I went to get a couple beers, and the box was wired and he opened up the box, fucking blew his body all over the place. He's laying there and he's fucking screaming—there's pieces of him all over me and I'm trying to pull it off and it's my friend that's all over me! He's got blood and everything and I'm trying to hold him together and put him together and his fucking insides keep coming out and nobody would help. He keeps screaming I wanna go home I wanna go home, he keeps calling my name, I wanna go home Johnny, I wanna drive my Chevy. I said with what? I can't find your fucking legs. I can't find your legs. I can't get it outta my head. It's nearly seven years. Every day it happens. Sometimes I wake up in the morning, I don't talk to anybody. I can't put it out of my mind.

The idea that the Vietnamese are so inscrutable and so fanatic that they would sacrifice their own children in this way is perversely persistent in American representations of the war.[12]

In *Rambo: First Blood Part Two* (1985), Rambo gets to return to Viet Nam. Still, however, the Vietnamese do not figure into the storyline in important ways. Rambo's real adversary is the Russians, who are clearly running the show, with the Vietnamese as their primitive flunkies.

After Rambo parachutes into Viet Nam, he runs into his native contact, who turns out to be a woman, Co. The inevitable romance begins to blossom. In this film, however, the Vietnamese woman cannot aspire to America and domesticity. Earlier Co has posed as a prostitute, riding a scooter to enter the prison camp and free Rambo, but now, instead of the exotic sexuality of Asia, she represents a desire to assimilate into American culture. The xenophobic American society of the film will not permit any such assimilation, and so she must die. While Co and Rambo are escaping their pursuers, she convinces him to take her back to America with him. When Rambo agrees, she says, "You make good decision," kisses him, and heads down the trail, straight into an ambush. The antimiscegenation message is clear. As soon as Co has transgressed the sexual role assigned to her as prostitute, not as wife/ mate, death immediately follows. In this film, America is unwilling to absorb Vietnamese refugees or acknowledge Vietnamese participation in the war.

The primitiveness of the Vietnamese is shown in their "crude" form of torture—suspending Rambo in a pit of pig shit—as opposed to the Russians' "sophisticated" form of torture—electrocution on an old and rusty box spring. (I wonder about that box spring—did the Russians import it?) The Vietnamese are obsequious to the Russians, ignoring their insults (the Russian colonel comments directly on the crudeness of the Vietnamese torture methods, suggesting that he and Rambo have more in common.) As soon as the Russians enter the picture, the Vietnamese disappear.

A recurring theme in films and narratives is the invisibility of the enemy; in this film, however, the invisibility of the enemy is appropriated by Rambo himself, who has "gone native." (Like his iconic predecessor, Billy Jack, Rambo is part American Indian.) When sought by Russian troops, Rambo becomes the invisible presence lurking in the jungle. This motif is carried to absurd lengths in a scene in which he melds himself into a mudbank and slithers out behind a Russian soldier to kill him silently with his knife. Rambo plays both sides—the invisible, primitive killer of Russians and the visible, technological killer of Vietnamese, exemplifying the contradictions in the U.S. response to Viet Nam. He takes on the Vietnamese strategy to kill the Russians and the American strategy to kill the Vietnamese. When he faces a Vietnamese officer who tries to shoot him with a pistol, he stands fully exposed, knowing he is out of range. The Vietnamese empties his clip at Rambo anyway (Vietnamese may *possess* our technology, but they do not know how to use it), then Rambo raises his bow and exploding arrow and the Vietnamese flees in terror. Rambo shoots him, and he is literally demolished. Rambo thus appropriates both sides of the war: he does visually what *Platoon*'s Chris Taylor does verbally.

While *Platoon* and *Rambo* may be at opposite ends of the spectrum as far as critical appraisal is concerned, their attitude toward Vietnamese is remarkably similar. Film, even more than literature, is guilty of relying on stereotypical, stock images of Asians and is unable to bring new light to old representations. (Even *Alamo Bay*, the one American film that really tries, fails.) All American films depicting the war and its aftermath rely on the same cultural attitudes manifested in *Platoon* and *Rambo*.

The sentiment that Viet Nam was the antithesis of something called "civilization," which was represented by what was known as "The World" in the soldiers' argot (that is, the United States), informs American films' portrayals of the Vietnamese. American films depict Vietnamese as other, but other in a specific way: as primitive in contrast to America's civilized technological, tall, clean-cut white boys. An analysis of the position of the Vietnamese in these films shows that within the realm of the primitive in which they are portrayed is the locus of sex, and of death, and of sex-and-death. These films simply cast Viet Nam as the heart of darkness, either self-consciously, as does *Apocalypse Now*, or unselfconsciously.

The patterns in print media are more diverse than those in films, but the historic pattern of racism is deeply ingrained in the majority. Some of the main themes in this pattern are ethnocentric attitudes toward the Vietnamese language, the portrayal of Viet Nam as a "second-rate" place, of

Vietnamese men as small, slanty-eyed "little brown brothers," and of Vietnamese women as prostitutes. These themes appear in many works; a few notable examples are cited here.

Some books rely on American ignorance of Viet Nam and the Vietnamese. Jeff Danziger's *Rising like the Tucson* is one example. A black comedy in the tradition of *Catch-22*, it is mostly a funny, pointed, and effective satire of the American military presence in Viet Nam. One section, however, which pokes fun at army language school, falls flat for any reader with even the most rudimentary knowledge of Vietnamese.

> The teachers . . . resolutely refused to explain anything, insisting instead that crazily untranslatable blocks of vocabulary be repeated endlessly. It was, for Kit and the others, a mass of silly codes to be memorized, words such as *do* and *da* and *dong*. Impossible to take seriously.
>
> Vietnamese, Kit learned, is a tonal language—a fact that any American could live a long and rewarding life without ever knowing. The words, like Chinese words, had tones. The word *do*, for example, has six tones, and six separate meanings. The word *da* also has six. The word *dong* has six tones, as well. In fact, every word had six tones. Sentences—nay, whole paragraphs—could be written using just *do* and *da* and *dong*. And there were eleven vowels, and several extra consonants. Thus, the number of permutations on a basic word was staggering.
>
> Kit worked hard at memorizing sentences such as:
> *Da dau dau dong da dong do dau dong da.* (18)

First, the attitude that Americans can live perfectly well without knowing anything about tone languages deserves to be satirized, but instead Danziger is sympathetic to it. Rather than setting the character of Kit up as a booby (which he is) unable to master another language, the author writes Kit as a hapless but well-meaning bumbler who is likable and in the right for not being able to master such a "silly" language. Second, Danziger's description of Vietnamese is supposed to be funny, but it is really not. Mark Twain's parody of German in "The Awful German Language" is funny because Twain knows enough German to hit home with his parody. Danziger, in contrast, relies on American ignorance of Vietnamese and on American bigotry about non-Indo-European languages.

Not every Vietnamese word can take all six tones—in fact, words that take the whole paradigm are rare. Nonetheless, the language is still more complicated than Danziger describes. There are two sounds represented by *d* in Vietnamese. In Northern dialect, *d* is pronounced similarly to the sound represented by *z* in English (in Southern dialect it is pronounced like English *y*), and *d* is pronounced similarly to English *d*. Of the words in the quotation, only *do* can take all six tones. But, as Danziger mentions, there are eleven vowels. Vowel quality differences are represented by diacritics. *Đo* can also be *đô*. Further, many of the words formed by adding various tones to the words above are particles—parts of compound words. Therefore, none of the "sentences" that Danziger produces could remotely be Vietnamese sentences. In addition, none of the words Danziger cites, if pronounced correctly, sounds alike. They only look alike when printed without the diacritics, as they usually are in books published in the United States. Danziger's parody relies on ethnocentric publishing practice as well as ethnocentric language attitudes for its humor.

This is not to deny that Vietnamese is a difficult language for English speakers to learn to hear and to pronounce, but part of our difficulty is our prejudices. Because Americans tend to hear Asian tone languages as "gobbledygook chatter," they have a very hard time learning to hear those languages as languages. Danziger is playing to that American prejudice about Asian languages. If a reader possesses that prejudice, he or she will find Danziger's passage funny. Timothy Lomperis notes the linguistic arrogance of the United States: "Almost to a man and woman, none of [the] journalists knew Vietnamese. For the military, especially after the large units arrived, Vietnam was all 'Indian country.' Except for superficial and awkward episodes in the towns, the troops kept to themselves. They gave everything American names" (64). This linguistic imperialism is in the same mold as Danziger's attempted parody.

In a kind of ironic contrast to the American renaming of Viet Nam, Americans tended to regard Viet Nam as a second-rate place, a place that no one would want, and which was consequently not worth fighting for. In the soldiers' argot, "The World" meant the United States, as in the common phrase "back in The World." Viet Nam was not in the world, and therefore was hell, or another planet, or no place at all. This attitude is present in one of the early personal narratives, Richard Tregaskis's 1962 *Vietnam Diary*: "I was lucky enough to find a seat, my over-all objective being to get a firsthand, eyewitness look at the strange, off-beat, new-style war in which we find ourselves engaged in the miserable little jungle country called Vietnam, which our nation's leaders have decided is pivotal and critical in our Asian struggle with Communism" (quoted in Pratt, *Vietnam Voices*, 113). Tregaskis's characterization of Viet Nam as not only "miserable" and "little" but a "jungle country" also epitomizes a typical American misperception. Viet Nam contains jungle, but also river deltas and beaches; the dominant image, however, is of jungle—the most "un-American" of Viet Nam's ecological spheres.

In a letter home in 1968 an American private first class writes, "Further, if the Kommmunists (sic) want to take over the world, I would rather wait and fight them in my back yard than in this hole" (quoted in Pratt, *Vietnam Voices*, 345). The soldier is reiterating the sentiment that Viet Nam is not worth fighting for, even in the supposed defense of America—the soldier's own back yard—against the spread of communism. This attitude makes Viet Nam the most valueless place imaginable.

Sometimes the negative sentiment about the country is placed in the mouth of a Vietnamese character, as in Thomas Fleming's *Officers' Wives*. After the coup in which President Diem is killed, and after President Kennedy's assassination, a Vietnamese woman, Thui Dat, talks to Joanna, wife of a U.S. officer. Thui Dat asks Joanna if she thinks Kennedy was killed by traitorous generals, as Diem was.

"No!" Joanna said. "Such a thing is—really quite impossible."
Thui heard the words as a rebuke. She nodded sadly. "You mean such things occur only in wretched countries like Vietnam," she said. "You are no doubt correct." (quoted in Pratt, *Vietnam Voices*, 151)

Euro-American authors "confirm" their own perceptions of the country by placing those perceptions in the mouths of Vietnamese characters. In so doing, Fleming overlooks the participation of the United States, and the Kennedy administration in particular, in Diem's assassination.

In American representations, Viet Nam is not only a nameless and placeless place, it is an uncivilized place. (There is general agreement among Vietnamese refugee writers and Euro-American writers that the *war* was uncivilized; many Euro-American writers, however, see not just the war but the entire nation of Viet Nam as uncivilized.) This attitude is clearly stated in a letter from the marine lieutenant Kenneth Babbs ("later to become known as author Ken Kesey's friend and bus driver") to John Clark Pratt, compiler of the anthology of "fragments," *Vietnam Voices*: "One of my stories, for instance, is designed to show the way the squadron camaraderie was breaking down the longer we stayed in Vietnam (another theme, the same as *Heart of Darkness* . . . we went over there to civilize them and ended up getting barbarized)" (quoted in Pratt, *Vietnam Voices*, 116; ellipsis in original). Perhaps Babbs's assessment is only slightly off—rather than "getting barbarized," maybe the barbarity behind the notion of "civilizing" another people was revealed in the attempt.

These ethnocentric and demeaning views of Viet Nam are not limited to "older" representations of the war or to pulp novels: one of the most famous and widely read books about the war, Michael Herr's *Dispatches* (1978), is one of the guiltiest.[13] It was published in a period during which our image of the fragmented, rock-n-roll war was formed. Two of the main contributors to this image were Herr's *Dispatches* and *Apocalypse Now* (1979), for which Herr wrote the voiceover narration. Both works show the war as surreal, incomprehensible, a black comedy of sorts, and both were taken seriously by critics. *Apocalypse Now* has been written about by film critics more than any other Viet Nam film except *The Deer Hunter* (1978), and *Dispatches* is one of the most studied books on the war. Suddenly, in the late seventies, works about Viet Nam were gathering both a wide popular audience and critical attention. The criteria for judging them had become how "accurate" or "true" they were—in other words, how much they said about the "real" war; the war itself, rather than representations of it, was being constructed as a "surreal" experience.

That "accuracy" was, of course, filtered through American prejudices. Here is what Herr has to say about Viet Nam:

It was late '67 now, even the most detailed maps didn't reveal much anymore; reading them was like trying to read the faces of the Vietnamese, and that was like trying to read the wind. We knew that the uses of most information were flexible, different pieces of ground told different stories to different people. We also knew that for years now there had been no country here but the war. (1)

With the phrase "no country here but the war," Herr takes an influential step in the process of the erasure of Viet Nam the country and its replacement, in the American cultural imagination, by "Vietnam" the war.

Susan Jeffords writes: "Michael Herr's declaration that 'trying to read the faces of the Vietnamese . . . was like trying to read the wind' reinforces the (con)fusion of the status of fact and fiction by suggesting that Vietnam was an unfamiliar world in which expected definitions and conclusions would appear alien" (30). Jeffords thus identifies the way Herr creates a world in which he can be sole arbiter of judgment and truth, in which there are no moral obligations but those he chooses to acknowledge. Herr, most prominently among canonical writers on the war, acknowledges no obligations whatsoever toward the Vietnamese.

When Asians are not completely erased from representations of the war, they are portrayed in ways that reflect standard stereotypes. When they are on "our side," they are "little brown brothers." In Smith Hempstone's 1966 novel, *A Tract of Time*, a CIA adviser tries to persuade a Montagnard village chief to take the side of the Republic of Viet Nam:

"The Viets are your enemies, Ye."

"Why, Erohe, tell me why."

"Because they are Communists. Because they will enslave you. Because they will steal your land and make cattle of you. You know all this." As he enumerated each point, Harry unbent a finger from his clenched fist and when he had finished held the three fingers close to Ye's face, as if to force the truth on the chief through the physical proximity of his hand. Ye wrinkled his brow and studied the designs he had etched in the sand, as if hoping to find there the answers to the questions which afflicted him.

"Communists?" We do not know what this means. Your words may be true but we do not know it. What we do know is that the Yoane, the yellow Annamese of the plains, have been our enemies since these hills were young. The Vietcong come from the north, from the mountains. From that direction we have not been threatened since the time of the men you call Mongols. And who amongst us can remember that time?" (in Pratt, *Vietnam Voices*, 102)

The portrayal of the Montagnard chief smacks of Orientalism. He is the stereotypical slow but deliberate Oriental who clings to his ancient "wisdom" even in the face of Western intelligence. Harry, the CIA agent, tries to force Ye to see things his way through physical force (the proximity of his hand), but, in the stereotypical way of the unmovable Oriental, Ye remains unmoved, studying the designs he draws in the sand. Ye is mystical, Harry is logical. The line given to Ye, "since these hills were young," sounds like the sort of speech often attributed to equally inscrutable American Indians.

Harry has his doubts about trying to enlist the Montagnards (whom he thinks of as "primitive tribesmen") because he suspects the war cannot be won, and he does not want to be responsible for the Montagnards committing themselves to a losing side. He carries out his assignment, however, because he has been instructed to do so by his superior. This is his strategy: "What we've got to do, Harry thought, is to recreate the circumstances of the twelfth century, when the montagnards fought with the Vietnamese against the Hindu Chams" (103). Because Harry sees the Montagnards as primitive, it makes sense to him to deal with them by going back to the twelfth century. (It does not seem to bother him that the war in which the supposed alliance between Montagnards and Vietnamese that he wants to recreate took place resulted in the genocide of the Chams. Worse, he has history wrong—the Montagnards actually allied with the Chams against the Vietnamese.)

After reflecting on his strategy, Harry turns again toward Ye: "And yet Harry knew that the little brown man in front of him was no fool. Ye would do what seemed best for his people and Harry respected him for that. That was what he himself wanted for them, too, he guessed" (104). Harry is caught up in the contradictions of his colonialist, Orientalist, paternalist attitude. It is impossible to "respect" someone one regards as a "little brown man." Harry uses size and color, two of the most common markers of otherness in the minds of Americans regarding Southeast Asians, to describe Ye. Yet he aligns himself with Ye in a paternalistic way—as Harry feels responsible for Ye, so Harry conceptualizes Ye being responsible for his people. It is in this shared paternalistic role, as Harry envisions it, that he can identify with Ye, although he clearly regards Ye as his "little brown brother." Such are the contradictions of Orientalism.

The representation of Vietnamese as small, and therefore helpless or inferior, and as beastlike extends across political positions and exists even in writers who exhibit great sympathy for Vietnamese, including writers of the antiwar movement. Robert Bly, in his introduction to *A Poetry Reading against the War*, writes, "One repulsive novelty of this war is the daily body-count. We count up the small-boned bodies like quail on a gun shoot" (in Pratt, *Vietnam Voices*, 229). Bly uses the smallness of the Vietnamese to inspire pity or sympathy for them. In so doing, however, he obscures their humanity. The Vietnamese were not quail, but simply human beings who are generally smaller than Americans in part because of Americans' greater access to nutrition as children. One dead Vietnamese is absolutely equal to one dead American, regardless of the size of their bones. Bly's formula does not grant the Vietnamese this equality.

Michael Bibby's excellent article " 'Where Is Vietnam?': Antiwar Poetry and the Canon," confirms that racism exists across the political spectrum. Bibby points out how even antiwar poetry falls prey to "the reinscription of dominant Western paradigms which position the Vietnamese as the 'oriental other' " (166) by the "fetishization of the 'primitive' as the realm of radical otherness," which comes from the "hierarchical dichotomies paradigmatic of colonialist thought and the Western habit of constituting Third World cultures as shadows of First World civilization" (167). Bibby is particularly critical of Bly, giving a brilliant reading of Bly's "Johnson's Cabinet Watched by Ants" in which he identifies the colonialist subtext of the poem and shows how the poem "transforms the Viet Cong . . . into a non-human caricature, small forest animals and barbarians" (169).

Bibby further shows how Bly's antiwar poetry is deeply enmeshed in a racist paradigm in his discussion of "Driving through Minnesota during the

Hanoi Bombings": "This poem can be said to reproduce a discourse in which the struggle for the Western individual's self-knowledge is central, whereas the Vietnamese and the war America waged against them are marginal" (171). It comes as no surprise, then, that Bly should choose to emphasize Vietnamese smallness and compare the Vietnamese to quail in his prose, since his poetry does not transcend racist paradigms.

Not only is smallness emphasized in many Euro-American portrayals of Vietnamese, but so is the shape of their eyes, which becomes a code image for untrustworthiness: "The Americans always gotta stick together. No telling what we're gonna find in there. These fucking slopes will bug out on you in a second," says Sergeant Kobus, the main character of Bo Hathaway's *A World of Hurt* (in Pratt, *Vietnam Voices*, 182). In a scene from Derek Maitland's *The Only War We've Got*, two American civilian officials are presented satirically. Maitland is clearly criticizing their conduct of the war and their treatment of the Vietnamese. Yet by presenting the Vietnamese character as exactly the kind of buffoon the Americans imply that he is, the narrative concurs in their attitude. Goldblatt is the ambassador; Risher is the head of the Civil Operations and Revolutionary Development Support program.

"But look at it this way, Goldblatt. These slant-eyes have got pride, you know. . . ."

"Let's get on with the briefing," Goldblatt snapped.

"O.K." cried Risher, and he beckoned to a grinning black-clad Vietnamese who stepped into the room. "Mr. Goldblatt, I'd like you to meet Colonel Nguyen Be who'll be heading the training side of our new programme. He's a great little guy—hates the Communists and speaks English almost as goddam well as me."

"Hi, Midder Ambassador," the colonel grinned, shaking hands with Goldblatt. "How's your hammer hanging?" Goldblatt recoiled with shock and Risher muttered: "He's spent a lot of time with the goddam Peace Corps."

"V.C. number-ten-guddem-cucksuckers!" the colonel chanted.

"I see what you mean," Ambassador Goldblatt breathed. (in Pratt, *Vietnam Voices*, 261)

Everyone in this scene is being satirized. Goldblatt and Risher are clowns because they are exaggerated types and clearly incompetent, unlike the standard picture of an American; the Vietnamese colonel, however, is presented in terms of the standard stereotypes—slant-eyed, small, speaking pidgin—and this presentation is supposed to be enough to serve as satire. Colonel Be is a clown simply because he is Vietnamese.

One particularly interesting portrayal of a Vietnamese character appears in

Nicholas Proffitt's novel *The Embassy House*. In this depiction, the Vietnamese is neither small nor slant-eyed; yet still he is the embodiment of the Orientalist stereotype of the untrustworthy Asian. Proffitt, author of *Gardens of Stone*, was a journalist in Viet Nam during the war. *The Embassy House* is an action novel that relies for much of its tension on the stereotype of the sneaky, inscrutable Asian.

In the traditional formulation of Asian/American relationships, according to Elaine Kim, "the Asian brute serves to demonstrate by starkest contrast the wholesome intelligence and heroism of his Anglo-Saxon counterpart" (*Asian American Literature* 6). *The Embassy House* departs from this tradition by representing the American and the Vietnamese as of equal intelligence and heroism (if not of wholesomeness on either part). The Vietnamese character Dang appears at first to be the "good Asian" sidekick to the American hero, Gulliver. They are teamed up as counterparts, Dang the Vietnamese leader and Gulliver the American advisor. In the confused and corrupt world of Saigon, they trust and respect only each other. Dang is the typical inscrutable Asian, but with a difference:

The tall Vietnamese named Dang checked the hang of the sun and spoke in a low voice to the American, whose name was Gulliver: "We have one hour of light left. How do you want to do this? An X and the usual way?"

Gulliver shrugged and smiled. "It's your team, Dang, not mine. How do you want to do it?" They spoke in English, the language they most often used around the other members of the team, the language of leadership.

Dang did not smile back; Dang never smiled. But there was a teasing note in his voice. "You are a terrible adviser, Sandman. You never advise" (9).

The way he checks the "hang of the sun" and announces the time of day is reminiscent of portrayals of Indian scouts in westerns. Dang never smiles, but he is able to tease with his American patron; he appears to be a thoroughly domesticated sidekick. Yet Dang's inscrutability is intact: Gulliver does not suspect that Dang is the spy his headquarters is looking for. Dang is referred to repeatedly as "the tall Vietnamese," and his height is the first tipoff that he might not be what he seems. Sidekicks, like Charlie Chan, are usually shorter than Americans. Villains, like Fu Manchu, are usually tall.

Paradoxically, although Dang turns out to be a Viet Cong spy, he does not quite turn out to be the villain. The bumbling bureaucrats, Vietnamese and American, are the real villains of the novel. The identification between Dang and Gulliver is very strong. They even share the same lover, a fairly inscrutable and exotic Vietnamese woman. Unbeknownst to Gulliver she is Dang's wife, whom Dang has set to spying on Gulliver. In the end, when Gulliver discovers that Dang is the spy, he lets him go. In the final confrontation with the CIA flunky who has betrayed them both, they are presented as equally heroic. *The Embassy House* performs the difficult feat of granting grudging respect to a thoroughly Orientalized character.

In American writing, one of the most common portrayals of Vietnamese is as prostitutes. This is not surprising, since GIs were quite likely to have more contact with prostitutes than with any other Vietnamese. Nor is it surprising that, more often than not, the descriptions of these encounters are heavily weighted with sexism and racism. The characters in the works, and the authors, too, dehumanize these women, as in this scene from Steven Smith's *American Boys*, where one character, Morg, is buying the services of a prostitute for his friend, Clampitt:

He waved five hundred piasters in front of her. "Come on, special chop-chop just for my friend."

"No chop-chop. You number ten thou."

"Six hundred p. chop-chop, boom-boom." He grabbed her shirt and waved the money in her face.

"Let me take my time, Morg," Clampitt said. "You know these buddhist chicks don't blow. Only the Catholics do."

He started to put the money in his pocket.

"Six hundred p.?" the girl said.

He winked at Clampitt. "That's right, Baby-san. Okay? You take care of my friend. You're not about to reach nirvana anyway." He dangled the bills in front of her again.

A few minutes later, Morg picks up a prostitute for himself.

She pulled off her pink blouse and black pajama bottoms and flopped on the mat. He removed his shirt and slid his pants and drawers below his knees, leaving his boots on. He looked at the girl, raised the can to his lips, then leaned over and spit a mouthful of beer on her stomach. . . .

He swung his feet over the pallet thinking how much better it was just whacking off.

"Jesus Christ," he said when she pulled an Army canteen cup half full of water from under the pallet and splashed her crotch. "You got some real good hygiene here."

"You like boom-boom, GI?" (408–9)

In these passages, not only do the characters treat the women in a dehuman-izing way, but the author invites his readers to share that point of view. It is illuminating to compare this passage to the sections in Le Ly Hayslip's auto-biography in which she describes her experiences as a bar girl and prostitute. The last paragraph, where Morg criticizes the prostitute for her inade-quate hygiene, is worthy of particular notice. He sees her as inferior; he does not see his own culpability in her situation. He has no curiosity for where she might have come from, or what her life is like, and the author's narrative discourages the reader from having any such curiosity, either. Morg is un-aware that it is the American presence in Viet Nam that has created a huge demand for prostitutes at the same time that it has caused huge inflation in the Vietnamese economy and so has forced many women into prostitution. It is the American presence, in other words, that has created the dehumaniz-ing conditions of this woman's life. Rather than recognizing this cause and effect, Morg blames the victim, and we, as readers, are invited to take a similar view.

Vietnamese men are often feminized in American representations. Philip Jason points out how enemy Asians are feminized: "In the crude semantic of the battlefield, killing gooks is the same as fucking them. . . . And to the 'white-bread' American grunt, the dusky Vietnamese man—small-boned and sparse in facial and body hair—was a figure simultaneously effeminate and menacing, whether friend or foe" (126). In his study of POW narratives Elliott Gruner shows how these narratives tend to feminize the Vietnamese captors. He describes one particularly over-the-top case in which the POW author, Charles Plumb, casts doubt on the "masculinity" of his captors as a strategy "to assert himself as superior to the culture which imprisons him" (102). Not only does Plumb criticize the Vietnamese because the women seem to be more sexually aggressive than the men, he identifies the men as homosexual because he sees them holding hands and walking arm in arm. Gruner comments, "However exciting it might be to reverse the observa-tion vector between guard and prisoner, his observations assume that the social practices and sexual stereotypes that exist in his America are universal and apply directly to the people of North Vietnam" (102). Gruner later quotes Plumb as saying, "Once again his [an interrogator's] devious Asian mind was too much for me to fathom" (133); Gruner notes also that Plumb has appeared as an "expert" on the MacNeil/Lehrer Newshour.

Susan Jeffords shows how patriarchal American culture attributes the same negative, "feminine" characteristics to women and to the Vietnamese: " 'Vietnam' is typified in American veterans' accounts by this elusiveness, deceit, and treachery" (147). Jeffords argues that this typical presentation of Vietnamese is "racism that is transfigured as gender" (151).

I turn now to an extended analysis of three books that are thoroughly enmeshed in the cultural attitudes I have been discussing: *The Ugly American* (1958), *The Green Berets* (1965), and *Close Quarters* (1977). I choose these three as representative works across time and across genres. *The Ugly American* is a political novel, *The Green Berets* is an action novel by a journalist, and *Close Quarters* is a critically acclaimed combat novel by a veteran. These works also represent a spectrum of political opinions. By general consensus Lederer and Burdick are cold war liberals, Moore is an ultrapatriotic right-winger, and Heinemann is a disaffected, slightly to the Left writer.

Lederer and Burdick's *The Ugly American* was the first novel of American authorship to deal with U.S. involvement in Southeast Asia. The book eventually sold four million copies, making it one of the most popular books in American history.[14] *The Ugly American* was an influential document. John Hellmann credits it with helping to create the whole Kennedy atmosphere of service and sacrifice, classes it with *Uncle Tom's Cabin* and *The Jungle* in its effect on American political debate, and cites mention of the book by President Eisenhower, Senator John Kennedy, Senator Russell Long, Senator William Fulbright, and presidential candidate Richard Nixon. The book has also been influential in shaping the paternalistic way Americans have regarded Asians. As Richard Drinnon points out, the real battle in this novel is between the United States and the "supersubversive" Russians. Drinnon contends, correctly I believe, that in life as well as in fiction Americans see Asians as dehumanized puppets and objects that can be manipulated. Drinnon accurately analyzes the novel's categorization of good and bad Asians as "the short step between overt and covert racism" (375).

The Ugly American is set in the fictional Sarkhan, "a small country out toward Burma and Thailand" (14). Although Viet Nam is mentioned in the novel, Sarkhan seems to be, in large part, an analog for it: Sarkhan has "border difficulty with the Communist country to the north" (20). Lederer and Burdick criticize U.S. policy because its means are incompetent to achieve its anti-Communist aims. One of the bases of the critique is the easy U.S. dismissal of the natives; however, Lederer and Burdick replace dismissal with paternalism.

The Ugly American is meant as political intervention; it begins with a "note from the authors": "This book is written as fiction, but it is based on fact. . . . The names, the places, the events, are our inventions; our aim is not to embarrass individuals, but to stimulate thought—and, we hope, action" (9). Despite the preposterousness of much of the novel, Lederer and Burdick also append a "factual epilogue" establishing their authenticity: "The authors have taken part in the events in Southeast Asia which have inspired this book" (229).

The novel focuses on two U.S. ambassadors to Sarkhan named Sears and MacWhite. Sears, the first ambassador, is ineffective, partly because he is only waiting out two years at the post until he is appointed a federal judge, which is his true ambition. Another part of the reason is that he consistently regards the Sarkhanese as "little monkeys," and no one in his embassy speaks the language. When appointed to the ambassadorship, Sears's comment was, "Now, you know I'm not prejudiced, but I just don't work well with blacks" (14). He sends a memo to the state department in which he writes: "These Sarkhanese are really tricky. Sometimes I think they're all Commies" (64). While it is clear that the real problem is that Sears is incompetent, the text portrays the Sarkhanese as "tricky," thus undercutting its own critique.

Sears is contrasted with Louis Krupitzyn, the Soviet ambassador to Sarkhan. Before assuming his ambassadorship, Krupitzyn spends two years, along with his wife, at the Moscow School for Asian Areas.

They learned to read and write Sarkhanese. They learned that the ideal man in Sarkhan is slender, graceful, and soft-spoken; that he has physical control and outward tranquility; that he is religious (Buddhism is the prevalent religion); and that he has an appreciation of the ancient classical music.

The Ambassador-designate molded himself into this pattern. He dieted and lost forty pounds; he took ballet lessons. He read Sarkhanese literature and drama, and became a fairly skillful player on the nose flute. (32)

The notion that the Sarkhanese are primitive in such a way that they could not possibly understand or accept difference is repeated throughout *The Ugly American*, as in the case of OSS agents who parachute into Sarkhan during World War II: they had been carefully prepped for their assignment—they spoke Sarkhanese, and "they all had approximately the same size and stature of the average Sarkhanese man. Their faces had been dyed the light brown of the native Sarkhanese" (16). This is a patronizing attitude, denying any possibility that a Sarkhanese might be able to take a cosmopolitan view. Assuming the analogy to Viet Nam, this attitude is patently absurd in light of the fact that the leaders of both the DRV and RVN—Ho and Diem—had spent most of their adult lives abroad.

Ambassador MacWhite, Sears's successor, differs from both Sears and Krupitzyn:

MacWhite was, from his first day in the State Department, a professional foreign service officer. He needed no breaking in. He was competent, exact, and highly efficient. He was also courageous and outspoken, and he had imagination. During the McCarthy excitement he kept his head and ran his desk smoothly. By 1952 he had served as Consul General in four large foreign cities, as Deputy Chief of Mission in two cities, and was regarded by his superiors as a comer. (79)

MacWhite prepares for his assignment to Sarkhan by learning Sarkhanese, reading about its history and politics, and talking to "anthopologists, sociologists, political scientists, diplomats, and businessmen who had visited Sarkhan in the last several years" (80). He is already a "recognized expert" on communism.

MacWhite prepares to battle against the Communists for the future of Sarkhan. He wants to enlist the ethnic Chinese population of Sarkhan in this battle.

As he looked out of the plateglass window of the Embassy Residence, Ambassador MacWhite was aware of the fact that Donald and Roger were in the room behind him. Somehow the small pitter-patter noises that they were making were a comfort to him. Donald and Roger were both elderly Chinese. The only English words they knew were the names given them by their American employers and a few necessary household terms. . . . They worked with an efficiency, dedication, and kindliness that never failed to touch Ambassador MacWhite. They often helped Molly with the boys. They were both excellent cooks and superb butlers. They were, somehow, a symbol of the decent Asian, and they made the entire struggle in which Ambassador MacWhite was engaged meaningful and important. They represented the honor and morality which had been taught by Confucius. (81–82)

This loaded paragraph is revelatory. The only "decent Asian" is a servant, a sidekick, one loyal to his white masters. Donald and Roger are childlike, emasculated, safe. It turns out, however, that they are inscrutable. They are Communist spies, but are only revealed as such by another Asian, Li, an old friend of MacWhite: "MacWhite . . . was startled by the change in Li. Li had always struck him as Anglicized, as open and straightforward. Li knew American jokes, English ballads, Irish dialects. He was as American as a tractor salesman. But now he looked menacing, hooded, tight with cruelty"

(86). No Asian can ever be truly Anglicized, assimilated, in Lederer and Burdick's world—they are always capable of "reverting," of becoming Fu Manchu stereotypes.

The conclusion MacWhite draws from this episode is that "he did not know enough about the Asian personality and the way it played politics" (90). MacWhite destroys the possibility of any variation within the vast region of Asia; he creates instead "the Asian personality," something that Americans seem to have believed in for almost two hundred years. It is a belief in "the Asian personality" that allows Lederer and Burdick to create the characters of Roger, Donald, and Li.

MacWhite learns a thing or two from Colonel Hillandale in the Philippines—Lederer and Burdick's thinly disguised version of Col. Edward Lansdale.[15] Hillandale persuades people of a province that has previously been swayed by Communist propaganda to vote for Ramon Magsaysay and his pro-American platform simply by hanging out and playing on his harmonica and making them like him because he is not a "rich and bloated snob," as they have been told all Americans are (95). Hillandale is a sort of pied piper, and the natives are simply children.

Hillandale reappears later in Sarkhan, where he brings about similar miracles by astute feats of palmistry. He concludes, after seeing astrology shops in the capital, that Sarkhanese take palmistry seriously, so he uses the occasion of a state dinner to do some creative palm reading on the Sarkhanese prime minister. After this session, "the Prime Minister was gazing up at The Ragtime Kid with obvious awe" (152); notice Lederer and Burdick's usual construction of the small Asian overawed by the large American. In inspiring this awe, however, Hillandale has been dishonest and manipulative. He describes palmistry as "a key" that will open the heart of Sarkhan. Using the right key, Hillandale claims, "you can maneuver any person or any nation any way you want" (153). He has done some detective work and found out that the prime minister has planned a secret trip; he pretends to read this fact in the man's palm and so earns the "awe" of the prime minister.

Here we have the spectacle not only of the Asian as childlike and simple, but also of the American cheating in order to pursue "higher" ends. Lederer and Burdick present Asians who believe in palmistry and Americans who do not, just like the books' presumed readers—this chapter is like a gigantic wink at its readers, enlisting them in scorn for the gullible Asians, even while working for globalist ends. Hillandale's ultimate goal with his palmistry shuck has been to read the king's palm and get him to send the Sarkhanese army on maneuvers that will make it look like Sarkhan is pro-American rather than pro-Soviet. The character who is criticized in this story is Swift, the American chargé d'affaires, who does not understand that the Sarkhanese take palmistry seriously and blows Hillandale's opportunity to read the king's palm. The real problem as presented in the narrative is not an American charlatan's manipulating Asian beliefs (those beliefs constructed by Lederer and Burdick out of the standard stereotype), but an American official's failure to see how easily manipulable the Asians are. This point of view ignores the fact that there is also an enormous market for fortune telling among Americans—former president Reagan, for example, consulted an astrologer.

The characterization of the real Lansdale given in William S. Turley's *The Second Indochina War* reveals how fanciful Lederer and Burdick's imaginations were:

> Immortalized in *The Pentagon Papers* as the mastermind of a plot to bring Hanoi to a standstill by sugaring its petrol supply, Lansdale was reputed at the time to be a counterinsurgency expert and skilled intelligence operative. It was Lansdale who headed off one coup against Diem by offering the plotters free trips to Manila; Lansdale who raised the money to bribe the sects; and Lansdale who journeyed into the jungle to offer the bribe. (16)

The historic Lansdale's methods were more prosaic and less Orientalist.

This paternalistic racism exists in the book despite Lederer and Burdick's protestations to the contrary. Asch, a character presented as effective and correct, presides over an armaments conference and warns British and French delegates that the Asians are "big boys now, and they should know what they're getting into. And don't kid yourself, gentlemen; unless you *feel* they're equals and act on that feeling, they'll never respond" (167; italics in original). Yet nothing in the novel presents Asians as equals or encourages readers to "feel" their equality. (Two pages after this declaration the narrative describes a Hong Kong woman doctor as looking like "an oriental miniature"; she, of course, turns out to be an inscrutable, seductive Communist spy.)

After visiting the Philippines MacWhite travels to Viet Nam just in time for the fall of Dien Bien Phu. There he meets another "good" American—Tex Wolchek, an army major who, in the Korean War, had "led his patrol through the Chinese like a haymower through a fresh field. . . . they also killed 120 other Chinese" (98). After being wounded, he is assigned as an observer with the French fighting in Viet Nam. In a talk with Wolchek, MacWhite identifies the Americans with the French. The French war, as constructed by Lederer and Burdick, prefigures the American war:

But even more frustrating than constant defeat was the fact that at the end of three weeks of fighting, they had not once seen the enemy. The fire-fights always took place at night and were over by dawn; the enemy always slipped away, taking his dead with him; and the men felt they had participated in phantom engagements. The only thing that made it real were the dead Legionnaires. (105)

Lederer and Burdick envision the world entirely in globalist terms, as communism versus democracy. This vision makes the Third World merely a playing field for the United States and Soviet Union, so much so that all Third World people are construed to be on either one side or the other, with no possibility of occupying for themselves a position that is not either "with us or against us." Consequently, Hanoi is filled with a "feeling of impending defeat which was shared by everyone—Vietnamese, French, and American" (105). Catholic and Buddhist, Communist, nationalist, peasant, intellectual—all Vietnamese are swept together in this sentence. Characterizing all Vietnamese residents of Hanoi as feeling defeated on the eve of independence is unbelievable, but Lederer and Burdick see events as the victory of communism, not the winning of independence.

Monet, the French officer, says, "Imagine a nation which produced Napoleon, Foch, and Lyautey being beaten by so primitive an enemy" (107). The authors' description of the enemy's movements—"Out in the hill country and plains behind Hanoi thousands of Communists were slipping over paddies, around rocks, down ravines" (108)—sounds like an invasion of serpents, not men. And how could the Vietnamese invade their own country? Only through a belief in the right of France to its colony could the Vietnamese presence be seen as an invasion.

Not only are the "Viet Communists" primitive, but they are savage. They capture some legionnaires and their Vietnamese scout (nicknamed "Apache"). They gouge out a legionnaire's eye, cut out the scout's vocal chords, and send them back as a "lesson." Later, when Hanoi is turned over to the Viet Minh, the legion marches out as if it were on parade. Then the Viet Minh march in.

Tex had the feeling that he was looking at people who were fighting a war that should have taken place three hundred years before. These men traveled on foot and carried their total supplies on their backs. They looked harmless and innocent, indeed they almost looked comical. But these were the men whom he and Monet had been fighting for months, and whom they had defeated only once.

The officer on the bicycle held up his hand. The line of men paused, and then, as fast as the slithering of lizards, they disappeared into doorways and gutters. . . . Tex was aware that around all of Hanoi a huge, silent, and featureless army of men, each of them no more impressive than these, were oozing into the city which they had conquered. (120–21)

Thus do Lederer and Burdick describe the victorious army of Vo Nguyen Giap, arguably one of the greatest military geniuses of the twentieth century. The authors do not even mention him.

MacWhite ends up resigning his ambassadorship, because his ways are out of sync with the foreign service. He warns in a letter to the state department: "If we cannot get Americans overseas who are trained, self-sacrificing, and dedicated, then we will continue losing in Asia. The Russians will win without firing a shot, and the only choice open to us will be to become the aggressor with thermonuclear weapons" (227). The authors clearly conceive of the world as a chess game between the superpowers, with Asian countries as pawns. Throughout the book, Asians are never given agency or independent thought.

A subplot involves John Colvin, an OSS agent who had parachuted into Sarkhan in 1943 and worked with a native guerrilla, Deong. Colvin and Deong run around sabotaging Japanese military efforts in Sarkhan; Colvin is notorious, and a "special detail of antiespionage troops . . . had been flown in from Indonesia for the specific purpose of running Colvin to ground" (17). In this formulation the American is "helping" the Sarkhanese, thereby reversing history: the Vietnamese, specifically Vo Nguyen Giap and his fledgling army, helped the Americans by recovering downed pilots and smuggling them to China.

Lederer and Burdick also subscribe to the "no regard for human life" cliché, although they polish up its surface: when a Buddhist monk dies under questioning by a Japanese officer in a temple in which Colvin and Deong are hiding, "Deong patiently explained the beauty and grandeur of death in the land of Sarkhan" (18).

In 1952, when Sarkhan is having trouble with the Communists, Colvin develops a capitalist scheme to help them out—he imports Texas cattle so that the "people of Sarkhan could be taught to use milk and its byproducts" (20). Lederer and Burdick approve of this scheme, displaying their ignorance. Most Asians are lactose-intolerant by adolescence. Deong has become a Communist and tries to sabotage Colvin's scheme by making him mix ipecac (a vomit-inducing agent) into the powdered milk he is distributing so that Sarkhanese will not develop a taste for it. Deong says, "Look, John, you took me off the back of a water buffalo and taught me about the big outside world. And I learned that the side with the most brains and power wins. And, John, that's not your side anymore. . . . America had its chance and it missed. And now the Communists are going to win" (22). Agency is again removed from the Asian—it is Colvin who is responsible for Deong's "education." They fight, and Colvin is wounded. Ambassador Sears sends him home.

U Maung Swe, a Burmese journalist, advises MacWhite to bring Colvin back: "Ideas like Colvin's are basic. When we've licked the basic problems, we can move on to grander projects. But we have to start with the little things which are Sarkhanese" (130). The absurdity of Lederer and Burdick putting these sentiments into the mouth of an Asian character is patent. Not only does it betray their ignorance of the lactose-intolerance problem, but to call a project in which someone first changes local dietary habits, then imports a foreign animal to supply them as "Sarkhanese" illustrates the kind of globalist thinking that steamrolls over local niceties.

While the novel heaps criticism on the American government and foreign service, it picks out alternative approaches to praise. One of the characters designed for this purpose is Father Finian, SJ, who thinks of communism as a "political plague . . . the face of the devil" (41). Finian works in Burma to fight communism. He gathers eight Burmese men to work with, and asks what they want to do.

"It is not for me to say," Finian said flatly. "It is for all of us. It is your country, your souls, your lives. I will do what we agree upon." . . .

This was, he was sure, the first time that these men had ever been told by a white man that a big and important decision was entirely their own . . . and would be followed by the white man. (47)

Despite this claim, Finian guides them through their discussion, leading them as if they were children. An even greater paternalism is the idea that if the Burmese want to oppose communism in their country, they are unable to organize themselves and must wait for an American to bring them together.

The quintessential example Lederer and Burdick offer of good Americans is the ironically named title character: Homer Atkins, the ugly American. Atkins is a physically ugly man and in all other ways a good one, whereas those characters who may be handsome and slick are the truly ugly Americans. Homer Atkins, however, is also the primary example of paternalism in the novel.

Atkins is a retired engineer, a millionaire ("every penny of which he had earned by his own efforts" [175]), serving as a building consultant in Southeast Asia. He recommends small, low-tech projects to help the local people; his suggestions are ignored by high-level bureaucrats who want showy projects like dams and big roads. He warns the French and Americans in Viet Nam about the Ho Chi Minh Trail, but the bureaucrats claim that it would be impossible to build a road through the jungle.

At Ambassador MacWhite's invitation, Atkins goes to Sarkhan, where he works on designing a pump to raise water into terraced rice paddies, using locally available materials, which he will be able to train the Sarkhanese to run, because "whenever you give a man something for nothing the first person he comes to dislike is you. If the pump is going to work at all, it has to be their pump, not mine" (183). But, like all other "good" Americans in the novel, Homer ends up tricking the natives to get them to use his pump. He goes to a small village and pretends he needs their help to perfect an invention he is working on, enlisting the aid of a native mechanic, Jeepo. The natives are impressed with the pump, and Atkins and Jeepo go into business producing the pumps.

Meanwhile, Atkins's wife, Emma, has a project of her own. This story is the low point of the novel's paternalism. Emma notices that all the old people of the village have bent backs and use short-handled brooms to sweep with. She goes out and finds tall reeds, transplants them to the village, and begins sweeping her own house with a long-handled broom made from these weeds. The natives all copy her new broom. Four years later, back home in America, Emma receives a letter from the headman of the village thanking her for unbending the backs of the old people. The arrogance of this incident as constructed by Lederer and Burdick is almost beyond comment—while it is a true observation that many old Asian peasants have bent backs, the source is certainly not traditional short-handled brooms. It is a lifetime of hand labor in the rice fields and probably osteoporosis from a calcium-deficient diet; a facile alteration of supposed tradition by a superior American intellect will not fix a problem caused by poverty.

The film version of *The Ugly American* (1962), starring Marlon Brando and the Japanese actor Eiji Okada, spectacularly reenvisions the relations of Asians and Americans. The film preserves little of the book and presents Sarkhan much more clearly as an analog of Viet Nam. In the film Ambassador Mac-White and John Colvin are merged into one character so that MacWhite

(Brando) has spent time during World War II in Sarkhan and was a friend of Deong (Okada), who has been a leader in Sarkhan's battle for independence and is now an unofficial national spokesman. When MacWhite returns to Sarkhan as ambassador he talks with Deong and comes to believe that he is a Communist; MacWhite commits the United States to back the corrupt government of Kwen Sai. Deong, meanwhile, is duped by the real Communists into leading a revolt against Kwen Sai; North Sarkhanese paratroopers enter the country, violating an agreement Deong has made with the combined Communist powers: representatives from the Soviet Union, China, North Sarkhan, and the South Sarkhanese Communist guerrillas. In the end, the treacherous Communists assassinate Deong.

While the film retains many clichés—the assassin is Deong's inscrutable young protégé, for example—it does depict Deong as the true equal of MacWhite, a lesson that MacWhite learns only at the end, when Deong is dying. In two important confrontations between Deong and MacWhite, Deong declares that American democracy is only for white people, and "I'm not your little brown brother."

The film retains the cold war point of view of the novel; the lesson is that Americans must not treat Deong like a little brown brother in order to save nations like Sarkhan from communism. Despite the film's age, it remains the most politically complicated American film about U.S. involvement in Viet Nam, and Okada's Deong is still the most fully realized Asian character to appear in any such film.

Robin Moore's novel *The Green Berets* was a phenomenal best-seller and remains the best-selling novel about the war ever published in the United States.[16] It is a love song to the Special Forces, celebrating the role of John Kennedy's favorite fighting force in the war against communism. John Wayne's film version, a simplistic story of good guys versus bad guys, was universally abhorred by critics when it appeared in 1968. It was a hit, however, and earned $9.75 million in domestic rentals in its original release (it cost $6.1 million to make).[17]

The novel is set in the Republic of Viet Nam in 1964, during the advisor phase of the war. The Green Beret units work closely with ARVN troops, acting as advisors to their Vietnamese counterparts. No important Vietnamese characters appear in the book, however; the Vietnamese remain abstractions. Moore begins by constructing himself as an insider privy to secrets and therefore an expert writing from his firsthand experience. In the preface he describes his introduction to the Special Forces and tells the story of going through their airborne training and guerrilla warfare school, the only civilian to have done so. Claiming that "*The Green Berets* is a book of truth," he then explains that he "could present the truth better and more accurately in the form of fiction" (9). As he explains, Green Beret methods are "unconventional," and he does not want to "embarrass U.S. planners in Vietnam" or "jeopardize the careers of valuable officers" (10).[18] Since he details illegal operations in Cambodia, Laos, and even the DRV(!) and double-dealing with Vietnamese counterpart officers,[19] the reasons for his concerns are clear. He justifies these operations with statements such as: "A few highly placed Americans were wise enough to realize that the Communists might not abide by the agreements they had signed" (167); as a result, the Americans do not abide by them either. The circular (non)logic of this would be funny, if it were not tragic.

Moore is straightforward about the nature of the secrets he reveals through fiction: "I saw too many things that weren't for my eyes—or any eyes other than the participants' themselves—and assisted in too much imaginative circumvention of constricting ground rules merely to report what I saw under a thin disguise" (10). In this passage Moore accomplishes at least two things. First, he establishes his own authority as a participant and witness. (At the end of the book he reports, "The proudest possession I own is the green beret given to me by an A team in a heavy combat zone" [333].) He goes to ridiculous lengths to build his own credibility on the basis of experience: "A detachments [the Special Forces combat units] began paying me the supreme compliment of sending me in place of another sergeant as the second American with an all-Vietnamese or montagnard patrol" (15). Second, he is brazenly reporting to his readers that U.S. Special Forces conduct illegal operations in order more effectively to carry out their war.[20] What is startling about this report is that Moore constructs the Special Forces' actions as heroic. He invests them with a right beyond political "restrictions," diplomatic negotiations, national sovereignty, or international law, by right of their superior experience and their superior capacity to use both cunning and force to win their battles. This vintage right-wing, stab-in-the-back theory is that the regular army and its conventions, along with political restrictions, handicap the Green Berets' efforts to win the war.

Moore deliberately keeps his narrative pinned firmly to the level of personal experience, his own and that of the characters he creates—fictional, he tells us, but based on fact. He and his characters are scornful of politics, which they perceive as getting in their way. These narrative devices allow Moore to construct the war precisely as he sees it. He perceives it in terms of

American mythology and cold war globalist consciousness, which he brings with him, intact, through his military training and his experience in Viet Nam. John Clark Pratt writes of this novel: "Moore's Americans hardly try to understand their environment or the implications of their presence in Vietnam; instead, they shape Vietnam and Laos to fit their own myths" (Lomperis 131). It is clear throughout Moore's narrative that he and his Green Berets conceive of the situation as their own war against communism (a disembodied entity not directly connected with Vietnamese people), with their Vietnamese allies as playing pieces in the game. The American agenda is what is important. They are resentful when Vietnamese politics and religion get in the way of their battle. In his preface Moore calls Vietnamese politics a "yo-yo" after describing the coup against Diem and the subsequent coup against his successor; he sees this yo-yo as an impediment to the fight against communism. However, he fails to note the role of the United States in the creation and maintenance of the RVN governments. Rather, he sees Vietnamese politics as annoyingly "Asian."

He also falls for President Diem's propaganda disinformation that the Viet Cong were mostly northerners infiltrating the South, rather than southerners forming their own organizations. For Moore, the northerners are "hardcore," and the Communist presence in the Republic of Viet Nam is an invasion by a "neighbor," not a civil uprising. Much of the anti-Communist justification for U.S. action in Viet Nam is based on this falsehood, which Moore perpetuates.

Religion also obstructs the Green Berets' war against communism. One chapter, "The Cao-Dai Pagoda," details the sneaky Viet Cong attempt to infiltrate a Special Forces camp that has a Cao Dai pagoda in it. The camp commander tells the Moore character: "The Cao-Dai elders say we unenlightened Americans have desecrated their temple" (93). As it turns out, the commander built the camp around the temple because it was the most strategic site, and, anyway, only one old woman was currently worshiping at the temple, and she said it would be okay. Now the Viet Cong, masquerading as Cao Dais, want entry to the base to worship at the temple. The Americans lure two NLF spies into the temple, then blow it up, making it look like a Viet Cong attack was responsible. During the course of this chapter one American says, "It's a goddamned tragedy if we're going to let religion and politics lose us big hunks of this war" (96).

One of the games the Americans are playing is Cowboys and Indians. The first sentence of chapter 1 reads: "The headquarters of Special Forces Detachment B-520 in one of Vietnam's most active war zones looks exactly like a fort out of the old West" (25). Another model that Moore builds his tale on is the legend of the French Foreign Legion. So many of his Green Beret characters are foreign-born nationals who have entered the U.S. Army to get citizenship that his Special Forces resembles the Foreign Legion: a Finn who joined the German army in World War II to fight the Russians, then joined the U.S. Army; a Frenchman; a Hungarian, whose "somewhat Oriental appearance" Moore attributes to "centuries of invasions and population movements in the Balkans" (108); a Syrian intelligence specialist who pushes the limits even of Moore's ethical standards; a German, who had been with the Hitler Youth before his family moved to Milwaukee in 1939; and a Filipino, who, although American by nationality, is described in strongly ethnic terms and spends much of his time passing for a Montagnard.

These Americans and Europeans stand in contrast to Moore's Vietnamese, who are constructed as unrelentingly primitive. "Many of the local people have never seen anything more modern than a crossbow before a Special Forces A detachment comes to their area" (17), he tells us in his factual preface. Later in the novel a Green Beret sergeant remarks that he does not trust Vietnamese to read their compasses correctly. Moore consistently emphasizes the contrast between American technology and Vietnamese "primitiveness," the latter which he attributes to some sort of intrinsic, stubborn backwardness rather than to poverty and the history of colonialism. "The low, white buildings with dark roofs which rose above the mud walls of Phan Chau, and the tall steel fire-control tower were visible from the airstrip" (32), the fictional character Robin Moore tells us on his arrival at the A-team camp of his friend Kornie. Notice that the clean, white American structures rise above the mud of Viet Nam; the narrator's relief at being able to spot these buildings from the airstrip is palpable. All else is "scrub-brush jungle" (32).

A lengthy description of Sergeant Ngoc's pin-under-thumbnail torture of a suspected Viet Cong infiltrator is followed by the Moore character's comment, "I've been around some damned crude sessions. Ngoc is more refined than most" (50). Ngoc's torture scene is followed by an American interrogation, carried out with superior American technology—a polygraph. Moore expresses no moral objection to torture; the contrast is between the inefficient physical brutality of the Asian and the technological efficiency of the American. The psychological torture is the same—the Americans tell the Vietnamese suspect that the blood pressure cuff of the polygraph will blow his arm off if he tells a lie. (In a later interrogation scene the Americans use sodium pentathol, a far more humane and efficient technique, proving that their own brutality with the polygraph is also outmoded and unnecessary.)

Captain Kornie's A team are "teutonic knights" (45), "Vikings" and "giants" (67), in sharp contrast to the small, dark Vietnamese. Kornie is the Finn who has previously served with the German army. He has built an A team comprised of Nordics like himself, except for Rodriguez, the demolitions expert. Moore suggests that Rodriguez is the ethnic exception on the team because demo experts have to be cunning and slippery. These "teutonic knights," fettered with their incompetent Asian allies, do battle against the forces of darkness. John Hellmann notes that the novel has an "underlying theme of 'Germanic' Anglo-Saxon racial superiority leavened only by sentimentality" (57).

Moore's belief in the incompetence of Asians leads him to include a chapter about a Caucasian Viet Cong—a Frenchman who acts as an advisor and who personally takes operational control of a Viet Cong battalion. In explaining that the Viet Cong have French advisors with operational control, a Green Beret officer named Scharne says, "They're more realistic than we are" (146), echoing Graham Greene's notion that European colonialism is older and wiser in dealing with the "natives." In this chapter Moore is setting up a battle of white men versus white men—much more gripping than yellow men fighting each other. (Later works, like *Rambo*, use the same strategy.) Scharne envies the Frenchman: "If I had operational control of a Vietnamese Ranger battalion . . . I could tear up anything the VC had" (147). He lies to his Vietnamese counterpart and to higher-ups, in effect to take operational control and lay an elaborate trap to kill the Frenchman (fancifully known as "the Cowboy," because he wears a Stetson and cowboy boots), and thus Moore can stage a battle between white leaders of native troops. John Hellmann contends that the real sin for which the Frenchman must die is "the betrayal of the white race" (Hellmann 62), citing the description of him as he dies: because of his wounds he is "barely recognizable as a Caucasian now" (166).

In addition to being primitive, the Vietnamese are corrupt. Moore notes that it is a triumph for Americans to build orphanages, since the normal Vietnamese practice is for families to take in orphaned children as "slaves." He takes this conceit too far, however, in a chapter where the Green Berets conspire to evacuate fourteen wounded Montagnard children to an American hospital, against Vietnamese orders that civilians not be transported on medevacs. Once the children are at the base camp, Captain Nim tries to prevent them from being taken to the American orphanage. "He wants those kids for slaves" (235), Captain Locke says. Moore misses an important cultural point and betrays how imaginary his Vietnamese are: Vietnamese would never take in Montagnard children. The whole episode exists to show the supposed moral superiority of Americans. Captain Locke says, "I and most Americans love all children" (236). The children are taken to the orphanage, although they are not even orphans: their relatives saw them off when they were evacuated.

In his preface Moore mentions a little political and historical background, including information about Special Forces' work with the Luc Luong Dac Biet (LLDB), the Vietnamese equivalent of Special Forces.

When U.S. Special Forces teams began setting up camps on a large scale, their job of fighting Communist guerrillas was made far more difficult and dangerous because Diem saddled them with the untrained, combat-shy, and—by U.S. standards—corrupt LLDB as counterparts. . . .

Obviously, strife and ferment often resulted from such diametrically opposed philosophies. (20)

The Special Forces imagine "their job" to be fighting communists; they do not conceive of "their job" to be training and advising the LLDB, but see the LLDB as getting in the way of their own war.

Because of these ethnocentric and globalist attitudes, Moore and his characters are caught in a contradiction that remains invisible to them. They do not see that the "ferocious, suicidal Communists" (67) are the same people as the LLDB. Instead, the Americans' consciousness bifurcates. They view the LLDB as "typical Asians"—primitive, corrupt, and incompetent, their terrible fitness as soldiers due to their racial makeup. At the same time, they see the enemy as "Communist guerrillas," with their identity as Communists obscuring their racial identity. Because they are wily Communists, they are competent, dangerous adversaries.

This bifurcation of consciousness prevents Moore and his characters from making a potentially disturbing political analysis. If they were to see the NLF as primarily Asians, rather than primarily Communists—that is, the same way they see the LLDB—they would realize that their stereotypes about Asians did not adequately explain the LLDB's corruption and bad soldiering, and would have to look elsewhere for an explanation. This would lead to a line of questioning outside the parameters of a globalist mindset.

Moore's attitude also manifests itself in the consistent portrayal of ARVN officers and enlisted men as cowards.[21] A nickname for the LLDBs is "lousy little dirty bug-outs" (75). An American advisory on how to deal with snipers by sending squads out after them is rendered by Vietnamese translators as directions to withdraw (251). Captain Kornie says of his counterpart, "He maybe don't like patrols himself, but if the Americans want to kill themselves and only a reasonable number of strikers, that's our business by him" (35). Kornie says this by way of explaining that this counterpart is better than his predecessors, whom he describes as "cowardly." Later, when Kornie goes out with a patrol, the Vietnamese commander elects to stay in camp, in case the B team needs to reach him. "Very good thinking, Captain," Kornie says, and Captain Lan misses the sarcasm and is pleased with the compliment. This is one of many examples in the book of the white man easily manipulating the yellow man while winking at his fellow whites, including the readers of the novel.

In a similar instance of duping, an American interrogator knows one sentence of Vietnamese: "We want to ask you some questions. If you tell the truth you won't be hurt" (52). He says this to prisoners before beginning with his polygraph, and the Vietnamese believe he understands what they say even though he has an interpreter. This subterfuge is presented in an admiring tone. Despite the Special Forces emphasis on languages (every Green Beret must be at least bilingual), very few of them seem to be able to speak Vietnamese.

The Americans complain repeatedly of ARVN cowardice: "The Viet battalion commanders won't fight like men and push the VC out of the village in man-to-man fighting" (126). Again because of Moore's globalist vision, it never occurs to anyone to question why the ARVN are so cowardly, while the NLF are so brave. The answer the novel presents is simple (and simplistic): the ARVN are just inferior Asians; the NLF are Communist supermen. This portrayal echoes the simultaneous sub- and superhuman images of Japanese during World War II.

Not all ARVN are corrupt and cowardly, though. The American officers occasionally praise a Vietnamese officer. Inevitably, that Vietnamese officer is someone who emulates the Americans slavishly. Kornie likes Captain Lan's subordinate, Lieutenant Cau: "Cau here is one of the tigers. If they had a few hundred more like him, we could go home. He went through Bragg [U.S. Special Forces school] last year" (39). Lieutenant Cau is just like an American, and if there were more like him, the Americans could leave. In other words, Viet Nam cannot manage on its own unless it becomes more American. Another Green Beret, Captain Farley, also praises a Vietnamese officer in the same vein: "Minh's the kind this country needs if it's ever going to become a modern nation" (84).

Moore is unabashed in his use of stereotypes. A Cambodian outlaw paid off by the Green Berets is a "sinister little brown bandit" (43). A corrupt Vietnamese officer pulls off a profiteering scam by having soldiers come through the pay line more than once. The American supervisors suspect, but have trouble knowing for sure, because it is hard to tell Vietnamese apart (81). A Chinese cook in a Special Forces camp grins and bows, his eyes crinkling, "apparently with pure joy at dispensing more of his food" (226).

Women, both Vietnamese and Montagnard, are tools to be used brutally by the Americans, both for sexual and intelligence purposes, then sacrificed or discarded. Sergeant Ossidian recruits female agents in Saigon by showing them pictures of their brutally murdered families in their home villages. In his elaborate system, he gets to them first with the news; that way they will be putty in his hands. Ossidian sacrifices these women without regret so he can carry out operations like the kidnapping of a Viet Cong officer. On another operation, Captain Arklin goes to live secretly among the Meo tribe in Laos to organize them into anti-Communist brigades. In order to fit in, he takes a Meo wife (who is conveniently half-French—the book has a plentiful stock of half-French women, but no half-French men). When his mission is over he leaves her to return to his stateside (white) wife.

Moore not only constructs Vietnamese and Montagnard women as sexually pliant, he constructs Vietnamese and Montagnard men as oversexed. A Communist official is kidnapped literally out of the bed of his secret-agent girlfriend, who has orders to get him involved in sex at a precise hour. She has no trouble with this, as he responds like a rutting bull to her every overture. Captain Arklin, out on a patrol with his Meo soldiers, cannot convince them that they need to hurry back to camp until he tells them he has to get back because he "promised Ha Ban I'd give her the biggest loving she ever had before daylight tomorrow" (197). This being a motivation they can understand, they immediately set off.

Moore also employs the notion of a reified "Oriental mind." At one point the Moore character reports that "I had learned to understand the deviousness of the Vietnamese mind" (85). Another Green Beret explains an action a Vietnamese has taken as "part of this Oriental face thing" (110). When the torturer, Sergeant Ngoc, says the polygraph method is no good because "if they are truly the enemy they should be tortured anyway," the American interrogator replies, "Now we get the Oriental mind at work. . . . If we stay here twenty years we won't change them, and God save us from getting like them" (54). The "Oriental mind" is a transcendent category, unaffected by history or anything else, that cannot be changed in twenty years. It is also a loathesome thing, which Americans should work hard not to be contaminated by.

It is important to note, however, the ways in which this book differs sharply from later portrayals of the war. Viet Nam the country is the abode of inferior little brown men, in Moore's formulation, but it is not the heart of darkness that later narratives present. "Vietnam" the war is a battle that makes sense, one that the Special Forces soldiers understand and to which they are dedicated, rather than the senseless maelstrom that exists for no other purpose than as a personal trial for the protagonists of later works. *The Green Berets'* racism is not attributable to the horror and brutality of the war: despite the horror and brutality, the characters are professional soldiers who are not overwhelmed by what they see (although they are sometimes disgusted, sometimes saddened, and always frustrated, they are nonetheless portrayed as in control of at least themselves, if nothing else).

The racism of *The Green Berets* is more akin to that of *The Ugly American* than to that of many of its successors. These two novels share the same globalist worldview, in which the Asian participants are simply pawns in the chess game (or, perhaps, domino game) played by the superpowers. As such, Moore has no need to represent Asians in any but the time-tested, most stereotypical ways.

Between the time of the publication of *The Green Berets* in 1965 and the making of the loosely adapted film version in 1968, enough had changed that a new perspective was needed. Instead of the insider-journalist narrator, the film uses a different device. David Jansen plays a liberal journalist who does not approve of the war; by the end of the movie he has been won over by the valor of the Green Berets (and the audience is supposed to be won over with him). The change in perspective, though, does not include a change in racism. Although the ARVN soldiers are now more noble than cowardly, they are portrayed as little brown sidekicks, who must constantly be taught moral lessons by the Americans. The plot of the movie bears little resemblance to the book. The major similarities between the two are their conceptions of Americans as tall and heroic, of ARVN as sidekicks, and of Communists as sneaky, brutal, and tough. That is, for Wayne's production company, the substance of the book translated into film seems to consist entirely of the stereotype. I want to emphasize here that the two *Greet Berets*, book and film, need to be taken seriously. They represent the most influential early view of the war.

In Larry Heinemann's *Close Quarters* the main characters have completely racist attitudes toward the Vietnamese. The novel, narrated in the first person by Philip Dosier, a young soldier, presents no picture of the Vietnamese independent of its narrator's and characters' attitudes toward them. Therefore, a reader imbibes the characters' views with nothing to contradict them. The characters' attitudes are perhaps even more extreme than the dominant American view. Philip Jason has written of Heinemann's novel that it

presents a horrifying vision of how attitudes toward orientals and women are heightened by the war experience. The narrator's inflection is so flat that one can not be sure if the horror is only the reader's. The protagonist's behavior is presented as a series of consequences, rather than a series of choices. This naturalistic perspective, then, assumes the animal in human nature and treats the combat zone as a return to the wild. (129)

Close Quarters is among the most savage of American representations of the war.

Dosier's friend Cross says, "I never met a squint-eye that I would call anything but gook" (19). Cross bears a grudge against the Vietnamese because they killed his friend, Murphy. He describes Murphy's death—Murphy has jumped out of his Armored Personnel Carrier to chase a Viet Cong through the woods: "One of the goddamedest things I seen *anybody* do. An' that chicken-shit gook turned on his fucken heel and shot Murph square in the neck" (20). Note the double standard Cross implies: he grudgingly admires his friend's crazy action, but the Viet Cong, who does what one would expect any soldier to do—defend himself—becomes "chicken-shit" in Murphy's eyes. Cross's (and the novel's) racism extends to African Americans, as well. Cross blames Sergeant Surtees, a black man, for being slow to call in a medevac after Murphy is wounded, causing him to bleed to death. Cross proclaims, "[If] I get about half a chance I'm gonna do a number square on his nappy fucken head" (20).

The characters in the novel seem to spend most of their tours of duty commiting illegal acts. One of the chief of these is killing a prisoner (an egregious violation of the Geneva Convention). Cross explains his attitude to Dosier:

He was giving away our position. . . . He was dying anyway. I seen it enough to know it when it comes stumbling out of the woodline. And besides, it was a gook. You give gooks a break like that and you ain't gonna last. Listen, I took a chance for Murphy, I'll take a chance for Atevo, and I'll take a chance for you, but don't ask me to take a chance for gooks. (63)

Among Cross's multiple justifications for his action, the fact that the man was merely a "gook"—a nonhuman to Cross—is his most important argument.

When the wounded man is first taken prisoner, the medic has treated him and "tried to talk to the man, in a light tone of voice like you would soothe a frightened dog or a lathered, skittish horse, but the man did not seem to hear" (61). This passage contains an interesting tension: although Dosier refers to the prisoner as "the man," Dosier and the other soldiers clearly see him as an animal, because he does not speak English, because he is "foreign."

The disdain Cross and Dosier show for Vietnamese is not limited to enemy Vietnamese. In an encounter with some ARVN troops in a bar, Dosier looks them over and thinks, "No helmets, no gear, no guns. Underfed, doe-eyed, skittish and fretful, with pegged pants and black high-topped gym shoes or shower thongs. Christ, no wonder we're over here busting our ass" (81). Cross calls the Vietnamese bartender Chingachgook. Another soldier explains to the ARVN why: "He reminds Cross here of his great white father, the last of the fucken Mohicans and a champion bartender from Washington. He lives in this boo-coo numba-one hooch, painted white with a twenty-four hour generator. Dig? Changachgook here same same three brain cells, white apron, goofy-looking feet, shiteating grin. Everything same same" (81). The equating of Vietnamese and American Indian in this passage harks back to Richard Drinnon's view of American attitudes toward Vietnamese being an extension of American attitudes toward Indians.

The perspective of Quinn, Dosier's best friend, is similar to the others, but marked even more clearly by petty sadism. Dosier recalls:

Another time we were running convoy and the road was crowded with dink kids, begging C rations just like always. Quinn was a gunner on the Cow Catcher by then. He took a full boxed meal and dangled it over the side just out of reach of this one kid, all the while tossing fifty-caliber cartridges at the kid's head—first with a light snap of the wrist, then flicking them, harder and harder, sidearm hard. After the kid had humped a good half a mile, fighting off other kids and ducking fifty brass, Quinn flipped it out to him. Big deal. Ham and lima beans, GI white bread, crackers, and apple jelly. (97)

Dosier condemns not Quinn's sadism—but the Vietnamese child for being desperate enough to suffer Quinn's abuse for a prize that Dosier himself disdains, because he has plenty. Dosier's and Quinn's lack of compassion, the men's inability to see the child as a starving boy in a ruined land, lies at the heart of the dominant American attitude.

Dosier's buddies are equally brutal in their attitude toward Vietnamese women. They call one prostitute who serves American troops "Claymore

Face" because she carries pox scars, and they call a young girl who sells them Coke "No-tits." The daughter of the woman who runs the base laundry tries sincerely to make friends with Dosier, but he can only see her as a potential prostitute: "She called me 'Serg'n' all the time and smiled every day when I dropped in. I kept asking her if she'd like to make a quick five hundred P. . . . She kept saying no. She was a convent girl, saving her pennies to go to France and be a model. Well, Chingachgook! I says, here's the easiest five hundred you'll make today" (272). The adolescence of Dosier's attitude illustrates one of the major problems in the literature of the war—dominant American views of Vietnamese seem to be stuck in just such adolescence. The critical emphasis on "authenticity" in portrayals of "experience" as a preeminent criterion for judging Viet Nam War literature has meant that this adolescent perspective is the only one granted legitimacy.

Dosier's perception of the Vietnamese language is that it is not speech, but gibberish—"the buzz and hum of gobbledygook chatter" (79). A group of ARVN's "quacked and cackled and yammered and wouldn't shut up the whole trip" (123). When called upon to use Vietnamese place names, the soldiers respond in an extremely juvenile and ethnocentric way: "All the way to the Suoi Cut. (We said the name of the place like we were calling hogs, 'Soo-wee! Soo-wee!')" (226).

The one time Dosier is able to feel some compassion, some identification with a Vietnamese, it practically costs him his soul because it comes too late. (There is an important point to be taken here.) He shoots and kills a lightly wounded prisoner. The prisoner, a young boy, has command-detonated a mine that has blown up members of Dosier's platoon. Dosier is guarding the prisoner with a shotgun, full of rage: "You fucking little squint-eye. Move, kid. Just move. . . . It would be so easy to kill him and say he made a grab for the gun" (217). Eventually Dosier does kill him. Although he suffers no legal consequences—all the soldiers, and his lieutenant, take his side and believe the prisoner tried to escape—he is haunted by moral consequences: "Vengeance is that quick vicious turn of anger that swings and hacks until you cannot step but on corpses. The day after Christmas I stood over a weak wounded kid and saw his grave and my grave, and the grave of those around me—a deep smooth-sided shaft and you will never fill it" (220).

Heinemann's second novel, *Paco's Story*, won the 1987 National Book Award. It is a sensitive, and sometimes brilliant, portrait of a returned veteran who is literally haunted by his past. Although Heinemann's writing about American veterans has sharpened and deepened between the two books, his portrayal of Vietnamese has not. *Paco's Story* epitomizes a disturbing tendency of recent U.S. Viet Nam War fiction: the practice of attempting to humanize Vietnamese characters by showing them as victims, only to make the American characters and readers feel guilty, if not responsible or repentant, for all the terrible things "we" did to "them." This type of representation does nothing to break down that us-them duality or to attempt to make rounded, authentic portrayals of the Vietnamese characters.

Heinemann's own attitude, as reported in interviews with him and articles he has written, reveals a good deal of confusion. While criticizing American policy and the behavior of Americans in Viet Nam, he does not seem able to separate himself from the horrors he describes:

But when you're there, and you're a grunt, there is no morality. If you try to resist the war, the evil simply blows through you, and you get killed. It doesn't matter about politics and morality. All you know is, the only thing dumber than going to Vietnam is being killed there.

Everybody knows what was different about Vietnam from, say, Korea or World War II or any other war was that there was no reason for it. To say we were saving the world from Communism was buls——. We were hired to kill gooks, and that's it.

At the same time, there was this sense of carte blanche. You could do anything, stand naked in the street and piss if you wanted; there was the broadest possible permission. If you killed the wrong person, that's too bad. That was a body count. So we got brutal and mean, and the evil of it was, we really began to like it. (quoted in Holt 12).

The "permission" that Heinemann describes depends on pervasive racism, and not all American soldiers fell into that moral trap, as we will see in this chapter's next two sections. Those who did fall into it did so because they saw the Vietnamese in the same light that Dosier sees them. To recognize that, as a soldier, one had been betrayed by the American government (in Heinemann's terms, "hired to kill gooks") meant for some a descent into a moral abyss created by the shared racism of government and individual soldier. In another interview Heinemann said, "I never hated anyone the way I hated the Vietnamese" ("Vietnam Horror"). Another attitude is possible, however, one that Heinemann never recognizes or acknowledges in either of his novels. This perspective is voiced by Sven Eriksson in Daniel Lang's nonfiction account *Casualties of War* of the abduction, rape, and murder of a Vietnamese woman:

All that many of us could think . . . was that we were fools to be ready to die for people who defecated in public, whose food was dirtier than anything in our garbage cans back home. Thinking like that—well, as I say, it could change some fellows. It could keep them from believing that life was so valuable—anyone's life, I mean, even their own. I'm not saying that every fellow who roughed up a civilian liked himself for it—not that he'd admit in so many words that he didn't. But you could tell. Out of the blue, without being asked, he'd start defending what he'd done maybe hours ago by saying that, after all, it was no worse than what Charlie was doing. I heard that argument over and over again, and I could never buy it. It was like claiming that just because a drunken driver hit your friend, you had a right to get in your car and aim it at some pedestrian. (Lang 21)

The attitude about retribution that Eriksson criticizes is decidedly adolescent and recalls the teenage perspective of all of Heinemann's characters.

Eriksson does not lose his moral compass because, although touched by American racism, he is not consumed by it. His method of dealing with what he witnesses in Viet Nam is to draw an analogy to the world he knows back home—the drunk driver parallel—and this allows him to steer clear of the moral abyss he sees others falling into, as does Heinemann's character, Dosier, who is unable to draw any parallels between Vietnamese people and "back home." Eriksson, a witness to the rape and murder, turns in his guilty friends and testifies against them, securing their convictions.

Eriksson also says,

We all figured we might be dead in the next minute, so what difference did it make what we did? But the longer I was over there, the more I became convinced that it was the other way around that counted—that *because* we might not be around much longer, we had to take extra care how we behaved. . . . We had to answer to something, to someone—maybe just to ourselves. (110)

This notion of answerability is missing in Heinemann's characters, and they lack it in part because they are teenagers who think and behave like teenagers (for all the racism of the soldiers portrayed in *The Green Berets*, at least they exhibit a more mature sense of responsibility for their actions). Deep-seated American racism provides them with a justification for their lack of answerability, just as it provides the men of Eriksson's squad the freedom from moral vision that allows them to commit their crime.

In an essay about *Close Quarters*, Cornelius Cronin makes the tired and self-serving argument that the American war in Viet Nam was different from all previous American wars, to which he attributes Dosier's viciousness:

"The ubiquitous presence and pressure of the body count forced the American combat soldier to see himself as primarily a killer" (128). Such arguments displace the historic role of American anti-Asian racism in the collective and individual American experience of the war in Viet Nam. In fact, this war was not startlingly different from previous American wars; Dosier's attitude closely resembles that of Americans toward Filipinos during the Philippine revolt and toward Japanese during World War II.

Cronin, in effect, apologizes for and justifies Dosier: "Dosier's actions are monstrous because man in war is monstrous" (128). This statement is a liberal cover-up for racism, and a lie besides. People are not always monsters in war (Eriksson in *Casualties of War* is an example of someone who firmly resists becoming a monster, despite the opportunity to do so). The idea that people are always monsters in warfare is pseudo-liberal, pseudo-pacifist falsehood. Modern warfare has rules and conventions to protect civilians, and in the U.S. Army those rules are taught as part of basic training. War is not unbridled savagery; rules in warfare are not a contradiction or absurdity. It is a postmodern idea to think that warfare has no rules or conventions, one that arises with the Nazis.[22] Dosier violates the rules (the text makes no note that there are rules or that he violates them) because he is killing *gooks*, not people. His actions are monstrous because of the racism of the war.

In *Paco's Story*, Heinemann includes an extended incident illustrating this type of treatment of Vietnamese in the chapter called "Good Morning to You, Lieutenant," which has been published separately as a short story in *Harper's*. The scene is of the rape of a Viet Cong woman:

Her eyes got bigger than a deer's and the chunks and slivers of tile got ground into her scalp and face, her breasts and stomach, and Jesus-fucking-Christ, she had her nostrils flared and teeth clenched and eyes squinted, tearing at the sheer humiliating, grinding pain of it. (Paco remembers feeling her whole body pucker down; feels her bowels, right here and now, squeezing as tight as if you were ringing out a rag, James; can see the huge red mark in the middle of her back; hears her involuntarily snorting and spitting; can see the broad smudge of blood on the table as clear as day; hears all those dudes walking on all that rubble.) (181)

This is not an Asian who is impervious to pain. The woman is portrayed as brave, even heroic, and somehow superior to the American soldiers. The main character, Paco, is a basically decent young man, who has been unalterably scarred by this and other memories of barbarity committed by

American soldiers. Yet the scene is told very much from the point of view of the soldiers (the narrator is someone who was in Paco's squad and died—he is narrating in retrospect, from a sort of modified first-person plural perspective). The woman never quite becomes truly human, truly a character in the novel—she remains a symbol of American guilt, a construct of that American guilt.

To be fair and complete in discussing Heinemann, it is important to note that he may have experienced an apotheosis and a turnaround in his vision. In an article in *Harper's* he describes his trip back to Viet Nam in 1990. "Could it be that veterans of the war in Vietnam are more intimately connected with the Vietnamese than with our own people and country?" he asks ("Making One's Way" 76). "For twenty-three years it was the war that was real and Vietnam that was the dream. But since coming home a second time, it is now the war that seems more a dream and Vietnam—seen by me as if for the first time—that is real" (76).

The stereotypes of Vietnamese explored here are not restricted to popular culture or literature; they affected the U.S. conduct of the war, and they continue to affect national discourse about Vietnamese immigrants and about the reestablishment of diplomatic relations with Viet Nam. William S. Turley gives an excellent example of how these attitudes influenced the conduct of the war:

Bombing advocates argued that the North could be pushed to some sort of psychological "breaking point." But just what that point was and exactly how the bombing was to push the North over it—something that conventional bombing had never done to any society before—were questions U.S. strategists never posed. Nothing more clearly revealed U.S. arrogance than the facile assumption that the North Vietnamese would succumb to pressures that the British and Germans had survived in World War II. (89)

An example of the ways such attitudes continue to be reflected in American culture is a newspaper article that displayed typical stereotypes of Asians. In a *San Jose Mercury News* article of 7 March 1988, titled "A Vietnamese Power Broker," San Jose businessman Doanh Chau is described as inscrutable, although not in so many words. "You never know exactly what he's doing," one Euro-American businessman is quoted as saying. In a box story about the three chambers of commerce serving the area, emphasis is put on numbers: "Seven years ago, the Vietnamese business community in Santa Clara County consisted of about 100 merchants. . . . Today there are more than 1,500 businesses." This statistic uncomfortably echoes the nineteenth-century mania with counting the incoming "Yellow hordes."

Trying, but Failing, to Break the Mold

> If, in trying to write about Vietnamese, they still look at us with "numb stares," then we have illiterate imaginations.
> —Timothy Lomperis, *"Reading the Wind"*

Brothers in Arms, William Broyles's narrative of his return to Viet Nam fifteen years after his war experience, opens with a prologue that stands as a metaphor for one segment of American consciousness of the Vietnamese. During the war, the young Lieutenant Broyles goes down a tunnel to check it out. He senses a presence in the dark, although he cannot see or hear anyone: "I felt a bond with that other human being down in that tunnel. How long had he been there, in the darkness? What was he like? Did he write poetry? Was he married?" (4). Broyles goes back down the tunnel and sets an explosive charge; he warns the "presence" in the tunnel to "didi"—to go away. That evening, Broyles says, "I had already begun to bury him in my memory, just as I had most likely buried him in the earth" (5). Significantly, the presence in the tunnel, despite Broyles's strong feeling of connection, remains a mystery in the dark.[23] For many American writers, attempts to illuminate that mystery in the dark ultimately run aground on the shoals of stereotype and ingrained ethnocentrism.

One such author is Philip Caputo. In his best-selling memoir *A Rumor of War* (1977), Caputo proclaims both his guilt and his harmlessness. In the story of his tour of duty as a U.S. Marine second lieutenant, he takes on American guilt about the war by telling of his court-martial for ordering the killing of a Vietnamese civilian. At the same time he tames the image of the killer by overtly not being a figure like Lt. William Calley, perpetrator of the My Lai massacre. He was, instead, an average American boy, a well-educated and civilized boy who could use lines from Shakespeare as the epigraphs to his chapters. In this respect he transcended the image of the crazy veteran and contributed to the rehabilitation of the image of veterans. But he does not do as well with the image of the Vietnamese.

Caputo portrays Vietnamese passivity, describing an incident in which several marines searched a hut in which a young woman sat:

The girl just sat and stared and nursed the baby. The absolute indifference in her eyes began to irritate me. Was she going to sit there like a statue while we turned her house upside down? I expected her to show anger or terror. I wanted her to, because her passivity seemed to be a denial of our existence, as if we were nothing more to her than a passing wind that had temporarily knocked a few things out of place. I smiled stupidly and made a great show of tidying up the mess before we left. See, lady, we're not like the French. We're all-American good-guy GI Joes. You should learn to like us. (83–84).

The young Caputo sees the Vietnamese woman's manner as alien, and while he wants her to understand he is one of the "all-American" good guys and means her no harm, the only mode of perception available to him causes him to be irritated by what he interprets as indifference on the part of the woman. He does not consider that the woman might, indeed, be terrified, but that her cultural pattern for reacting to terror might not be the same as his. He cannot make the shift that would allow him to engage in the contact with her that he clearly desires.

A poem by a veteran writer, Bill Jones, states the problem clearly:

> ### The Body Burning Detail
>
> Three soldiers from the North
> Burned for reasons
> of Sanitation.
> Arms shrunk to flippers
> Charred buttocks thrust skyward
> They burned for five days.
> It was hard to swallow
> Difficult to eat
> With the sweet smoke of seared
> Flesh, like a fog,
> Everywhere.
>
> Twenty-five years later
> They burn still.
> Across sense and time
> The faint unwelcome odor
> Rises in odd places.
> With a load of leaves
> At the city dump

A floating wisp of smoke
From the burning soldiers
Mingles with the stench
Of household garbage.

Once, while watching young boys
Kick a soccer ball,
The Death Smell filled my lungs.
As I ran, choking
Panic unfolded
Fluttering wings
Of fear and remorse.
A narrow escape.

A letter, snatched from the flames
The day we burned them
Is hidden away
In a shoebox
With gag birthday cards,
Buttons, string, rubber bands.
A letter from home?
The Oriental words,
Delicately framed
Are still a mystery.

This poem makes the leap that Caputo's text cannot and notes the inter-twinedness of the speaker with the three "NVA" soldiers—he literally inhales them, and they reside within his memory for twenty-five years. Still, they remain "inscrutable"—the "Oriental words" remain "a mystery." The speaker of the poem does not have either the resources or the imagination to find a translation of those letters, to go beyond the surface of the words—the surface of the dead bodies—to find a meaning. He ends with the statement of his distance from the letters, thus showing his consciousness of the problem, but he cannot take a step toward solution of the problem.

Robert Mason's personal narrative of his war experience as a helicopter pilot, *Chickenhawk*, similarly embodies all the contradictions of a person who is trying to overcome what he knows to be racist stereotypes, while succumbing to them all the same. This description of a work crew fits into the worst of traditionally racist works: "Black pajamas and conical hats piled out of the trucks and hurried purposefully off in all directions while the boss yelled orders. . . . In less than five minutes I was standing in the center of a circle of Vietnamese peasants armed with slashing machetes and flashing axes, watching the edge of the clearing dissolve as they hacked away like large, maddened termites" (89). Mason first uses a metonymy that completely erases the existence of the Vietnamese as people and replaces them with their clothes, then he portrays them as insects. In another instance he describes them as crabgrass (302). Yet simultaneously he expresses an interest in the Vietnamese. He starts learning Vietnamese words from a young girl: "She told me her real name but insisted that I call her by an American name. This beautiful and innocent girl on the other side of the world insisted that I call her Sally. It was depressing" (91). The entire scene of supervising the work crew is illustrative of American stereotypes about Asians. After patiently learning words from Sally, Mason is informed by Nguyen, the Vietnamese foreman, that one of the workers is dead. When Mason talks to him about it, he thinks, "This dumb gook doesn't know what I'm saying" (92). He makes no connection between his patience with and interest in Sally and his impatience with Nguyen.

The dead worker has been bitten by a snake: "He had been bitten, killed the snake, and then sat down to die. His friends working around him did not stop their work to help. They knew, and he knew, that when that snake bit you, you died. So he did" (93). Mason seems to attribute the lack of reaction among the workers to some sort of Oriental stoicism which he cannot understand. An alternate explanation never occurs to him, although he has presented all the details. Nguyen, under Mason's observation, has been brutally keeping the people at work. He has "kicked one of them in the ass" (89) and kept up a steady harangue. Perhaps, rather than Oriental stoicism, it was terror of the Americans and their overseers that kept the dead man's fellow workers working while he died. Whatever the Vietnamese were thinking, Mason does not know. Even after his laborious attempts at communication with Sally, he does not ask Nguyen, or Sally, or any of the other Vietnamese what they are thinking about the death—he simply rests on his assumptions.

Nonetheless, Mason is acutely aware of racism. He describes an acquaintance talking to an ARVN lieutenant in a bar.

"We see Americans as being apelike, big and clumsy with hairy arms," a Vietnamese lieutenant was saying to Kaiser. "Also, you all smell bad, like greasy meat."

Kaiser had got into a conversation with a racist of the opposite race. I watched the two men hate each other while I drank the genuine American bourbon that the Vietnamese lieutenant had so kindly bought us. . . .

The two men continued to trade heartfelt insults, the gist of which revealed normally submersed beliefs. (224)

Mason carefully distances himself from the two racists; he shows no sympathy for Kaiser, but at the same time he appreciates his "genuine American bourbon." While he repudiates racism, he implicitly maintains his ethnocentrism, remaining loyal to American products, American culture, and American paradigms.

At one point he makes a trip into town, where he perceives all the Vietnamese as sellers and himself as buyer. He sees them as shopkeepers and prostitutes, all with something to sell to him. He observes a young girl doing something which he interprets as trying to sell a baby. Full of moral certitude, he explains, "I had started to tell her that it was wrong to do what she was doing," but he notices that the baby is dead (115). He wonders, "How could you do this?" but neither he nor his companion try to ask her—instead they ask each other.

Mason continues to want to make contact with Vietnamese. At one point he has an opportunity to talk with an ARVN interpreter. He asks him how he thinks the war is going, but it soon becomes clear that the "interpreter" does not really speak English. Mason is frustrated and motivated to cruelty— he begins teasing the man in front of an audience. Someone ends the game by calling, "Hey, Nguyen," to the interpreter, who runs back to his tent. "At least he knew his name," Mason remarks, conflating ignorance of English with ignorance (172).

Mason comes face to face with his ethnographic dilemma when he participates in the massacre of some villagers who are standing in front of a Viet Cong gunner, shielding him from the helicopters. The Viet Cong has just shot down some helicopters. Mason has instructed his gunner to shoot at the ground first, to scare the people away.

The bullets sent up muddy geysers from the paddy water as they raged toward the group. The VC gunner was concentrating on another ship and didn't see Rubenski's bullets yet. I really expected to see the black pajamas, conical hats, and the small children scatter and expose the gunner. Were they chained in place? When the bullets were smashing fifty feet in front of them, I knew they weren't going to move. They threw up their arms as they were hit, and whirled to the ground. After what seemed a very long time, the gunner, still firing, was exposed. Rubenski kept firing. The VC's gun barrel flopped down on its mount and he slid to the ground. A dozen people lay like tenpins around him. (268–69)

This incident haunts Mason, because he cannot figure it out. He talks about it with his copilot.

"Why didn't they duck?" I sat in my seat staring into the night.
"The VC forced them to stand there."
"How can you make people stand up to machine-gun bullets?"
"He would have shot them if they had run."
"But if they had all run, he couldn't have shot them, not with us right there shooting at him."
"Obviously they were more afraid of him than they were of us."
"That was it? They were so afraid that they would get killed that they stood there and got killed?"
"Orientals don't think like we do."
Firefights chattered all night, but I didn't lie awake because of that. I kept replaying the scene. The faces were clear. One old woman chewed betel nut and nodded weakly as the bullets boiled in. One child turned to run, chewed up even while he turned. A woman shrieked at the child, then she was hit, too. The gunner kept firing. I saw it over and over, until I knew everybody in that group. And they all knew me and nodded and smiled and turned and whirled and died. (269)

Mason knows that his companion's theory about the way Orientals think is inadequate to describe what he has seen—he cannot dismiss it so easily, but he also cannot figure it out. In the end, he does not know everyone in the group, he knows only his image of them, which haunts him because of its inexplicableness. There is a compensatory quality to his saying that he knows them; it points to their mutual lack of knowledge, to his futile desire to compensate for that unbridgeable gap. It does not occur to Mason that the gunner has counted on the Americans' refusal to shoot civilians; but because helicopters have been shot down, the Americans do shoot the civilians. The ramifications of what those mutual assumptions and actions mean do not enter into Mason's consideration of the incident, perhaps because he cannot imagine the assumptions of the Vietnamese.

Finally, Mason makes the connection he has longed for, but it is a connection with artifacts, not with human beings, who have turned out to be too complicated, too unreachable. He is exploring an abandoned village. He finds an old woman and her grandson; he is unable to talk to them, so moves on to explore an empty house.

The last hooch I examined was the home of a master carpenter. I discovered his box of tools. . . . The wide selection and the quality of their tools told me that these people, or at least this person, were definitely not savages.

I had never heard of a gook or a slope-head or a slant-eye or a dink who did anything but eat rice and shit and fight unending wars. These tools and that waterwheel convinced me that there was successful way of life going on around us, but all we saw were savages, backward savages fighting against the Communist hordes from the North. . . .

The carpenter had made a bench whose parts fit so well that it didn't need any nails to hold it together. . . . I saw this as an enlightening symbol of the true nature of the Vietnamese people, so I stole the bench. . . . I walked over to my helicopter and put the bench in the shade of the rotor, sat down, and said, "Look, no nails." . . . Kaiser came over to see. "See, they put this together so well it doesn't need nails," I said.

"That's because they have to. Dumb gooks don't know how to make nails," said Kaiser. (312–13)

This passage sums up Mason's contradictory attitudes. He is definitely critical of Kaiser's typical American racism, but Mason does not have an adequate replacement for it. Even while he shows some ironic self-awareness about stealing the bench because he liked it so much, his theft reveals that he has made only part of the journey away from Kaiser's attitude. Further, he can connect with the Vietnamese only in the abstract; his ethnography has progressed from an early attempt to speak with Sally to a disembodied analysis of the handiwork of an absent craftsman.

The clearest example of a work that tries and fails to understand the Vietnamese is Tim Mahoney's 1988 novel *We're Not Here*. In this book, the main character, Sergeant Lemmen, wants to bring his American bubble with him to Viet Nam and live there monoculturally, not biculturally. His interest is in economic exploitation of Viet Nam, not in negotiations with Vietnamese culture as he encounters it in the persons of his friend, Nuong, and his lover, Hoa.

Westerners often fail to see that when Asians adopt aspects of Western philosophy or material culture, the Asians become more complex than Westerns who do not adopt Asian things. When Euro-Americans look at Asians, the Euro-Americans do not see Asian culture, which seems invisible; the Euro-Americans see only the adopted Western traits, which makes Asians seem simple, flat, derivative. This is the portrait of Asians that *We're Not Here* offers.

Lemmen has a dream of retiring in Viet Nam after the war and living like some of his old friends, "sergeants who retired to Korea, and they're all living great" (30). But, of course, the United States and the Saigon regime lose the war, and in the chaos of the final days of Saigon, Lemmen loses his girlfriend, the Vietnamese orphan boy he wants to adopt, and his colonialist dream. The book critiques the U.S. blindness to the realities of Viet Nam and the war there, and attempts, by telling parts of the story through the eyes of Lemmen's girlfriend, Hoa, and his interpreter, Sergeant Nuong, to critique American perceptions of Asians. Ultimately the novel fails to transcend the boundaries of American stereotypical representations of Asians, and the Vietnamese are presented only in the clichéd terms that the book seeks to critique. Although this is a text that uses Vietnamese characters in major roles, it is not a bicultural text.

Lemmen's dream of remaining in Viet Nam is the dream of a colonialist whose American money gives him great buying power in the colonized country. He is serving his second tour in Viet Nam, in 1975, when there are supposedly no more Americans in the delta (hence the novel's title). He remembers his first tour, in 1969: "Delta Town had once been a good home, with a decent PX, a tolerable mess hall, and that fine NCO club. . . . Where else could a man find a life so good and so easy?" (49). He sees the colonized Viet Nam of 1969 as a paradise and mourns its passing; since the slow withdrawal of American troops, leaving behind only "Operation Scarecrow," consisting of Lemmen's commander and himself and a few ARVN troops, all the good life is gone. He also waxes nostalgic over the "Pacex" catalogue: "Amazing what guys ordered from that catalogue: refrigerators, diamond jewelry, Seiko watches, cameras and lenses, color TVs, air conditioners, and, of course, stereos, stereos, stereos. Back in '69, his squad owned enough electronic stuff that Lemmen had wondered whether he was in a war zone or a stereo zone" (64).

Lemmen wants to be "somebody," to have power. He tells Nuong, "In the States, I'm a nobody" (155). In Viet Nam, as an American, he sees himself in a position of power, because he conceives of power solely in terms of money. It is clear that Lemmen wants in Viet Nam a cheaper version of the life he could have in the United States. In Viet Nam, his American dollars give him almost unlimited buying power. While the text shows us Lemmen's naïveté, it constructs him as a hapless victim of the evil or merely incompetent U.S. government. Lemmen's dream is seen as unrealistic only because it is in Viet Nam, rather than Korea or the Philippines, where he wants to retire. The text does not critique the whole colonialist paradigm; it critiques only the conduct of the war in Viet Nam.

During his 1969 tour, Lemmen eventually grew bored with the domestic comforts of Little America and began "craving Vietnam . . . to get a taste of the real thing" (105). He does not recognize that the Saigon he sees is also a colonized zone, peddling the GIs a mixture of familiar goods and prepackaged exoticism—"orange soda, Seiko watches, prerolled marijuana cigarettes, jade jewelry, military medals and patches, ice-cream bars, cameras, carved walking sticks, loafers and sneakers, rice cakes, chess sets, bronze statuary, photo scrapbooks, ivory statuary, blacklight posters, peace symbols, blue jeans, and cassette tapes" (105). Lemmen sees Viet Nam as one huge shopping list. He comes from a poor background, having had a father who failed to provide and then abandoned the family: Lemmen's history of (relative) deprivation makes the colonized Viet Nam look like paradise to him. He never notices how little the Vietnamese have. The novel does not blame Lemmen for his predicament—he is a perfectly ordinary guy, who, like all Americans, wants upward mobility. He does not and cannot see, since he trusts his country, that a large portion of his upward mobility is attained at the cost of the Vietnamese. The novel does not provide any analysis of the relationship between the U.S. underclass and Third World peoples. Whereas Lemmen might identify with the Vietnamese, because they are poor, as he was poor, he does not. The novel might make an argument about power relations and exploitation, but it does not; as a novel it is much less complex than that.

Lemmen's colonial vision must change in 1975, when all of his PX dreams have gone with the American troops. His colonialist vision changes, but it does not disappear. The dream becomes pastoral, a romanticized notion of living in peace on the land. He wants to retire to Hoa's home village: "I wanted to live along the Mekong. I've been dreaming about it for years. I used to be freezing, up in the mountains of Colorado, and I used to dream about it. Palm trees. The river. Boys fishing. Water buffalo. People keeping hogs and chickens" (118). But Lemmen is blind to the real situation. The war that he has participated in, the war that has allowed his colonialist dreams to flourish, has also destroyed Viet Nam. Hoa's home village is deserted now, occupied only by the old village headman. All the other houses are empty. There are no boys fishing, no water buffalo. The people, including Hoa's mother, have become refugees in Saigon. His very presence as an occupying soldier has made impossible his dream of peace and economic security as an American retiree in a colonized country.

Eventually, he recognizes something of the actual situation. It becomes clear that the United States will pull out of the delta and perhaps even out of Saigon. He realizes that he will have to leave, and with that realization his eyes begin to open a little bit to the world around him. He looks at Hoa and sees "a Vietnamese peasant. A revelation! She speaks English and listens to rock 'n' roll but she's a rice paddy girl. Why hadn't he ever seen that in the [bar]?" (179). Lemmen, partaking of the privileges of the occupying army, had never been able to see Hoa for who she really was in the setting of the bar she ran for GIs. With the bar closed, with Lemmen's dreams of the good life of retirement in a peaceful Viet Nam gone, he can finally see her a little more clearly. He remembers his arrival in Viet Nam, when a little boy had thrown a rock at him: "If he had been thinking, he would have known the moment that boy let go of the rock that he wasn't wanted here, was hurting the same people he was supposed to help . . . if he'd only admitted that what he saw with his own eyes was true—and to hell with what he'd been told" (229). His vision is still as narrow as it has ever been: originally he saw Viet Nam as a paradise in which he wanted to stay, now he can only see it as a hellhole to be gotten out of. There is little subtlety or nuance to his vision. He represents the United States in this respect. The novel portrays the U.S. military presence as either crushing or abandoning Viet Nam, with no sensitivity to the country itself. This is the black and white vision that Americans have been raised to believe in—the absolute good versus absolute evil polarity of the cold war, which fails to admit any complexity.

Along with his dawning recognition of the world around him, Lemmen develops a desire to do "one decent thing" before he leaves. He wants to rescue an orphan boy, Van. The irony is that in order to do what he considers a "decent thing," removing Van from a country Lemmen can now see no good in, he must lie, steal, become a criminal: "He would become a thief, and maybe even a murderer, but what difference did that make now?" (221). It does, of course, make a difference. Lemmen's actions again reflect the behavior of the United States in Viet Nam—in order to do "one good thing" (save Viet Nam from communism) the United States became criminal. Lemmen fails to see any contradiction in becoming a criminal in order to do a "decent thing," and the tone of the text reflects pathos rather than irony, suggesting that we are meant to see it Lemmen's way.

Lemmen never gets a chance to do his decent thing, never gets to "rescue" Hoa or Van, just as the United States was unable to "save" Viet Nam from communism. The novel attributes Lemmen's failure to his commanding officer, just as many representations of the war attribute the U.S. failure to a stab in the back by (depending on their politics) the media, the protestors, the government, or the military. The novel fails to see, as Lemmen fails to see, that destroying something in order to save it does not save it at all.

The Vietnamese characters are presented in ways that are conditioned by ethnocentric stereotypes. *We're Not Here* tries to critique America through its Vietnamese characters, but it falls short, because Nuong and Hoa lack depth. The novel, like Lemmen himself, can only perceive them as "inscrutable Asians," can only present them as "Little People."

Lemmen never notices the poverty of the Vietnamese, but Nuong does, and although his attitude should work in the novel as a critique, it is not entirely successful because it comes out in terms of self-hatred. Nuong has become "worldly" and his travels have made him despise his homeland: "Now he was traveled—California, Hawaii, Singapore—and it seemed that even in a simple thing like brewing beer, his people were hopelessly behind" (33). Nuong is unable to bridge the two cultures. Living in America, where he has had more comforts than he ever had at home, has marked him. He knows that, because of American racism and xenophobia, he can never be an "American," and that in his own country, the privileges of the colonizers are not available to him. Lemmen takes him to the recreation area in Little America but cannot, because of regulations barring natives, invite him into the swimming pool. Nuong feels trapped between the two cultures, and while he and Lemmen are in an ARVN outpost, reflects on this predicament: "Nuong often had the feeling that he no longer belonged anywhere; no matter how good his English or how much time he spent with GIs, he would never be American, and in a camp like this he was considered something of a traitor—as if living in America had ruined him as a loyal Vietnamese" (111). Nuong has internalized the American disregard for Viet Nam, making him unhappy in his own country. He wonders "why these big, rich people had sent their sons to die in his little nothing of a faraway country" (150). He remembers his time in California "fondly." The comparison with California, the land of supermarkets and restaurants, makes his own country seem like a "little nothing" to him.

Compared with the complex, wrenching cultural negotiations that the character Minh undergoes in *Blue Dragon, White Tiger*, this description of Nuong's bicultural experience is revealed for the simplistic counterfeit that it is. Nuong does not try to balance his two cultures; he does not feel the pull of Viet Nam against the pull of the United States. He simply disregards Viet Nam, as an American might.

Hoa, too, dreams of America. Her vision of California is as unreal as Lemmen's vision of Viet Nam. She dreams of "beautiful houses and big cars and buildings taller than Saigon," which she would be happy just to see, but Lemmen's vision of the United States is purely economic: "Hoa, I can't afford a beautiful house and a big car" (29). The portrayal of Hoa is reminiscent of Graham Greene's Phuong in *The Quiet American*; both writers present their characters as shallow, materialistic opportunists, who are also sweet and cheerful.

Nuong and Hoa are "simple peasants." Hoa has no curiosity and is devoid of emotions. The only time she does express any emotion—anger at Lemmen for not marrying her—the description follows an old stereotype: "He saw that look he'd seen enough times in this country, the eyes of an iron-willed fanatic" (179). Again it is useful to compare *We're Not Here* with *Blue Dragon, White Tiger*, which also presents characters who might be called "iron-willed fanatics," but the difference between them and Hoa is immense and is a matter not of the social class, but of narrative presentation of the characters. Minh's old love Thai is a fanatic in her devotion to the Party, but she is given motivation for her fanaticism, which makes her a comprehensible character. Hoa is merely a cliché.[24]

Hoa's single goal, pursued relentlessly, is to get Lemmen to marry her and take her to the United States. She does not miss her mother, who has gone to Saigon. She has the stereotypical simplemindedness of a "simple peasant." The major, whom she works for, asks her to bring fresh cookies for a congressman and his female aide. The aide grabs Hoa's wrist and objects to the major addressing her as "Sweetheart": "The woman let go of Hoa's wrist. 'I'm in full solidarity with you,' the woman said. Hoa backed away, rubbed her wrist—it was all red. She tried to figure it out—did they want fresh cookies or not?" (172). The scene is meant to make the Americans look absurd, but it also makes Hoa look absurd. In the last sentence, the "it" Hoa is trying to figure out at first seems to be the situation—the interchanges between the woman and the major. It turns out it is only the cookies she is trying to figure out—Hoa is not allowed to have any curiosity, any intellect at all.

The Vietnamese are often described in the book in terms of animals. Lemmen muses that all Vietnamese women smell like fish. A group of ARVNs crossing a bridge look like "monkeys in helmets" (118); the ARVN password is "birdlike" (133); Hoa feels like she is a "chicken in a coop" (223). And Lemmen sees a group of girl singers in a bar as food: "Their skin like Hershey bars. Their eyes like almonds. Their lips, cherries. Their tits, bouncing plums. Lemmen, a starving man!" (153).

The inability of the novel to transcend the paradigm it critiques is clearest in the opening chapter, which is set in 1982, seven years after Lemmen has lost Hoa in the delta. Lemmen is building his own Viet Nam in his room, but he is building it out of kitsch items:

Asia picture calendars are tacked to the walls; plates and bowls are piled in one corner; end tables are crowded with little things: bronze statues, incense burners, ceramic monkeys, tigers, and elephants. Woks and bamboo steamers—overflow from a closetlike kitchen—sit under a carved coffee table. A straw sleeping mat covers the wornout sofa, which sits next to a two-foot-high Buddha holding a begging bowl. In the Buddha's bowl are a Seiko watch and a gold crucifix on a gold chain. (8)

Now retired from the army, he is searching for Hoa in the Vietnamese community in San Francisco. Lemmen is "the kind of white man who can tell at a glance: Chinese from Korean, Thai from Viet, Filipino from Cambodian" (3). Yet, even so, these people stay foreign, unassimilable. "Near Eddy and Larkin it looks like another nation" (3). The immigrants do not become Americans, do not enter the melting pot. When Lemmen leaves that neighborhood and enters Union Square, he sees "all those bright American faces" (6).

The chapter reifies an "Asian" character: "Enough Oriental has seeped into [Lemmen's] mind and heart" (5), as if "Oriental" were a definable commodity. And again: "Something about her face is all Asia: scarred and anxious, tired and suspicious" (7). There is some Oriental/Asian quality—the quality of the other.

Viet Nam remains unnamed in the first chapter, although the references to it are clear. "A woman comes into the store and talks in the only foreign language Lemmen even dimly understands" (4). Lemmen asks, " 'What town are you from?' he does not want to add *over there*" (5; italics in original). He looks into a bar and sees "the remnants of Thieu's army" (6). "Typed under the picture are the words *Hoa Muon, Vinh Long, RVN*" (8). Why must the name Viet Nam not be used in this first chapter? Because, as the title says, "we're not here." Viet Nam remains unknowable in this novel; the Vietnamese characters remain flat and limited, built within the clearly defined limits of American representations of Asians. While the novel succeeds in exposing the insanity of America in Viet Nam, it teaches us nothing about Viet Nam itself.

Neither does Tim O'Brien, the most critically acclaimed fiction writer of the war, teach us about Viet Nam. O'Brien does not distinguish between Viet Nam the country and the American war in Viet Nam, even when he is talking about the country as well as the war: "I think that two hundred years, seven hundred years, a thousand years from now, when Vietnam is filled with condominiums and we're all going there to vacation on the beautiful beaches, the experience of Vietnam—all the facts—will be gone" (quoted in Lomperis 54). When O'Brien says "the experience of Vietnam" he means the experiences of individual American soldiers in the war in Viet Nam, but for him, as for so many Americans, Viet Nam the country is simply synonymous with "Vietnam" the war.

O'Brien's novel *Going after Cacciato* makes extensive use of Vietnamese characters, but, like Mahoney's book, does not fully realize them in the way it realizes its American characters. This novel stands near the center of the canon of literature of the American war in Viet Nam: it is the most written-about of Viet Nam War novels, O'Brien the most celebrated of veteran fiction writers. The novel's protagonist, Paul Berlin, imagines himself going on a journey with his squad to bring back Cacciato, a soldier who has deserted and is walking on an absurdist journey to Paris. Berlin remembers his war experiences in chapters that alternate with the imaginative and surreal journey to Paris. He is imagining this journey while he spends a night on guard, and several chapters take place in the observation post where he is on duty.

We are alerted from the beginning that Berlin's journey to Paris is imaginary, but it is more than an idle romp: "No, it wasn't dreaming. It was a way of asking questions" (46). The major question driving him is whether he, too, should desert, and what his obligations and possibilities are. His questioning turns out to be inconclusive. Given the conditions of the novel, it can only be inconclusive, because it is carried out in the absence of any political analysis, any consideration of the issues of the war, any knowledge of the people and the politics being fought against. O'Brien takes the idea of the war as the United States versus the United States even further by embedding it in the conscience of a single American individual, making it the battle of man versus himself. It is significant that it remains imaginary. Berlin never translates his dreams into action. At the end of the novel, we are returned to "reality"—Cacciato has slipped away from the patrol just at the Laotian border, and Berlin has experienced an episode of panic when the squad moves in on Cacciato, and he has not done his part. O'Brien's questioning of the war turns out to be nothing more than a test of courage for an individual.

O'Brien's own sense of history and politics, as he has expressed them in an interview, is embedded in the minutiae of individualism:

Based on my own experience, not many of the soldiers believed that Vietnam was an evil war. Most people fighting there—the ordinary grunts like me—didn't think much about issues of good and evil. These things simply didn't cross their minds most of the time. Instead, inevitably, their attention was on the mosquitos and bugs and horrors and pains and fears. These were the basic elements of the Vietnam war, and the same were present at the Battle of Hastings or Thermopylae or wherever. (McCaffery 134)

One of the major problems with *Cacciato* (as with most American representations of the war in Viet Nam) is that it is, indeed, focused on the "mosquitos and bugs and horrors." *Cacciato* still appears to be a first reaction to the war, yet it is O'Brien's third book about the war and was written ten years after his war experience. The U.S. discourse has so far been unable or unwilling to look beyond this first-reaction response to the war, to look beyond simple dichotomies such as all soldiers are victims, all authorities are victimizers, and only the American side can be or should be or needs to be examined. Further, for O'Brien to suppose that William the Conqueror's aristocratic knights or the Spartan elite at Thermopylae did not know what they were doing and why is for him to write American ignorance into the history of warfare. Hastings and Thermopylae, battles that took place in pre-Napoleonic warfare, are not parallel to the American war in Viet Nam; the personal experience of warfare is not a timeless and transcendent category, and O'Brien's claims to the contrary add to the mystification of warfare that clouds the issues of the American war in Viet Nam.

In *Cacciato*'s conception of the war as the United States versus the United States, the squad is battling with Lieutenant Martin. Berlin is battling with himself. In the imaginary journey to Paris, the squad is chasing not the enemy, but one of its own men. And in a scene where the death of one member of the squad is described, the man, Pederson, is killed by machine-gun fire from one of his own helicopters. Dying, he shoots back at the helicopter. The war is neatly transformed into United States vs. United States, and nothing else needs to be looked at. Indeed, in the national paradigm, nothing else can be looked at. Thus O'Brien's attempt to represent the other side fails.

Two Vietnamese characters have speaking parts in the novel. One is a woman, Sarkin Aung Wan (not a phonetically possible Vietnamese name), who serves as Berlin's guide and sweetheart on the journey to Paris. She is never anything more than Berlin's imagining, a projection the book acknowledges but does not critique. When she is introduced, she is a refugee, fleeing with her two aunts. A member of the squad shoots one of the refugees' water buffaloes, then the squad continues on with the refugees in their wagon with their remaining buffalo. Sarkin Aung Wan is beautiful and inscrutable, embodying all the American clichés about Asian women. She would "dearly like to be a refugee in Paris" (79). Many U.S. authors seem to be able to imagine Asia only as a place from which people want to flee, and the West only as a desirable place to flee to. The novel maintains an ongoing contrast between "civilization" and Viet Nam, which is something other than civilization: "Already he anticipated the textures of things familiar: decency, cleanliness, high literacy and low mortality, the pursuit of learning in heated schools, science, art, industry bearing fruit through smokestacks. Wasn't this the purpose? The goal? Some vision of virtue? . . . *Even* in Vietnam—wasn't the intent to restrain forces of incivility?" (328; emphasis added). *Even* in Vietnam, a place somehow outside of civilization. (Viet Nam's literacy rate is, in fact, 94 percent; it is 96 percent in the United States. This literacy is invisible to Berlin, however, because it is literacy in Vietnamese.)

Sarkin Aung Wan, even though she is Berlin's imagined creation, is completely unknowable. "What did she want? Refuge, as sought by refugees, or escape, as sought by victims? It was impossible to tell" (304). "He would ask her to see the matter his way. . . . Were her dreams the dreams of ordinary men and women?" (313). Notice that "ordinary men and women" are American men and women. Berlin does not ask if her dreams are those of "familar" men and women, of "men and women I know," but whether they are those of "ordinary" men and women.

Berlin's imagination is very convenient where Asian characters are concerned. The two aunts completely disappear from the narrative, without explanation.

Not only is Sarkin Aung Wan unknown and, more important, unknowable, Viet Nam itself is unknowable: "They [U.S. soldiers] did not know if it was a popular war, or, if popular, in what sense. They did not know if the people of Quang Ngai viewed the war stoically, as it sometimes seemed, or with grief, as it seemed other times, or with bewilderment or greed or partisan fury. It was impossible to know" (310). It may be impossible for Paul Berlin, completely caught up in his own interpretive framework, to know, but Viet Nam certainly is not unknowable in any transcendent way. The perceptions American soldiers brought with them, conditioned by American ethnocentrism and the history of stereotyping of Asians, made it seem impossible to know Viet Nam; Americans tended to see what they had been conditioned to see, and they tended to cling to their prefabricated vision even in the face of counter evidence.

Perhaps a better gauge of the novel's failure to imagine the other side is embodied in Li Van Hgoc (another naming error—he asks to be called "Van," his middle name, which is not a possible form of address for a Vietnamese; "Hgoc" is likewise not a possible Vietnamese name, and "Li" is a Chinese spelling). Li Van Hgoc is a deserter (another error; Van is introduced as a Viet Cong major, but later he turns out to have been born in Hanoi, and drafted, meaning he would have been drafted into the PAVN, not the Viet Cong). He has been sentenced to live in a tunnel for ten years. In a surreal sequence the squad has fallen into this tunnel. Members of the squad converse with Li Van Hgoc.

"The soldier is but the representative of the land. The land is your true enemy." . . . nodded Li Van Hgoc. . . .
"So the land mines—"
"The land defending itself."
"The tunnels."
"Obvious, isn't it?"
"The hedges and paddies."
"Yes," the officer said. (107–8)

While U.S. soldiers might often have felt that the land itself was the enemy, to put those words into the mouth of a Vietnamese soldier is to be guilty of an erroneous political analysis, which devalues the war efforts of those very Vietnamese soldiers. The land itself did not recycle American C ration cans into booby traps—Vietnamese soldiers did. By presenting Li Van Hgoc as a deserter like Cacciato and Berlin's squad, the novel is trying to show a commonality between soldiers, but through the conversation about the land, it simultaneously denies the Vietnamese their role as soldiers.

Further, placing Li Van Hgoc as a prisoner in the tunnels held there by his own government obscures the real role of the tunnels. "The land, Paul Berlin kept thinking. A prisoner of war, caught by the land" (121). Vietnamese soldiers who worked in the tunnels were held prisoner there not by their land, but by U.S. bombing. The tunnels were constructed as a way to survive U.S. munitions. Thus, in a clever step, O'Brien neatly obscures U.S. responsibility in the war.

Tim O'Brien has said in an unpublished interview that he "dealt with the Vietnamese people. . . . more closely than I would have liked to."[25] O'Brien explains:

I didn't know them. They didn't know me. One can't pretend to know what one doesn't. One can use one's imagination and try to identify with villagers and with particular human beings, soldiers who are Vietnamese. But to do it successfully you have to somehow be grounded in that which would somehow fuel their imaginations. One can't simply impose a Western civilization imagination on those people and come up with anything meaningful. . . . If I were capable as a person of imagining the Vietnamese I would do it. But I'm not. . . . I think by and large, in American fiction that has tried to render the Vietnamese people, they have ended up as stereotyped cartoon figures or as puppets.

He says in the same interview that he never does research: "If I don't know it I just make it up." It is not surprising that he finds himself incapable of imagining the Vietnamese. Nevertheless, in *Cacciato* he has done exactly what he describes as being meaningless—applied "a Western civilization imagination on those people" in the creation of Li Van Hgoc and Sarkin Aung Wan, who appear as cartoons or puppets in his novel.

The ethnocentricity of O'Brien's position emerges even more clearly when his attitude toward representing Vietnamese is contrasted with his attitude toward writing American female characters. He says it seems "more artistic, more beautiful, to include as much as possible the whole of humanity in these stories. Also, it's interesting to test in one's imagination . . . the reactions of a female heart." For O'Brien, "the whole of humanity" seems to include women and men, but only American ones, and he feels no limitations on his imagination in relation to American women. The barrier seems to be a cultural one, a barrier that he reifies with his mystification of the Western imagination and the Asian imagination, as if these were two material unitary entities incapable of knowing one another.

Yet O'Brien is more knowledgeable and sensitive about the overall costs of the war than are many American writers. In the same unpublished interview he says, "When we speak of Vietnam we still talk about the 48,000 Americans who lost their lives there. But we don't talk about the death of 400,000 South Vietnamese soldiers, or the more than 900,000 enemy soldiers who were killed, let alone all of the civilians." However, he seems unable to turn this knowledge toward a more culturally permeable view of the war.

Despite O'Brien's recognition of the costs of the war to Viet Nam, *Cacciato* remains a deeply apolitical novel. The lack of political analysis and the belief in the American mythology produce Paul Berlin's musing after his contrasting of "Vietnam" and "civilization," quoted earlier:

Even in Vietnam—wasn't the intent to restrain forces of incivility? The *intent*. Wasn't it to impede tyranny, aggression, repression? To promote some vision of goodness? Oh, something had gone terribly wrong. But the aims, the purposes, the ends—weren't they right? Wasn't self-determination a proper aim of civilized man? Wasn't political freedom a part of justice? Wasn't military aggression, unrestrained, a threat to civilization and order? Oh, yes—something had gone wrong. Facts, circumstances, understanding. But had the error been wrong intention, wrong purpose? (328)

Berlin believes the bill of goods sold him by the U.S. government in order to carry on its war. He believes in America's good intentions, or at least wants to believe so much that he cannot bring himself to believe anything else, as his series of questions underscores. Of course, even a cursory familiarity with the history of Viet Nam and the history of U.S. intervention in Viet Nam shows that self-determination and freedom were never elements of the South Vietnamese state that the United States created. It is convenient and easy for Americans not to have that familiarity with history, however, since the facts of U.S. history run counter to America's mythology about itself. Despite O'Brien's extensive portrayal of Vietnamese characters, *Going after Cacciato* ends up extending the status quo in U.S. Viet Nam War discourse.

A novel that comes from a different political point of view, James Webb's *Fields of Fire*, also uses Vietnamese as major characters, but also flattens them out into the usual stereotypes. Webb, a former secretary of the navy who resigned over a conflict about appropriations, remains the most outspoken critic of the Vietnam Veterans Memorial—he thinks it is unpatriotic because it is not a heroic statue. Webb is an avowed conservative.

Fields of Fire traces the fate of several members of a "melting pot" marine platoon, including Snake, the corporal, a white boy from the ghetto; Lieutenant Hodges, inheritor of a long southern tradition of military service; Goodrich, the Harvard dropout; Speedy, the Chicano; and Cannonball, the black. To this standard mix, Webb adds Dan, a Hồi Chánh (a former Viet Cong who has "volunteered" to serve with the Americans as a scout).

For Webb, the Viet Cong are reprehensible not because they are Asians with "no regard for human life," but because they are Communists with no regard for human life. (Webb's characters consistently use the word *gook* to mean Viet Cong, not all Vietnamese, thus making a distinction between Communists and others.) He has included the character of Dan to create a complete, for him, and nonracist portrayal of the war. He lets Dan speak for the Vietnamese, whose war Webb sees this as, unlike the view of many American writers, who see it as their own war. Racism, both against Asians and against African Americans, is a major issue for Webb: one of the important themes of the novel is the racial tension among Americans, and although he does not portray the radical black agitator Rap Jones sympathetically, he does recognize the injustice of white racism in the military and the necessity for whites and blacks to work together.

Webb shows how little attention Americans paid Vietnamese: "Those who had known Dan intimately would have noticed that he was nervous underneath his calm mask. The only hint of nervousness in Dan was in the eyes. His wife would have noticed that they flitted anxiously along the trail, and had lost their usual acquiescence. But no one noticed today" (172). This passage illustrates the duality of Webb's conception—even while he points out how little Americans notice about Vietnamese, he buys into the stereotype of Oriental "acquiescence." Dan had two brothers, one of whom died of cholera, one of whom was shot by the U.S. Marines. "There is no difference," Dan thinks (176). This statement conveys a fatalism constructed by Western stereotypes and assigned to Asians. Narratives like Le Ly Hayslip's reveal that Vietnamese see a great difference between dying of disease and dying because of the war.

Webb relies heavily on this idea of Asian fatalism. He describes a night in Dan's village when the marines are firing Harassment and Interdiction rounds: "They were meant to discourage enemy troop movements. The villagers did not know that. They viewed the rounds as one would view a rainstorm. Some nights there were artillery rounds. Some nights there were no artillery rounds. It did no good to question it" (182). Dan's village has close ties to the Viet Cong; the villagers would certainly know the purpose of the rounds. All of the narratives by Vietnamese exile writers show that Vietnamese did question and evaluate the war and the competing sides in the war. Webb's characterization is a gross oversimplification.[26]

Webb's interest in portraying the inside of Vietnamese village life is rare among American writers; even if he gets it mostly wrong, the attempt is still important.[27] In addition, Webb does try to explain behavior that many Americans found incomprehensible:

[Dan] was effective, if somewhat unpredictable, with the villagers. There were times when he remembered the valley as it was before a brother would kill a brother for the sake of discipline, and he was gentle and loving, one of them. But there were other times when he could not view a villager but as the wife or child or parent of one of the soldiers who had killed his family and driven him from his land. (190)

Although Dan's motivations may be oversimplified, Webb acknowledges that this Vietnamese character possesses motivations that the American characters do not understand, because they do not ask. Dan has learned how to deal with the Americans by putting on a "jive act"—they have decided his haircut makes him look like one of the Beatles, so they call him Ringo. Fully aware of what he is doing, Dan plays along in order to stay safe with them.

In the moral universe of Webb's novel, the soldiers are forced into morally untenable situations by the nature of the war being fought. Most of the characters respond with cynicism, which they develop to a fine art in the name of self-protection. The moral dilemma faced by the Harvard dropout Goodrich is the heart of the book. He has two moral decisions. First, his squad murders two Vietnamese civilians in retribution for the killing, by the Viet Cong, of two squad members. Goodrich decides to turn his squadmates in for murder. Second, Goodrich inadvertently causes the death of one of his squadmates when he prevents him from shooting at a little girl; the American is then killed by a Viet Cong hiding behind the girl. In this passage Webb extends the stereotype of the dangerous Vietnamese child.

For all of Webb's attempts to portray the moral complexity of the war and to criticize American racism, he succumbs to racism himself, especially in his portrayal of Lieutenant Hodges's Okinawan girlfriend. Hodges's "seduction" of this young woman, a virgin, is more akin to rape. Yet Mitsuko apparently falls in love with Hodges, as he with her, and they get engaged. Mitsuko is the stereotype of the pliant, subservient, sexually exotic Asian woman. Unlike Dan, she is a flat, two-dimensional character, unknowable to both Hodges and the reader.

Webb, like the other writers discussed in this section, simultaneously seeks to transcend, yet remains enmeshed in, the dominant paradigm of U.S. representations of Asians. The examples of O'Brien, a liberal, and Webb, a conservative, remind us that the political position of the writer does not guarantee his stance vis-à-vis the Vietnamese. While O'Brien uses Vietnamese characters to show the insanity and pointlessness of the war and the complicity of the United States, concluding that it therefore should not have been fought, Webb uses Vietnamese characters to show the insanity and evil of the war, as embodied in the Communists who victimize ordinary Vietnamese, concluding that the war should have been fought better. Despite their differing projects, and despite obvious efforts to the contrary, both writers end up with Vietnamese characters who remain cardboard cutouts.

An American poet, Elliot Richman, has attempted a unique project—a series of poems written from the point of view of various Vietnamese characters. These poems are collected in a volume titled *A Bucket of Nails: Poems from the Second Indochina War.* In his subtitle Richman expresses his effort to adopt a new perspective on the war by referring to it by its more international designation. The collection begins with a startling poem that emphasizes American ignorance of Viet Nam:

> *This Is No Country For The Young*
>
> The American boys pay no attention
> to me, an aged man dozing in the shade,
> a bag of bones in a loin cloth. They do not know
> my oldest son died with his bayonet
> in a Jap's face. They do not know
> my father was executed by the French
> for the Plot of 1907. They do not know
> that at night these wrinkled but steady fingers
> place detonators in land mines
> that will make bones of their young bodies. (3)

The poet's main point is that American ignorance of Viet Nam and American prejudices cause the soldiers to disregard the old man, and it is this disregard that will kill them.

After this promising start, however, the poems descend into exoticism and stereotypes; the subsequent Vietnamese voices seem to emerge more from American mythology about Vietnamese than from true knowledge. A prostitute has "ten thousand years of Asian sex/in each finger tip." (4), and Vietnamese children sabotage American vehicles. Women are repeatedly killed by wounds to the vagina. A Viet Cong truck driver feels remorse after watching a prisoner being skinned alive. A Viet Cong soldier envisions the war as a John Wayne movie he has once seen in Saigon: "This war would be different. The Apaches would win" (16). The wife of a political official remembers her young lover, killed at seventeen, and reflects on how things are now:

Our troops are fighting our Vietnam War in Cambodia.
My serene philosophy is like teak splinters
in the jungle. (18)

A Vietnamese woman would hardly think of the occupation of Cambodia as "our Vietnam War," and the "serene philosophy" is an old and tired Western stereotype of Asians. While Richman's project is original, and he certainly attempts to show his readers the war from another perspective, his effort is hindered by his unfortunate use of clichéd and mythological images of Vietnamese.

A recent novel by a nonveteran, Susan Fromberg Schaeffer, tries to draw a much more holistic picture of "the Viet Nam experience" than does most of the literature by veterans. The majority of novels and personal narratives by veterans begin and end with the war. Schaeffer's *Buffalo Afternoon* encompasses the childhood, war experiences, and later life of its protagonist, Pete Bravado, and also includes an important Vietnamese character, Li, who serves as a first-person narrator in sporadic chapters throughout the book. The novel takes its title from Li saying that the "buffalo afternoon" is "when the work is done and the buffalo head straight for their wallows. . . . When evening arrives, they turn homewards, and no matter how far they have gone, they know their way home. . . . So it was with the water buffalo and so it was with us. Days would pass and pass and we would grow older and for us, it would be buffalo afternoon" (9). Although some of Li's story verges on fetishized exoticism, Li emerges as such a complete and appealing character that the tendency toward exoticizing her and her Vietnamese milieu is forestalled by an emphasis on her basic similarity to Pete.

The similarities between Li's peasant life and Pete's working-class urban life are clear: Li's family first rejoices when Li's mother has four sons in a row, a sign of good fortune, then laments when a fifth son is born, a sign of coming ruin. Pete's family is also "superstitious." Pete is the fifth child; his grandmother reads his palm and tells him he will have a black year.

In Li's first chapter, the war comes to her village when her family's water buffalo is shot by American soldiers while she is riding it. A fortune-teller prophesies that Li will live among the white people. She foresees her life among whites: "I saw myself describing to them things they did not see, although they looked" (12). Schaeffer uses Li as a vehicle to critique the Americans' inability to understand Viet Nam.

Li resurfaces after a hundred pages spent describing Pete's childhood. For her, no time has passed; she describes her spiritual malaise after the killing of the buffalo. In this and subsequent sections interspersed with the story of Pete in the war, her story unfolds. Pregnant out of wedlock, she leaves her village to avoid shaming her parents. She goes to find the white men: "I was going to those who had placed the mark of the ghost on me. I was already a ghost" (153).

She and Pete meet in a whorehouse. When she asks if he will come back, he replies that his unit is going out on patrol for two or three months. She says she will find him.

No one could find him. Not even his mail could find him.

"The villagers do your laundry?" she asked, and when he said yes, they did, she said, "Then they must find you to ask for payment, and they will find you, and through them, I will find you." He looked at her and shook his head. So it was true; if you lived your life in this heat, sooner or later you went off your head. (173)

Li is not off her head—the simple, prosaic mechanisms through which Vietnamese were able to accomplish what Americans considered either mystic feats or Communist intrigue (that is, finding Pete in the field) are revealed as simple, homey practicalities.

Li wants to make this connection with Pete because she perceives that, like her, he is missing a soul. In fact, Schaeffer conceives of the whole novel as a ghost story. For example, she explains the American soldiers' custom of never knowing a man's full name: "To know a man's name was to know the man, and to know another man was to give his ghost terrible power once he was gone" (210). The plot is full of ghostly events.

Li does find Pete in his armored personnel carrier. The squad decides to take her on as a sort of Kit Carson scout. She cuts her hair, wears a uniform, and becomes one of them. Li shows them things they could never otherwise have seen—an Esso gas station on the Ho Chi Minh Trail, Viet Cong in a village at daylight. She tells Pete stories about her life, adding to the ghosts already haunting him. He asks her repeatedly why she followed him, and she gives him various, unsatisfying answers. To herself she thinks, "I came because I wanted revenge, although even now I do not know who I wanted to revenge myself against. My own people? The people who bombed my village? I want revenge against the world itself and yet I want to protect everything that walks upon it. My soul is ripped in two" (251).

When she joins the men Li is pregnant, and, out in the field, she gives birth. The men watch the birth and are, briefly, amazed and rejuvenated by the baby.

And the baby waved its little fists and stopped time for them, and they stood, still and peaceful in the light.

The Chief took the baby from [Pete], and one of the ARVNs, the one whose father had been the village chief disemboweled by the VC who came to ask for volunteers, took the baby next, and he looked at it a long time, and later no one knew why they didn't watch him with the child, or even why they'd let him stay there, but all their eyes were on Li, who was smiling and wiping her eyes at the same time, and none of them wanted to say, *I don't like this place no more*, not now. For a while it was washed away. Everything was clean and new as the baby. And then the ARVN who was holding the baby stepped through the back hatch of the track, carrying the child, and Sal went for him, but it was too late. (257)

The ARVN soldier, who has been made crazy by the war, kills the baby and puts an end to the symbolic hope the baby raises. Pete then kills the ARVN soldier. The important element in this passage is the American soldiers' willingness to stop hating the place they are in, if they can only get far enough from the war and close enough to normal life. This narrative recognizes that Viet Nam does not begin and end with the war, that there is normal life in Viet Nam, and that Americans, given the opportunity, could build connections to that normal life. The war will not let them, though— the war has warped and destroyed American and Vietnamese alike.

After the death of her baby Li has a vision: when she dies she will come back as a kinaree, a half-bird, half-woman spirit who will "exact vengeance": "People in the villages would try to placate her. They would put sacrifices on their altars. They would give gifts to the monks and the monasteries but she would not be appeased. . . . Between them, the Americans and the Vietnamese had fashioned her destiny, but now she belonged to neither" (258). Li becomes the spirit of the war, shaped out of the shared evildoing of the Americans and Vietnamese. The narrative recognizes the shared responsibility and agency of Americans and Vietnamese.

Li disappears, as does the Chief, the Native American soldier from Pete's armored personnel carrier. Immediately after their disappearance, reports start coming in about sightings of a "White Man," a man who looks like a mummy. Some people think he is a Viet Cong, and some think an American deserter. His indeterminate identity is a further symbolic interlinking of the Vietnamese and Americans in the novel (the White Man turns out to be the Chief).

In another section of her own narration, Li makes a surreal transformation into a ghostlike being who travels, with the White Man, and witnesses the atrocities of the war. "We came to see the war as an animal with a life of its own, whose breath was fire, whose eyes saw no difference between the living and the dead, because to stay alive a man had to let much of him die, and those who lived had seen so much death, had lived so surrounded by the dead, they felt closer to the dead than to the living" (293–94). Shortly after Li disappears, Pete goes home. Two hundred pages of narrative detail his life after the war, a section of the book in which Li has no part.

She reappears when the survivors, including the Chief, have a reunion. Her fate is unclear. The Chief recounts:

"Oh, we roamed around together for a while and she got thinner and thinner, not like a normal person, but like something the light was coming through, and then one day she was just drawn there on the light and when the sun came up, she was gone."

"She's dead?" Sal asked.

"I didn't say that," the Chief answered. "She's gone." (519)

The reunion turns surreal; Pete's dead grandparents appear, along with others, including Li. This symbolic reintegration serves as a healing process for Pete, but for the Chief and Li, there is a surreal, indeterminate ending: she appears to the Chief as a kinaree, and he goes with her again, by stepping out an open window "into Li's outstretched arms" where she hovers on her wings (531). It is not clear whether the Chief is already dead, is committing suicide by jumping out the window, or if something else is afoot, just as the exact nature of Li's presence is unclear. For Pete there is a realistic ending of healing and reconciliation.

While *Buffalo Afternoon* does much to show the shared destinies, the entangled fortunes of Vietnamese and Americans, Li remains for the most part a symbol rather than a character on the level of the other characters; she is an artifact woven in and out of the narrative whenever her presence is necessary to the main thrust of the narrative—Pete Bravado's life. Even though she speaks in her own voice, she is ultimately a cipher, a ghost. Although the descriptions of her village and her life have some texture, they are essentially a representation of a generic Third World peasant society without any real, accurate detail. The word *kinaree* is not a phonetically possible Vietnamese word, nor is "Li" a possible Vietnamese name. The novel would have required more research to go beyond good intentions into fully realized and accurate representation.[28]

Representations of Vietnamese characters have recently moved out of war novels and into other streams of American literature. *Spartina*, a novel by John Casey, includes a Vietnamese character who exists in an unremarkable way, as part of the multiethnic world of the Rhode Island fishing community on which the novel centers. Captain Dick Pierce, the main character, has been one of the few able to save his boat from a hurricane that has destroyed most of the fishing fleet's lobster pots. Pierce's wheeler-dealer friend, Parker, brings him a new deckhand, Tran:

The Vietnamese man spoke up. Dick didn't understand him, thought he was speaking Vietnamese. The man repeated himself. Dick understood that the man was trying to introduce himself. Dick looked him in the face. The man said his name a third time. Something something Tran. Tran something something. Dick liked that the man said it just as slow and patiently the third time. Dick said, "I'm Dick Pierce." Tran's hand moved at his side and Dick stuck out his hand. (322)

Dick Pierce is measuring Tran by his own "swamp-yankee" standards, and Tran measures up—Tran's idea of politeness and Dick's mesh in a workable way when Tran continues to repeat his name slowly.

One of the major themes of the novel is class conflict—Dick Pierce is a working-class man who is both involved with and enraged at people he thinks of as spoiled and rich. He has been employing a deckhand who he consistently calls "Keith college-boy." Dick feels a much closer affinity for Tran: "Dick gave Keith credit, though he still didn't like him. Dick did like Tran" (324).

Parker has set up Tran's family, whose house has been destroyed in the hurricane, with a makeshift "factory" in a barn where they are making lobster pots. Parker is paying them piecework, and Dick is afraid Parker is exploiting them. His sympathies lie with them because they are working people, like himself. He knows what piecework is like because his wife has done it in a crab processing factory.

Dick visits the lobster pot factory, where he meets Tran's father. Dick is paying Tran a half-share for his work on the boat.

The old guy said, "When you you pay Tran a full share?"

"The more he learns, the more he earns."

"Christmastime?" The old guy said.

Dick hoped the old guy was as pushy when he was dealing with Parker. Dick said, "He's still the boy. That's just one week he's put in."

"Twenty years old. You call him boy?"

"He's the boy till he can do all the stuff needs to be done. I'll teach him. He pays attention, he'll be full-share in a year."

The old guy spoke softly, but he kept coming. "Tran spent time on fishing boats, more than a year, three years." The old guy held up three fingers. "How long you have your boat? Captain Parker says your boat is brand-new."

Dick said, "Goddamn." Trans spoke to his father in Vietnamese. Dick said, "Goddamn!" more angrily, but he kept his temper. He looked at Tran and shook his head. "You tell your old man not to screw up a good thing. I'll see you day after tomorrow." (331)

Dick is angry because the old man does not know the New England fishing etiquette—what to bargain over and what not. Later he thinks back on the incident and is ashamed of himself, because hs sees that he has taken the same attitude toward Tran and his father that authority figures have taken toward him.

With a little jolt Dick saw himself as Captain Texeira when Captain Texeira fired him. As the loan officer at the bank pursing his mouth. As Joxer Goode asking about collateral. . . .

Dick still couldn't figure what he liked so much about Tran. Part of it was Tran reminded him of when he'd been the kid on board. Let the kid do it, that way he'll learn. And Tran reminded him of a different way to take it—he wasn't as sour as Dick had been. Tran was quiet and serious and earnest about it all, reminded Dick of Charlie. (332–33)

Charlie is Dick's son. There is a slight suggestion in this novel that Tran will become a sort of surrogate son to Dick, since Charlie and Tom, his own sons, are bound for college and will not be working on the boat with him. In addition, the last third of the novel is about second chances and emotional reconciliation, so Dick seeing himself in Tran, but seeing Tran as a better version of himself—"less sour"—is significant.

Keith college-boy leaves the crew and Dick hires "an old Portuguese who suited Tran and him fine" (337), and they settle in hauling lobster pots for the winter. The novel ends with the suggestion that this crew will work on in harmony.

If these aspects were all there was to the portrayal of Tran, this book would represent a major step in integrating representations of Vietnamese immigrants into mainstream American literature. All the positive, nonracist, aspects of this portrayal, however, are undercut by the feminization of Tran, as "sidekick" Asian characters have traditionally been feminized.

Tran is consistently identified with Elsie, Dick's extramarital lover. When Dick first meets Tran and shakes hands, "Tran's hand was as small as Elsie's" (322), "and for all his being a bronze-colored fellow, what with his small hands, his small bones dwarfed in the foul-weather jacket, he reminded Dick of Elsie" (332). One of the rich people Dick has dealt with is a documentary film producer, Schuyler, who has, earlier in the book, shot footage of Dick fishing for swordfish. On that filming expedition Elsie has been along; at one point she was out in a skiff following a harpooned fish. Schuyler has shot some film of her, but he did not want it to be obvious that it was a woman in the boat, so he has taken only long shots. Dick watches the finished film in a bar with other fishermen. When the scene in which Dick lifts Elsie from a shark-encircled skiff comes on, one of the guys says, "Ain't that the Vietnamese kid that's the boy on *Spartina*?" (347).

The dual identification of Tran with Elsie and Dick's son Charlie is both confusing and strange, since Tran is simultaneously identified as a son-surrogate and as a feminized stand-in for Dick's lover. Yet there is no suggestion of a homoerotic bond between Dick and Tran. If there were, it would be a narcissistic one, since Tran also reminds Dick of his younger self, but in the spaces where such a homoerotic attraction might surface in the narrative, the identification with Dick's son surfaces instead. I suggest that the author is not in complete control of his descriptive prose when Tran enters the narrative—the feminization, the identification with Elsie, do not make sense in the rest of the novel's symbology. Rather, I suggest, the inevitable feminization of the Asian sidekick is cultural baggage that intrudes inappropriately into the narrative.[29]

In this section, I have examined works that have taken steps toward abandoning the history of negative stereotypes, which has burdened the history of American representations of Asians. None of these works has entirely succeeded in breaking out of the old cultural patterns of thought regarding Asians and has not, therefore, made truly significant contributions to changing the nature of the U.S. discourse about the war. These works take some steps toward transforming "Vietnam" the war into Viet Nam the country, but they do not make the whole journey.

Subtracting the Fear from the Landscape

> The struggle for political control is the struggle for the images in our heads.
>
> —Timothy Lomperis, *"Reading the Wind"*

> It seems to me that this country has reached a point of empire where it is absolutely crucial for it to understand what other people think. . . . Literature, I think, can address that. . . . It isn't just that we lost the war, but it is also that they won it. It seems to me that a lot of our fiction talks about Vietnam as if it were something that went wrong in Alabama. . . . To understand the Vietnam War more fully, with greater instruction, we have to understand the Vietnamese.
>
> —John Balaban, quoted in Lomperis, *"Reading the Wind"*

> Rhetoric makes people killable; literature makes people believable, and lets them live.
>
> —John Balaban, *Remembering Heaven's Face*

> Full circle vets are those men and women who recognize and understand this need to go from warrior to peacemaker. . . . This requires an examination of the whole war: the beginning, the middle, and the end. We have to stop pretending that we can do this without including the other side.
>
> —Greg Kleven, "Vietnam Echoes"

Poet and memoirist John Balaban writes:

For the many millions of Americans who went there, and for the millions who watched on television, Vietnam is the name of a war. . . . Few of us had any sense of the people, their language, their history, their beliefs. For many who went there, the landscape was a confusion of crushing heat, monsoons, malaria, bad water, sawgrass, snakes and leeches, where ambushes or booby traps lay waiting in flooded rice paddies, in bamboo thickets along canals and slow muddy rivers, and under the triple canopy of the mountain jungles. But take away the war—

subtract the fear from the landscape—and it was beautiful, as soldiers often discovered when they were safe and dry and fed, and free, for a moment, to look at another Vietnam. (Clifford and Balaban 14; emphasis in original)

In this section I look at works by writers who have subtracted the fear from the landscape and seen the beauty. These Euro-American writers have transcended the paradigms that entrapped the writers examined in the previous two sections of this chapter. They write, at the least, nonstereotypical portraits of Vietnamese; at the most, they achieve the same bicultural understanding as in the best of the Vietnamese exile writers' work.

Edward Said says of Westerners writing about the Orient: "What he says and writes, by virtue of the fact that it is said or written, is meant to indicate that the Orientalist is outside the Orient, both as an existential and as a moral fact" (*Orientalism* 21). The writers examined in this setion have made the leap of perspective that has allowed them to recognize that they are not outside the "Orient"; in their works, the division between Viet Nam and "The World" (an artifact of soldiers' argot that informs most American writing about the war) does not exist. For these writers, Viet Nam is part of the world. They have experienced not only the war fought on Vietnamese soil, but also Viet Nam and the Vietnamese.

Timothy Lomperis said at a conference addressing the literature of the war,

I don't think that we can ever approach the ending of this war for us until we can view it in a larger context. . . . We also need to remind ourselves most forcefully that this wasn't just an American war in which we can contemplate exclusively our own hang-ups and societal malaise. This war occurred in a country called Vietnam. It impacted as well on a culture and on a society that is Vietnamese. And until we bring these two highways (or experiences) together, we won't put either war to rest. (64–65)

Lomperis describes the subsequent discussion among the conference participants (including most of the famous names in U.S. Viet Nam War literature), recounting a vehement debate that ended with a whimper: "Arnold Isaac's wry reminder that the Vietnamese never mattered to the Americans effectively closed the argument, and brought everyone around to a pessimistic harmony over such lamentable neglect" (65).

Not all Euro-American authors have treated Viet Nam and the Vietnamese with lamentable neglect. The authors who do not are those most similar in point of view to the Vietnamese exile writers: Bruce Weigl, W. D. Ehrhart, Yusef Komunyakaa, John Balaban, Robert Olen Butler, and Wayne Karlin.[30]

Bruce Weigl is one of the most highly regarded veteran poets. His poetry has been published widely in periodicals, and he has won the Pushcart Prize as well as the Academy of American Poets Prize. Weigl served with the First Air Cavalry in 1967–68. His poetry moves beyond the recounting of experience into a realm of speculation that transcends that of much of the poetry of the war. His poem "Him, On the Bicycle" sets up an interesting dynamic. The speaker, an American soldier riding in a helicopter, is very distant from the Vietnamese soldier he is looking at, although the speaker conceptualizes his own survival as a necessary bonding with the Vietnamese soldier:

> In a liftship near Hue
> the door gunner is in a trance.
> He's that driver who falls
> asleep at the wheel
> between Pittsburgh and Cleveland
> staring at the Ho Chi Minh Trail.
>
> Flares fall,
> where the river leaps
> I go stiff.
> I have to think, tropical.
>
> The door gunner sees movement,
> the pilot makes small circles,
> four men running, carrying rifles,
> one man on a bicycle
> in the midst of the jungle,
>
> he pulls me out of the ship,
> there's firing far away,
> I'm on the back of the bike
> holding his hips.
> It's hard pumping for two,
> I hop off, push the bike.
>
> I'm brushing past trees,
> the man on the bike stops pumping,

he lifts he feet,
we don't waste a stroke,
his hat flies off,
I catch it behind my back
put it on, I want to live forever!

Like a blaze
streaming down the trail. (*Song of Napalm* 9)

From the beginning of the poem, Weigl juxtaposes American realities and Vietnamese realities. He moves between the "foreign" and "exotic" (liftship, Hue) and the familiar (the driver, Pittsburgh, Cleveland), then throws that familiarity into the Vietnamese landscape (the Ho Chi Minh Trail).

The "I" enters the poem in the second stanza, a stanza marked by fractured and elusive syntax. Do the flares fall where the river leaps, or does the "I" go stiff where the river leaps? Or both? What relation does the word *tropical* bear to the sentence in which it appears? To some extent, these questions remain unanswerable. The introduction of the "I" in the midst of this elusive syntax makes it impossible for the reader to settle in to a comfortable identification with the speaker of the poem.

The speaker's surreal journey from the helicopter (the symbol of American mobility in the war) to the back of the Vietnamese soldier's bicycle (the symbol of the PAVN's determination in the face of its lack of technology), bridges the seemingly unbridgeable gap between the American soldier and the Vietnamese soldier. Their journey is a model of cooperation—the speaker, recognizing that "It's hard pumping for two," pushes the bike. The rider, recognizing the speaker's pushing of the bike, "stops pumping / he lifts his feet." Their cooperation is successful and efficient: "we don't waste a stroke."

Then the speaker moves from cooperation to identification when the rider's hat comes off, and the speaker puts it on. The act of putting it on culminates in the exclamation "I want to live forever!" Wearing the rider's hat, pushing the bicycle, the speaker experiences a sort of fusion of identity. He wants to live not just forever, but forever "Like a blaze / streaming down the trail." It is in his union with the "enemy" soldier that the speaker finds life.

This poem's attempt to bridge the gulf between an American in a helicopter and a Vietnamese on a bicycle reaches across distance, across cultures, and across the politics of the war for a symbolic fusion that proclaims the necessity of communality. In this poem it is the American door gunner and pilot who are "other," rather than the Vietnamese "enemy" below.

W. D. Ehrhart is another American poet whose work has moved beyond the cultural framework of stereotype in which it began. A prose writer as well as a poet, Ehrhart's war memoir, *Vietnam-Perkasie*, shows him to have been caught up in the American way of seeing that caused Vietnamese to appear to him as "gooks" during most of his war experience. An experience that sets him on the road toward a transformation of attitude occurs when he talks with Sergeant Trinh, an ARVN assigned to Ehrhart's marine unit. Trinh has refused to work with the Americans any more. As he explains to Ehrhart why he has refused, citing the Americans' brutality toward his country, Trinh excoriates Americans for their lack of cultural sensitivity and their blundering, well-meaning actions: "None of you mean any harm; you just do not think" (146). Ehrhart's interaction with Trinh starts him thinking and eventually leads to a change of attitude that leads him into the antiwar movement.

A series of Ehrhart's poems exhibits a movement toward understanding and de-alienation of the Vietnamese. The first poem, "Making the Children Behave," contains a subtle but vital change in point of view:

> Do they think of me now
> in those strange Asian villages
> where nothing ever seemed
> quite human
> but myself
> and my few grim friends
> moving through them
> hunched
> in lines?
>
> When they tell stories to their children
> of the evil
> that awaits misbehavior,
> is it me they conjure? (*Carrying the Darkness* 97)

In the original scene of the poet's war experience, only he and his American friends seemed human: but the wrenching point of view shift in the second stanza records a change of awareness; perhaps the villagers saw themselves as human and saw the American invaders as monsters, now enshrined in myth in the form of the bogey-man who will punish misbehaving children. In the turn this poem takes, Americans change from human to monster, while Vietnamese change from nonhuman to human.

Again, in "Letter," Ehrhart invests the Vietnamese with a possible moral superiority. The "letter" is addressed to a PAVN soldier who fired a rocket that was a near miss, almost killing the speaker.

Letter

to a North Vietnamese soldier
whose life crossed paths with mine
in Hue City, February 5th, 1968

Thought you killed me
with that rocket? Well, you nearly did:
splattered walls and splintered air,
knocked me cold and full of holes,
and brought the roof down on my head.
    ★ ★ ★

But I lived,
long enough to wonder often
how you missed; long enough
to wish too many times
you hadn't.

What's it like back there?
It's all behind us here;
and after all those years of possibility,
things are back to normal.
We just had a special birthday,
and we've found again our inspiration
by recalling where we came from
and forgetting where we've been.
Oh, we're still haggling over pieces
of the lives sticking out
beyond the margins of our latest
history books—but no one haggles
with the authors.

Do better than that
you cockeyed gunner with the brass
to send me back alive among a people
I can never feel
at ease with anymore:

remember where you've been, and why.
And then build houses; build villages,
dikes and schools, songs
and children in that green land
I blackened with my shadow
and the shadow of my flag.

Remember Ho Chi Minh
was a poet: please,
do not let it all come down
to nothing. (*Carrying the Darkness*, 98–99)

Here, the poet has despaired of America and demands of his unknown adversary that he build a future in Viet Nam that will make meaning of the war. The poet is reaching for a place to make meaning, and finds that place in a still distant, still anonymous Viet Nam.

"Making the Children Behave" and "Letter" are both early works. In a later book of poetry, *Just for Laughs* (1990), Ehrhart's relation to Viet Nam has changed, following a trip back to that country in peacetime. Now, the people he has conjured in imagination exist in the flesh, in particular persons, such as Nguyen Van Hung, to whom "Second Thoughts" is dedicated:

You watch with admiration as I roll
a cigarette from papers and tobacco.
Hanoi. The Rising Dragon. 1985.
You can't do what I can do
because it takes two hands

and you have only one, the other
lost years ago somewhere near Laos.
I roll another one for you. You smile,
then shrug, as if deformity from war
were just a minor inconvenience.

Together we discover what we share:
Hue City. Tet. 1968.
Sipping *lua moi*, we walk again
familiar ground when you were whole
and I was whole and everything around us

lay in ruins, dead or burning.
But not us. Not you or I. We're partners
in that ugly dance of men
who do the killing and the dying
and survive.

Now you run a factory; I teach and write.
You lost your arm, but have no
second thoughts about the war you fought.
I lost a piece of my humanity,
its absence heavy as a severed arm—

but there I go again; those second thoughts
I carry always like an empty sleeve
when you are happy just to share
a cigarette and *lua moi*, the simple joy
of being with an old friend. (27)

This poem explores the classic theme of combatants who have more in
common with each other than with noncombatants on either side. This is a
poem in the tradition of Thomas Hardy's "The Man He Killed." There are
remarkably few such poems of the American war in Viet Nam—not many
Americans have found a bridge for that gap. Ehrhart emphasizes the communality of the two old soldiers in this poem: they are "partners," they
are "old friends." The poet envies Mr. Hung his composure and serenity,
despite his physical handicap. "Second Thoughts" is a fulfillment of "Letter." Mr. Hung may have been the unknown gunner; he has, indeed, built
what the poet exhorted him to build—peace. In the last stanza of "Second
Thoughts" the poet tries to share some of that peace by stressing the common bond.

Yusef Komunyakaa is another poet whose war experience seems to have
enabled him to look at things from a perspective different from the norm.
His poems reflect his awareness of his position as an African American
soldier in a white man's war. He served as a combat correspondent in Viet
Nam and received a Bronze Star. Komunyakaa's book of war poems, *Dien
Cai Dau*[31] (Vietnamese for "crazy" and the correct spelling of the pidgin
phrase "dinky dow" often used in U.S. narratives), often turns its point of
view toward Vietnamese—poems attempt to see a rape from the standpoint
of the victim, to see the lives of bar girls. These attempts mostly remain

outside, though, and the Vietnamese remain mysterious. In "Re-creating the Scene," a rape is described:

> They hold her down
> with their eyes,
> taking turns, piling stones
> on her father's grave.

When the woman reports the crime, though, she disappears before the trial is finished:

> on the trial's second day
> she turns into mist—
> someone says money
> changed hands,
> & someone else swears
> she's buried at LZ Gator. (19–20)

Not only is her fate unknown and mysterious, but she herself "turns into mist," an image that perpetuates an image of Vietnamese as inscrutable and mysterious.

In "The Edge," the bar girls are identified with the Vietnamese landscape:

> . . . Their real feelings
>
> make them break like April
> into red blossoms.
>
> Cursing themselves in ragged dreams
> fire has singed the edges of,
> they know a slow dying the fields have come to terms with. (32)

It is unusual for an American writer or filmmaker to stretch far enough to see a Vietnamese woman's point of view at all.

One poem, "*Dui Boi*, Dust of Life,"[32] addresses the responsibility of Americans for their Amerasian children:

> You drifted from across the sea
> under a carmine moon,

framed now in my doorway
by what I tried to forget.
Curly-headed & dark-skinned,
you couldn't escape
eyes taking you apart.
Come here, son, let's see
if they castrated you.

Those nights I held your mother
against me like a half-broken
shield. The wind's refrain
etched my smile into your face—
is that how you found me?
You were born disappearing.
You followed me, blameless
as a blackbird in Hue
singing from gutted jade.

Son, you were born with dust
on your eyelids, but you bloomed up
in a trench where stones were
stacked to hold you down.
With only your mother's name,
you've inherited the inchworm's
foot of earth. *Dui boi.*
I blow the dust off my hands
but it flies back in my face. (58)

This poem addresses the racism of both Vietnamese and Americans, situating the black Amerasian child as a victim of both sides. The Amerasian child also stands as a symbol of the permanent link between Viet Nam and the United States—the speaker tries to blow the metaphoric dust off his hands, but it will not be so easily shaken.

One of the most contentious postwar issues has been the fate of the supposed MIAs—the missing in action. Komunyakaa adopts a new perspective on that issue in his poem "Missing in Action."

Men start digging in the ground,
propping shadows against trees

outside Hanoi, but there aren't
enough bones for a hash pipe.
After they carve new names
into polished black stone,
we throw dust to the wind
& turn faces to blank walls.

Names we sing in sleep & anger
cling to willows like river mist.
We splice voices on tapes
but we can't make one man
walk the earth again.
Not a single song comes alive
in the ring of broken teeth
on the ground. Sunlight
presses down for an answer.
But nothing can make that C-130
over Hanoi come out of its spin,
spiraling like a flare in a green sky.

After the flag's folded,
the living fall
into each other's arms.
They've left spaces
trees can't completely fill.
Pumping breath down tunnels
won't help us bring ghosts
across the sea.

Peasants outside Pakse City
insist the wildflowers
have changed colors.
They're what the wind
& rain have taken back,
what love couldn't recapture.
Now less than a silhouette
grown into the parrot perch,
this one died looking up at the sky. (59–60)

This poem brings Viet Nam and America together through the bodies of the
American MIAs, still present in the country of Viet Nam and changing the

color of its wildflowers with their decomposition. The imagery of "polished black stone," the Vietnam Veterans Memorial, and of the shadows of Vietnamese engaged in digging for American remains in Viet Nam, come together to suggest a continued shared destiny and presence in each other's fates.

A poem by John Balaban takes an interestingly similar, yet distinct, view of the MIAs.

For the Missing in Action

Hazed with harvest dust and heat
the air swam with flying husks
as men whacked rice sheaves into bins
and all across the sunstruck fields
red flags hung from bamboo poles.
Beyond the last treeline on the horizon
beyond the coconut palms and eucalyptus
out in the moon zone puckered by bombs
the dead earth where no one ventures,
the boys found it, foolish boys
riding their buffaloes in craterlands
where at night bombs thump and ghosts howl.
A green patch on the raw earth.
And now they've led the farmers here,
the kerchiefed women in baggy pants,
the men with sickles and flails, children
herding ducks with switches—all
staring from a crater berm; silent:
In that dead place the weeds had formed a man
where someone died and fertilized the earth, with flesh
and blood, with tears, with longing for loved ones.
No scrap remained; not even a buckle
survived the monsoons, just a green creature
a viny man, supine, with posies for eyes,
butterflies for buttons, a lily for a tongue.
Now when huddled asleep together
the farmers hear a rusty footfall
as the leaf-man rises and stumbles to them. (486–87)

Here, there is no American context at all, only the Vietnamese context, and the leaf-man is wholly without identity—the American MIAs and the Vietnamese MIAs have blended together in the earth—nothing, "not even a buckle" remains of the man's original identity as to ethnicity or side of the war. The MIA problem in this poem is not an American one, but a Vietnamese one—their land haunted by the ghosts left without burial, without proper tending.

Balaban is also the author of perhaps the only memoir by a Euro-American to achieve true bicultural understanding, *Remembering Heaven's Face: A Moral Witness in Vietnam*. Balaban's story puts him in a unique position from which to write. As a conscientious objecter, he served in Viet Nam first with International Voluntary Services (IVS), then with the Committee of Responsibility for War-Burned and War-Injured Children (COR). Later during the war, and by that time a fluent Vietnamese speaker, Balaban spent a year in Viet Nam as a National Endowment for the Humanities fellow, gathering *ca dao*, peasant oral poetry. In 1989 he made a fourth trip there with the dual purpose of addressing the Vien Van Hoc (Institute of Literature) in Hanoi and revisiting some of the children COR had sent to the United States for reconstructive surgery during the war.

Gloria Emerson, author of *Winners and Losers*, is quoted on the dust jacket of *Remembering Heaven's Face*, writing that it "is a book of immense beauty and wit and pain by an American who plunged so deeply into the lives of the Vietnamese, who understood their language and their dreams so well, that Vietnam became his country too." The dust jacket includes also a quotation by Tran Van Dinh, author of *Blue Dragon, White Tiger*, who comments that

Balaban succeeds, as no writer has before, in blending into one story the soul of Vietnam with his own soul. His fusing of *Tinh* (Feeling) and *Ly* (Reason) helps the reader to absorb the true nature of the Vietnam War in its most fundamental aspects: the tears and the laughter, the fear and the hope of the common people, the inhumanity of the war planners, the torment of the moral witnesses on both sides of the conflict.

Balaban's works as a whole reflect his difference. He has written three volumes of poetry: *After Our War, Blue Mountain*, and *Words for My Daughter*. He has published *Ca Dao Viêtnam: A Bilingual Anthology of Vietnamese Folk Poetry* and written the accompanying text for *Vietnam: The Land We Never Knew*, a book of photographs by Geoffrey Clifford, as well as a novel, *Coming Down Again*, set in the aftermath of the war.[33] The unusual aspect of Balaban's work is that his face is turned as much toward Viet Nam as toward America.

The difference in *Remembering Heaven's Face* is also immediately apparent in the typography: the book includes diacritics for the Vietnamese words, one of only a handful of U.S.-published books that do so. Balaban's prose is laced with Vietnamese proverbs, and his title reappears in discussions of fate and the will of heaven in the Vietnamese sense, not the Western version.

Balaban's prose is often poetic; it is important to note that, along with everything else, this is a beautiful book. Many of the descriptions and incidents in the book also appear in Balaban's poetry. The prose narrative and the poems, read together, illuminate each other. Although I do not offer extended readings of Balaban's poetry here, it, like his narrative, exhibits a bicultural point of view that sets it apart from the bulk of American poetry about the war. His poetry is particularly notable for its extensive use of ghosts—an especially Vietnamese point of view.

Balaban's perspective differed from that of most Americans from the beginning of his involvement with the war and the country. On deciding as a young man that he is a conscientious objector and opposed to the war, he also decides that "the only place to learn anything, to *do* anything about Vietnam was in Vietnam" (33). Instead of serving his CO obligation stateside in a VA hospital, or in the war as a medic, he travels to Viet Nam with IVS to teach English.

In Viet Nam, IVS prepares him to "live like Vietnamese. One old IVS hand told me he wished he could *be* a Vietnamese" (34). He soon learns to see himself through Vietnamese eyes. He can speak some Vietnamese, but this skill is so rare among Westerners that in public places Vietnamese talk about him as if he cannot understand. In a market he overhears a woman call him and his American companion "Ghê qúa," disgusting, and he sees through her eyes: "two 'disgusting' Big Noses with inhuman blue eyes, hairy ape arms, and preposterous, large, sweating bodies" (42). Later, as a COR representative, he habitually eats breakfast in the market and overhears people saying, "Look, the Americans are using chopsticks" (175), as if it were a miraculous event.

Once he goes into a restaurant with three AWOL American soldiers; one of them had not known that Vietnamese could "sit at tables or eat with knives and forks. He didn't mean that as a racist joke; it was real wonderment. His only sense of Vietnam and the Vietnamese had come from his months of humping the countryside, suffering ambush after ambush" (184). Through the telling of these incidents Balaban demonstrates that definitions of "civilized" behavior are all culturally constructed, that Americans and Vietnamese alike felt prejudices formed by their lack of experience with each other.

Balaban's perspective allows him to see the country that is not the war—"a Vietnam whose beauty was beyond the reach of the war, a beauty so captivating that I came to measure everything against it" (40). Like most Americans, he is astonished by the ancientness of the place, but, unlike most Americans, he has knowledge of the true history of the place. He spends most of his time in the delta, and he knows that although civilization there is ancient, it was not always Vietnamese civilization: in his narrative he teaches about the kingdom of Champa, the Khmer kingdom, and the Vietnamese march south. His specificity and sense of history allow him to marvel at the age of things (like the ribs of a sunken boat that have sat in the Mekong since A.D. 1177), but also allow him to see the progression of history, rather than constructing an Orientalist picture of an "unchanging East."

The American Balaban most admires (and to whom the book is dedicated) is Dave Gitelson, an IVS volunteer who speaks fluent Vietnamese and wanders through the delta as a sort of itinerant farm advisor. He is known as "Mỹ Nghèo," the Poor American, because he lives exactly like the poor farmers he advises. It is rumored that he has a safe pass from the local Viet Cong. Balaban sees Gitelson as having "really entered their world, maybe the only one of us who had" (63). The U.S. military hates Gitelson; an American colonel calls him "that guy, who looks like a bum, who goes around like Santa Claus with a sack" (79), but *Time* magazine had earlier called him "the most effective American of all the thousands involved in Delta pacification" (83). Gitelson is murdered out in the countryside. Balaban and another IVS volunteer go to try to reclaim his body. Balaban believes that he may have been murdered by Americans, because Gitelson had been reporting to Ted Kennedy about atrocities committed by the United States. Years later, Balaban suspects that Gitelson might have had early knowledge of the Phoenix program and might have been assassinated by its agents.[34]

Finally, Balaban settles for a Vietnamese philosophical explanation for Gitelson's death: " 'Happiness or misfortune,' we are told paradoxically in *The Tale of Kieu*, 'are prescribed by the law of Heaven, but their source comes from ourselves.' . . . In Vietnam, under the prospect of Heaven, the scrutiny of Mr. Sky, Gitelson had achieved a life of fateful clarity, redolent with moral choice, with risk, and with humane purpose" (89). Passages such as this highlight the bicultural understanding that informs Balaban's book. In 1989, on his return journey to Viet Nam, Balaban attempts to find out once and for all who had murdered Gitelson; he fails in the attempt. A Vietnamese says to him, "A lot of us don't know where our friends are" (331).

Despite Balaban's different perspective, when he first goes to Asia he must learn about the culture he is entering, like anyone else. In Japan, en route to Viet Nam for the first time, he realizes that he has no knowledge of Asians: "I realized that I didn't have a clue as to their emotions" (23). As soon as he arrives, he begins to learn:

Despite the initial sense of dislocation I'd felt in the cities, here [in the delta] I began to see that Vietnamese lives were lived not on a Spenglerian trash heap of history but, rather, in a dense spiritual continuum in which ancestors guided them and history reflected destinies cast in heaven. . . . Next to this antiquity and preposterous resolve, the jets diving on the horizon seemed so many gnats. (25)

This description is reminiscent of the image Hayslip uses of the U.S. elephant stomping on the Vietnamese ant hill.

Throughout his narrative, Balaban insists on the complexity of the war. One of his first American friends in Viet Nam is a CIA agent, to whom the other IVS volunteers will not even talk. Much to Balaban's surprise, the CIA agent is largely opposed to the war and is being transferred because he has refused to help the local province chief assassinate his enemies. Balaban also meets another CIA agent, an interrogator with no respect for the Vietnamese. Balaban muses on these seeming contradictions early in his narrative; he sees things at a much higher level of complexity than most American writers, who tend to oversimplify to a cartoonish level. Balaban also does not try for a false, forced resolution of these contradictions—he lets them lie, disturbing as they are.

One of the major contradictions he explores is the ways in which the war itself effectively prevented American-Vietnamese relationships from developing. During Tết Mậu Than, the offensive of 1968, he is living in an apartment complex with Vietnamese neighbors. When the fighting starts, he goes to his neighbors: "My presence . . . was a liability to these decent people. . . . Still, instead of letting me head out onto the uncertain streets nattering with gunfire, my neighbors were offering me their protection, which seemed neither decent nor wise for me to accept" (95). He has celebrated Tết with them the night before; he has come as close to joining their society as he can, but the war tears him away. In order to protect them, he leaves. He never sees them again.

Balaban's life is changed forever by Tết Mậu Than. He spends several days assisting a medical team treating civilian casualties:

What collective karma, what shared fate, could Ông Trời [Mr. Sky] have been weighing to have judged these innocent people so harshly? An elderly intellectual once told me that the war was the Vietnamese punishment for their destruction of the Khmer and Champa kingdoms centuries before. But for me, after Tết, no philosophy or ideology—least of all, crusading American democracy—could justify or even remotely explain the slaughter of those civilians. From that day on, I had no facts or beliefs except for what had been done to those people. (105)

Acting on his new perceptions, he resigns from IVS and joins COR, acting as a field officer trying to facilitate the transfer of critically wounded children to the United States, where they could receive treatment unavailable in Viet Nam.

He is stonewalled by both United States and RVN officials; his contempt for them has nothing to do with ethnicity. He scorns Americans and Vietnamese alike who impede COR and praises those who help. He also has no use for U.S. liberal critics of the war, who claim that "not only were we creating a cruel, war-perpetuating illusion of American concern and responsibility (just look at our name!) but we were helping save these kids' lives only to corrupt them culturally in the United States and so make it impossible for them to live happily in Vietnam again" (189). Balaban takes this charge seriously and discusses frankly the effects on very young children of so much cultural dislocation. He describes the case of one boy he escorts home after the boy's stay in the United States who seems thoroughly Westernized but quickly, if not easily, reassimilates after a few weeks back home. Balaban's moral compasss is firmly tied to one fact: "My yardstick on the rightness of what we were doing, even assuming some inevitable cultural erosion and deracination, was that we were at least saving their lives. That mattered first. Later we could anguish over the spiritual damage to those lives" (191). Balaban also subtly points out the cultural egotism of the critics who think the pull of American culture is insurmountable. They are akin to the U.S. authors (such as Mahoney) who create Vietnamese characters who easily prefer the United States to Viet Nam and never feel the pull of nhớ nhà, homesickness. Balaban describes the "vibrant tangle of love and obligation" (192) that is Vietnamese family life and quotes several exchanges of letters that show the sufferings of Vietnamese families, temporarily without their children, and of American foster families, who come to love the children, then lose them. Again, Balaban does not shrink from complexities and contradictions.

After two years in Viet Nam, first with IVS, then with COR, Balaban is released from his Selective Service obligation and goes home, where he suffers from much of the same isolation and post-traumatic stress syndrome that returning veterans suffered from. He marries, teaches at Penn State, then, in 1971, decides to return to Viet Nam with his wife.

> When Lonnie and I decided to go, it seemed like the only honest thing to do for citizens of a society raging at itself as it killed hundreds of thousands of anonymous little people halfway around the world. Those people weren't anonymous to me. From my point of view, the best thing I could do now to help stop the war was gather the poetry made by ordinary folk in Vietnam and bring it before Americans. However insignificant this effort might be, the more human Vietnamese seemed to Americans, the harder it might be to slaughter them. (225)

His return journey does much to heal the spiritual wounds inflicted on him by his earlier experience, even though he suffers another trauma when his wife has a miscarriage, for which he blames himself.

What made Balaban so different? His text does not address that issue, but it is interesting to note that despite his Harvard University education, he grew up poor in a housing project, in a world saturated by violence. He was drawn into the civil rights movement and attracted to the Society of Friends. His structural position within American society placed him in a similar position to the Vietnamese civilians he saw brutalized by the war.

Finally, the most important aspect of Balaban's narrative is its function as the American side of a possible bridge. Together with the works of Le Ly Hayslip, Tran Van Dinh, and Vo Phien, Balaban's book represents continuity rather than discontinuity. It is my hope that those of us who teach about the war might take these few, frail books, link them together into just such a bridge, place them at the center of the canon, and reformulate American understandings.

Balaban is not entirely alone among American prose writers; the novels by Lloyd Little, Robert Olen Butler, and Wayne Karlin also deserve to be located in this new canon.

Lloyd Little's *Parthian Shot* (1973) is an early novel that takes a different perspective toward the Vietnamese from most of the work contemporary with it. This novel is a black comedy, a satire on the ludicrousness of the American and the South Vietnamese war effort. It centers on a Special Forces A team that, due to a bureaucratic snafu, is left behind in the village of Nan Phuc. The U.S. command believes the team has already rotated home.

The Special Forces members must fend for themselves, and they do so by inadvertently waging the war in the way that it should have been waged, had the United States lived up to its own propaganda: they set up private enterprise, employ the local villagers, raise everybody's standard of living—thus promoting capitalism—and form an effective alliance with the local private army of the Hoa Hao.

Little served as a medic with a Special Forces A team during the early part of the war. The experience of the men in these teams was different from that of the majority of U.S. soldiers, because they did have close contact with Vietnamese people. Especially in the "advisor" phase of the war, but continuing into the early period of U.S. combat troops' presence in the war, these A teams lived with the Vietnamese, spoke the language, got to know the culture, and carried out a program that resembled what the United States said it meant to do in terms of winning the "hearts and minds" of the South Vietnamese people. It is not surprising, therefore, that a novel written by a veteran whose experience of the war was one such as this should differ radically from the general run of U.S. representations in its depiction of the Vietnamese.

It is also not surprising that the book's dedication mentions a Vietnamese as well as Americans: "To Lô Thành Lân, the men of Special Forces Detachment A-16, IV Corps, and to my wife, Drena." Given the book's early publication date it is astonishing that Lan's name appears with diacritics. And although the Vietnamese phrases throughout the rest of the book do not appear with diacritics, the narrator constantly gives pronunciation guides for the terms he introduces.

Little's representation of his characters is balanced—the American and Vietnamese characters have equal depth, and there are bad guys and good guys on both sides. Bureaucratic stupidity—the main target of the novel's satire—is not restricted to either side.

The book begins with a geographic description of the Mekong River, on which the village of Nan Phuc lies. By setting the Mekong Delta of Viet Nam within the context of Asia, Little resists the American tendency to think of the United States as "The World" and of Viet Nam as nowhere. This beginning sets the tone for the novel. The narrator, Staff Sergeant Phil Warren, continually insists on the beauty of Viet Nam and at one point says, "This is my country, I thought. Vietnam. My delta" (59). Warren does not mind staying on in Nan Phuc; he prefers it to spending his last nine months in the army at Fort Bragg, because he likes the Vietnamese town, an attitude hardly found among the protagonists of U.S. Viet Nam War fiction.

Little satirizes the government of the Republic of Viet Nam and the U.S. military equally:

Nan Phuc needed a policeman like it needed more rain. But Vietnam's former prime minister, Ngo Dinh Diem, in a futile effort to establish rapport with the common folk, had appointed the son of the village chief as Nan Phuc's official police captain two years ago. Since then our man in khaki had not heard a single word (except for his monthly salary of three thousand piasters) from the government. He had no idea what a police captain did, so he bought a pool table and set it up in his living room. (5)

When the top sergeant returns from a trip to Da Nang to find out why the A team has not been relieved yet, he tells the soldiers that he has found out that

"The six of us are back at Fort Bragg."
"Come on, Top. Quit kidding," said Wheaty, grinning.
"That's exactly what I told the captain, the major, and the colonel, and damned if they almost didn't convince me we're not here anymore." (7)

By satirizing both bureaucracies, Little accurately places his black-humor barbs where they are most deserved and avoids racist bias when satirizing the absurdities of the RVN government.

Little also shows a nonracist understanding of the practices of the other side in a description of a battle in which some of the A team had been involved: "[The VC] left behind seventy-three CIDG, six dead Americans, and more than two hundred of their own. And when you figure the VC carry off as many of their own dead as possible, it was a costly victory indeed" (13). The Vietnamese practice of carrying off their dead and wounded is often reported as frustrating for American soldiers (who also, of course, carry off as many of their dead and wounded as possible, only they do it with helicopters rather than bare hands). The narrator of *Parthian Shot* displays none of the irrationality of this frustration; rather, he understands the meaning for the Viet Cong of the bodies left behind.

Further, the novel shows American characters through Vietnamese eyes when the narrator explains to a female American visitor why the village children follow her around: "We're funny-looking in their eyes. Big, hairy, coarse people with long noses and sickly-looking skin" (133–34). He also confronts the common American complaint about Vietnamese using human waste as fertilizer when the top sergeant advises them to do so: "I've been trying to convince the farmers to save their shit and use it. But they believe it's dirty and unclean" (159).

The novel criticizes characters that it presents as racist, particularly a CIA operative who says, "These gooks are so fucking lazy. As bad as niggers." The angry reaction of Hood, a member of the A team, is " 'We have worked with these people'—he emphasized 'people'—'and found them not particularly better but certainly no worse than the average U.S. Army recruit" (108). The novel thus equates U.S. racism against blacks and that against Asians; the book, like Hood, puts the emphasis on "people," in order to satirize and criticize racism.

Little reveals a fairly deep knowledge of Vietnamese culture and history, and periodically interrupts his narrative to insert informative asides. In one of these, he gives a detailed account of the founding of the Hoa Hao religious movement by Huynh Phu So. His knowledge allows him to place his narrator into the position of identifying more with some Vietnamese than with some Americans: "There was some sense of identity between us and the Hoa Hao. . . . The regular Army attitude toward Green Berets, in spite of clever public relations, was one of suspicion and dislike. It was easier for us to sympathize with the problems of the Hoa Hao than the problems of the latest coup winner in Saigon" (23). This narrator is able to make distinctions both among groups of Vietnamese and among individual Vietnamese that other representations are unable or unwilling to make.

For example, this is the description of Major Choi, the Hoa Hao camp commander: "Choi was tall for a Vietnamese—about five feet nine. His smooth brown skin and coal-black hair belied his forty-two years. He was a handsome man, not so much in classic good looks, but in his friendly eyes, tiny smile wrinkles, and his open personality. He had the quiet but forceful manner of a good leader. One you trusted" (54). This description is remarkable not only in that it neither feminizes nor demonizes Choi, but also because it describes a Vietnamese military officer as someone to be trusted. In this respect, it is a passage perhaps unique in U.S. Viet Nam War representations.

Racial identity in the novel is fluid. Two characters have theories about their own racial identities: "Hood, who thought he was black, was really white. Santee, who was really black, thought he was Oriental" (98). This fluidity satirizes U.S. racism. The characters have constructed their own identities in opposition to the way that racial identity is constructed from the outside and forced upon people.

Little seemingly recognizes the forces stacked against any such resolution of racial conflict, though. The novel ends on an extremely bitter note, with a news report that Nan Phuc has been mistakenly bombed by the U.S. Air Force, demolishing the textile factory and killing Major Choi and the two Americans who have chosen to stay behind, along with more than one hundred other people.

Robert Olen Butler is a Euro-American writer who has included complex portrayals of Vietnamese characters in more than one of his several works concerning the war. Three of his books, *The Alleys of Eden, Sun Dogs*, and *On Distant Ground*, form a trilogy of sorts, because they deal with a set of characters who were together in Viet Nam. Cliff Wilkes, Wilson Hand, and David Fleming all served in the same intelligence unit. Each of the three novels alludes to the same incident: Wilson Hand is abducted by the Viet Cong, Cliff Wilkes and Capt. David Fleming inadvertently kill an informant during questioning, Cliff Wilkes deserts and David Fleming rescues Wilson Hand. Each novel concentrates on one of these main characters. Butler's most recent novel, *The Deuce*, is a departure from these novels and is a better book in many ways. Butler's most recent book, *A Good Scent from a Strange Mountain* (1992), crosses completely over—it is a collection of stories narrated from the points of view of a group of Vietnamese immigrants to the United States.

With *The Alleys of Eden* (1981), we are clearly in a territory different from that of most U.S. fiction about the war. The title offers the first hint: Viet Nam is usually conceived of as hell, not Eden.[35] This novel tells the story of Cliff, an army deserter who, in April 1975, has been living in Saigon for several years with his girlfriend, Lanh, a Saigon bar girl. Knowing that the end of the war is near, Cliff and Lanh must decide whether to go or stay, to split up or remain together. For both of them, this decision entails questions of culture, identity, selfhood.

Cliff has largely acculturated to Viet Nam. He speaks fluent Vietnamese and has been happy in Saigon: "He'd held to this place—and the place had held to him—better than any before" (4). When he and Lanh first met, she teased him:

—You're skinny like a Vietnamese.
—I eat a lot of Vietnamese food.
—Maybe that's it, Lanh said. You weighed more when you first came here.
—Yes.
—Three hundred pounds. Right?

—Yes . . . Uh, yes, three hundred pounds.

—Very fat. Typical American.

—Then I ate cha gio and bun bo and ban xeo.

Lanh laughed at his knowing the foods. Good, she said. Good. And you lost two hundred of your American pounds. The one hundred left is the Vietnamese who was inside you waiting to get out.

—Vietnamization. Cliff used the word that filled even the Saigon newspapers. (9)

Cliff is serious about his transformation, although Lanh does not completely believe in the change. Later she says, "That was a joke. The heart doesn't change" (11). But Cliff's heart has changed: "Saigon was his home now. He felt that strongly" (69). When he meets with an American reporter in Saigon, her voice "was foreign to him now, but he sensed a danger in letting it reassert its claim to the movement of his mind" (71).

Cliff had deserted because he, as an interrogator, had participated in the accidental death of an informant who had information regarding the capture of Wilson Hand. He held the man down while Captain Fleming placed a wet handkerchief over his face; the man died as a result, because he had a weak heart. This incident has driven Cliff to make a separate peace and has led him to Lanh.

Lanh is a complicated woman, who both resists and plays with stereotypes. "I'm not a Vietnamese woman. Just a Saigon bargirl," she says (9). Lanh hates Saigon, because she has, ironically, learned to see it as Americans do:

One time I saw the city in a different way. . . . Then I grew up and you Americans came who knew other ways, more advanced. And I learned from you. I began to see the city through your eyes. The city is choking on filth from machines that are treated like lovers by fools with sunglasses and pointy shoes. It's filled with these tiny brown animals always grubbing after anything they can get to hoard to themselves. (11–12)

For Lanh, the American presence in Saigon has resulted in self-hatred; she has associated with Americans and internalized their perceptions. In this way she is similar to the woman in *Blue Dragon, White Tiger* who wants to have cosmetic surgery to make her look more Western.

Lanh plays the role of a Saigon bar girl, which to her is something artificial, cheap, in contrast to a Vietnamese woman. She is conscious of her identity as a construction. She suffers from internalized oppression, believing herself not to be as beautiful as American women: "I've seen the pictures of women that were so beautiful they would not be denied. They would not lose a man to anyone like me" (15). Cliff is dismayed by her attitude, because he has made a cultural crossover, and finds Lanh and Saigon to be more beautiful, more of a home, than America.

Her relationship with Cliff is both comfortable and difficult. When she first agrees to let Cliff live with her, an interchange between them portrays her slipping in and out of identities:

—I'm not just a whore, Lanh said sharply. I make all the money I need in the bar. GIs like to talk to me. They buy me Saigon Teas and I do all right.
—Of course.
—But for you I can make an exception, if you want. You can live here all right, but you pay by the hour. Okay?
—I wish you'd make up your mind what you want from *me*, Cliff said. You're angry because I talked money. But talking money is talking straight, isn't it?
—I'll give you a special deal. The hours out of bed—half price. Pretty good, GI?
—I think we were too quick in having me stay. Maybe I better go. I won't be a GI to you.
—And I won't be a whore to you. (18)

Cliff and Lanh are both caught up in the roles prescribed for them, and both fight to get out of those roles. Lanh has clearly been damaged by working as a prostitute and bar girl, though she fights to maintain her integrity and selfhood.

—I'm a good girl, Lanh said, her anger suddenly vanishing, her voice husky.
—I know.
—Then you know wrong, she said, suddenly sharp again, pulling away from his hands. I'm a bad girl. The worst. We'll stay up tonight and I'll tell you about all the men, all their requests. (132)

In her struggles over her identity and the person the war has forced her to become, she resembles Wayne Karlin's Xuan (discussed later): she puts on and takes off the prostitute role, and keeps the man who loves her at a distance because of her own destroyed self-image.

During the night Cliff spends trying to decide what to do, whether to stay or to go, he imagines a dialogue between Lanh and himself:

Go, she would say. What is this place and its people to you? The best of you, the most compassionate of heart, the most tolerant and appreciative of mind, have come here and used Vietnam as a stage to play the high drama of your own conscience. A place to suffer grandly, to define the limits of your own goodness, to confront the traces of your own evil, and then to leave. To leave utterly. And whether you treated us good or treated us bad, it makes no difference. You used us. You came and gave us scraps of your awareness, one year each of your heart. You came and made us feel, feel deeply, stirred us, set us seeking new things, and then you go. Vietnam is a foreign place to you. You feel here, suffered, for a time, but you return to a home far away. But there is no home away from here for me. You come and you make me suffer, I suffer with you, you give me joy, we share joy, and all those things alter this place for me. The sun shows differently on the clouds now, the trees are different. You go back to other places, old feelings. It was a terrible thing you suffered here. But it was only a dream, after all. It was another time, another place, the far side of the world, and it is all over. Go back. It is all you can do. But I hated you and loved you and I cannot be the same and there is nowhere for me to go.

Yes, Lanh, Cliff answered in his mind. You're right about us in many ways. And you're right to treat me like an extension of all the others. I only gave you a few more years of my heart. But what happened to you happened to me as well. And not just here. . . . I've spent a lifetime collecting scraps of awareness, changing my heart, seeing the world change around me, and I held people to me, held them close and then they were gone and I had nowhere to go. But I still have nowhere. What I've sought has always been on the far side of the world. (86)

Such are the factors that bring them together and tear them apart. The war, their two cultures, and their gender roles all work to unite them in false, temporary ways. They fight against these forces to try to come together more genuinely, but in the end they are defeated.

Out of fear of being killed, Cliff decides to leave with the last of the Americans. Lanh, against her better judgment, decides to go with him, and so begins a transformation for both of them. They make it to the United States, after separating during the helicopter-lift from the embassy. Cliff slips back into America with a false ID he obtained from the editor of the leftist paper he has written for while he was in Saigon; Lanh is sponsored by a church in Speedway, Illinois. They reunite and live together in Speedway, but they are unable to live together in America as they did in Saigon.

For Cliff, the questions of identity are acute. Is he American, or Vietnamese, or some hybrid? He approaches the American embassy in Saigon on the last day of the evacuation: " 'Sergeant,' Cliff shouted. He waited a moment and then realized he'd shouted in Vietnamese. 'Sergeant,' he cried in English" (104). In the helicopter he feels more Vietnamese than American; he feels small and thin next to the American marines. "Too much bun bo," he thinks (111), making reference again to losing weight on Vietnamese food, thus becoming more Vietnamese.

The United States is as dangerous to him as Saigon would have been after the liberation. He must conceal his identity and live as a fugitive, because he is a deserter. He is forced back into his American identity during the time he is separated from Lanh and staying with a leftist underground organization. Yet he remains Vietnamese in his perceptions: "Mindy was young—early twenties—and he knew she was pretty, though he was conscious that this reaction was an intellectual one now—the American women he'd seen on the streets in the past few hours, and now this one leaning very near to him, all seemed outsized, rough-skinned, all fist and jaw" (144). When he rejoins Lanh in Speedway, he finds them a "tiny room in a city-noisy place" like their place in Saigon, but as he stands in the room, he hears the whir of the refrigerator: "From the start there had been no way to reproduce Saigon here, he told himself. The refrigerator would be convenient" (172).

For Lanh, the loss of the power and control that she had in her own culture defeats her. As they are leaving Viet Nam she says to Cliff, "And what if I change there? . . . You love Lanh but if I go to a place like that, what if it changes me?" (107). She does change. Her English is very poor; Cliff has never realized how little English she knows, because in Saigon they always spoke Vietnamese. Lanh has used English only when she has taken on her bar girl persona. "I'm just a goddam whore in English," she says (218). In Speedway, she feels terribly isolated, handicapped, helpless: "She had no language now and her mind, her heart, had been sealed shut—she had no country now and everything was alien to her and turned her into a stranger" to Cliff (239).

The crisis comes when they meet people. Cliff befriends an American, Quentin, and he and Lanh eventually go to Quentin and his wife June's house for dinner. "Cliff felt a curious shift in his identification as he heard June speak. For a moment he felt included in June's 'we' " (190). For him, a transformation has begun.

He and Lanh begin to fight; she is angry at him for excluding her in the conversation with Quentin and June, he is angry at her for not being willing to learn more English immediately. Lanh finds out that there is a Vietnamese family in Speedway. Cliff is annoyed at her reaction.

"You lit up at the thought of seeing other Vietnamese. But in Saigon you avoided them. You talked as little as possible with the old women. You and I were enough."

"I know."

"You come to this place . . ."

"I don't understand it myself," she said. "I did not feel Vietnamese in Vietnam. I felt part of you and that was all . . . But now, even this moment, speaking of the Vietnamese family makes my heart flutter." (198)

In Saigon, Lanh has been separated from her Vietnamese identity by her work as a bar girl, which is shameful in her culture. In America, she can leave her bar girl past behind her and rejoin her Vietnamese culture. Lanh's feeling about her identity is reminiscent of Minh in *Blue Dragon, White Tiger*, who feels that he can be truly Vietnamese only in exile in the West.

Cliff continues to become more Americanized, taking a job with Quentin's company as a salesman (what could be more American?). He and Lanh meet the Vietnamese family, who are amazed that Cliff speaks Vietnamese.

All of Binh's family hooted in delight and Cliff felt a surge of pleasure—he thought for a moment that he'd had an instant remission of his alienation—he felt an intimate connection to this group of people—this group of simple, intensely friendly, loyal people. But Binh said something quickly that Cliff did not catch and he found himself thinking in English about the sounds he'd just heard. A momentary crossover of languages—a minor thing, a common thing—but it pulled him back and the connection he'd felt in this room was broken. . . . He wanted—desperately wanted—to connect again to these sounds, to these people, but he sat in the chair they offered him, and in the core of himself, away from the conversation he was conducting, he felt numb. (209)

Yet he cannot maintain his American identity, either. At a sales seminar, "He'd actually begun to think in Vietnamese, all at once, and the seminar leader suddenly had become a foreigner speaking an utterly incomprehensible tongue" (222).

Lanh decides to leave Cliff and move in with Binh's family. Cliff visits his American ex-wife and finds no refuge there; instead his status as a fugitive is reinforced by this encounter. He returns to his apartment and sees Lanh. In a tour de force section of the novel, Butler explores the questions of identity as Cliff makes love to Lanh for a last time.

He had a vision of Vietnam. A flash of sunlight in his first moments of flight, the sun flaring from a pond, a water buffalo beyond, a palm frond, an empty sky, the heat, he felt them all again now, he lay down on the bed, held Lanh; and he swelled with the countryside, with the sprawl of the city, Saigon, their race through the alleyways, he wanted to go back, go back to their alley room, that was their place. Lanh had made him love the very smell of the air, the very heat that beat down the stone walls. This was why his penis rose now, why he pressed against her with a low cry, his breath twisted tight in his chest. In her body he was Vietnamese. . . . She must have known how important this was, the accumulation of countless nights and mornings, the weight of all their years together and apart, of all the accumulated clutter of culture that they tried to sort out and then join by this joining of their bodies.

. . . He wanted to be Vietnamese again. More than that—he wanted to be human again, connected to a woman only, just a woman. But he heard a car horn bark in the street, and once more he heard the refrigerator grinding away—trivial things, they mean nothing, he cried to himself, but they were the things that were imprinted in him—the synapses of culture—the tracks that caught him and pulled him away, back to the dinner table, large there himself, a tall man, taller by a head than the president of Vietnam or Chairman Mao—he tried to wrench himself back, these things had nothing to do with him. But he heard the silence again on the porch just moments before Lanh came down and they were rejoined. He was an American.

. . . Cliff cried out again, raised his head and shook his mind clear. He was not an American. It had all run out—all the power of his past—all the meaning of his own fields, his own rivers, his own buildings and food and dinner conversation. . . . He came. The release squeezed and squeezed and he found himself attaching only to his own thoughts—and they were full of detritus. Pot shards, bone fragments, a vanished civilization. (241–44)

In this passage Cliff fights to find the markers of a stable identity within language, culture, landscape, custom, architecture, his own body, and can find it in none of these. He is Vietnamese; he is American; he is neither. At the end of the novel, Lanh moves in with Mr. Binh's family, and Cliff goes to Canada, which will also not be a home for him, as he tells Lanh. The book ends in desolation; neither character finds a home, a culture. *The Alleys of Eden* is unusual in that not only does it present a nonstereotypical portrait of a Vietnamese character, but it takes seriously the possibility of an American assuming a Vietnamese identity, the possibility of an American loving the country of Viet Nam.

In *Sun Dogs* (1982) the protagonist, Wilson Hand, has maintained no connection to Viet Nam, but continually has flashbacks to the time he was a prisoner of the Viet Cong, although he never achieves any sort of reintegration of meaning. He dies in a plane crash in Alaska, where he has been employed as a private detective to find leaks in an oil company's security system protecting exploration information. As it turns out, the oil company and the government have been deluding the public, and Wilson has been a pawn in the game. In a way, he dies in a surrogate Viet Nam War in Alaska, in another example of the U.S. government using and abusing its people. Viet Nam itself, however, plays only a small role in this book.

In each of these novels, the story is told completely through the perceptions of the main characters (although the narratives are in third person). Consequently, the last book in this "trilogy," *On Distant Ground* (1985), appears at first glance to reverse all the cultural understanding Butler displayed in *The Alleys of Eden*. If the whole text is read, though, as David Fleming's attitudes, then it can be seen as a parable of the larger U.S. attitudes about the war. Fleming can be seen as representing, in his attitudes, America as a whole. He is not a sympathetic character—he remains distant, cut off, emotionally isolated, something of a jerk. Butler is walking a thin line and taking a huge chance in this novel. If read alone, outside his oeuvre as a whole, *On Distant Ground* seems like just another American ethnocentric novel with good intentions and poor execution.

As the novel opens, David Fleming is being court-martialed for freeing a Viet Cong suspect from a Republic of Viet Nam prison. During his trial in April 1975, his American wife gives birth to a son, and he comes to the realization that he has another son in Viet Nam; he makes a plan to go and get his Vietnamese son before the fall of Saigon. He is found guilty in his court-martial, but sentenced only to be reduced in rank and dishonorably discharged. With help from a CIA friend he gets to Saigon and finds his son, whose mother has died, but the city is liberated before he can get out. David encounters Tuyen, the Viet Cong man he had freed and who is now an official in the new government. Tuyen, in turn, allows Fleming to go free, and he makes it to Bangkok with his son.

David's lover in Viet Nam, Suong, was an aristocratic woman, part French; she presents the stereotypical image of the exotic métisse: "He could see her face: her eyelids rounded from the French blood in her family, her jaw strong for a Vietnamese, a surprisingly Western face but for her tawny skin and the long, straight black hair and the tilt to her eyes and her wide, sullen mouth" (35). Although this is David's perception of her, we are offered nothing else, so she remains, for the reader, a cipher. When he returns to Viet Nam and traces Suong's mother, Madame Trung, he again exoticizes Asia: "Here was the picture of Suong's father, the picture David remembered. The man's face was long-jawed, almost Western; Suong had her father's face, not her mother's; this woman who was motioning for him to sit was from the world of golden dragons, mandarin robes, her face was round, finely etched, the delight of emperors, not businessmen" (192–93); later he actually sees her face as "inscrutable" (200). He is equally alienated when he first sees his son: "The face was all wrong. . . . It was very round, evenly sallowed with the Orient; the nose was snubbed and wide-nostriled; the eyes showed their lids when open, almost Western eyes, no more than Suong's own eyes. There was nothing of David in this face at all. Nothing" (195).

David has come seeking an image of himself, but finds his son's Vietnamese identity to be intractable. He struggles with the thought that perhaps the boy is not his son, but ultimately he knows that he is. Fleming wants an American son in Viet Nam, not a Vietnamese son: "Perhaps that was why they were cluttered together, the ones who should be part of him and the ones who were strangers. None of them truly engaged him. None of them moved him. Not even his son" (200). David Fleming is the mirror image of Cliff Wilkes: Cliff's cultural boundaries are so permeable that his identity shifts fluidly; David's are so impermeable that he is moved by almost no one but himself, and sees strangers wherever he does not see his own image.

The novel can be read as an allegory: David's original quest, to find the prisoner whose cell graffito has intrigued him, and his second quest, to find the son who he hopes will be in his own image, can be seen as symbolizing America's quest to find a Viet Nam in its own image, a Viet Nam it can understand without effort. David has originally sought out Tuyen, tracing him through the prison system, because in David's filthy cell he has found the graffito "Hygiene is healthful." He sees Tuyen, on the basis of this graffito, as being like himself—detached, ironic. David knows that Tuyen will die in prison; he wishes to seek him out and free him because he identifies with him.

Interestingly, David Fleming remains in Saigon after 30 April to face what Cliff Wilkes fled from. He is on the street and afraid, realizing that he has come too late, but he is reassured by a stranger:

David looked up into the face of a Vietnamese man. A round, dusky, foreign face.

"It's all right," the man repeated in flawless English. "They're not hurting anyone caught behind. Or anyone else." (197)

In this interchange, Butler attempts to show that it is David's attitude that makes the man "foreign," but there are too few such instances of Vietnamese characters speaking against David's preconceptions to rescue the novel entirely.

Tuyen is now director of security for Saigon-Gia Dinh; David sees him in a parade. The climax of the novel comes when David begins to experience some self-realization.

> After twice seeing the child, twice seeing Tuyen, and still remaining cut off from them both, David knew he had to resolve all this. He was in a room alone, with his own mind. He'd been alone often enough in his life—he'd sought that isolation—and his own voice would be sufficient now. He had two Vietnamese to understand.
>
> "Khai and Tuyen." He spoke the names and this linkage made him rise from the chair.
>
> "Look at what you've done," he said aloud to himself. "You've put the two together. Before, you'd thought of them separately." (222)

He begins to recognize that what he is looking for are reflections of himself: "I love my child only because I see myself in him. I cannot love Khai because there's nothing of me to see there" (223). Thinking about why he wanted to free Tuyen, he thinks, in a dialogue with himself,

> "You're talking to yourself," he said.
>
> "That's because your own mind is the only one you've ever felt you could talk with."
>
> "Except when you were thinking about Tuyen. Imagining him. And later, by the stream on Con Son Island."
>
> "And you knew him from the wall."
>
> "Yes."
>
> "And what was there?"
>
> "His mind."
>
> "More."
>
> "My mind."
>
> . . . David had seen himself on that cell wall; he'd seen the pattern of his own mind, in its aloofness, its irony. Tuyen was not a face, he was a mind, and David had seen himself here as clearly as he'd seen himself when his [American] son was lifted by the nurse. (225)

In this passage David reflects the solipsism of America in its adventures in Asia. David, however, acts to overcome his solipsism. Despite his lack of feeling for his son, he agrees to escape with the boy, whose grandmother knows that Amerasian children will have a hard time in Viet Nam and that she, his only relative, will not live for many more years. Ironically, David plans an escape on a boat, thus aligning himself with the Vietnamese. David, who sees only the alienness of Viet Nam, almost becomes a Vietnamese "boat person."

During his escape across Saigon to the dock, the reluctant American adopts Viet Nam. When Khai cries, David considers abandoning him: " 'Grandma,' the boy said again, lower, but his voice full of tears, the Vietnamese word sounding alien, the pitch of the voice making David's teeth hurt. Run away. Run. But David made his own hand come up, made himself gently press the boy closer, made his hand stroke at the back of the child's head" (244). He is caught by the police, however, and taken for interrogation to Tuyen, in a reversal of power roles from the war years. David feels caught in his own trap.

He realized he was foolish to expect anything from this man. If David had seen his own mind—seen himself—in Tuyen's words on the cell wall, then of course there would be no feeling now, only thought, only distance, at best some irony between them. As he sat, David smiled faintly: he had sought and freed the very sort of man who could remain aloof at this moment. (251)

But David is wrong, wrong altogether, and ironically this misperception leads to his salvation rather than his destruction. It turns out that Tuyen did not write the graffito on the cell wall. David had not found his own image in Tuyen; Tuyen is a different man altogether.

Tuyen was suddenly unpredictable, was suddenly alien to David, no different from any stranger in this country. But so was Khai. Khai had once been an alien as well. But now: just thinking of the child made David stir, made him focus on Tuyen's averted eyes, his silence; these eyes, this silence, were great dangers now, these threatened to separate David from Khai forever. (258)

David is wrong again, as usual. Tuyen is a different man, and that means David's and Khai's freedom, not incarceration.

The novel ends with David feeling some rapprochement with both his son and Tuyen. The interview with Tuyen ends on a note of self-discovery and discovery of the other:

Tuyen closed his eyes briefly, as if he were in pain. "I was very frightened there. . . . I just wonder who it was that could write something like that. What sort of man?"

"I thought it was you."

Tuyen smiled. "I wish it could have been so."

"Couldn't it?"

"No. Not at all. I am not that brave a man. I am too close to the pain. . . . The man who wrote those words was very brave."

David felt drawn again to Tuyen. "When I saw the words on the wall I thought I knew you," David said. "Now I think that again." (260)

David learns a lesson in acceptance of otherness: he can know Tuyen, even if Tuyen is not his twin; he can accept his son, even if the son is not his image in miniature.

This change is a paradigm of the transformation that America as a whole could possibly undergo, but the novel is not clear enough in its point to perform the transformative function that it sets up.

The Deuce (1989) is a complete departure for Butler. It breaks away from the interwoven events of his earlier novels; none of the characters in *The Deuce* has appeared in the earlier works. Also, this narrative is told in first person, in the voice of an Amerasian teenager who lives in Point Pleasant, New Jersey, with his American father.

In *The Deuce* Butler returns to the theme of dual identity that he introduced in *The Alleys of Eden.* "I wish it was simple just to say who I am," the novel begins,

just to say my name is so-and-so and that makes you think of a certain kind of person and that would be me. . . . But me, I've got three names. And so I've got to go through all this bullshit just to start talking. I'm Anthony James Hatcher, Tony. I'm Võ Đình Thanh. And I'm the Deuce. Don't ask me which one I use. It's too early for that. I've got to tell you some things first. (7)

"The Deuce" is the name given to Forty-second Street by its denizens; Tony/Thanh is given that name when he runs away to New York. He is named by Joey, a beggar who uses his identity as a Viet Nam War veteran as a begging line and becomes Tony/Thanh's surrogate father.

The Deuce's identity remains dual; he does not go one way or the other. In the course of the book, he learns to accept his dual identity. In addition to being an Amerasian, he is also a wise-guy teenager with a sarcastic mouth. In Viet Nam, he would have been a Saigon cowboy. In New York, he is a street-tough runaway. The suburban Point Pleasant of his district attorney father, Kenneth Hatcher, is a bad fit for Tony/Thanh.

The me that's Tony Hatcher is from the Jersey Shore. . . . The Deuce is from Forty-second Street, the street that gave me the name. . . . And Võ Đình Thanh is from Saigon, Republic of Vietnam, now known as Ho Chi Minh City, named after a man who had the stupidest-looking beard in history. . . .
But that's where I was born, in Saigon. You ask almost anybody hanging around the Port Authority or out on the Deuce where they were born and they give you a who-gives-a-shit shrug, but when I say I was born in Saigon, it's not just that you can look at my face and see that I'm not any all-American, it's also that I can sit back in my head and I can be in Saigon as clear as any damn place in New Jersey. Even as clear as New York. (8)

The Deuce can always be in two places at once, is always divided, but by the end of the novel he has taken on this duality not as an impediment to his identity, but as his identity:

And now I know what voice I have, and who it is I am. A guy on a beach in Vung Tau tells me I'm Vietnamese. A civics teacher in Point Pleasant tells me I'm American. Kenneth James Hatcher tells me I'm his son, and I'm the son of a woman named Võ Xuân Nghi who's lost somewhere half a world away. I'm a lot of things but I'm one thing, and I have no doubt about that. I'm The Deuce. (303)

Thanh had been living with his mother in Saigon until his father, Kenneth Hatcher, returned to Viet Nam to get him. His mother, Nghi, is a prostitute and a drug addict; Kenneth takes Thanh but leaves Nghi behind, for which Thanh resents Kenneth. Thanh is doomed by heritage to wander. Kenneth comes first to see him in Saigon on Wandering Souls' Day. Tony, looking back, does not believe in that "Vietnamese voodoo" (18), but by the end of the novel, The Deuce has reached peace about his lost mother and lost culture: "And I'm going to figure out when Wandering Souls' Day is and I'll say some kind of prayer for her, just in case she's dead and just in case the Buddhists are right about all that. She believed in it, even if I don't, so it's the least I can do for her" (302). Without integrating his multiple identities, he accepts his multiple heritages.
The Deuce resists stereotypes that might be forced on him:

Do you take me for that? A Vietnamese kid who's an American now? The newspapers and magazines love us American-Asian kids. We're smart as hell. You can see us on the cover of Time. Look at these kids. They don't really look like Americans, do they? But surprise. They are. And because they don't look

279

American, they don't look all that smart, either, right? Surprise again. That's why they're such a big deal on the cover of this magazine. And I *am* smart, like it says right here.

But there's something a little different about me. Those are good, obvious Asian faces on the magazine cover. You look at me and there's something a little odd. (26)

As Tony in Point Pleasant, he is seeking a purely Asian identity, which he cannot quite capture. When a Chinese American girl becomes a new student at his high school he is excited, seeing her as similar to himself. He approaches her after class and asks her name. When she says, "Nancy," he is appalled and demands to know how she can be named Nancy if she is Chinese. Nancy replies that she is not Chinese—she was born in Hackensack and demands, "What's *your* name?" He thinks, "If I weren't so conscious at that moment of how really off-the-wall I'd been acting, I might have said it. As it was, the answer actually shaped itself in my mouth and when I realized it, it scared the shit out of me. Tony, I was going to say" (62–63).

Living life as "Tony" is driving him crazy, so he runs away, asserting his Asian identity in his goodbye note to his father: "So long, Kenneth. Thanks for the education. Since by the time you read this I'm long gone and for good, you won't have to marry fat Tracy so I can have a mother. It wouldn't have worked anyway. I'm Vietnamese" (67). His plan is to go to New York, then on to Montreal: "I figured since I wasn't American, there was no sense in staying in America" (71). He plans to join the Vietnamese community in Montreal as a Vietnamese, not as an Amerasian.

He is robbed in the Port Authority bus terminal, so he never makes it farther than New York. In New York, however, he finds links back to his other city, Saigon, in the smell of incense rising from the display of a sidewalk merchant. Walking through the back alleys of New York in search of a place to sleep,

there was a real bad little moment then because you don't look at scrounged-up shacks without thinking of Saigon and you don't look at whores without thinking of your mother and the two of them together made me imagine her in the doorway of a shanty on stilts out over the Thi Nghè River and nobody stopping in to fuck her because there was garbage running in the river under her bed. (112)

He comes to feel at home in New York because it reminds him of Saigon— he has found the underside of America, a place he finds more genuine than the suburban emptiness of Point Pleasant.

He is still maintaining his pure-Asian identity when he meets Joey, the veteran and beggar who gives him his new name. Joey is begging in the Port Authority terminal, using the line "I fought for you in Vietnam."

. . . I say, "You didn't fight for *me* in Vietnam."
He throws his head back and laughs a laugh as tight and dry as his face and says, "I can see that."
"What can you see?"
"You're half Vietnamese, aren't you?"
"I'm Vietnamese." (118)

When Joey asks his name, and he is tongue-tied for an answer, Joey names him The Deuce: "You watch out for the motherfuckers out there who want to eat you alive. But that street is still the Mekong, the river that runs right through all of us around here. And something else, and you're going to get pissed off at me again. You can't bullshit me. You're two things. You're Vietnamese and you're American. A deuce" (122). It is Joey, the surrogate father, who teaches The Deuce to accept his dual identity.

Joey himself is two things: a veteran and a liar. He was a soldier, but not a combat soldier. The stories he tells and the pose he strikes as a beggar are all lies. Like The Deuce, Joey is neither all one thing nor another—neither all fake nor all genuine. Joey is an alcoholic, but it is not his war experience that has made him into who he is. "It's not Vietnam," he says, explaining his alcoholism, "it's just me. All Vietnam did was give me the only beautiful thing I ever had" (245). Eventually he admits all of this to The Deuce after they have been living together in an abandoned building, after he has taught The Deuce the ways of the street. But The Deuce accepts him as a surrogate father, bonds with him in a way he had never bonded with Kenneth, because there is one thing that Joey is not lying about: he really was in love with his Vietnamese girlfriend, a woman who refused to accompany him to America when he left Viet Nam. All these years later, he still carries her picture, just as The Deuce carries a picture of his mother.

Joey tells the story of how he loved this woman, who then left him. The story pulls at the strings of The Deuce's identity:

I'm glad Joey felt good about himself in Vietnam. I still like him for loving a Vietnamese. But at the moment all that doesn't count for much with me because I'm not feeling Vietnamese myself and because I'm getting real mad at the whore in the story he's telling. But I don't know why the hell I should be mad at her.

She made Joey feel good for a year. What's so bad about that? I look at him and he's staring out the window and his tears hold the sky like the photo did in my hand. (188)

The Deuce wishes that Kenneth loved his mother the way Joey loved this woman. That, for him, would make a whole identity. When The Deuce returns to his real father at the end of the novel, he finally begins to accept him when Kenneth admits for the first time that, like Tony, he, too misses Nghi. This is the broken link that Tony has been unable to live with, and that The Deuce has made whole again.

For all the novel's sophistication and antistereotypical cultural portrayals, it is distressingly homophobic. The Deuce becomes the object of desire of Treen, a sado-masochistic homosexual rapist and murderer of young boys. This element of the plot gives the novel its denouement, when Treen kills Joey, who has warned him away from The Deuce, and then, in turn, The Deuce leads Treen to his death in revenge for Joey. One possible interpretation is that Treen's pursuit of The Deuce puts him in the same position as his mother—as a potential prostitute—but textual evidence does not support this generous interpretation. The Deuce is not paired with his mother in this way, or with Norma, the runaway who becomes a hooker and gives The Deuce his first sexual experience. Rather, Norma is paired with his mother. The portrayal of Treen merely fits the stereotypical image of the murderous homosexual pederast and is the one unfortunate note in an otherwise brilliant piece of bicultural writing.

It is, in fact, Norma who provokes The Deuce to take his first step in accepting his dual identity: "What do I look like to her? I realize I'm hoping it's not Vietnamese, and that gives me a little twist of guilt. . . . and if I have to be American to get her to like me, then goddamit, that's what I'll be" (149–50). Norma later thinks he is Puerto Rican. He never tells her what he really is; "Frankly, I'm a little confused myself" (199). Later, when she rejects him, he takes on that identity and says to her, "They've got better whores than you in San Juan" (252).

He moves further toward dual identity in an encounter with a Korean grocer.

"Okay. So what am I? You take a guess."
. . . "I think maybe you Vietnamese."
When you consider what I was trying to do when I ran away from Jersey, you'd expect this to please me. I sure expect it as I stand there by the salad bar in

those first few seconds after Sung declares me to be Vietnamese. But then it dawns on me as Sung waits for an answer that nothing's happening in me. At least not what I expect. There's no fucking flash of light or ringing bells or any goddam thing. . . . Am I Vietnamese? Am I Võ Đình Thanh after all? What the fuck good would that do me? (209)

Later he reflects on this encounter:

If I'd gotten on that bus and gone to Montreal, would I be Vietnamese right now? Could I have done it? Could I have been Vietnamese? I try to see myself. . . . My skin is starting to tingle, it's starting to fucking peel away and fall off and underneath, instead of being white, it's even darker, and I look at my reflection in the window and you can see the skin falling off my face and the eyelids fall away and underneath, my eyes are purely Asian, like my mother's and it's true after all, I'm Vietnamese, and by the time we get to the bus station in Montreal the whole world can know me at a glance and so can I.

And of course all this is bullshit. I know it even as I let myself see it in my head. I had a chance not so long ago, I remind myself. And I told Mr. Sung to get fucked. (222)

With his letting go of the dream of a purely Vietnamese identity, he starts to become comfortable with his duality.

When The Deuce sees a picture of himself on a runaway poster, he looks at the eyes and they change back and forth, like a moving hologram: "These are the eyes of an American, then they're the eyes of a Vietnamese" (237). Joey's death catalyzes his dual identity: "I'm both crying these tears and standing back watching, like I'm two different people inside here, and I wonder who's who, probably the American is crying for Joey Cipriani and the Vietnamese is watching and saying, Head for the alleys, get the fuck out of here or you'll be back where all they can do is kill your luck" (256).

When he is thoroughly dual in his identity, he begins to reconcile not only himself, but the two cultures. He spends a night in the abandoned room he and Joey have shared and believes he sees Joey's ghost: "That's something Nghi would believe in and probably all the other whores in Saigon, and I guess all the Buddhists in Vietnam, for that matter, with their little shrines to their ancestors. But a bunch of Christians in America do, too. The Catholics think they can talk to the saints, and those are just ghosts hanging around, if you look at them close" (262). He thus views neither culture as alien. In a larger sense, that is what the whole novel seeks to do. Butler has drawn the two nations, the two peoples, together in the body of one boy. The Deuce stands as a symbol of the intertwined fates and destinies of the two countries. Once, to pass time, The Deuce has gone to the New York Public Library and looked at an atlas in the map room. He has seen pictures of countries paired on the pages—implicitly, in the novel, Viet Nam and America are also paired, just as in all the narratives by the Vietnamese exile writers.

One of the many remarkable aspects about this book is that all the Vietnamese words are printed with diacritics, and the diacritics are clearly hand-drawn. This illustrates the lengths to which Butler has gone in this novel to attempt to produce a bicultural text.

The diacritics in *A Good Scent from a Strange Mountain* are typset, marking a move in the publishing industry rather than in Butler's writing. This collection of stories won the 1993 Pulitzer Prize, bringing Butler a level of recognition he had not previously enjoyed. The stories are narrated in the voices of Vietnamese immigrants living around New Orleans in the Buddhist community in Gretna, the Catholic community in Versailles, and the industrial town of Lake Charles. Some of the narrators are male, some female, and they range in economic status from a transplanted Saigon "bar girl" who is now an exotic dancer in New Orleans to a successful businessman who buys a shoe that John Lennon was wearing the day he was killed, paying "much money" for it (139).

For a reader familiar with Vietnamese exile writers, Butler's stories are at first very strange, not because of their representation of Vietnamese culture and the dislocations of exile—about which they are, for the most part, quite accurate—but rather because of their style. Butler's stories tend toward the minimalist, the postmodern; they have abrupt and indeterminate endings and focus on character and symbol rather than plot. In these features they differ strongly from the short stories of exile writers such as Vo Phien, or the writers in Nguyen Ngoc Bich's anthology *War and Exile*, who write in a more traditional story form in which the endings tend to be tied up more neatly and the plot usually advances in a linear way.

The style of Butler's stories in no way undermines them. It makes them unique—Vietnamese cultural experiences put to distinctly American fictional purposes—but this presents one way immigrants have been incorporated into American culture, when others write in their voices. Objections may be raised to Butler's use of the first-person Vietnamese narrator, but, since culture is learned and not inherited through the genes, Butler, who knows the language and has clearly familiarized himself with the culture, can write as appropriately in this voice as in any other he has created.[36]

Some of the stories in this collection succeed better on their own terms than others, and some of the narrators are more engaging than others. The most succint and pointed of the stories is "Letters from My Father," in which an Amerasian girl learns of her father's love for her through copies of old letters he wrote in his attempt to bring her and her mother over from Viet Nam. There are also two memorable ghost stories. The longest piece, "The American Couple," warns of the dangers of being too seduced by the surfaces of American culture.

A few seeming lapses appear in the creation of the Vietnamese personas. One of the most notable of these is an emphasis on size, which is more American than Vietnamese. The narrator of "Crickets" says, "I am the size of a woman in this country" (60), and the narrator of "Love" describes his rival for his wife's affections as "a tall man, nearly as tall as an American" (78). Vietnamese tend, in fact, to view Americans' size as ungainly rather than enviable. Also, Butler always describes Western features in Vietnamese faces as beautiful, as in "Preparation": "Her closed eyes showed the mostly Western lids, passed down by more than one Frenchman among her ancestors. This was a very attractive thing about her" (145). Vietnamese standards of beauty uphold racial purity, not racial mixing, as the ideal.

Nonetheless, the emphasis in most of these stories is on the richness of the possibilities of cross-cultural experience, as in "Snow," in which Miss Giàu is a lonely waitress in a Chinese restaurant. She meets Mr. Cohen, a Jewish American Holocaust refugee originally from Poland, and the possibility of love develops between them. On the night of their first date she listens to the grandfather clock ticking as she waits for him to pick her up to celebrate New Year's Eve: "The Vietnamese New Year comes at a different time, but people in Vietnam know to celebrate whatever holiday comes along. So tonight Mr. Cohen and I will go to some restaurant that is not Chinese, and all I have to do now is sit here and listen very carefully to Grandfather as he talks to me about time" (135). Overall these stories suggest that understanding is possible, if we are open to the possibilities.

Wayne Karlin has also produced a remarkable and polyvocal novel. *Lost Armies* is a mystery novel in which the plot depends on the merging of identities of an American and a Vietnamese. One of the novel's epigraphs is from Joseph Conrad: "It was, in the night, as though I had been faced by my own reflection in the depths of a somber and immense mirror." Multiple mirrorings abound in this novel, across multiple cultural and racial lines.

The novel's main characters are Wheeler, a veteran and former journalist; Dennis, his childhood friend and fellow veteran; Xuan, a refugee and Dennis's former lover; and Tho, Xuan's brother, who had been Dennis's "Kit Carson" scout in Viet Nam. The focus of the multiple identities is Dennis, who is dead throughout the novel, but whose death is not discovered by the narrator, Wheeler, until the end; indeed, the mystery plot revolves around Dennis's whereabouts. Dennis has been something of a "crazy vet." In the past, he has cut the tongues out of deer and dumped them in the town square (a sort of replication of an incident in Viet Nam). The novel begins when someone, presumably Dennis, begins leaving dead deer with their tongues cut out in public places. He had done this once before, years ago. But this time, it is Tho, impersonating Dennis. Another way to see the situation is that Dennis is not "really" dead until the end of the novel, with the death of Tho, who has taken on Dennis's identity. As the action of the novel develops, with the tongueless dead deer appearing again, the sheriff asks Wheeler to help him find Dennis.

Dennis and Wheeler grew up together in coastal Maryland and went to Viet Nam together, along with Willy Looms, a black man from the same town. Dennis, seemingly a typical redneck, becomes friends with Willy across racial lines, and when Willy is killed, Dennis christens his Hồi Chánh[37] scout "Willy the Gook." This Willy is Tho (a fact unknown to Wheeler until the novel's end). Tho has betrayed Dennis in Viet Nam, setting an ambush for him: Tho is a fake Hồi Chánh, still loyal to the Viet Cong. Dennis believes, however, that Tho was the victim of treacherous villagers, rather than the opposite, and, in revenge he kills a number of the villagers and cuts out their tongues. Tho and Dennis each feel terribly guilty about the other. Dennis finds Tho and his sister Xuan in a refugee camp after the war and brings them back to Maryland, believing that Tho miraculously survived the villagers' betrayal and still not knowing that Tho betrayed him.

Wheeler teaches English as a Second Language at a junior college. Xuan has come to him as a student; they eventually become lovers, and she introduces Wheeler to her brother, Tho. Wheeler's position as an English teacher serves as an opportunity for the narrative to comment about American perceptions of Vietnamese:

Wheeler smoothed the paper on the desk top, his pen a slim, predatory wraith, hovering and darting. Dinh's eyes were fastened to it, cloudy with apprehension. Wheeler circled a singular subject, drew an accusatory arrow from it to a plural pronoun, shot a significant glance at Dinh.

. . . The first essays assigned were to be about personal experiences ("let the student deal with subject matter that is familiar to her/him," the text urged).

What she/he wrote were pleas. Here I am, on this paper. See me, not the child I am in your language. The papers were pits of pain. Wheeler didn't know what to say to Dinh. He didn't have the language. "You see, when you write here about your wife in the water it doesn't directly support your topic sentence about the Thai fishermen, and your verb form isn't parallel. You lose unity, coherence." He felt ridiculous.

"Look, Mr. Dinh, I want you to understand something. The corrections I make, it's not that I don't have any feelings about what you write. But the best way I can help you is to show you your mistakes."

"Yes," Dinh looked at the essay about the murder of his wife. "My mistakes." . . .

Wheeler's vision fled from his pleading eyes, brushed the rows of VDT screens in the study carrels, their blank green faces glowing behind Dinh's head, squat demons guarding the gates Dinh wished to enter. (2)

This passage at the beginning of the book establishes the history of the Vietnamese refugees, rather than the history of the American veterans, as the center of attention. Wheeler, the veteran and teacher, is inadequate in the face of Dinh's history and Dinh's immediate need to communicate with Americans. Ironically, Dinh, in his poor English, manages to carry out his half of the communication; it is Wheeler who can formulate no adequate response. In this respect, Wheeler certainly stands for America as a whole.

Further, this passage establishes the role that language will play in the novel: it will always be inadequate to convey the feelings of the characters, despite their seeming articulateness. Xuan and Tho were educated, articulate people in their own language and culture; in Maryland, they are poor residents of a trailer park, their verbal eloquence stripped by their linguistic isolation. Wheeler, an English teacher and former reporter, does not possess the words to deal with his students, or with Xuan, or Tho, or Dennis. Dennis (or his ghost) uses no words: his language is action, his language is killing. The passage about Mr. Dinh also decenters its "American" context. The line about the VDTs as demons is quite literal; it is the harbinger of all the ghosts to come in the novel.

Dennis is a ghost throughout the novel; in a way, Tho is possessed by Dennis's ghost, and it is Dennis's ghost (in the form of booby traps he has left behind) who kills Tho in the end. (When Tho chases Wheeler, trying to kill him because he has been sleeping with Xuan, Wheeler runs into the forest and finds Dennis's grave. Tho follows him and trips a booby trap that Wheeler knows Dennis had laid before his death.)

Wheeler sees the Vietnamese residents of Maryland as "an odd haunting . . . Asian ghosts that had followed him to the altars of his ancestors" (3). Note that Wheeler is thinking of his home country in terms of a Vietnamese paradigm, as the "altars of his ancestors." Wheeler is both wrong and right to see the Vietnamese immigrants as ghosts—in some ways, they are, but in other ways it is they who are alive and he who is the ghost—a ghost of his former self, living a lonely and isolated life. He sees the Vietnamese immigrants' material success as "inevitable as justice in a fairy tale, to take over dreams he no longer had" (3). The refugees are becoming the new Americans, to live American dreams, and he is fading away.

Whereas Wheeler is a metaphoric ghost, Dennis is a literal one. Dennis first reappears as a message on a postcard in Wheeler's mailbox: "The handwriting suggested Dennis's, but only as if he were a spirit directing someone else's hand; the big, bold letters were his, but weakly scrawled" (4). This description is at once the literal truth and an artful piece of misdirection, since it is not Dennis but Tho who has written the postcard, and Tho has, indeed, been guided by Dennis's ghost.

Another clue about Dennis occurs in a conversation Wheeler has with Ben Campeau, editor of the local newspaper, who wants Wheeler to write a story about Dennis. Ben says of Dennis, "The Corps never leaves its dead, but what if the dead walk out by themselves, right? What do we do with the walking dead?" (9). Wheeler remembers that the first time he saw the Vietnam Veterans Memorial, he thought Dennis's name should be on it (58).

When Wheeler sees one of the dead deer, its tongue cut out, at the Vietnamese trailer park in Rector's Point, he walks away from it, out to the shore, which he perceives as "layers of murder"—a land embedded with fossils, a land that held a Union POW camp where three thousand Confederate soldiers had died, a land that entombed a "race of Indians under soil enriched by the corpses of murdered prisoners that supported the ghosts of murdered Vietnamese, trapped in the bodies of deer" (27).

Wheeler's position as English teacher also provides the opportunity in the narrative for Xuan's voice to intrude in its subversive way. Xuan first approaches Wheeler as a potential student. When he asks for a writing sample, this is what she writes for him:

I am asked to write who I am, but what I am now does not define me. I will tell you what does. Once upon a time and far away I was a whore for Americans. I let them empty their nightmares of the murder of my people into me. Then I made them look into my eyes until they saw me. I knew that one day they would raise a weapon and see me again in the face of their enemy and they would hesitate and die. When they left I knew I had birthed their corpses. (13)

Xuan steals a workbook and continues to write "essays," which appear throughout the novel. Xuan is thus given her own voice. In her essays she works out her identity, but she lies, from the first. She resists having an identity ascribed to her:

My "lover's" myth, his legendary boyhood friend Wheeler translated to flesh, was a darker, leaner soul than I expected, a sickness of lust for me stamped in his rain ghost's eyes like an insidious invitation: Come, he said, and I'll teach you my monkey demon's language, I'll ensnare you with my words so I may trap your soul in this red and gray prison, this web of books in whose center I sit. So I stole his magic instead: this book I write in now—*Gateway to English*, it proclaims. An exercise book. Stealing it was my first exercise. (21)

Within the text, Xuan resists being stereotyped, demands to create her own identity, just as the creation of the character, the interpolation of sections in which she is given her own voice, resists the sort of pigeon-holing and stereotyping that U.S. fiction usually imposes on Asian characters. She is a trickster, who eludes both Wheeler and the reader. Xuan comments on the way representation supplants memory:

I sit in the dark tunnels of theaters and I watch the dream form in front of my eyes. . . . We are all dreaming at once. The same image is left in all our minds, like the dust of a single dream. We see a strange land that is supposed to be my homeland. Pictures form that might be glimpses of my homeland reflected by the shattered, jagged fragments of a thousand broken mirrors, the dragon teeth of broken glass. Like something strong once seen and dimly echoed forever at night, in sleep. Distorted evil suggestions of an evil dream. Dust as I am dust. I wish to say this: what we dream is not my country. Its trees are not my trees nor its sounds nor its colors. Yet the colors of this dream are stronger than the colors of my memory. And because of their strength I fear that the dream will become my memory. It will replace my country. (54)

She exposes the American representation of Viet Nam as a forgery.

Xuan has hopes that Wheeler will be able to see through her poses and see through the stereotypes their cultures have erected around them. She writes a fantasy of standing on a Saigon street, dressed as a hooker, and Wheeler walking toward her: "Unlike the others, this soldier would be excited by my humanity—it is the elusive gem the country has been hiding from him" (68). She hopes that if they can see each other through the roles prescribed for them, they can touch each other in a way that she and Dennis could not.

Karlin, too, comments on representation and reality. In a passage describing Wheeler's war experience, he writes,

One day, soon after the squadron had lost five helicopters and crews on the DMZ, his crew chief machine-gunned a woman, clearly pregnant, who'd been working a paddy in which they'd made a forced landing. Wheeler had heard all the stories, but then there it was, in the flesh, bleeding into the green shoots of rice. Do you think this is a story, any of this? He didn't know what he was supposed to do about it. What was he supposed to be, GI Joe or the terror of their lives? (57)

Who is the "you"? The sentence "Do you think this is a story, any of this?" appears in the paragraph as a ghostly interpolation—who is the "you"? Who is the implied "I" asking the question? It can only be Karlin himself intruding into the construction of his own narrative to directly ask you, the reader, where you position yourself in relation to what you are reading. Do you think this is a story? Any of this?

Another of the major Vietnamese characters is Lily Minh, a successful businesswoman, involved with a congressman and willing to exploit Vietnamese or Americans equally for profit. She is not stereotypically portrayed; instead, she uses Americans' stereotypical perceptions of Asians to manipulate them into doing her will. Yet she is not a dragon lady—she is a modern American businesswoman. Thus the text makes another meta-comment on stereotypes.

In the course of trying to find Dennis, Wheeler talks to Hallam, the sheriff, whom he and Dennis had known, but not liked, when they were all kids. Hallam displays a typical American attitude, and then an awareness about that attitude. When he asks Wheeler if he still speaks Vietnamese, Hallam says,

"I used to know a few words myself. 'Halt,' 'Hands up,' 'Suck my dick.'" . . . Hallam looked surprised at his own words. "Hell, listen to me. I get out to Rector's Point yesterday—all those damn names. Phuong and Huong and Nguyen and Pham Dam and Phuc Duc and Duct Tape and Fuck a Duck. It's a time trip. I've got a master's in public administration, I go to a health club, I've even been known to drink fucking Perrier, and I get with those people and suddenly I'm sounding like a redneck jarhead again." (16–17)

Despite Hallam's self-knowledge, he cannot tear himself away from his ethnocentric attitude; unlike Wheeler, unlike Dennis, he has not crossed over in his perceptions. Wheeler sees the similarity of Americans and Vietnamese: he sees the immigrants as the new Americans, supplanting the descendants of the "Catholic boat people who'd come ashore in 1634" (37). Wheeler has had a career as a reporter for the *Washington Post*; he has sacrificed that career because he was called by ghosts.

Back in 1975 he'd applied to cover the fall of Saigon and had been turned down then also, but the reports of the latest Vietnamese migrations—no longer only the upper classes and the ethnic Chinese, but now the people in the villages— had again pushed into him a need to close a door in his life that had never been closed, to physically witness an ending. It hadn't worked out. The rapes and murders of the refugees by Thai and Malaysian fishermen, the packed hopelessness of the camps he'd visited, called too many other memories to his mind to close any doors; instead they had only given him new ghosts to replace his ancient ghosts. . . . When he'd run out of money, he'd come back to find the people he'd gone to write about waiting for him on his own ground. (41)

In Lily Minh's house he sees a woven fish trap; it reminds him of seeing them in Viet Nam. From a fishing area himself, "He'd tried to regard them as one of the connections that he'd sought between himself and Vietnam: the traps worked on the same principle as a crab pot" (72). In his Maryland trailer park home, Tho has been weaving fish traps, but his are crazy, "uneconomical, unfunctional, un-Vietnamese" (73).

Wheeler comes into contact with Xuan again in the process of searching for Dennis. He is led to her because she had been Dennis's girlfriend, and he goes to see her at the Vietnamese restaurant in Washington where she is a waitress. They play an avoidance game having to do with naming, which draws on Wheeler's knowledge of Vietnamese culture. He asks her what her full name is, knowing that it is rude to do so. She tells him and says,

"This is the name I took when I left Vietnam. There's nothing more real than a death name."
"Xuan means spring, doesn't it? That's a strange death name."
. . . "Yes, you're right. Perhaps I'll change it to something more fitting. To *Lon.*"
It meant vagina. "And I'll change mine to *Cat.*" Penis. . . . "Why do you want to insult yourself with something like *Lon*?"

She laughed harshly. "You know I was *me my.*" It was slang for a GI's woman. . . . "*Lon* is fine. Your given name is Emmett, isn't it? Yet you don't use it, Dennis told me. That's very Vietnamese, not to use your name so that you misdirect malevolence."

It was also the reason to give children nicknames like *Lon.* Which, he supposed, made him the evil spirit she feared. (48)

She tells him that she met Dennis at a refugee center in Oakland, and that Dennis had been in Thailand. Wheeler asks why Dennis had been there.

"Once he told me that he'd gone there to look for a Vietnamese friend. A Vietnamese with a foolish name."

"Willy," he whispered.

She nodded. "Perhaps it was just a name to confuse the spirits also—like Wheeler. Like Xuan."

"He was Dennis's Kit Carson scout. Dennis called him Willy the Gook."

"Yes. Willy the Gook and Xuan the Gook. . . . He went looking for this dead man, this Willy the Gook, but he had to come home to find Xuan the Gook instead." (49–50)

Although Wheeler does not know it yet, Xuan is both telling him that she is "Willy the Gook's" sister and explaining her relationship to Dennis. It turns out that Xuan is the "foolishly romantic name your foolishly romantic friend gave me" (51).

Xuan tells Wheeler that she and Dennis lived in the forest for weeks, "like shadows, like forest spirits. . . . And then one day he was gone" (51). Wheeler asks why, but Xuan turns the question around, demanding, "You tell me." Xuan is being completely truthful, but also not telling the whole story. She knows that Dennis is dead. Then the text does the same thing—tells the truth but not the whole story—with the first appearance of Tho:

She stood up, her face draining as if she'd seen a forest spirit.

"Here's my brother," she said. "Tho."

Her liquid, piercing eyes gleamed in the face of the man walking toward them. He was wearing a white shirt and black pants and a busboy's apron that seemed ridiculous after Wheeler saw his face. It was the carved face of a temple god who had been forced to experience the earth. (51)

The narrative pairs Dennis and Tho as forest spirits. First Dennis is mentioned as a forest spirit, then Tho appears, and Xuan reacts as if she'd seen a forest spirit. Tho and Dennis are the same person, the same vengeful, tortured spirit.

When Wheeler leaves the restaurant, he says, "You know why I'm here—your people are being terrorized—probably by Dennis," and Xuan replies, "You say that as if it's something new in the world" (52) It is not, of course, something new in the world. Dennis has a dark secret, a dark secret he shares with Tho, although Tho knows all of it and Dennis does not. Wheeler writes up his story about Dennis for the local paper, and as part of it, he must tell what he knows of Dennis's dark secret, of what Dennis did at a place called Trung Toan.

He put on display the fictive character Dennis had reduced himself to and put him back in the jungle, finally Jim Bridger, the knower of the land's secrets, the only white man the tribes trusted. He described Dennis's relationship to Vinh, Willy the Gook, the two of them fibered together with the expectations, the myths that each had of the other: the cowboy, the native scout. . . . He told about the sullen, squalid villages, the closed faces, the silent walls of hatred and contempt, and how Trung Toan had finally opened to Dennis and Willy like a flower, the villagers telling Willy where an NVA cadre would be passing by that night. He wrote how Dennis must have felt when the villagers betrayed him, his ambush itself ambushed and only he surviving it, hiding out in the jungle that night and coming back to find his mutilated dead along the trail, the ace of spades pinned to them, and Willy the Gook missing, only a blood trail where he'd been, and Dennis had known what they'd do to Willy, to one of their own who'd defected. He told how Dennis had waited next to the trail until the first group of people from Trung Toan passed by on the way to market, how he'd ambushed them in turn. . . . Then he left his own calling card on the corpses by performing the mutilation that years later he would perform on deer in Wheeler's readers' backyards—an Indian punishment for betrayal that Dennis had read about in one of the mountain man books that had shaped his boyhood. (59–60)

Dennis's relationship with his scout is both genuine and an artifact of representation, because it is fashioned on stereotypes. Dennis's tragic response, massacring the villagers and cutting out their tongues, comes from stories he has read as a child: motivated by real emotion, by the real knowledge that if the Viet Cong have recaptured Willy they will torture and kill him, Dennis invents a response out of fiction. This response haunts Tho, because Tho knows where the real betrayal lies and Dennis does not. Tho has been a false Hồi Chánh; he has remained loyal to the Viet Cong, and he, not the villagers, has betrayed Dennis.

Up until this point Dennis and Tho/Vinh/Willy have remained separate people, bound together but not merged. At the point of Tho's betrayal, one of them must be dead, and yet they are both still alive. Therefore they merge, they take on each other's identities, and this carries itself out to its conclusion: they must kill each other, the drama of betrayal begun in Trung Toan must play itself out, and it does.

Xuan comes to Wheeler's house to offer herself to him, sent by Dennis's ghost. She brings Wheeler a poem by Dennis.

> Wheeler,
>
> Do you remember Kin Village on Okinawa
>
> How the bar girls saw us away?
> And we threw them the silver off our eyes
> And mistook their laughter
> For temple bells?
>
> Do you remember rites of reunion
>
> On Kin sheets wet with the semen of dead men
> And girls who never realized they were part of a ceremony
>
> But maybe someday they would have a reunion too. (64)

The poem recalls Wheeler's ultimate merging with Dennis, a time in transit, after Trung Toan, both of them haunted already. Wheeler recalls,

They shared the room with the ghosts of Trung Toan and Willy the Gook and of Dennis's team and his own squadron. They fucked death, Dennis said. . . . At one point all the divisions between them melted away—watching the undulating thrust of Dennis's body into his girl's was to Wheeler like watching himself; he felt what Dennis felt and what she felt and what his girl felt, and afterward the four of them slept like that. (65)

This is a classic act of men joining through the mechanism of women's bodies, and Wheeler is about to replicate it by taking Xuan, Dennis's lover, for his own, although the presence of too many ghosts in the room prevents them. Wheeler fears the ghosts Dennis's poem has conjured—"spirits of the drowned, *ma da*, waiting to pull others into the water after them; *tinh* spirits that pulled souls through open mouths; spirits of the restless, murdered dead who'd never been soothed by worship or vengeance: the whole gang, the whole lost army" (66)—and Xuan has come not for Wheeler, but to try to recreate Dennis. The gulf is too wide, yet, for Xuan and Wheeler to bridge.

Later they do connect, but their relationship is fragile and perilous. He wonders if "what they had started in this bed were even possible, if their hearts and minds wouldn't always be cluttered with the angry spirits conjured by the contrast of their joining flesh, the colors of their skins" (116). In other words, is it possible for individuals to transcend stereotypes assigned to them by culture?

The denouement occurs after Xuan and Wheeler become lovers. Tho tells Wheeler that Xuan has lied about being a whore in Viet Nam—that she has only become a whore, in Tho's estimation, in America, first with Dennis, then with Wheeler. Tho tells Wheeler the real story of their family: their father was a minister in the Republic of Viet Nam government, a position taken to protect his children, who rebelled and joined the Buddhist peace movement. Tho and Xuan were both arrested and tortured, and when Xuan was released, she was "what my American friends would call a basket case" (128).

Tho explains why he and Xuan left Viet Nam:

> "Because there was nothing left of me for my country. . . . Because I'd become *me my* also . . . I was often with the Americans. . . . They had certain expectations of me that were so strong I was ashamed not to live up to them. I fought against my country being a whore when I was in the peace movement, but I didn't know how to fight against their love.
>
> ". . . You Americans have the freedom to invent your own lives—it gives you the illusion you can invent other people's lives also. Invent them and grow tired of your inventions. You came to us to kill us and to love us, all to prove some idea you had about yourselves. But we were nothing to you. Only your dreams, your shadows, your whores." (129)

Tho sums up the truth about American involvement in Viet Nam in these lines. This passage is reminiscent of what Cliff imagines Lanh saying to him in *The Alleys of Eden*, when Cliff considers leaving his lover in Viet Nam.

The action climaxes on Trung Nguyen, the day of wandering spirits, when "the gates of hell are open . . . and errant spirits look for a cult, for worshippers, for an altar" (130). "We try to give them peace," Tho says, "so they will leave us alone" (130).

Tho killed Dennis because he is finishing what he began in Trung Toan, because he believes that Dennis is using Xuan as a whore, and because he and Xuan are trying to build new identities, new lives, and Dennis is preventing him, because Dennis asserts, builds, and assigns identities to them. Xuan has said, "He made up Willy Looms. Just as he made up Willy the Gook. They bled for him more than he did for them. . . . He made me up too. As his redemption" (83). In order to be who he is, Tho must reveal himself as the false Hồi Chánh, and, in so doing, he must kill Dennis. But Dennis's ghost is powerful and it possesses Tho, leading him to seek out Wheeler through the dead deer. Dennis's ghost seeks Wheeler through its possession of Tho's body, perhaps desiring revenge on Wheeler for surving; Tho must try to kill Wheeler to end his possession, but the only way for Tho to end his possession by Dennis's ghost is to let Dennis, posthumously, kill him with one of his "consequences"—Dennis's name for booby traps. Thus Dennis's ghost is appeased by vengeance, and Dennis and Tho are both at rest, leaving Wheeler and Xuan to try to build on the ruins.

For any of these characters to find peace, there must be a double joining, in death and in love. The Americans and the Vietnamese must recognize each other, incorporate each other's mutual guilt, and go forward, connected in love.

FIVE

Conclusion: *Bạn tri âm*
"the one who hears your sound"
(friend)

How small and sour-grapes seems our postwar punishment of
Vietnam, our trade and diplomatic embargoes that keep the
country in economic ruin. How self-punishing and miserly in
American spirit are these policies. How much better it would be for
our national pride if we offered the country our help, for it is we
and those who threw in their lot with us who seem to dwell in
needless quandary, who live lives punctuated by active resentments
and pain. Go visit Vietnam, I'd tell the troubled vets. Go visit, if
you can, and do something good there, and your pain won't seem
so private, your need for resentment so great.

—John Balaban

It is important to remember, to spell the names correctly, to know
the provinces, before we are persuaded that none of us were in such
places.

—Gloria Emerson

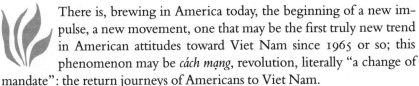 There is, brewing in America today, the beginning of a new im-
pulse, a new movement, one that may be the first truly new trend
in American attitudes toward Viet Nam since 1965 or so; this
phenomenon may be *cách mạng*, revolution, literally "a change of
mandate": the return journeys of Americans to Viet Nam.

This return has embraced several categories of Americans: U.S. war veterans and civilians, and Vietnamese immigrants, now naturalized United
States citizens. The representation of these return journeys has taken the
form of books, television documentaries and news reports, newspaper articles and feature articles in magazines. One U.S. veteran, Gordon Smith, who
returned with the Vietnam Reconciliation Project to construct a medical
clinic in Vung Tau, has been presenting a slide show to both U.S. veterans'

organizations and Vietnamese organizations in California.[1] This return is a hopeful trend in two ways. First, in the reports about Vietnamese immigrants making return journeys, they are presented as *Americans* returning to their land of birth; this emphasis is reflected in the title of one PBS documentary, "A Chicagoan Goes Home," a film about Lam Ton, a successful immigrant, on his first return to Viet Nam. Second, the most prevalent themes in all these accounts are of healing and reconciliation.

Pham Thanh is the subject of a PBS documentary called "Thanh's War." Wounded as a twelve-year-old in 1968, he was brought to the United States by the Committee of Responsibility.[2] Orphaned at the same time he was wounded, he was taken in by an American foster family and made his home here. In 1980, he traveled back to his village in Viet Nam; he has since made several return trips to tend his family's graves and to marry. Thanh's story is especially poignant: because there are no diplomatic relations between the two countries, Thanh's wife has not accompanied him to the United States—if she did and decided she did not want to emigrate, she would be unable to return to Viet Nam. In a *New York Times* editorial written during the Persian Gulf War, Thanh responds to Bush's proclamation that the "Vietnam syndrome" is dead:

Americans must understand, not bury, the Vietnam experience. We need normal diplomatic relations and an end to the trade embargo so that the metaphor "Vietnam" loses its charge and the country Vietnam takes on reality. . . .

Our separation mirrors the gulf that must be bridged to heal each country's soul. I will return home, finally, to propitiate my ghosts. For others haunted by Vietnam, closer ties with it can do the same. (19 April 1991)

The documentary covering Thanh's return to Viet Nam takes a step in the direction of propitiating America's cultural ghosts by humanizing, normalizing, and making familiar both an immigrant who is now an American and the country from which he came.

In an article about Asian-American veterans of the war, Peter Nien-chu Kiang describes the importance of return journeys to Viet Nam for this group of U.S. veterans:

For veterans who continue to experience some degree of PTSD, the Full Circle Recovery project hypothesizes that returning to the scene of the battlefield enables veterans to recall images of war, death, and destruction which they still carry with them, and replace those images with new ones of a people and a country at peace. Instead of seeing the dehumanized enemy, one sees farmers and families. One returns to the U.S. a second time, completing the full circle with these new images as a foundation for healing. (34)

The idea of full circle recovery applies to U.S. veterans of all ethnicities, and many have been making return trips since 1985.

Several organizations have been founded in recent years to facilitate re-establishment of diplomatic relations between the two countries, as well as to funnel aid to Viet Nam and help veterans, educators, and other Americans travel to Viet Nam. Among them are Le Ly Hayslip's East Meets West Foundation, the U.S.V.N. Friendship & Aid Association of Southern California, the Veterans' Viet Nam Restoration Project, the Fund for Reconciliation and Development, and the U.S.-Indochina Reconciliation Project, which sponsors trips to Viet Nam, Cambodia, and Laos for American professionals, teachers, students, and veterans. These organizations seek aid for the very poor country of Viet Nam and work with both nations to try to bring about diplomatic relations, which would take a large step in ending Viet Nam's poverty through the end of the United States–sponsored trade embargo. Viet Nam also has an organization, based in Hanoi, the Viet Nam–United States Association (Việt Mỹ), which works with the American associations.

Some of the books that I have mentioned previously are, at least partially, narratives of return: Le Ly Hayslip's and John Balaban's both contain sections detailing their return journeys years after the war. Both make the same request of their readers: see this country, see the scars of a cruelly prolonged war, and make change now to move away from the past and into the future.[3]

Not all return narratives reach the levels of communality and biculturality found in Hayslip's and Balaban's books, but they all stand above the standard run of war narratives: they are, as a group, remarkably free of racism and ethnocentrism; the writers are able, finally, to sort out what is the war and what is the country. And veterans who were more open to alternate worldviews are beginning to speak out and be heard; Robert Jenkins, a veteran who is now a theater arts professor, directed a college production of a play of the same name based on the oral histories of the women in *A Piece of My Heart*. A newspaper story quoted Jenkins as saying, "I liked the Vietnamese people, I liked the food. . . . It would be a gross generalization to say I liked the Asian worldview, but I had developed a flickering interest in Buddhism. . . . I guess I loved being Asian" (Green 44). While Jenkins's feelings have not changed over the years, his access to media attention has. Ten or fifteen years ago, veterans with opinions like his simply were not quoted in mainstream media.

One of the earliest return narratives was William Broyles's *Brothers in Arms* (1986). Broyles, a former marine lieutenant and former editor of *Newsweek*, was one of the first U.S. veterans to return to Viet Nam. He remains staunchly anti-Communist throughout his narrative, delighting, at times, in reporting his conversational one-upmanship with Party members, but he is not anti-Vietnamese. He says that the Communist leaders "were ruthless and insulated from suffering" (86), but he makes a separation between Communists, by whom he means high-echelon leaders, and Vietnamese people. It seems as if he has merely transferred the no-regard-for-human-life stereotype, but his trip leads him to conclude that Americans and their former enemies are, as his title proclaims, "brothers in arms."

In addressing the question "Why go back?" Broyles writes, "A soldier's best weapon is not his rifle but his ability to see his enemy as an abstraction and not as another human being. The very word 'enemy' conveys a mental and moral power that makes war possible, even necessary. I had never known my enemy, and I wanted to" (11). Broyles does not comment on the fact that Americans not only did not know their enemy, but also did not know their ally. Nonetheless, while looking at the Vietnam Veterans Memorial, Broyles has a revelation: "And then I realized that other names weren't there—the names of the men and women we fought, our enemies. They died by the hundreds of thousands, but they remain abstractions. Who knows their names?" (12). And so he arranges a trip to Viet Nam.

In Viet Nam, Broyles is aware of his own ethnocentrism and lack of understanding. In one revealing paragraph he seems to simultaneously embrace and repudiate his ethnocentric view, but behind his confusion lies a quest for greater understanding.

I know how brave and resourceful the North Vietnamese soldiers were. But I couldn't understand how this backward place could have taken those boys riding placidly on the backs of water buffalo and made them antiaircraft gunners and platoon commanders. . . . It simply didn't compute. In combat the North Vietnamese troops had seemed so motivated, as if history were riding on their shoulders. Tiny men, no bigger than boys, they drove out a race of giants. But this pastoral, timeless landscape that had nurtured them seemed outside of history. Nothing, I thought, ever happens here. (20–21)

Broyles struggles with the limited, stereotypical, Orientalist view of Asians that is all his culture has provided him with to understand a series of events inexplicable within that framework. He knows that his paradigm is unworkable, but he does not yet have anything to replace it with; a replacement is what he has come to find.

A Party official later says to him, "The French laughed at us. . . . They saw us only as little people with primitive weapons. You made the same mistake" (62). As more and more Vietnamese tell him the same thing, he begins to see. He has a conversation with a former Viet Cong, who might have fought against him in the same battles. They talk about weapons. Broyles asks, "What was your best weapon? He smiled. Then he pointed to his heart" (185).

He is stunned by the friendliness with which he is greeted. One of the only phrases he learns in Vietnamese is "Khong phai Lien Xo" (30), meaning "I'm not Russian." He finds that the Vietnamese hate Russians because they are "cheap"; his hosts react enthusiastically when they find out he is American. Broyles begins to achieve a little perspective when a small boy stares at him on the street: "I finally locked eyes with one of them. . . . To my surprise, he didn't even blink. . . . I was not another human being looking back at him, but a different creature" (59).

He meets Kim Phuuc, the woman who was photographed as a girl running down a path after her clothes had been burned off by napalm (he does fail to mention that this famous photograph was taken by a Vietnamese photographer, Nick Ut). He meets a woman whose husband was away fighting for nine years; during that time, she received only one letter from him. To Broyles's stunned amazement over her sacrifice she replies only, "Everyone did it" (67). He meets a survivor of the massacre at My Lai, Vo Thi Lien, and goes into the tunnels at Cu Chi, preserved now as a war memorial.

All these experiences act cumulatively on him: "I left Vietnam with a sympathy for my old enemies I had not had before. I found myself wanting to share in their war experience, since it seemed so much better than mine" (257). Since he remains so staunchly anti-Communist—his parting remark to his guide was "You are a good guy—for a communist" (252)—this sentiment can only come from his recognition of the Vietnamese as human beings like himself, not tiny, primitive aliens.[4]

The *San Francisco Examiner* ran a series of articles in 1989 about a correspondent's return to Viet Nam. The first installment appeared in the Sunday magazine, *Image*, featuring a cover photograph of two Vietnamese children with the caption, "Vietnam alive: Fourteen years after the fall of Saigon," as if, for U.S. readers, Viet Nam were being resurrected from some oblivion. Viet Nam's aliveness, its contemporary existence, is presented in this feature as news, as indeed it must have been news to many of the *Examiner's* readers, for whom Viet Nam had disappeared for fourteen years.

The photo essay presents Viet Nam both in terms of "normalcy"—life as American viewers would recognize it, as in photographs of rice workers and a dance club in Hue—and in terms of Viet Nam as the victim of the United States, especially on one page that features a grisly photograph of a room in a hospital lined with jars of deformed fetuses, a result of Agent Orange. Set next to this image is a photograph of a mournful-looking Amerasian teenager holding a picture of his GI father. The photo essay seeks to transcend stereotypical images, while simultaneously maintaining a view of the United States as powerful and Viet Nam as weak and victimized. Even two photographs of a military unit focus on very young-looking soldiers' faces.

This series of articles, titled "Vietnam: The Road Back" and written by Edvins Beitiks, a wounded veteran, keeps looking for the war in Viet Nam, but finding peace instead. In a bizarre touch, the story is written entirely in the second person. On the one hand, this construction brings the reader into Beitiks's experience; on the other, it serves as a distancing device, since the writer is talking of his own experience as if he were not himself. He looks for the war by searching for the battlefield where he was wounded, but finds that all the tree lines look alike, and he cannot recognize the particular place of his wounding: "You squinted toward a string of palms about a half-mile off the road, thinking it worth a try. As you started toward it a woman pulling rice stalks stood up, saw you staring and smiled, waving a hand. Children came running, giggling, whispering to each other, reaching out to touch the hair on your arms. It didn't happen the way you thought it would" (A14). Viet Nam defeats him, over and over again, as he searches for his war but finds peace in its stead.

He tells stories of many NLF and PAVN veterans he meets on his trip, but he displays intractable American ignorance. He describes "Maj. Gen. Tran Cong Man, who joined the North Vietnamese army in World War II" (A17). Of course, Viet Nam was not divided in two until 1954, so Man could not possibly have joined anything called the "North Vietnamese army"; he had probably joined the Viet Minh.

Nonetheless, Beitiks does work to present a picture of the war as experienced by all sides, telling the stories of PAVN veterans, ARVN veterans, and his own U.S. platoon. The series as a whole seeks to make visible what had remained invisible to the United States since 1975, through words and pictures. This in itself is a turnaround.

Morley Safer's account of his return trip to Viet Nam, *Flashbacks* (1990), while providing a thoroughly nonracist view, does not offer much for a reader interested in contemporary Viet Nam. *Flashbacks* is self-consciously an old man's book, tinged with nostalgia, as the title suggests. Safer is more interested in his memories than in his current journey. He does, however, have some interest in the present as an antidote to the past:

Hanoi at last, via twenty-four years of curiosity that amounts to almost yearning to just look at these men in their natural state. I have seen them before only as piled-up corpses at the edge of bomb craters or as frightened young men, hands tied behind them, being urged on by the muzzle of a South Vietnamese or American rifle. After spending so many years of being briefed on how they are the faceless menace or mindless pawns of evil masters or cowardly bastards who will not stand up and fight, I feel a need to engage them in the most banal kind of conversations. (2)

Safer hopes to heal his memories of the war by engaging with the simple humanity of the former enemy.

Safer runs into an American veteran also traveling in Viet Nam, who tells him, "Everybody has a sense of unfinished business. I've longed for Vietnam ever since I came home . . . I think when I go home, the chapter will be over" (76). The unfinished business of the veteran is the same as Safer's—they are looking for the country that is not the war.

Safer tries to counter stereotypes, even while he falls prey to them: he decides that "Vietnamese have no sense of time the way we understand it" (4), then three pages later ponders, "Why is it we assume enemies cannot have lives at least as complicated as our own?" (7). He recognizes, in retrospect, American ignorance: "Even the smartest of us knew so little," he reflects (55). He then becomes a teacher, inserting passages that instruct about Vietnamese history and culture. He tells the story of the Trung sisters leading an uprising against the Chinese two thousand years ago, and attempts an explanation of the Vietnamese version of Buddhism and how it is intertwined with Confucianism.

The Vietnamese to whom Safer talks insist on the communality of the war experience—a Hanoi doctor tells of his trip to the United States, where he met surgeons whose articles he had read in a medical journal during the war. Dr. Tung says, "We were fighting each other with the same weapons and saving lives with the same medicine" (14). Safer himself experiences feelings of this communality, such as when he visits the Trung Son Cemetery, which reminds him of "Arlington or Verdun or St. Laurent-sur-Mer in Normandy"

(108). Safer's Vietnamese companion, Hung, says, "Ten thousand, ten thousand of my family. They were the best sons and daughters of Vietnam"; this line immediately reminds Safer of words he has heard from an American visitor to the graves of the American casualties of the D-Day invasion of Normandy (108).

The idea of communality is also expressed in a poem by Van Le, a filmmaker in Ho Chi Minh City, which Safer quotes in full:

> There's an American soldier
> Who returns to northern Cu Chi.
> He bends his back to the tunnels.
> What does he see? What does he think?
>
> There's a Vietnamese hero
> Now a grandfather.
> He asks the American to share wine
> Outside the tunnel.
>
> Each man is silent
> As he looks into the other's eyes.
> Something is rising like a deep pain.
>
> The war was terrible
> All that time past.
> The dead lost their bodies.
> The living lost their homes.
>
> How many American soldiers
> Died in this land?
> How many Vietnamese
> Lie buried under trees and grass?
>
> The pain still lingers.
> Why should we remember it?
> We are old, our era past.
> Our mistakes belong to bygone days.
>
> Now the wineglass joins friends in peace.
> The old men lift their glasses.
> Tears run down their cheeks. (250–51)

Safer is moved by Le's recitation of the poem; later, in response to another incident, he says, "For a hardened people, the Vietnamese are easily touched. So are we, I guess" (323). There are many aspects of the book for which Safer can be faulted— especially a paternalistic sexism that causes him, for example, to describe his interpreter as "cute-as-a-button Miss Mai" (116). The book is also marked by a generalized xenophobia, directed most prominently at Russians, and a liberal attitude that resists the notion of American defeat and Communist victory, and persistently overlooks the United States–generated causes for the Vietnamese poverty that Safer notes everywhere.

In contrast to Safer's focus on the past, W. D. Ehrhart's account of his return, *Going Back* (1987), is focused on the present. He, too, is looking for the country that is not the war; his attitude is summed up when he says, "Show me what you've done with this country *since* the war; that's what I came here to see" (23). Unlike many other Americans who expected to see Viet Nam preserved in time, the bomb rubble unmoved, Ehrhart wants and expects to see rebuilding. He reaches his personal reconciliation at the end of his text, when he gains a perspective that allows him to see that in Viet-namese history, which goes back to "bronze age drummers on the hills overlooking the Red River Valley, the French—and even the Americans— are just another chapter. Already a new chapter is being written" (176).

The whole presentation of the book proclaims its difference. The cover picture is not of the war (as on Broyles's book) or the author (as on Safer's), but of an elderly Vietnamese woman standing outside her house. The first chapter of the book—the only one outside the chronological structure of the narrative—begins with a reference to that woman: "Nguyen Thi Na is 67 years old" (1), rather than beginning with the narrator's "I." Mrs. Na lost all five of her sons in the war. She says to Ehrhart, "And you did this to me" (1). Ehrhart uses this statement as an immediate form of dislocation for the reader, just as it was a form of dislocation for him. He quotes his own poem, "Making the Children Behave" (discussed in chapter 4). Thus he introduces the themes of the book: seeing the previously unseen, knowing the pre-viously unknown, and gaining a previously unheld perspective.

He begins with a revisionist history of his own military service:

I had been told that the people of Vietnam wanted and needed our help, but I found that most people in Vietnam hated us because we destroyed their forests with chemical defoliants, and burned their fields with napalm, and called the people of Vietnam gooks, chinks, slopes, and zipperheads, turning their sons into shoeshine boys and their daughters into whores. And most people in Vietnam, from what I could see, wanted little else than for us to stop killing them and go away. (5)

Ehrhart has returned to Viet Nam to see what else they wanted, to see what they have done with their victory that cost both them and him so much.

Ehrhart traveled to Viet Nam with fellow American poets Bruce Weigl and John Balaban (this trip is the same one Balaban refers to at the end of *Remembering Heaven's Face*). His poetry serves as an entry point to make real contact with Vietnamese, as he desires: he has brought a translation of one of his poems, "Making the Children Behave," done by a Vietnamese friend back home in Pennsylvania, which ends up winning several friends for him on the trip. In one instance, a Vietnamese poet, Te Hanh, excitedly shows Ehrhart an English translation of one of his own poems, called "Questions Underground," in which a child living in tunnels during the war repeatedly asks when they will be able to go aboveground again. The last stanza reads:

> When there are no more bombs,
> shall you let me go up on the earth again?
> Why do you keep asking, little one . . .
> I want to see the uncles and aunts I loved,
> are they still fighting, Mama?
> I want to see the Yankee,
> Mama, does it look like a human being? (82)

The similarity between this poem and Ehrhart's is striking, a coincidence noted with amazement and appreciation by both poets.

As much as he can, he makes this a bicultural text. He explains his desire to return to Viet Nam with a Vietnamese proverb: "Go out one day; come back with a bucket full of knowledge" (6). Like Safer, he includes a lot of lessons in Vietnamese history and culture, and criticizes America for its ignorance: "If only American policymakers had taken the time to learn what every Vietnamese schoolchild knows, how different for both our countries might have been the course of the past 40 years" (56). He has the ability to imagine himself into Vietnamese shoes: "And what would I have been, had I been one of Mrs. Na's sons? I know what I would have been" (125).

Ehrhart also maintains a comparative perspective; when he is deluged with a bit too much Party rhetoric, he ponders, "Is General Chi's language anything more than a mirror image of what I've heard in my own country all my life?" (29). When he thinks about the treatment of American prisoners in the "Hanoi Hilton," which he is scheduled to visit, he again summons a comparison: "Yet how did we treat *our* prisoners? Many an armed Viet Cong captured in the field never even made it to the rear alive" (46). He returns repeatedly to comparisons in order to achieve a perspective, not usually available in American texts, that gives credit where credit is due but holds both sides equally accountable for their actions.

He stresses themes of communality. He tells of meeting Nguyen Van Hung (the man to whom his poem "Second Thoughts" is addressed): "The more we talk, the more a kind of brotherhood of adversaries takes root between us" (54). This passage expresses a tone somewhat similar to that of Broyles, except Broyles is looking for brothers in arms, whereas Ehrhart is looking for brothers in peace. He goes on to explore what it is exactly that he and Hung share:

Why am I so attracted to this man? I lost so many friends to men like him. But then, how many friends did he lose to men like me? It was all so long ago, and we were very young. Here at last is a direct link with my own past. . . .

When the evening ends, he takes my hand and squeezes it. "I'm glad you weren't killed," he says. He breaks into a broad, toothy grin, and I embrace him with both arms, happy that both of us are alive to share this moment. (54)

Ehrhart finds that the common experience of the war, now so many years in the past, is enough to build a bridge between them. Both men were common soldiers, out of control of their own destinies, and both suffered. Rather than building a warrior mystique, as Broyles does, Ehrhart leaves it at that. For him and for Hung, that is enough.

It is easy to see why the accounts by Safer and Broyles are published and sold in supermarket racks, and Ehrhart's is published by a small press and poorly distributed—Safer's and Broyles's politics are standard liberal anti-communism. Ehrhart's views are much more radical. As he repeatedly points out in the Hanoi portion of his trip, he does not like socialist-drab architecture or socialist speechifying, but he does not disagree with the Communists' basic view of the war and of the world.

Although Ehrhart's politics certainly play their part in fueling his passionate interest in the Vietnamese, Safer is also interested in Vietnamese individuals—old friends and new—on his trip, as is Broyles, whose political position is somewhat similar to Safer's. Clearly, radical politics are not the only road to nonracist viewpoints.

Bruce Weigl has also written of the trip to Viet Nam he took with Ehrhart and Balaban, in an article called "Towards a Biography of Place: Notes on Discovering My Country," published in an anthology called *American Writers Abroad*. Weigl is one of the least likely candidates to write a bicultural narrative, since he says of himself, "I haven't lived for any length of time outside the United States except for my year in Vietnam as a soldier" (156), and yet he discovers that he has two countries. "Because I feel so connected to the two places of my life [Viet Nam and an Ohio mill town], when I am away from them, which is most of my waking hours, I long to be back there" (156).

In Viet Nam, Weigl spends time with Miss Tao, a woman who was imprisoned for several years in the notorious tiger cages of Con Son Island.

I'd gone back to Vietnam with my self at the center of my thinking. Gradually as I met people who had been my invisible enemy sixteen years before the self began to lose its importance. In the face of the enormous struggle these people had endured all of their lives, my involvement, my sacrifices seemed less and less significant. Miss Tao pushed me over the edge into understanding. (157–58)

Concluding his essay, Weigl echoes Andrew Lam, the Vietnamese exile writer who wrote, "I am of one soul . . . two hearts." Weigl writes that his poems "all seem haunted to me, they seem the voice of an exile looking for home. Miss Tao helped me find that home, my country, which is the heart split in two" (160).

Retired army colonel David Hackworth, "America's most decorated living veteran," has also written of his return in a *Newsweek* article. Certainly neither leftist nor radical, Hackworth nevertheless has nothing but compassion for contemporary Viet Nam and finds himself identifying with the former enemies he meets at the site of his most costly battles. He cheerfully compares scars with Vietnamese veterans. He visits the Trung An Military Cemetery where thirteen thousand Viet Cong are buried. He and Col. Bay Cao light incense, and Hackworth "felt the tears well up, and I relieved the wrenching experience I'd had at the black wall of the Vietnam Memorial in Washington: all these dead, all this waste, and to what end?" (47). Hackworth brings Viet Nam and America together through the similarity of his feelings for the dead of both sides. He ends his article with a quote from a Zippo lighter that he bought in Saigon: "Vietnam—1968. When the power of love overcomes the love of power, Vietnam will know peace" (48). And so, Hackworth implies, will America.

Perhaps these narratives of return journeys represent a hope that, all these years later, for America, "Vietnam" the war will finally become Việt Nam the nation.

Notes

Introduction

1. Viet Nam is not a "little" country, as John Kennedy and so many other Americans would have it. American conceptions of Viet Nam as a nation are shaped largely by this sort of paternalism. The 1990 estimated population of Viet Nam, according to the *World Almanac*, was 68,488,000, and the country is 128,401 square miles, or roughly the size of New Mexico. By contrast, El Salvador, with a 1990 estimated population of 5,221,000, is a small country. Viet Nam is about the size of France, a country that would not normally be referred to as little.

2. The American tendency to call the war "Vietnam" or "the Vietnam War" obscures the fact that there was a series of wars in Southeast Asia. The First Indochina War is the anticolonial revolution against France. The Second Indochina War is the war between the Democratic Republic of Viet Nam (North; henceforth abbreviated DRV) and the Republic of Viet Nam (South; henceforth abbreviated RVN) together with its allies, the major one of which was the United States (Australia, South Korea, New Zealand, Thailand, and the Philippines also sent troops). The Third Indochina War is the invasion of Viet Nam by China in 1979. In Viet Nam, the war carried on between 1961 and 1975 is usually called the American War.

3. I have adopted the spelling *Viet Nam*, because that is the Vietnamese spelling. (Vietnamese is written in Roman characters, with its own set of diacritics.) "Vietnam" is the French usage, which has been adopted in the United States. Most of the texts I quote employ the spelling "Vietnam," so the name of the country will appear both ways. "Vietnamese" is an American word, not a Vietnamese one, so I have adopted that spelling for it (*Viet* is the usage in Vietnamese).

4. See, for example, Nguyen Thi Dinh, *No Other Road to Take*, Vo Nguyen Giap, *How We Won the War*, and Van Tien Dung, *Our Great Spring Victory*.

5. *NVA* (North Vietnamese Army), the usual term, implicitly sanctions the separation of Viet Nam into North and South. Both the RVN and DRV claimed to be the legitimate government of all of Viet Nam; the creation of a permanent, independent South Vietnamese state was an American, not a Vietnamese, dream. Therefore I have adopted the term *PAVN* (People's Army of Viet Nam), which is what that entity called itself.

6. Practices such as this mass burial—without the collection of identification—contributed to the large number of Vietnamese MIAs (more than two hundred thousand).

7. As Tassilo Schneider has noted, those reviewers and critics who have praised *Platoon* for representing the Vietnamese as "able fighters" and for portraying them, as well as the Americans, as victims, are misreading the film. Schneider's observations are worth quoting at length:

> During the . . . raid on the Vietnamese village . . . the viewer gets the impression that it is, above all, the American soldiers that suffer, not their Vietnamese victims. It is the G.I.s who get the closeups, showing their faces shocked and horrified. . . . When Chris witnesses his comrades raping a Vietnamese woman, we do not see one single shot of the victim but, instead, get plenty of opportunity to contemplate *his* moral despair; and, while the Vietnamese seem to die quickly and painlessly, the film is full of shots depicting Americans in agony and death-struggle. . . .
>
> . . . Vietnamese and American soldiers are killed in a ratio of at least ten to one. . . . The Vietnamese soldiers are a faceless, anonymous enemy. Stone thus progresses from the traditional war film convention of showing an enemy with an ugly face to showing one with no face at all. (51)

8. Even the cities can be transformed into metaphoric jungles, as in the film *Full Metal Jacket*; although the battles take place in the city of Hue, it is a heart-of-darkness jungle.

9. This particular item of faith is demonstrably untrue on many levels. A careful reading of World War II novels, such as those by Norman Mailer, James Jones, and Thomas Pynchon, shows that the soldiers' experience of battle is as chaotic as that of the "Vietnam" soldiers, that military life is just as senseless, and that overriding idealism does not ameliorate these facts. Further, as Mardi Horowitz and George Solomon report in a 1975 article, military psychiatrists did not treat soldiers in Viet Nam for stress disorders with the same frequency as was done during World War II—a direct result of the army's famous one-year rotation policy, which was put in place as a response to the high number of stress disorders suffered by soldiers who spent extended periods in combat during World War II.

10. The visual arts may be leading the way in this arena. A provocative exhibit called *As Seen by Both Sides: American and Vietnamese Artists Look at the War* toured the country in the early 1990s; an annotated catalogue is available from the University of Massachusetts Press.

11. There is no book-length memoir by a Latino veteran in print. There is one oral history, *Soldados*, by Charlie Trujillo—which, after numerous rejections by publishers, he put into print himself—and there is one novel, *Oddsplayer*, by Joe Rodriguez. *Welcome to Vietnam, Macho Man*, by Ernest Spencer, is the only

book-length memoir by an Asian American veteran. There is no book-length work by an American Indian veteran, despite the fact that American Indians served in greater proportion to their representation in the population than any other minority group. Several works by African American veterans have been published, but none of them has received good distribution or critical attention; the only book about African American participation in the war to make much impact is Wallace Terry's oral history, *Bloods*.

12. Michael Herr is the only writer on the war in Viet Nam to be anthologized in the new "expanded canon" *Heath Anthology of American Literature*, in which an excerpt from *Dispatches* appears.

13. For example, A. R. Flowers's *DeMojo Blues*, a novel by an African American veteran that diverges from the usual story of American innocence facing disillusionment in revolutionary ways, is long out of print. Howard University Press recently reprinted four works by African Americans, and John A. Williams's novel *Captain Blackman* was recently republished by Thunder's Mouth Press. *Remains*, by William Crapser (Satchem Press), *Redemption*, by Bob Dagget (Veterans for Peace), and *F.N.G.*, by Donald Bodey (Ballantine), represent works by white working-class veterans. How many unpublished or unwritten works do these few represent?

14. See Lisa Hsiao, "Project 100,000," and Christian Appy, *Working-Class War*, for further details on the service of blacks in Viet Nam. As Appy points out, blacks did comprise 20 percent of combat deaths in the early part of the war, and 12.5 percent over the entire period of the war, out of a civilian population of 11 percent (19). Hsiao and Appy both cite reliable studies for their figures.

15. See Jean-Jacques Malo and Tony Williams, eds., *Vietnam War Filmography*.

16. One of many examples of this constant replaying of American myth is the protest against and defense of the Mexican-American War being replicated with uncanny similarity in the protest against and defense of U.S. intervention in Viet Nam, despite the participants in the twentieth-century version having no consciousness of their forebears in the nineteenth-century version.

2. Vietnamese Exile Narratives

1. This chapter makes an argument for reading the works of Vietnamese immigrant authors in English. An additional argument can be made that we should read Vietnamese literature. American ethnocentrism makes French literature and other European literatures important. We pay some attention to Chinese literature, and now, with the rising political and economic importance of Japan, to Japanese literature. Viet Nam also has a long and significant literary history. A good place to start in Vietnamese literature is with the national epic

The Tale of Kieu, available in several English translations. Vietnamese perspectives on what they call "the American war" can be found in a series of short story collections published by the Foreign Languages Publishing House, Hanoi, including *Back to His Home Village*, *The Ho Chi Minh Trail*, and *After So Many Years*.

2. Although Vietnamese exile literature has been ignored, Vietnamese immigrants have not been; there is a wide sociological literature on settlement patterns and the effects of the escape from Viet Nam upon the escapees. Although Vietnamese American people have not been ignored, the Vietnamese American community has not been recognized yet as a producer of literature.

3. I have included diacritics in quotations whenever the source uses them, and have omitted them when the source does; in any instance where the use of Vietnamese is my own, I have used diacritics, except in words that have been adopted into English, such as Viet Nam, Viet Cong, Viet Minh, and so on.

4. My own work is, as far as I know, the first of its kind to be published. "The Unheard: Vietnamese Voices in the Literature Curriculum" appears in the National Council of Teachers of English (NCTE) anthology *Cultural and Cross Cultural Studies and the Teaching of Literature*, edited by Joseph Trimmer and Tilly Warnock. "*Blue Dragon, White Tiger*: The Bicultural Stance of Vietnamese-American Literature" appears in *Reading the Literatures of Asian America*, edited by Shirley Geok-lin Lim and Amy Ling. Professor Qui-Phiet Tran of Schreiner College is writing a book-length study of the works of Tran Dieu Hang, who publishes in the United States in Vietnamese.

5. One promising note for the future is the special issue of *Amerasia Journal* published in 1991 titled "War and Asian Americans," in which three stories by Vietnamese American writers appeared: "The Tradition That Was Grandmother," by Don T. Phan, "Forget Me Not—Vietnam," by Van Luong, and "Of Luggage and Shoes," by Thuy Dinh. It can be hoped that this appearance marks the beginning of a new emergence of Vietnamese American writers on the Asian American literary scene.

6. Vu-Duc Vuong ran for the board of supervisors in San Francisco in 1990, the first Vietnamese American candidate for a U.S. public office. Vietnamese fishermen are challenging discriminatory and selectively enforced U.S. fishing laws. The Vietnamese American community is waging its own political conflicts, especially over the issue of normalization of relations with the Socialist Republic of Viet Nam; several Vietnamese Americans involved in this conflict, including writer Doan Van Toai and columnist Triet Le, have been killed or wounded.

7. There is also in the United States a nonbicultural Vietnamese community of authors who write and publish in Vietnamese-language newspapers and periodicals. Dr. Nguyen Manh Hung lists in his 1984 article on Vietnamese refugee scholars nine Vietnamese-language magazines and ten Vietnamese-language

newspapers that were currently being published. Here I am addressing only those authors who publish in English.

8. Not only Vietnamese refugee writers, but also Vietnamese living in the SRV take this stance of communality. Pham Van Dong, former prime minister, wrote this statement to introduce a book of photographs of Viet Nam: "As for myself, in so far as I appear in these photographs, mine will be the gladness of meeting a myriad of Americans from all walks of life. . . . And to them I shall tell a tale of friendship and mutual understanding, of the multi-faceted ties that link both our people, the Vietnamese and the American peoples" (Clifford and Balaban 125).

9. Oliver Stone's film of Le Ly Hayslip's story does try to present Viet Nam as central to the war; unfortunately, *Heaven and Earth* was the first of his post-*Platoon* films to be a box-office failure.

10. Vietnamese names follow the pattern of family name, middle name, given name. Because there are very few surnames in Viet Nam, it is the formal and proper Vietnamese practice to refer to people by their given names; if a person has a title, he or she is referred to by title and given name. Thus Tran Van Dinh is Professor Dinh; Dinh is his given name and Tran is his family name. I have adopted Vietnamese practice for all the writers except Hayslip, who goes by her American married name.

11. In this aspect *Blue Dragon, White Tiger* can be seen as a rewriting of *The Tale of Kieu*, in which three men represent various twists in the heroine's fate; Dinh has reversed the genders in his appropriation of the tale.

12. I am indebted to Leslie Bow for suggesting this idea to me.

13. In 1991, Dr. Vien was arrested for criticizing the government. As of this writing, he is still in prison in Viet Nam. Dr. Vien is a scholar born in colonized Viet Nam in 1913 who lived in France for twenty years. In 1961 he returned to the Democratic Republic of Viet Nam. During the American war he continued to publish in France; the first American translation of his work appeared in 1974. He has maintained ties to Europe and the United States while continuing to live in Viet Nam.

14. W. D. Ehrhart records in his memoir of his 1985 trip to Viet Nam that he asked Communist officials about Tang's allegations that northerners took all the power after the war. They responded that the charges are false, and that Tang left because he "wanted more power than he had" (102). They never suggest that Tang was not who he claims to be in his book.

15. The comparison of Ho and Lincoln is not uncommon among Vietnamese. Thu Huong, one of the women who broadcast as "Hanoi Hannah," said in a 1990 interview with Don North in *Indochina Newsletter*, "I have always compared our traditions of liberty, like those of Abraham Lincoln and Ho Chi Minh."

16. Ngan now lives in Canada; the book was published simultaneously in Canada and the United States, but it is clearly aimed at an American audience.

17. Another such reference occurs in Nguyen Van Bong's story "After the Enemy Raid," published in *Vietnamese Literature*, edited by Nguyen Khac Vien. In that story the situation was equally clear: "In the district, manure was as precious as gold. The mountains were far away and the enemy had destroyed all the green trees in the village. It was impossible to find any greenery to make compost. People could now only rely on buffalo and pig manure, or human manure. But human manure was not very plentiful, and people rarely raised pigs, for fear of raids. As for the buffaloes, the soldiers in the post shot at them or came to steal them, so there weren't many left" (784).

18. Taking dead and wounded with them is a matter of pride for some Vietnamese veterans. Duong Quang Ngai was wounded by rockets that killed ten men and wounded forty. He says, "But we picked up every man when we withdrew. Every man" (quoted in Beitiks, A17).

19. Personal interview, 25 November 1990. Another issue often raised in connection with the book is whether she "really" wrote it, since she had a coauthor, Jay Wurts. Hayslip described her cowriting process to me as follows: she wrote the original manuscript and her son typed it on a word processor. They sent that version to Wurts, who edited the grammar and suggested places for expansion or revision. Hayslip then made those changes, and Wurts once again edited. The book's structure was Hayslip's idea: "It just came out that way," she said.

20. Phien is not the only Vietnamese exile writer who writes in Vietnamese but would like to reach an English-speaking audience. Tran Dieu Hang, a writer who has published Vietnamese-language novels in the United States, has told me that she wants very much to publish in English but feels she can write effectively only in her native language.

21. Sheryl A. Byrne, the president of TriAm Press, wrote to me (when I requested permission for Temple University Press to print quotations from *Blue Dragon, White Tiger* in a critical article): "I have always felt that [*Blue Dragon, White Tiger*]'s real value would come long after its publication date. Your scholarly work reassures me that this is so."

22. I am indebted to Leslie Bow for discussion of these ideas.

3. U.S. Wars in Asia and the Representation of Asians

1. These terms, while generally preferable to the old term *Oriental*, are still controversial. As Elaine Kim and others point out, these terms lump together a

large number of distinct cultures, nationalities, and ethnic groups. "To Asians," Kim writes, "all Orientals do not 'look alike' " (*Asian American Literature* xii). A tragic incident in 1982 conveys the Euro-American inability to distinguish Asians and their willingness to let one Asian stand for all: an unemployed Euro-American auto worker in Detroit beat a Chinese American, Vincent Chin, to death with a baseball bat, because he thought Chin was Japanese and he blamed Japan for unemployment among auto workers.

2. These representations occur in discourses ranging from political speeches to literature to advertising. A series of television commercials for Singapore Airlines in the early 1990s focuses on the exotic sexuality of the airline's female cabin attendants. They are shown in embroidered brocade robes and elaborate hairdos decorated with jewels, posing in subservient postures and offering trays of exotic-looking foods. Although this is an Asian airline, the commercials were designed for the American market by an American advertising company. The 1987 documentary film *Slaying the Dragon* is an excellent study of how portrayals of Asian women in films and television as passive and exotic affect the lives of contemporary Asian American women.

3. See Florence E. Baer's article in *Western Folklore* for an investigation into how a legend is transmitted and reified through storytelling, newspaper articles, and legal hearings. The particular incident Baer writes of is the growth of a representation and perception of Vietnamese refugees as eaters of pet dogs in Stockton, California. Without a truly discernible beginning, a story grew, took form, was reported in the local newspaper, returned to oral form, and came to stand as an icon of how the local citizens felt about the new residents of the town; eventually, everyone the author interviewed believed that the Vietnamese did eat dogs, although no one could cite a firsthand source for the story.

4. "The 'model minority' Asian," writes Kim, "by never challenging white society, at once vindicates that society from the charge of racism and points up the folly of those less obliging minorities who are ill-advised enough to protest against inequality or take themselves 'too seriously.' As a permanent inferior, the 'good' Asian can be assimilated into American life. All that is required from him is that he accept his assigned status cheerfully and reject whatever aspects of his racial and cultural background prove offensive to the dominant white society. And of course he must never speak for himself" (*Asian American Literature* 18).

5. That law was not repealed until 1952. A later law, the Cable Act of 1922, stripped citizenship from any woman who married "an alien ineligible to citizenship" (Takaki 15).

6. For discussions of Social Darwinism, see the writings of Steven Jay Gould, particularly *The Mismeasure of Man* and the essays in *Ever since Darwin*.

7. There is an interesting variant on these practices today in the current mania

with IQ testing and testing of scholastic achievement. Each time the results of math and science testing in the United States and Japan are published, with Japanese students outscoring American students, a fervent call goes out in the press for better education for American students. In a similar and related move, my stepdaughter's high school math teacher gave assembled parents a speech about how the school had revamped and improved its math program so that advanced students could finish calculus before going on to college, because all the students admitted to scientific and technical majors in the good colleges were named Nguyen.

8. The Chinese Exclusion Act was not repealed until 1943, when a small immigration quota for Chinese was set up. In 1952 the McCarran-Walter Act abolished race as a criteria but retained a national bias against Asian nations. That act was amended in 1965 to abolish the national-origin bias. Today one of the largest groups of immigrants coming into this country are Southeast Asian refugees, who are allowed entrance under a separate law, the Refugee Act; however, a 1990 act changed immigration quotas to allow a larger number of immigrants from western Europe to enter the country.

9. The English-as-official-language issue recurred in the 1980s, with the passage in California of the English-only initiative; while aimed largely at the eradication of Spanish in California, the next-largest language group affected is Chinese.

10. Lorelle's "The Battle of Wabash" (1880), Adah Batelle's "The Sacking of Grubbville" (1892), William Crane's "The Year 1899" (1893), and R. P. Pearsall's "The Revelation" (1911): all these works have a certain millenarianism about them, as well.

11. In the first half of the twentieth century, Asian Americans began writing their own narratives and poetry in English, although these early works had limited circulation and were not influential in challenging popular stereotypes. An examination of Euro-American portrayals of Asians contemporary with Asian American self-representations would be a productive and interesting study, but one that is beyond the scope of this book.

12. These quotations come from friends of my mother, native Californians of the generation that fought World War II.

13. Some Californians even feared that the rest of the country might be willing to sacrifice everything west of the Sierra Nevada, and I have heard from several Californians that they are positive they personally sighted Japanese submarines off the coast.

14. Compare that attitude with the joke in Derek Maitland's Viet Nam War novel *The Only War We've Got* (a joke that echoes a popular sentiment of the time): "The only way we're gonna win this war . . . is to tow this goddam

country out into the middle of the Pacific and bomb the shit out of it until it sinks" (quoted in Pratt, *Vietnam Voices* 262).

15. Takaki points out that Filipino immigrants were often referred to as "goo-goos" and "monkeys," and an immigration study called them "jungle folk" (325).

16. An American veteran of the war in Viet Nam once declared in a public discussion that it was simply impossible to take Vietnamese boys off the backs of water buffaloes and train them to be pilots. I told him I had read the story of Pham Tuan, a peasant boy who had grown up tending buffalo and had become a national hero of the DRV by, as an MIG-2 pilot, shooting down a B-52. The American veteran declared flatly that this was impossible. Pham Tuan has since become a cosmonaut.

17. It was particularly destructive because it completely undermined the ability of the allies to work together. Also, this racial stereotype blinded Americans to the possibility of looking at the reasons the ARVN was a bad army (i.e., because they were the military arm of a corrupt and unpopular government).

18. See Appy, *Working-Class War*, chap. 2, for a discussion of this issue.

19. Poverty enters into the "weak and helpless" image as well—Americans see poor Americans as "weak and helpless," too.

20. *Welcome to Vietnam, Macho Man*, by Ernest Spencer, a Korean-American. This book is out of print and unavailable, but as of 1995, more articles on Asian American veterans are seeing print. See, especially, Peter Nien-chu Kiang's 1991 article in *Amerasia Journal*.

21. Gloria Emerson, quoted in Gordon Taylor, "American Personal Narrative of the War in Vietnam," 295.

22. Quoted in Grahame Smith, *The Achievement of Graham Greene*, 130.

4. Euro-American Representations of the Vietnamese

1. I am aware that by using the terms "American" and "Vietnamese" here I am overgeneralizing—Americans of different race and class positions would, of course, not have identical cultural codings, nor would Vietnamese of different class positions. In the literature of the war, however, American writers have tended to come from a fairly culturally, if not politically, homogeneous point of view, as noted in my discussion of canon formation in chapter 1.

2. This study also found that negative attitudes toward Vietnamese were less prevalent among soldiers thirty years and older, especially among whites. These soldiers were mostly career military. They, too, are excluded from the canon, which is dominated by draftees and one-hitch volunteers, although many career military veterans have written memoirs.

3. Jeffords's own argument is America-centric, and, unfortunately, she does not always clarify the terms of her argument carefully enough, so she is led in to statements like this: "The war in Vietnam was an eruption of the gendered structure of American society" (84). The war in Viet Nam was about anti-colonialism, independence, communism, and several other issues; Jeffords's statement refers to *American participation* in the war, which she does not specify. Jeffords quotes Judith Stiehm on women and war: "Were women to enter combat, men would lose a crucial identity—warrior" (92). Vietnamese women did enter combat (see Mrs. Nguyen Thi Dinh's memoir, *No Other Road to Take*). Jeffords at one point talks about "both South Vietnam and the Republic of Vietnam," which are, of course, the same. I am not arguing that Jeffords falls into racism in her argument; rather, I am pointing out the huge effort that is needed to overcome America-centric assumptions that overgeneralize American experience.

4. This dominant orientation toward the war emerges in many of the book titles, in just this same way: the titles not only fail to distinguish Viet Nam the country from "Vietnam" the war, but reveal the overwhelming ethnocentrism of American views. Steven Phillip Smith's *American Boys* is similar to Nichols's *American Blood*. The title of George Donelson Moss's history *Vietnam: An American Ordeal* suggests that the sole significance of the nation of Viet Nam lies in the "ordeal" it presented America. Viet Nam is, typically, subsumed totally within America. Peter Goldman and Tony Fuller's *Charlie Company: What Vietnam Did to Us* takes a similar stance. The cover of this book proclaims: "To understand the war and the homecoming, this is the one book to read." The suggestion that a book focusing on Americans will explain the war is typical of U.S. discourse about the war. Chris Mullin's novel *The Last Man Out of Saigon* implies that only Americans are "men," since thousands of (Vietnamese) men remained in Saigon after the last Americans were gone.

5. From the transcript of an interview of John Nichols by Paul Skenazy, 7 May 1987.

6. It is also typical to portray them as "feminine," as Graham Greene did. Though Greene's is a far better book than Nichols's by any measure, the symbolic embodiment of Viet Nam in a "helpless" woman and a "helpless" child is part of the same Western worldview.

7. Several people have told me that they thought the young Vietnamese man was retarded, because of the way he grins. The script does not describe him as retarded; he is, rather, a cripple with one leg, a fact that does not show up clearly because of the dim interior lighting of the scene.

8. The significant exception is Oliver Stone's *Heaven and Earth*, based on Le Ly Hayslip's autobiographies. As Andrew Lam points out in a newspaper commen-

tary, however, Stone's film is "yet another narrative that puts America at the center of Viet Nam's history" (D7). One of the most egregious liberties taken by the film is its emphasis of the story of "Sgt. Steve Butler," the composite character who is based on at least four American men Hayslip was involved with. One of these men, a con artist, told Hayslip a story about being a Phoenix program assassin. Later, after she discovered his duplicity in every other aspect of his dealings with her, she doubted the authenticity of his story. In the film Stone gives the story total authenticity, and in a powerful scene in which "Sgt. Butler" tells the story to Le Ly, his wife, makes Butler the bigger victim of the war.

9. Both *Platoon* and *Rambo* were cultural phenomena as well as movies. *Platoon* became a rallying point for veterans to claim pride in their service. Made for $5 million and produced by a British film company (Hemdale) because no American company was interested, *Platoon* earned $110 million in domestic rentals. *Rambo: First Blood Part Two* cost $27 million and grossed $75.8 million in its first twenty-three days of release (Zoglin 72); it also became the most popular film ever to play in Beirut, Lebanon.

10. The character was created by David Morrell in the novel *First Blood* (1972).

11. This is a theme that runs through POW narratives and films. While it is true that U.S. prisoners in Hanoi were tortured by their captors, the image of the torturing Asian devil circulates freely, far beyond representations of POWs.

12. The sacrifice-of-children story surfaces in slightly different form in the critically admired film *Apocalypse Now*, when Colonel Kurtz tells the story of immunizing a village of children and returning to find that the Viet Cong had cut off all the immunized arms and left them in a pile. Kurtz, because he has entered this heart of darkness, admires the will and determination of the Viet Cong in carrying out this act.

13. Herr's view of the war has been enormously persuasive. Even Alfred Kazin accepted Herr's views, in a review published in *Esquire* (1 March 1978, 120–21): after calling *Dispatches* the "best book to come out of that lasting American trauma," he goes on to say that "Vietnam, being alien to Americans in terrain and in purpose and souping up every kind of racial touchiness into the general trigger-happy fear, became the ultimate no place to be" (121).

14. See John Hellmann, *American Myth and the Legacy of Vietnam*, 15, for the history of this novel.

15. Landsdale was an OSS operative during World War II; after that he helped Ramon Magsaysay put down the Huk rebellion in the Philippines. As a civilian he had been an advertising executive and in the OSS and later CIA was a true believer in psychological warfare. He went to Viet Nam in 1954 to work against the Viet Minh; later he helped establish Diem as prime minister of the Republic

of Viet Nam. He was a Pentagon advisor when Kennedy was elected; Daniel Ellsberg, who eventually leaked the Pentagon Papers, was his aid. Stanley Karnow, in *Vietnam: A History*, identifies Lansdale as the prototype not only of Colonel Hillandale, but also of Alden Pyle in *The Quiet American*.

16. It was fifth on the best-seller list for 1965; when it was issued in paperback the next year, 1,200,000 copies were printed in the first two months (see Hellmann 53). There were no best-selling novels about the war after *The Green Berets* until John Del Vecchio's *The Thirteenth Valley* in 1982.

17. Lawrence Suid, "The Making of *The Green Berets*," *Journal of Popular Film* 6 (1977): 106—25.

18. The Pentagon objected to the book when it was published, claiming that it contained security violations and distorted the Special Forces' role; the publisher felt compelled to put a label on the dust jacket emphasizing that it was fiction (Hellmann 54).

19. One of the more amazing cases of this is Captain Kornie mining the inside of Vietnamese gun emplacements, so that if the gun crews turn out to be Viet Cong infiltrators, he can blow them up. When his superior asks if Kornie has told his counterpart, he replies, "My God! . . . Tell the Vietnamese?" and the superior approves (72).

20. The long last chapter details guerrilla operations inside North Viet Nam in which Americans dye their hair and skin and pass for Montagnards. They blow up a generator and a bridge, and assassinate and capture political officers with the help of the Tai tribe. Moore's insistence that he is privy to secrets allows him to invent almost anything he wants.

21. Interestingly, no notion of cowardice attaches itself to the Americans, who have orders to "exfiltrate" (that is, abandon) the camp in case it is overrun. When things look bad and they tell Lieutenant Cau that they have to go, Cau says, "Yes, sir. We'll cover you" (70). Captain Kornie promises to have him promoted. The Americans' imminent bugging out thus looks gallant.

22. For example, international law defines civilians as "any person who does not take a direct part in the hostilities as an active member of the organized conventional or guerrilla armed forces. In order to enjoy complete protection, such persons must refrain from committing hostile acts" (Frey-Wouters and Laufer 131).

23. Doug Peacock, a Special Forces medic, describes a similar tunnel experience in his book *Grizzly Years*. Peacock had gotten to know the people living in the central highlands and had come to love the country Viet Nam where the war had not devastated it (52). Supplied with more information to feed his imagination that Broyles had, his tunnel musings are much more specific. Sensing the presence in the tunnel with him, Peacock thinks, "Whoever was there could

have killed me or tried to at any time. But he did not. Maybe the dead were his friends or even his family. He might have been paralyzed by grief or mourning his dead. The war could have been over for him. All I could hear was the regular sound of breathing. He did not move. He just sat there with the dead, and so did I" (57). Peacock's imaginings of the man in the tunnel with him are much more humanized than Broyles's.

24. In addition to the substantive limitations of the novel's view of Vietnamese, it also misuses Vietnamese names. Tranh Huu Nuong should be referred to formally as Sergeant Nuong and familiarly as Nuong, although the novel mistakenly presents Nuong as the family name and Tranh as the given name; a discussion of Sergeant Nuong and his brother, Albert reads: "They had gone to different schools—Albert for French and Tranh for English" (73). Hoa is a given name; the family name is Muon. However, her name is given as Hoa Muon, not Muon Hoa, as would be proper, and the village headman refers to her, incorrectly, as Miss Muon (85). Miss Hoa would be the proper form.

25. Quoted from the text of an unpublished interview with Steven Kaplan. I would like to thank Professor Kaplan for supplying me with a transcript of this interview.

26. Charles Gaspar suggested in a paper presented at the Popular Culture Association Conference (1992) that Dan serves as Goodrich's alter ego in that they are both noncommitted, in contrast to the other, committed, characters. In Gaspar's analysis, Dan's committed brother is the equivalent of Goodrich's roommate, Mark. While this analysis earns Webb more points on the good intentions scale, it nonetheless leaves the portrayal of Dan open to charges of stereotyping.

27. He gets not only tone and character wrong, but facts. The family of Dan's wife has been in their village "for five hundred years" (184). The nation of Viet Nam has not occupied the area of contemporary South Viet Nam for five hundred years; Webb follows the mistaken American practice of assuming everything in Asia is ancient and unchanged.

28. Schaeffer's previous novel, *Anya*, about a Holocaust survivor, reflected such accurate research that reviewers mistook her for a Holocaust survivor herself.

29. Dan Scripture has suggested an alternate explanation of this phenomenon: that it is Elsie who is masculinized, rather than Tran who is feminized. In other words, Dick sees Elsie as boyish, hence the identification with Tran.

30. More poets than prose writers seem to have made the imaginative leap over the stereotypical boundaries that constrain most Americans' understanding of the Vietnamese. Perhaps this is an artifact of form: the structure of the "war narrative" has such a long history of racism that it imposes that racism on all but the most transcendent of prose writers.

31. To be completely correct the words should read *điên cái đau*.

32. Oddly, there is a reversal of letters in these words; the words should read *bui doi* (*bụi đời*). I do not know whether the mistake is Komunyakaa's or the typographer's.

33. This novel might be the only one in which Americans are actually rescued by the PAVN. Two Americans held in a Thai prison for drug smuggling make a jail break with the aid of a third American and a group of local smugglers. They escape toward Laos and run into a PAVN patrol, which secures their escape from the pursuing Thais.

34. Phoenix was a CIA-sponsored program designed to destroy the Viet Cong infrastructure through assassinations. Stanley Karnow reports that by both CIA claims and Vietnamese Communist confirmation, sixty thousand Viet Cong agents were "eliminated" by the program (602).

35. References to Viet Nam as hell abound in U.S. Viet Nam War fiction. It is interesting to note that the titles of Vietnamese exile works and bicultural Euro-American works often refer, by contrast, to heaven: Nguyen Ngoc Ngan's *The Will of Heaven*, Hayslip's *When Heaven and Earth Changed Places*, Balaban's *Remembering Heaven's Face*. Heaven is *troi*, the decider of fate; *troi* is also sky. Eden is a place where human fate is decided. Thus there is a strong cross-cultural connection among these works' titles.

36. My own (as yet unpublished) novel includes four first-person narrators; one is a white female, two are white male Viet Nam veterans, and one is a Vietnamese female refugee. The ultimate outcome of the argument that one can write only about what one knows firsthand is that we are all completely atomized: Butler could only write about white male Viet Nam veterans from the South; I could only write about white female Irish-American working-class-turned-academic women from rural California. That is, I believe, a very reductive argument that oversimplifies the complexities of culture, identity, and the fiction-writing process.

37. A Hồi Chánh was a former NLF soldier who had surrendered and volunteered to work with the ARVN/U.S. The program was called "Chieu Hoi," literally, "open arms."

5. *Conclusion:* Bạn tri âm

1. Gordon Smith, a member of VFW Post 5888, Santa Cruz, California.

2. He is one of the children John Balaban brought over.

3. In February 1992, the U.S. government gave $25,000 in disaster aid to the victims of a storm in Viet Nam that killed 150 people and destroyed a large

amount of rice. This was the first U.S. government aid to the Socialist Republic of Viet Nam (*Los Angeles Times*, 2 February 1992). In July 1995, diplomatic relations with the SRV were finally established by the United States.

4. I have described only limited aspects of Broyles's book. He concludes that he and his former enemies are brothers because they have shared warfare together. Broyles privileges the experience of war, claiming the authority of the veteran to announce that only a veteran can truly understand another veteran. He sees that bond as cutting across nationalities and political boundaries. This is an untenable and war-mongering conclusion. See Susan Jeffords for a critique of this aspect of Broyles's work. My point is that if even William Broyles can change his perspective on the Vietnamese by going back to Viet Nam, there is much hope to be found in return journeys.

Works Cited

Allott, Miriam. "The Moral Situation in *The Quiet American.*" In Robert O. Evans, ed., *Graham Greene: Some Critical Considerations.* Lexington: University Press of Kentucky, 1963.

Appy, Christian. *Working-Class War: American Combat Soldiers and Vietnam.* Chapel Hill: University of North Carolina Press, 1993.

Baer, Florence E. " 'Give me . . . your huddled masses': Anti-Vietnamese Refugee Lore and the 'Image of Limited Good.' " *Western Folklore* 41.4 (1982): 275–91.

Baker, Houston, ed. *Three American Literatures: Essays in Chicano, Native American, and Asian-American Literature for Teachers of American Literature.* New York: Modern Language Association, 1982.

Balaban, John. *Ca dao Việt Nam: A Bilingual Anthology of Vietnamese Folk Poetry.* Greensboro, N.C.: Unicorn Press, 1980.

———. "For the Missing in Action." In Bill Henderson, ed., *The Pushcart Prize, XV.* New York: Simon and Schuster, 1990.

———. *Remembering Heaven's Face: A Moral Witness in Vietnam.* New York: Poseidon Press, 1991.

Barth, Gunther. *Bitter Strength: A History of the Chinese in the United States, 1850–1870.* Cambridge, Mass.: Harvard University Press, 1964.

Batelle, Adah F. "The Sacking of Grubbville." *Overland Monthly,* 2nd series 20, 1892.

Beidler, Philip. *American Literature and the Experience of Vietnam.* Athens: University of Georgia Press, 1982.

———. "Bad Business: Vietnam and Recent Mass-Market Fiction." *College English* 54.1 (1992): 64–75.

———. *Rewriting America: Vietnam Authors in Their Generation.* Athens: University of Georgia Press, 1991.

Beitiks, Edvins. "Vietnam: The Road Back." With photos by Kim Komenich. *San Francisco Examiner,* 6 August 1989, A14–17, *Image*; 9 August, A8, B1; 10 August, A8; 13 August, A1, A18.

Bergevin, Hue-Thanh. "Uncle Vy." *Porter Gulch Review* (spring-summer 1991): 38–40.

Berman, David M. "Teaching Vietnam through Vietnamese Sources." *Social Studies Journal* 14 (1985): 30–37.

Bibby, Michael. " 'Where Is Vietnam?' Antiwar Poetry and the Canon." *College English* 55 (1993): 158–78.

Bouvard, Marguerite, ed. *Landscape and Exile*. Boston: Rowan Tree Press, 1985.

Bow, Leslie. "Cultural Mediation and Le Ly Hayslip's Bad (Girl) Karma or 'How Much Can Have Happened to a Pretty Little Girl Like You?' " Manuscript, 1991.

Boyers, Robert. *Atrocity and Amnesia: The Political Novel since 1945*. New York: Oxford University Press, 1985.

Broyles, William. *Brothers in Arms: A Journey from War to Peace*. New York: Avon, 1986.

Buck, Pearl. *The Good Earth*. (1931). New York: Pocket Books, 1973.

Bundesen, Lynne. "Vietnam: One Woman's Story." *Los Angeles Times Book Review*, 25 June 1989, 4.

Butler, Robert Olen. *The Alleys of Eden*. New York: Horizon Press, 1981.

——. *The Deuce*. New York: Simon and Schuster, 1989.

——. *A Good Scent from a Strange Mountain*. New York: Henry Holt, 1992.

——. *On Distant Ground*. New York: Ballantine, 1985.

——. *Sun Dogs*. New York: Ballantine, 1982.

Caputo, Philip. *A Rumor of War*. New York: Ballantine, 1977.

Casey, John. *Spartina*. New York: Knopf, 1989.

Cheung, King-Kok, and Stan Yogi. *Asian American Literature: An Annotated Bibliography*. New York: Modern Languages Association, 1988.

Christopher, Renny. "*Blue Dragon, White Tiger*: The Bicultural Stance of Vietnamese-American Literature." In Shirley Geok-Lin Lim and Amy Ling, eds., *Reading the Literatures of Asian America*. Philadelphia: Temple University Press, 1992.

——. "The Unheard: Vietnamese Voices in the Literature Curriculum." In Joseph Trimmer and Tilly Warnock, eds., *Understanding Others: Cultural and Cross Cultural Studies and the Teaching of Literature*. Urbana, Ill.: National Council of Teachers of English, 1992.

Chu, Li-Min. *Images of China and the Chinese in the "Overland Monthly" 1868–1875*. San Francisco: R and E Research Associates, 1974.

Clark, Lucille Hanh. "Dowry of Myths." Senior thesis, University of California, Santa Cruz, 1993.

Clifford, Geoffrey. Text by John Balaban. *Vietnam: The Land We Never Knew*. San Francisco: Chronicle Books, 1989.

Conroy, Hilary, and T. Scott Miyakawa, eds. *East across the Pacific: Historical and Sociological Studies of Japanese Immigration and Assimilation*. Santa Barbara, Calif.: ABC-Clio, 1972.

Coolidge, Mary. *Chinese Immigration*. New York: Henry Holt, 1909.

Crane, William. "The Year 1899." *Overland Monthly*, 2nd series 21, 1893.

Cronin, Cornelius. "Historical Background to Larry Heinemann's *Close Quarters.*" *Critique* 24.2 (1983): 119–30.

Crown, Bonnie R. Review of *Blue Dragon, White Tiger. World Literature Today* 59.1 (1985): 160.

Daniels, Roger, and Harry H. L. Kitano. *American Racism: Exploration of the Nature of Prejudice.* Englewood Cliffs, N.J.: Prentice-Hall, 1970.

Danziger, Jeff. *Rising like the Tucson.* New York: Doubleday, 1991.

Del Vecchio, John. *The Thirteenth Valley.* New York: Bantam Books, 1982.

DeVitis, A. A. *Graham Greene.* Boston: Twayne Publishers, 1986.

Dooner, Pierton W. *Last Days of the Republic.* San Francisco: Alta California Publishing, 1880.

Dower, John. *War without Mercy: Race and Power in the Pacific War.* New York: Pantheon, 1986.

Drinnon, Richard. *Facing West: The Metaphysics of Indian-Hating and Empire-Building.* New York: New American Library, 1980.

DuBois. W. E. B. *The Souls of Black Folk.* In *Three Negro Classics.* New York: Avon, 1965.

Dunn, Ashley Sheun. "No Man's Land." *Amerasia Journal* 5.2 (1978): 109–33.

Durand, Maurice M., and Nguyen Tran Huan. *An Introduction to Vietnamese Literature.* Translated by D. M. Hawke. New York: Columbia University Press, 1985.

Eastlake, William. *The Bamboo Bed.* New York: Simon and Schuster, 1969.

Ehrhart, W. D., ed. *Carrying the Darkness: American Indochina—The Poetry of the Vietnam War.* New York: Avon, 1985.

———. *Going Back: An Ex-Marine Returns to Vietnam.* Jefferson, N.C.: McFarland, 1987.

———. *Just for Laughs.* Silver Spring, Md.: Vietnam Generation and Burning Cities Press, 1990.

———. *Vietnam-Perkasie: A Combat Marine Memoir.* Jefferson, N.C.: McFarland, 1967; reissued Amherst: University of Massachusetts Press, 1995.

Fiman, B. G., J. F. Borus, and M. D. Stanton. "Black-White and American-Vietnamese Relations among Soldiers in Vietnam." *Journal of Social Issues* 31.4 (1975): 39–48.

Fitzgerald, Frances. *Fire in the Lake: The Vietnamese and the Americans in Vietnam.* New York: Vintage, 1972.

Freeman, James. *Hearts of Sorrow: Vietnamese-American Lives.* Stanford: Stanford University Press, 1989.

Frey-Wouters, Ellen, and Robert S. Laufer. *Legacy of a War.* Armonk, New York: M. E. Sharpe, 1986.

Fussell, Paul. *The Great War and Modern Memory.* New York: Oxford University Press, 1975.

———. *Wartime: Understanding and Behavior in the Second World War.* New York: Oxford University Press, 1989.

Gaspar, Charles. "*Fields of Fire*: Stories into Histories." Paper presented at the Popular Culture Association Conference, 1992.

Gilman, Sander L. *Difference and Pathology: Stereotypes of Sexuality, Race and Madness.* Ithaca: Cornell University Press, 1985.

Glade, Jon Forrest. "All These Years Later . . ." *Vietnam Generation* 3.3 (1991): 79.

Goldman, Peter, and Tony Fuller. *Charlie Company: What Vietnam Did to Us.* New York: Ballantine, 1983.

Gordon, Elizabeth. "On the Other Side of the War." In Sylvia Watanabe and Elizabeth Bruchac, eds., *Home to Stay: Asian American Women's Fiction.* Greenfield Center, N.Y.: Greenfield Review Press, 1990.

Gould, Steven Jay. *Ever since Darwin.* New York: W. W. Norton, 1977.

———. *The Mismeasure of Man.* New York: W. W. Norton, 1981.

Green, Judith. "War Correspondence." *San Jose Mercury News,* 24 September 1993, I43–44.

Greenblatt, Stephen. "Towards a Poetics of Culture." *Southern Review* 20 (1987): 3–15.

Greene, Graham. *The Quiet American.* New York: Bantam, 1956.

Gruner, Elliot. *Prisoners of Culture: Representing the Vietnam POW.* New Brunswick: Rutgers University Press, 1993.

Gurr, Andrew. *Writers in Exile: The Identity of Home in Modern Literature.* Atlantic Highlands, N.J.: Humanities Press, 1981.

Hackworth, David H. "The War without End." *Newsweek,* 22 November 1993; 44–48.

Halberstam, David. *One Very Hot Day.* New York: Warner, 1967.

Hanley, Lynne. *Writing War: Fiction, Gender, and Memory.* Amherst: University of Massachusetts Press, 1991.

Harte, Bret. *Tales of the Argonauts and Other Sketches.* Cambridge, Mass.: Houghton Mifflin, 1903.

———. *Writings of Bret Harte.* Boston: Houghton Mifflin, 1906.

Hasford, Gustav. *The Short-Timers.* New York: Bantam Books, 1979.

Hayslip, Le Ly. Personal interview, 25 November 1990.

———, with James Hayslip. *Child of War, Woman of Peace.* New York: Doubleday, 1993.

———, with Jay Wurts. *When Heaven and Earth Changed Places: A Vietnamese Woman's Journey from War to Peace.* New York: Penguin, 1989.

Heinemann, Larry. *Close Quarters.* New York: Penguin, 1986.

———. "Making One's Way, Again, through Vietnam." *Harper's*, July 1991, 68–76.

———. *Paco's Story*. New York: Penguin, 1987.

Hellmann, John. *American Myth and the Legacy of Vietnam*. New York: Columbia University Press, 1986.

Herr, Michael. *Dispatches*. New York: Avon Books, 1978.

Ho Chi Minh. *Selected Writings*. Hanoi: Foreign Languages Publishing House, 1973.

Holland, William E. *Let a Soldier Die*. New York: Dell, 1984.

Holt, Patricia. "Viet Vet Sees War as a Moral Vacuum." *San Francisco Chronicle*, 26 November 1987, E12.

Houston, Jeanne, Wakatsuki. "A Woman of Two Worlds." *West Magazine*, 15 April 1984, 6–11.

Hsiao, Lisa. "Project 100,000: The Great Society's Answer to Military Manpower Needs in Vietnam." *Vietnam Generation* 1.2 (1989): 14–37.

Huynh Quong Nhuong. *The Land I Lost*. New York: Harper and Row, 1982.

Ignacio, Lemuel F. *Asian Americans and Pacific Islanders: Is there Such an Ethnic Group?* San Jose, Calif.: Pilipino Development Associates, 1976.

Irwin, Wallace. *Seed of the Sun*. New York: George H. Doran, 1921.

Isaacs, Arnold R. "Vietnam: The Sorrow and the Pity." *Washington Post Book World*, 16 July 1989, 1.

Jackson, Earl, Jr. "The Metaphysics of Translation and the Origins of Symbolist Poetics in Meiji Japan." *PMLA* 105.2 (1990): 256–72.

Jason, Philip. "Sexism and Racism in Vietnam War Fiction." *Mosaic* 23.2 (1990): 125–37.

Jeffords, Susan. *The Remasculinization of America: Gender and the Vietnam War*. Bloomington: Indiana University Press, 1989.

Jehlen, Myra. "Why Did the Europeans Cross the Ocean? Or, Montaigne's Dilemma." Invited public lecture at the University of California, Santa Cruz, 16 October 1990.

Jones, Bill. "The Body Burning Detail." *Vietnam Generation* 3.3 (1991): 68–69.

Kaplan, Caren. "The Poetics of Displacement: Exile, Immigration, and Travel in Contemporary Autobiographical Writing." Dissertation, University of California, Santa Cruz, 1987.

Karlin, Wayne. *Lost Armies*. New York: Henry Holt, 1988.

Karnow, Stanley. *Vietnam: A History*. New York: Viking, 1983.

Kiang, Peter Nien-chu. "About Face: Recognizing Asian and Pacific American Vietnam Veterans in Asian American Studies." *Amerasia Journal* 17.3 (1991): 22–40.

Kim, Elaine H. *Asian American Literature: An Introduction to the Writings and Their Social Context*. Philadelphia: Temple University Press, 1982.

———. "Defining Asian American Realities through Literature." *Cultural Critique* 6 (1987): 87–112.

Kingston, Maxine Hong. *China Men*. New York: Ballantine, 1980.

———. *The Woman Warrior*. New York: Vintage, 1976.

Komunyakaa, Yusef. *Dien Cai Dau*. Middletown, Conn.: Wesleyan University Press, 1988.

Kovic, Ron. *Born on the Fourth of July*. New York: Pocket Books, 1976.

Lam, Andrew. " 'Heaven and Earth' Centered in U.S." *San Francisco Chronicle*, 31 December 1993, D7, D9.

———. "My Vietnam, My America." *The Nation*, 10 December 1990, 724–26.

Lang, Daniel. *Casualties of War*. New York: Pocket Books, 1989.

Lederer, William J., and Eugene Burdick. *The Ugly American*. New York: Fawcett Crest, 1958.

Lifton, Robert Jay. *Home from the War: Vietnam Veterans: Neither Victims nor Executioners*. New York: Simon and Schuster, 1973.

———. "The Postwar War." *Journal of Social Issues* 31.4 (1975): 181–95.

Lim, Shirley Geok-lin. "Twelve Asian American Writers: In Search of Self-Definition." *MELUS* 13.1–2 (1986): 56–77.

Limerick, Patricia Nelson. *The Legacy of Conquest: The Unbroken Past of the American West*. New York: Norton, 1987.

Ling, Amy. "Asian American Literature: A Brief Introduction and Selected Bibliography." *ADE Bulletin* 80 (1985): 29–33.

Little, Lloyd. *Parthian Shot*. New York: Ballantine, 1973.

Lomperis, Timothy. *"Reading the Wind": The Literature of the Vietnam War*. Durham, N.C.: Duke University Press, 1987.

Lorellle. "The Battle of Wabash." *Californian* 2 (1880): 364–76.

Lowe, Pardee. *Father and Glorious Descendant*. Boston: Little, Brown, 1943.

Lucas, R. Valerie. "Yellow Peril in the Promised Land: The Representation of the Oriental and the Question of American Identity." In Francis Barker, ed., *Europe and Its Others*. Colchester: University of Essex, 1985, 41–57.

McCaffery, Larry. "Interview with Tim O'Brien." *Chicago Review* 33 (1982): 129–49.

McCarry, Charles. *The Tears of Autumn*. New York: Signet, 1974.

McWilliams, Carey. *Prejudice: Japanese Americans: Symbol of Racial Intolerance*. Hamden, N.J.: Archon Books, 1971.

McWilliams, Dean. "Time in O'Brien's *Going after Cacciato*." *Critique* 29.4 (1988): 245–55.

Maehara, G. Akito. "Think on These Things: A Perspective from a Vietnam Era Veteran." *Amerasia Journal* 17.1 (1991): 123–28.

Mahoney, Tim. *We're Not Here.* New York: Dell, 1988.

Marien, Mary Warner. "A Vietnamese Life Etched by War and Its Ripples." *Christian Science Monitor*, 3 August 1989, 13.

Malo, Jean Jacques, and Tony Williams. *Vietnam War Filmography.* Jefferson, N.C.: McFarland, 1994.

Marshall, Kathryn. *In the Combat Zone.* New York: Penguin, 1987.

Mason, Robert. *Chickenhawk.* New York: Penguin, 1983.

Maurer, Harry. *Strange Ground: Americans in Vietnam 1945–1975: An Oral History.* New York: Henry Holt, 1989.

Melling, Philip. *Vietnam in American Literature.* Boston: Twayne, 1990.

Miller, Christopher L. "Theories of Africans: The Question of Literary Anthropology." In Henry Louis Gates, Jr., ed., *Race, Writing and Difference.* Chicago: University of Chicago Press, 1986.

Miller, Joaquin. *First Fam'lies of the Sierras.* Chicago: Jansen, McClurg, and Co., 1876.

Miller, Stuart Creighton. *The Unwelcome Immigrant: The American Image of the Chinese, 1785–1882.* Berkeley: University of California Press, 1969.

Minh Duc Hoai Trinh. *This Side, the Other Side.* Montrose, Calif.: Occidental Press, 1985.

Mirikitani, Janice, ed. *Ayumi: A Japanese American Anthology.* San Francisco: Japanese American Anthology Committee, 1980.

Montero, Darrel. *Vietnamese Americans: Patterns of Resettlement and Socioeconomic Adaptation in the United States.* Boulder: Westview Press, 1979.

Moore, Robin. *The Green Berets.* New York: Avon, 1965.

Morrell, David. *First Blood.* New York: Fawcett Crest, 1972.

Morris, Jim. *War Story.* New York: Dell, 1985.

Moss, George Donelson. *Vietnam: An American Ordeal.* Englewood Cliffs, N.J.: Prentice-Hall, 1990.

Mullin, Chris. *The Last Man Out of Saigon.* New York: Bantam, 1986.

Mundo, Oto. *The Recovered Continent: A Tale of the Chinese Invasion.* Columbus, Ohio: Harper-Osgood, 1898.

Myers, Thomas. *Walking Point: American Narratives of Vietnam.* New York: Oxford University Press, 1988.

Nguyen Dang Liem. "Vietnamese-American Crosscultural Communication." *Bilingual Resources* 3 (1980): 9–15.

Nguyễn Du. *The Tale of Kiều.* Translated by Huỳnh Sanh Thông. New Haven: Yale University Press, 1983.

Nguyen Hung Quoc. "The Vietnamese Literature in Exile." *Journal of Vietnamese Studies* 5 (1992): 24–34.

Nguyen Khac Vien. *Tradition and Revolution in Vietnam.* Berkeley, Calif.: Indochina Resource Center, 1974.

——, ed. *Vietnamese Literature.* Hanoi: Red River, n.d.

Nguyen Manh Hung. "Refugee Scholars and Vietnamese Studies in the United States, 1975–1982." *Amerasia* 11.1 (1984): 89–99.

Nguyen Ngoc Bich, ed. *War and Exile: A Vietnamese Anthology.* Springfield, Va.: Vietnamese PEN East Coast USA, 1989.

Nguyen Ngoc Ngan, with E. E. Richey. *The Will of Heaven: One Vietnamese and the End of His World.* New York: E. P. Dutton, 1982.

Nguyen Thi Dinh. *No Other Road to Take.* Translated by Mai Elliott. Southeast Asia Program Data Paper Number 102. Ithaca: Cornell University Southeast Asia Program, 1976.

Nguyễn Thị Thu-Lâm, with Edith Kreisler and Sandra Christenson. *Fallen Leaves: Memoirs of a Vietnamese Woman from 1940 to 1975.* New Haven: Yale Center for International and Area Studies, and Boston: William Joiner Center, 1989.

Nichols, John. *American Blood.* New York: Henry Holt, 1987.

North, Don. "The Voice from the Past: The Search for Hanoi Hannah." *Indochina Newsletter* 63 (1990): 1–8.

O'Brien, Tim. *Going after Cacciato.* New York: Dell, 1978.

——. "How to Tell a True War Story." *Esquire,* October 1987, 208–15.

——. *If I Die in a Combat Zone.* New York: Dell, 1973.

Oehling, Richard. "The Yellow Menace: Asian Images in American Film." In Randall M. Miller, ed., *The Kaleidoscopic Lens: How Hollywood Views Ethnic Groups.* Englewood, N.J.: Jerome S. Ozer, 1980.

Peacock, Doug. *Grizzly Years.* New York: Kensington, 1990.

Pearsall, R. P. "The Revelation." *Overland Monthly,* 2nd series 58 (1911): 485–94.

Pelfrey, William. *The Big V.* New York: Liveright, 1972.

Pham Thanh. "My Two Countries, My Flesh and Blood." *New York Times,* 19 April 1991, A27.

Pike, Douglas. "Opinions of an Opportunist." *New Republic,* 29 July 1985, 33–38.

Pratt, John Clark. *The Laotian Fragments.* New York: Viking Press, 1974.

——. *Vietnam Voices: Perspectives on the War Years, 1941–1982.* New York: Penguin, 1984.

Proffitt, Nicholas. *The Embassy House.* New York: Bantam, 1986.

Ramirez, Juan. "A Personal History of a Chicano Vietnam Veteran before, during and after the War." Senior thesis, University of California, Santa Cruz, 1986.

Richman, Elliot. *A Bucket of Nails.* Monroe, Conn.: Samisdat, 1990.

Roberts, Alden E. "Racism Sent and Received: Americans and Vietnamese View One Another." *Research in Race and Ethnic Relations* 5 (1988): 75–97.

Rodriguez, Joe. *Oddsplayer.* Houston: Arte Publico Press, 1989.

Said, Edward. *Orientalism.* New York: Vintage, 1978.

——. "Through Gringo Eyes: With Conrad in Latin America." *Harper's,* April 1988, 70–72.

Safer, Morley. *Flashbacks: On Returning to Vietnam.* New York: St. Martin's, 1990.

Schaeffer, Susan Fromberg. *Buffalo Afternoon.* New York: Knopf, 1989.

Schneider, Tassilo. "From Cynicism to Self-Pity: *Apocalypse Now* and *Platoon.*" *Cinefocus* 1.2 (1990): 49–52.

Schroeder, Eric James. "Two Interviews: Talks with Tim O'Brien and Robert Stone." *Modern Fiction Studies* 30 (1984): 135–64.

Shipler, David K. "A Child's Tour of Duty." *New York Times Book Review,* 25 June 1989, 1.

Slotkin, Richard. *Regeneration through Violence: The Mythology of the American Frontier, 1600–1860.* Middletown, Conn.: Wesleyan University Press, 1973.

Smith, Grahame. *The Achievement of Graham Greene.* Englewood, N.J.: Barnes and Noble, 1986.

Smith, Steven Philip. *American Boys.* New York: Avon, 1975.

Snape, Ray. "The Political Novels of Graham Greene." *Durham University Journal* 75 (1982): 73–81.

Stratton-Porter, Gene. *Her Father's Daughter.* New York: Doubleday, Page and Co., 1921.

Tagatac, Sam. "The New Anak." In Frank Chin, ed., *Aiiieeeee: An Anthology of Asian-American Writers.* Washington, D.C.: Howard University Press, 1974.

Takaki, Ronald. *Strangers from a Different Shore: A History of Asian Americans.* New York: Penguin, 1989.

Taylor, Gordon O. "American Personal Narrative of the War in Vietnam." *American Literature* 52 (1980): 294–308.

Thomas, C. David. *As Seen by Both Sides: American and Vietnamese Artists Look at the War.* Boston: University of Massachusetts Press, 1991.

Thomson, James C., Jr., Peter W. Stanley, and John Curtis Perry. *Sentimental Imperialists: The American Experience in East Asia.* New York: Harper and Row, 1981.

Thornburg, Newton. *Cutter and Bone.* New York: Fawcett, 1976.

Thorpe, Stephen. *Walking Wounded.* New York: Doubleday, 1980.

Tollefson, James W. "Indochinese Refugees: A Challenge to America's Memory of Vietnam." In Michael D. Schafer, ed., *The Legacy: The Vietnam War in the American Imagination*. Boston: Beacon Press, 1990.

Tompkins, Jane. "West of Everything." *South Atlantic Quarterly* 86.4 (1987): 357–77.

Tran, Anh K. Review of *Ca Dao Việtnam: A Bilingual Anthology of Vietnamese Folk Poetry*, by John Balaban. *Amerasia Journal* 14.2 (1988): 149–51.

Tran Mong Tu. "A New Year's Wish for a Little Refugee." Translated by Huynh Sanh Thong. *Vietnam Forum* 1 (1983): 107.

Tran Tri Vu. *Lost Years: My 1,632 Days in Vietnamese Reeducation Camps.* Indochina Research Monographs No. 3. Berkeley: Institute of East Asian Studies, 1988.

Tran, Truong. "Ode to a Fruit Salad" and "The Day I Ran into Octavio Paz." *TWANAS* (spring 1991), a University of California, Santa Cruz, student publication.

Tran Van Dinh. *Blue Dragon, White Tiger: A Tet Story.* Philadelphia: TriAm Press, 1983.

———. "The Tale of Kieu: Joy and Sadness in the Life of Vietnamese in the United States." In Reese Williams, ed., *Unwinding the Vietnam War.* Seattle: Real Comet Press, 1987.

Trinh T. Minh-ha. *Woman, Native, Other.* Bloomington: Indiana University Press, 1989.

Truong Nhu Tang, with David Chanoff and Doan Van Toai. *A Vietcong Memoir.* New York: Vintage, 1985.

Turley, William S. *The Second Indochina War: A Short Political and Military History, 1954–1975.* Boulder: Westview Press, 1986.

Van Tien Dung. *Our Great Spring Victory.* New York: Monthly Review Press, 1977.

Vietnam Generation. Special issue: "Southeast Asian-American Communities," 2.3 (1990).

"A Vietnamese Power Broker." *San Jose Mercury News*, 7 March 1988.

"Vietnam Horror Inspired Prize-Winning Author." *San Francisco Chronicle*, 11 November 1987, E3.

Vo Nguyen Giap. *How We Won the War.* Philadelphia: RECON Publications, 1976.

———. *Unforgettable Days.* Hanoi: Foreign Languages Publishing House, 1975.

Vo Phien. *Intact.* Translated by James Banerian. Victoria, Australia: Vietnamese Language and Culture Publications, 1990.

———. "A Spring of Quiet and Peace" and "The Key." In Marguerite Bouvard, ed., *Landscape and Exile.* Boston: Rowan Tree Press, 1985.

Walker, Keith. *A Piece of My Heart: The Stories of Twenty-Six American Women Who Served in Vietnam.* Novato, Calif.: Presidio Press, 1985.

Webb, James. *Fields of Fire.* New York: Bantam, 1978.

Weigl, Bruce. *Song of Napalm.* New York: Atlantic Monthly Press, 1988.

———. "Towards a Biography of Place: Notes on Discovering My Country." In Eleanor M. Bender, ed., *American Writers Abroad.* Charlotte, N.C.: Heritage Printers, 1986.

Weimann, Robert. "History, Appropriation, and the Uses of Representation in Modern Narrative." In Murray Krieger, ed., *The Aims of Representation.* New York: Columbia University Press, 1987.

West, Morris L. *The Ambassador.* New York: William Morrow, 1965.

West, Richard. "Graham Greene and *The Quiet American.*" *New York Review of Books,* 16 May 1991, 49–52.

Whitney, Atwell. *Almond-Eyed: The Great Agitator.* San Francisco: A. L. Bancroft, 1878.

Woltor, Robert. *A Short and Truthful History of the Taking of Oregon and California by the Chinese in the Year A.D. 1899.* San Francisco: A. L. Bancroft, 1882.

Wong, Eugene. *On Visual Media Racism: Asians in the American Motion Pictures.* New York: Arno Press, 1978.

Wu, Cheng-Tsu. *"Chink!" A Documentary History of Anti-Chinese Prejudice in America.* New York: World Publishing, 1972.

Wu, William F. *The Yellow Peril: Chinese Americans in American Fiction, 1850–1940.* Hamden, Conn.: Archon Press, 1982.

Zo, Kil Young. *Chinese Emigration into the United States, 1850–1880.* New York: Arno Press, 1978.

Zoglin, Richard. "An Outbreak of Rambomania." *Time,* 24 June 1985, 72–73.

Index

Acknowledgments and Permissions

John Balaban, "For the Missing in Action," in *Words for My Daughter* (Copper Canyon Press, 1991), © 1991 by John Balaban. Used by permission of the author.

Robert Olen Butler, from *The Alleys of Eden* (New York: Horizon Press, 1981); *The Deuce* (New York: Simon and Schuster, 1989), and *On Distant Ground* (New York: Ballantine, 1985). Used by permission of the author.

W. D. Ehrhart, "Making the Children Behave" and lines from "Letter," in *To Those Who Have Gone Home Tired* (Thunder Mouth Press, 1984); and "Second Thoughts" from *Just for Laughs* (Vietnam Generation and Burning Cities Press, 1990). Used by permission of the author. The exchange between Te Hanh and W. D. Ehrhart appears in Ehrhart's *Going Back* (McFarland & Co., 1987). The English text of Te Hanh's "Questions Underground" appeared originally in *Vietnamese Literature* (Red River Press).

Jon Forrest Glade, "All These Years Later," in *Photographs of the Jungle* (Saint John, KS: Chiron Review, 1990), © 1990 by Jon Forrest Glade. Used by permission of the author.

Bill Jones, "The Body Burning Detail," in *Vietnam Generation* 3, no. 3 (1991): 68–69. Used by permission of the author.

Wayne Karlin, from *Lost Armies*, first published by Henry Holt, 1988. Used by permission of the author.

Yusef Komunyakaa, "Recreating the Scene," "The Edge," "Dui Boi," and "Missing in Action," in *Dien Cau Dau* (Wesleyan University Press) © 1988 by Yusef Komunyakaa. Used by permission of University Press of New England.

Janice Mirikitani, from "Loving from Vietnam to Zimbabwe," in *Ayumi: A Japanese American Anthology* (San Francisco: Japanese American Anthology Committee, 1980).

Elliot Richman, "This is no Country for the Young," *Green Fuse* 11 (Winter 1989); lines from "The Love Song of the Wife of an Assistant Deputy Minister of Justice," *Lactuca*, no. 14 (May 1991); "Jungle Ambush in the Monument Valley," in *A Bucket of Nails: Poems from the Second IndoChina War* (Monroe, CT: Samisdat Press, 1990); and "To the Old Tune, . . ." *Green Fuse* 12 (Spring 1990). Used by permission of the author.

Tran Mong Tu, trans. Huynh Sanh Thong, "A New Year's Wish for a Little Refugee," in *Vietnam Forum* 1 (1983). Used by permission.

Truong Tran, "Ode to a Fruit Salad," in *TWANAS* (Spring 1991). Used by permission of the author.

Bruce Weigl, "Him, On the Bicycle," in *Songs of Napalm* (New York: Atlantic Monthly Press, 1988). Used by permission of the author.